D1083669

Competitive Sports for Children and Youth

An Overview of Research and Issues

Eugene W. Brown, PhD
Crystal F. Branta, PhD
Michigan State University

Editors

Human Kinetics Books
Champaign, Illinois

Library of Congress Cataloging-in-Publication Data

Big Ten Committee on Institutional Cooperation Symposium on
   the Effects of Competitive Sports on Children and Youth
   (1985 : Michigan State University)
   Competitive sports for children and youth.

   (Big Ten body of knowledge symposium series ; v. 16)
   "Proceedings of the Big Ten Committee on Institutional
Cooperation Symposium on the Effects of Competitive Sports
on Children and Youth, held at Michigan State University,
East Lansing, MI, October 3-4, 1985"—T.p. verso.
   Includes bibliographies.
   1. Pediatric sports medicine—Congresses. 2. Sports
for children—Congresses. I. Brown, Eugene W., 1946-
II. Branta, Crystal F., 1954-   . III. Title.
IV. Series. [DNLM: 1. Sports—congresses. 2. Sports—
Medicine—in adolescence—congresses. 3. Sports
Medicine—in infancy & childhood—congresses.
QT 260 B592c 1985]
RC1218.C45B54 1985   617'.1027'088054   86-33728
ISBN 0-87322-105-2

Developmental Editor: Laura E. Larson
Production Direction: Ernie Noa
Projects Manager: Lezli Harris
Copy Editor: Judy Weidman
Typesetter: Sandra Meier
Proofreader: Linda Purcell
Text Layout: Denise Peters
Cover Design: Keith Blomberg
Printed By: Braun-Brumfield, Inc.

ISBN: 0-87322-105-2

Copyright © 1988 by Human Kinetics Publishers, Inc.

Printed in the United States of America

10 9 8 7 6 5 4 3 2 1

Human Kinetics Books
A Division of Human Kinetics Publishers, Inc.
Box 5076, Champaign, IL 61820
1-800-DIAL-HKP
1-800-334-3665 (in Illinois)

Contents

Contributors

Dr. Richard Boileau
Department of Physical Education
125 Freer Hall
906 South Goodwin Avenue
University of Illinois
Urbana, IL 61801

Dr. Brenda Bredemeier
200 Hearst Gym
University of California, Berkeley
Berkeley, CA 94720

Dr. Eugene W. Brown
Health Education, Counseling Psychology, and Human Performance
204 IM Sports Circle
Michigan State University
East Lansing, MI 48824

Dr. David Cunningham
Department of Physiology
Medical Science Building
University of Western Ontario
London, ON N6A 5C1
Canada

Dr. Paul A. Dyment
Chief of Pediatrics
Maine Medical Center
Portland, ME 04102

Dr. Martha E. Ewing
Health Education, Counseling Psychology, and Human Performance
201 IM Sports Circle
Michigan State University
East Lansing, MI 48824

Dr. Daniel Gould
117 Freer Hall
906 South Goodwin Avenue
University of Illinois
Urbana, IL 61801

Dr. Bernard Gutin
Teachers College
Columbia University
New York, NY 10027

Dr. John Haubenstricker
Health Education, Counseling Psychology, and Human Performance
128 IM Sports Circle
Michigan State University
East Lansing, MI 48824

Dr. Jon Kabara
Biomechanics
A 407 East Fee Hall
Michigan State University
East Lansing, MI 48824

Dr. Anne B. Loucks
Department of Reproductive Medicine
University of California, San Diego
La Jolla, CA 92093

Dr. Robert Malina
Institute for Latin American Studies
Sid Richardson Hall, Unit 1
University of Texas
Austin, TX 78712

Dr. Rainer Martens
Human Kinetics Publishers
Box 5076
Champaign, IL 61820

Dr. Doug McKeag
Family Practice
B100 Clinical Center
Michigan State University
East Lansing, MI 48824

Dr. Lyle Micheli
Children's Hospital Medical Center
319 Longwood Avenue
Boston, MA 02115

Dr. Alan D. Rogol
Department of Pediatrics
University of Virginia
Medical Center
Charlottesville, VA 22908

Dr. Allan Ryan
5800 Jeff Place
Minneapolis, MN 55436

Dr. Tara Scanlan
Department of Kinesiology
405 Hilgard Avenue
University of California, Los Angeles
Los Angeles, CA 90024

Dr. Rachelle Schemmel
Food Science & Human Nutrition
302 B Food Science Building
Michigan State University
East Lansing, MI 48824

Dr. Vern Seefeldt
Health Education, Counseling Psychology, and Human Performance
213 IM Sports Circle
Michigan State University
East Lansing, MI 48824

Dr. William Thorland
Center for Youth Fitness and Sports Research
135 Coliseum
University of Nebraska
Lincoln, NE 68588

Dr. Wayne Van Huss
Health Education, Counseling Psychology, and Human Performance
3 IM Sports Circle
Michigan State University
East Lansing, MI 48824

Dr. Christine Wells
Department of Health and Physical Education
Arizona State University
Tempe, AZ 85287

Mr. Chet Zelasko
Health Education, Counseling Psychology, and Human Performance
3 IM Sports Circle
Michigan State University
East Lansing, MI 48824

Editorial Board Reviewers

Preface

A rapid proliferation of sport programs for children has taken place over the past three decades. Presently, approximately 20 million children participate in various youth sport programs in the United States. Each of these young athletes is seeking to gain the benefits purported to be associated with sport participation. Our body of knowledge, associated with the many different aspects of youth participation in sport, however, has not kept pace with the growth of youth sports. Therefore, many important questions related to the benefits and risks of youth involvement in sport are unanswered.

The Youth Sports Institute at Michigan State University under its director, Vern Seefeldt, has taken a leadership role in expanding the knowledge about youth participation in sport. This symposium grew out of an attempt to increase our understanding of the influence that athletics has on children and youth. A Big Ten Committee on Institutional Cooperation Symposium presented a logical vehicle for a gathering of scholars from many disciplines to discuss these issues. The idea to convene such a symposium was accepted and supported by the faculty of the School of Health Education, Counseling Psychology, and Human Performance of the College of Education.

A proposal for financial support to hold a symposium to review the biological, psychological, sociological, and biomechanical research relating to the effects of competitive sports on children and youth was submitted to the Big 10 Committee on Institutional Cooperation. Acceptance of this proposal was followed by the formation of a local organizing committee composed of Crystal F. Branta, Eugene Brown, Mary Helfer, Vern Seefeldt, and Wayne Van Huss. Each committee member willingly assumed a variety of tasks in carrying the idea of an interdisciplinary symposium on youth sports to fruition. Appreciation is extended to the Big 10 CIC Symposium Steering Committee, Charles Mand, Ohio State University, chairperson, for their encouragement and support during the planning of this symposium.

From many perspectives, the resulting symposium on the "Effects of Competitive Sports on Children and Youth" was a success. It brought together invited scholars from several disciplines to share their research and knowledge. It resulted in thought-provoking interactions between presenters and attendees. Such interactions should precipitate additional interest and study of the young athlete. Finally, it resulted in the publication of this book, which should be of value to a broad array of scholars and practitioners interested in youth sports.

Eugene W. Brown

PART I

Body Composition and Nutrition

Problems Associated With Determining Body Composition in Maturing Youngsters

Richard A. Boileau
Timothy G. Lohman
Mary H. Slaughter
Craig A. Horswill
Rachel J. Stillman

Body composition assessment has become a vital component in the comprehensive evaluation of health, fitness, and physical performance. The recent interest in obesity, a primary nutritional, hypokinetic, and metabolic disease, has stimulated interest in the development of various body composition techniques to definitively assess overfatness. The reported prevalence of obesity in the pediatric population ranges from 5 to 30% in developed countries (Coates, Killen, & Slinkard, 1982; Ylitalo, 1981). The national importance of this problem is demonstrated by the fact that two recent physical fitness evaluations conducted on schoolchildren in the United States have incorporated measurements of body composition via skinfold thickness measures to identify obesity (The American Alliance for Health, Physical Education, Recreation and Dance Health Related Fitness Test [AAHPERD Task Force, 1980]; U.S. Public Health Service National Children and Youth Fitness Study [Pate, Ross, Dotson, & Gilbert, 1985]).

Another important aspect of body composition assessment is its use in providing information regarding minimal, ideal, and maximal body weight levels for effective performance in various sports. It is well recognized that physical performance can be strongly influenced by the relative amounts of the fat and fat-free components of body composition (Boileau & Lohman, 1977) in both the adult and the pediatric athlete. This fact has important implications for physical fitness testing in which performance-based items are employed. Specifically, past research has demonstrated that tasks requiring either vertical or horizontal translocation of body weight are generally performed more poorly by overweight and overfat individuals (Asmussen & Heeboll-Nielsen, 1955; Cureton, Boileau, & Lohman, 1975; Cureton, Boileau, Lohman, & Misner, 1977; Riendeau et al., 1958). On the other hand, a high fat-free weight may be a requirement for success in activities in which force must be applied against external objects. Another area in which body composition assessment has become useful is in those sports where weight loss may

3

be attempted due to an imposed weight classification system, as seen in the sport of wrestling (Clarke, 1974; Tcheng & Tipton, 1973). Identification of tolerable variability in body weight for this sport and others, based on body composition parameters, is needed to insure proper nutrition practices for normal growth and maturation of the pediatric athlete. Thus, body composition assessment appears essential to a comprehensive understanding and a prudent interpretation of the health and physical fitness status as well as performance aptitude for various sports.

Body weight composition is normally characterized in terms of its components: fat and fat-free body weight. The estimation of these components is typically accomplished by one or more of a number of standard measurement techniques including anthropometry, densitometry, hydrometry, potassium-40 (^{40}K) spectroscopy, and/or one of the newer techniques involving whole body imaging, electrical impedance, or conductivity (Lohman, 1984). In the young adult, these techniques appear to provide reasonable estimates of the fat and fat-free body components; however, assessment of these components in children appears to be complicated by the fact that growth and development processes evoke changes in body composition that affect the conceptual basis for estimating fatness and leanness (Lohman, Boileau, & Slaughter, 1984). In this review, a discussion of several problems associated with assessing body composition in maturing youngsters is undertaken, and alternative solutions are suggested.

Fat-Free Body Stability and Estimation of Body Composition

Densitometry, hydrometry, and ^{40}K spectroscopy are generally considered primary or criterion body composition techniques. In order for each technique to render valid estimates of fat and fat-free body (FFB), an assumption of chemical maturity and stability of the FFB must be made. The validity of this assumption is suspect, if not untenable, in children. For over 50 years, the general theory of Moulton (1923) that chemical maturity is achieved in humans by 3 to 4 years of age has been accepted. As a consequence, the adult body composition model has received widespread use in the pediatric literature, in spite of concern expressed from time to time regarding the validity of such practice (Boileau, Wilmore, Lohman, Slaughter, & Riner, 1981; Lohman, 1981; Pařízková, 1961; Wilmore & McNamara, 1974). The following mature adult values, based primarily on whole body cadaver analysis, provide an index by which FFB maturity and stability can be judged in the pediatric population: The FFB density has been computed to be 1.100 g/cc (Brozek, Grande, Anderson, & Keys, 1963); the water content of the FFB has been estimated to range from 71.8% (Osserman, Pitts, Welham, & Behnke, 1950) to 73.8% (Brozek et al., 1963); and the potassium content of the FFB has been placed at 2.66 g/kg FFB (Forbes & Hursh, 1963). Although few data pertinent to these indices are available for the maturing youngster (Fomon, Haschke, Ziegler, & Nelson, 1982; Haschke, 1983; Haschke, Fomon, & Ziegler, 1981; Heald et al., 1963; Young, Bogan, Roe, & Lutwak, 1968;

Young, Sipin, & Roe, 1968), evidence suggests that these constants reflecting chemical maturity of the FFB are inappropriate for the child. Moreover, by utilizing adult constants, body fatness may be overestimated by 7 to 13% with the density and potassium methods and underestimated from 3 to 6% by hydrometry.

Recently, additional data (Boileau et al., 1984; Lohman, Slaughter, Boileau, Bunt, & Lussier, 1984) have been provided on the variability of the fat-free body utilizing a three-component model in which the FFB is described in terms of water, mineral, and protein. These data included 292 male (n = 157) and female (n = 135) subjects, of which 54 were classified maturationally (Tanner, 1962) as prepubescent, 50 pubescent, 107 postpubescent, and 81 adult. The body composition of each subject was measured by several techniques including anthropometry, densitometry by underwater weighing, hydrometry by deuterium oxide dilution, bone mineral by photon absorptiometry, and body potassium by ^{40}K spectroscopy. The criterion measure of FFB was estimated by the method of Siri (1961) in which body density and relative body water content are utilized. This method does not require an assumption of water content stability but does assume a constant body mineral to protein ratio. From these data, it is possible to assess variability in the chemical composition of the FFB as a function of maturation with respect to FFB density, water, mineral, and potassium content.

Variability in FFB Density

Perhaps the most comprehensive index of FFB composition is represented by its density (D_{FFB}). The density of the FFB can be calculated from the fractions and densities of its components. Equation 1 illustrates the method employed to estimate FFB density (D_{FFB}):

$$1/D_{FFB} = f_w/D_w + f_m/D_m + f_p/D_p \qquad (1)$$

where f is the fraction of water (w), mineral (m), and protein (p), respectively, for total FFB, and D is the density of each respective component assumed to be 0.9934 g/cc for water, 3.00 g/cc for bone mineral, and 1.34 g/cc for protein (Brozek et al., 1963).

Density of the FFB as a function of age is shown in Figure 1 for the sample of 292 subjects. The reference sample of 81 adults (aged 19 to 30 years) is presented as two data points: one each for males and females. It is interesting to note that although the theoretical FFB density for the chemically mature individual is 1.100 g/cc, only the mean male value is at this level, and the adult female mean FFB density is estimated to be lower at 1.096 g/cc. Although substantial variability exists both across age groups and between the genders, the FFB density appears to increase dramatically during the pubertal period, ages 11 to 15 years. Fomon et al. (1982) have reported changes in the FFB density for males and females who range in age from 1 to 10 years. These investigators estimated the FFB density to increase from 1.063 to 1.068 g/cc during the 1st year

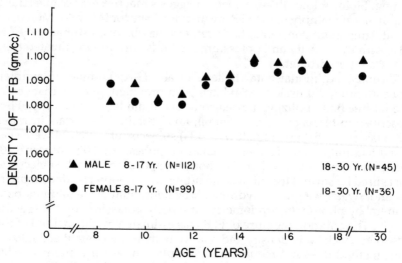

Figure 1 Mean fat-free body density values for children and youth (8 to 17 years of age) and adults (18 to 30 years of age). These values were computed from data presented by Boileau et al. (1984) and Lohman, Boileau, and Slaughter (1984).

of life, with the value by 10 years of age reaching 1.085 and 1.075 g/cc for males and females, respectively. Additionally, Haschke (1983) has shown the male FFB density to increase from 1.086 g/cc at 12.5 years of age to 1.093 g/cc at age 18.5 years. From these data it is appropriate to conclude that fundamental changes in FFB composition are taking place.

Instability in FFB composition, as seen in D_{FFB}, has an effect on estimation of fat as well as the total body composition. Therefore, it is important to account for variability in FFB if accurate estimates are to be made, particularly from whole body densitometry. The fat component, on the other hand, appears to be rather stable with a density of 0.900 g/cc. The following equation (2) by Siri (1961) is often used for estimating the fat fraction (f_F) of adults from body density (D_B), assuming an FFB density of 1.100 g/cc and a fat density (D_F) of 0.900 g/cc:

$$f_F = (4.95/D_B) - 4.500 \qquad (2)$$

This is derived from the following general relationship:

$$f_F = 1/D_B \left[(D_F \times D_{FFB})/(D_{FFB} - D_F) \right] - \left[D_F/(D_{FFB} - D_F) \right] \qquad (3)$$

The demonstrated variability in the D_{FFB} for age groups, maturational levels, and gender suggests that it is likely that a series of equations for estimating relative fatness from body density may be needed to provide more accurate evaluations of body fatness in the pediatric population. The following example illustrates the effect of assuming an adult FFB density when in fact the D_{FFB} is lower: If instead of a D_{FFB} of 1.100 g/cc, assumed for the adult, an 8-year-old prepubescent child has an actual D_{FFB} of 1.080 g/cc and a total body density of 1.052 g/cc, the percentage fat of the child using Equation 2 would be 20.5% fat. However, by adjusting Equation 3 for a D_{FFB} of 1.080 g/cc, fat content would be estimated at 13.3%, a difference of more than 7%, according to Equation 4:

$$f_F = (5.400/D_B) - 5.000 \qquad (4)$$

Equation 4 is only relevant to a D_{FFB} of 1.080 g/cc and should not be applied to children generally. The fact that the D_{FFB} appears to increase dramatically from prepubescence to postpubescence (Figure 1) suggests that a series of equations is needed for the maturing youngster.

The preceding analysis, together with an emerging pool of data describing the body composition of children and youth, indicates that the FFB is not chemically mature. A question then arises as to what the nature of change in the FFB is during the processes of growth and development. As described in Equation 1, the FFB chemical composition is defined in terms of its water, mineral, and protein components. Although all three components are increasing dramatically in absolute amount during growth and development, analysis of the relationship of each component to the other two components provides information regarding the relative change in each component with respect to the total FFB. Although protein constitutes a substantial portion of the FFB, ranging from 17 to 20%, variability in water and mineral content is more likely responsible for the major alterations in FFB composition from the prepubertal to postpubertal stages. The following is a discussion of the changes occurring in these two components.

Variability in FFB Water Content

Relatively small FFB water changes (percentage water-FFB) appear to have a large impact on the FFB composition because water is its largest constituent and has the lowest density. The water content of the FFB undergoes a tremendous decline from birth to adulthood, ranging from 81 to 72% water-FFB (Fomon et al., 1982; Osserman et al., 1950). Mean percentage water-FFB data for the sample previously described are presented in Figure 2. A substantial decrease in water content appears between the ages of 11 and 15 years. Overall, a decrease from 75.0 and 75.9% water-FFB for male and female prepubescents to 72.1 and 73.1% water-FFB for male and female adults was noted (Boileau et al., 1984). This drop in water content coincides with the abrupt rise in the mean FFB density seen between those ages in Figure 1, suggesting the importance of the water component to alterations in the total FFB. It should be mentioned, however, that although the mean data for both D_{FFB} and percentage water-FFB suggests a cubic relationship with age, this pattern could not be confirmed because regression analysis on individual data only describes a significant linear decrease of 0.38% water-FFB per year (Boileau et al.,

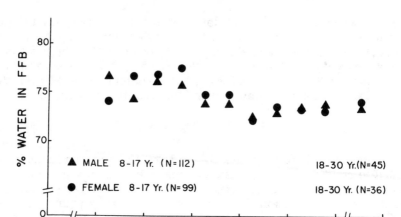

Figure 2 Mean percentage fat-free body water values for children and youth (aged 8 to 17 years) and adults (aged 18 to 30 years).

1984). Computing the FFB water content has also been possible from body density and body water data previously reported by Heald et al. (1963), Young, Bogan, Roe, and Lutwak (1968), and Young, Sipin, and Roe (1968). The data of Heald et al. on male subjects show a decrease from 75.5% water-FFB in the 12-year-old to 71.8% in the 18-year-old. Similarly, the data of Young, Bogan, Roe, and Lutwak (1968) and Young, Sipin, and Roe (1968) on female subjects showed a drop in percentage water-FFB from 77% at 9 years to 73.7% at 16 years of age. The effect of even a relatively small percentage water-FFB difference (3%), attributed singly to water content, has been estimated to result in an overestimation of relative body fatness by 4% or more with the densitometric method (Boileau et al., 1984). Moreover, by using body water directly to estimate body composition (hydrometric method), an underestimation of fatness by 3% or more is possible. Thus, it is clear that variation in the water content of the FFB must be considered in developing future body composition models for the maturing youngster.

Variability in FFB Mineral Content

Variation in the mineral content of the FFB (percentage mineral-FFB) also exerts an important influence on FFB composition. The mineral component is derived from both osseous (bone mineral) and nonosseous sources. The nonosseous source constitutes a rather constant and negligible fraction of the FFB, ranging from 0.6 to 1.2% (Brozek et al., 1963; Fomon et al., 1982). On the other hand, the osseous FFB content appears to be more variable, ranging from 2.6% at birth (Fomon et al.) to about 5.6% in the mature adult. Additional variability in mineral content appears to be introduced by race and gender, with blacks and males having

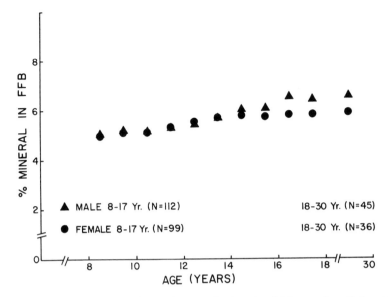

Figure 3   Mean percentage fat-free body mineral values for children and youth (aged 8 to 17 years) and adults (18 to 30 years).

higher values. In body composition work employing the two-component system of fat and FFB, the percentage mineral-FFB has been assumed to constitute 6.8% FFB, a figure based on adult cadaver studies (Brozek et al.). Although *in vivo* estimates of this component are difficult to achieve, use of photon absorptiometry in combination with other body composition techniques has made it possible to estimate the percentage mineral-FFB (Boileau, Lohman, & Slaughter, 1985; Lohman, Slaughter, Boileau, Bunt, & Lussier, 1984). Mean changes in this component as a function of age (8 to 18 years) are presented in Figure 3 for the sample previously described. As shown, both males and females increase somewhat linearly in FFB mineral content from ages 8 to 15 years. The tendency for males to have a higher FFB mineral content can be noted for both adolescents and adults. Fomon et al. (1982) and Haschke (1983) have calculated changes in FFB mineral content similar to those shown in Figure 3. Although the relative change in percentage mineral-FFB appears to be rather small, ranging from about 5.0% (8-year-old) to 6.2% (18-year-old), the influence of this change is substantial because of the high density of this component (3.00 g/cc). Therefore, it appears necessary that variation in mineral content as well as water content of the FFB be considered in developing appropriate models for body composition assessment in children.

It follows then that estimates of body fatness involving both the densitometric and hydrometric approaches need to be developed using a multicomponent model. One such approach in which the Siri (1961) density and water model has been modified to include variability in the body mineral content has been described (Boileau et al., 1985) and is given in Equation 5:

$$f_F = (2.747/D_B) - .727 \text{ (w)} + 1.146 \text{ (m)} - 2.0503 \tag{5}$$

Although more data, both cross-sectional and longitudinal, are needed to validate this approach and to further characterize the variability in FFB water and mineral fractions, it may be possible to estimate these fractions from other indices of growth and development such as maturational status, height, or age. Therefore, when reasonable estimates of the water and mineral fractions can be made, then only body density would need to be measured to resolve Equation 5.

Variability in FFB Potassium Content

Another demonstration of FFB variability in the maturing youngster is reflected in the change in FFB potassium (K) content. Most body K resides in the nonosseous tissues of the FFB and is negligibly found in adipose tissue. Thus, total body K is considered to be an index of FFB and, more specifically, of muscle mass. As indicated earlier, the adult FFB concentration of K has been given at 2.66 gK/kg FFB (Forbes & Hursh, 1963). Although this constant has been debated for the adult female, it is clear that this value is not applicable for children (Forbes, 1978). Fomon et al. (1982) reported FFB K content to range from 2.25 g/kg FFB at birth for both genders to 2.61 and 2.49 gK/kg FFB at 10 years for males and females, respectively. Haschke (1983) has also reported lower K values for the FFB than the adult value (2.66 g/kg FFB) in adolescents. In our previously described sample, values of 2.51 and 2.48 g/kg FFB were observed for prepubescent males and females, compared with adult values of 2.68 and 2.48 gK/kg FFB, respectively (Boileau et al., 1985). These data further indicate instability in the FFB composition and the inappropriateness of employing an adult body composition model to estimate fatness and leanness in the pediatric subject.

Use of Anthropometry to Estimate Fatness and Leanness in Maturing Youngsters

The use of body surface measures including skinfold thicknesses, body widths, and circumferences to estimate whole body composition and ideal body weight has become popular in schools, training rooms, field studies, and clinical settings. These methods are typically based on the relationship of one or more body surface measurements to criterion body composition techniques, particularly densitometry. The methodology, including its advantages and pitfalls, has been thoroughly reviewed by Lohman (1981). Specifically, this procedure is fundamentally based on the assumption that the relationship between the body surface measure(s) and body density is stable and applicable to the sample being studied.

There is evidence in the maturing youngster that this relationship may not be stable, and therefore, the use of anthropometry to estimate body composition may be unsound without consideration of potential violation of this assumption. Further, standard errors of estimating the dependent variable (density) can be substantial, and inter- and intratester variability, even among experienced investigators, can be large.

The relationship of the sum of four skinfold thicknesses (triceps, calf, abdomen, and thigh) to body density for the previously described sample has been reported (Slaughter, Lohman, Boileau, Stillman, et al., 1984). For males, the association between the sum of skinfolds and density was found to be significantly different for prepubescents, pubescents, and postpubescents, with the relationship being similar for postpubescents and adults. In females, on the other hand, the greatest change in this relationship was seen between prepubescents and pubescents. These inconsistencies demonstrate that a generalized equation to estimate either density or fatness may not be possible without considering both the apparent variability in the FFB composition and the changing relationship of subcutaneous fat to density.

The two national fitness evaluations previously mentioned (AAHPERD Publication, 1980; Pate et al., 1985) have utilized two skinfold sites to evaluate fatness in school children: the triceps and the subscapula. The sum of these skinfolds is used as a raw score and is compared to normative data for evaluative purposes. Moreover, the sum of these skinfolds is often used to estimate body fatness from equations developed on adult

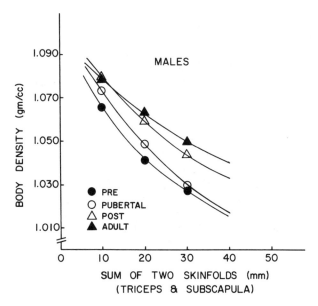

Figure 4   Relationship between the sum of two skinfolds and body density for males in four maturation groups.

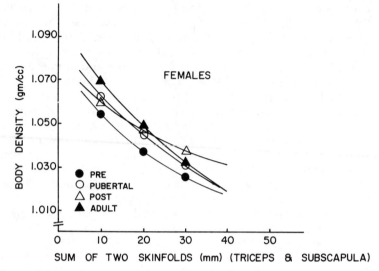

Figure 5 Relationship between the sum of two skinfolds and body density for females in four maturation groups.

samples. Utilization of the sum of these skinfolds to estimate body composition, specifically relative body fatness, is problematic in children. This procedure is debatable because the changing relationship between skinfolds and density will almost certainly lead to a gross overestimation of body fatness. The problem is illustrated in the sample described previously where the sum of two skinfolds is compared with maturation level for males (Figure 4) and females (Figure 5). The results of this analysis, which are generally similar to the data reported by Slaughter et al. (1984) on the sum of four skinfolds, indicate that prepubescent males and females and pubescent males are estimated to have a lower body density for a given skinfold thickness sum. It seems reasonable to suggest that this difference in relationship reflects an instability in the FFB density, and thus a given estimate of body density from skinfolds in maturing youngsters needs to be interpreted in light of changes in FFB maturity.

Recently, general equations for males and females have been proposed to circumvent this problem and to estimate the percentage of body weight that is fat (Boileau et al., 1985). Equation 6 (for 8- to 29-year-old males) and Equation 7 (for 8- to 29-year-old females) were developed by first estimating the f_F (Equation 5) from density, water, and mineral measures and then relating the sum of the triceps (Tri) and subscapula (Subsc) skinfolds to the percentage fat as follows:

$$\% \text{ Fat} = 1.35 \text{ (sum Tri + Subsc)} - 0.012 \text{ (sum Tri + Subsc)}^2 - 4.4$$
$$(6)$$

$$\% \text{ Fat} = 1.35 \text{ (sum Tri + Subsc)} - 0.012 \text{ (sum Tri + Subsc)}^2 - 2.4$$
$$(7)$$

Although these equations estimate percentage fat with relatively good precision, further modification of the intercept term may be needed for both genders at each stage of maturation (Slaughter, Lohman, Boileau, Going, & Horswill, 1984).

Summary

This review focuses on problems associated with the measurement of body composition in terms of fat and fat-free body in children and youth. Specific attention is given to the validity of fundamental concepts inherent in utilizing criterion body composition techniques, including densitometry, hydrometry, and ^{40}K spectroscopy, for the maturing youngster.

The importance of measuring body composition and identifying early predisposition toward overfatness is manifested by the fact that the most common hypokinetic and nutrition-related diseases are obesity and heart disease. Both of these diseases are often referred to as "adult-onset" diseases, although it has become apparent that their genesis can be traced to childhood. Early identification of overfatness and subsequent remedial nutrition and exercise therapy may have an important impact on future adult health status. Assessment of body composition has also been useful for the pediatric athlete. Estimation of minimal, ideal, and maximal body weight for effective performance can be enhanced through the accurate measurement of body composition.

A fundamental assumption in body composition assessment is that the constituents of the FFB are stable and chemically mature. The validity of this assumption in children and youth appears uncertain at best because there is growing evidence that the fat-free body components, which include water, mineral, and protein, are undergoing proportional changes during growth and development. In particular, data suggest that FFB water content decreases and FFB mineral content increases in such a way as to make accepted adult body composition models for criterion methods invalid and therefore inaccurate for the maturing youngster. Additionally, the use of skinfold thicknesses, body widths, and circumferences to estimate body composition appears to be influenced by the instability and chemical immaturity of the FFB in children. Although potential solutions to these problems are proposed, more cross-sectional and longitudinal data on various pediatric samples are needed to definitively deal with the above problems and to validate proposed solutions.

Acknowledgment

Supported in part by NIH Grant AM 35586.

References

AAHPERD Task Force. (1980). *AAHPERD health related physical fitness test manual* (pp. 12-17). Reston, VA: AAHPERD.

Asmussen, E., & Heeboll-Nielsen, K. (1955). A dimensional analysis of physical performance and growth in boys. *Journal of Applied Physiology,* **7**, 593-603.

Boileau, R.A., & Lohman, T.G. (1977). The measurement of human physique and its effect on physical performance. *Orthopedic Clinics of North America,* **8**, 563-581.

Boileau, R.A., Lohman, T.G., & Slaughter, M.H. (1985). Exercise and body composition in children and youth. *Scandinavian Journal of Sport Sciences,* **7**, 17-27.

Boileau, R.A., Lohman, T.G., Slaughter, M.H., Ball, T.E., Going, S.B., & Hendrix, M.K. (1984). Hydration of the fat-free body in children during maturation. *Human Biology,* **56**, 651-666.

Boileau, R.A., Wilmore, J.H., Lohman, T.G., Slaughter, M.H., & Riner, W.F. (1981). Estimation of body density from skinfold thicknesses, body circumferences and skeletal widths in boys aged 8 to 11 years: Comparisons of two samples. *Human Biology,* **53**, 575-592.

Brozek, J., Grande, F., Anderson, J.T., & Keys, A. (1963). Densitometric analysis of body composition: Revision of some quantitative assumptions. *Annals of the New York Academy of Sciences,* **110**, 113-140.

Clarke, K.C. (1974). Predicting certified weight of young wrestlers: A field study of the Tcheng-Tipton method. *Medicine and Science in Sports,* **6**, 52-57.

Coates, T., Killen, J., & Slinkard, L. (1982). Parent participation in a treatment program for overweight adolescents. *International Journal of Eating Disorders,* **1**, 37-48.

Cureton, K.J., Boileau, R.A., & Lohman, T.G. (1975). Relationship between body composition measures and AAHPER test performances in boys. *Research Quarterly,* **46**, 218-229.

Cureton, K.J., Boileau, R.A., Lohman, T.G., & Misner, J.E. (1977). Determinants of distance running performance in children: Analysis of a path model. *Research Quarterly,* **48**, 270-279.

Fomon, S.J., Haschke, F., Ziegler, E.E., & Nelson, S.E. (1982). Body composition of reference children from birth to age 10 years. *American Journal of Clinical Nutrition,* **35**, 1169-1175.

Forbes, G.B. (1978). Body composition in adolescence. In F. Falkner & J.M. Tanner (Eds.), *Human growth* (Vol. 2, pp. 239-272). New York: Plenum.

Forbes, G.B., & Hursh, J.B. (1963). Age and sex trends in lean body mass calculated from K-40 measurements with a note on the theoretical basis for the procedure. *Annals of the New York Academy of Sciences,* **110**, 255-263.

Haschke, F. (1983). Body composition of adolescent males. Part II. Body composition of the male reference adolescent. *Acta Paediatrica Scandinavica* (Suppl. 307), 11-23.

Haschke, F., Fomon, S.J., & Ziegler, E.E. (1981). Body composition of a nine-year-old reference boy. *Pediatric Research*, **15**, 847-849.

Heald, F.P., Hunt, E.E., Schwartz, R., Cook, C.D., Elliot, D., & Vajda, B. (1963). Measures of body fat and hydration in adolescent boys. *Pediatrics*, **31**, 226-239.

Lohman, T.G. (1981). Skinfolds and body density and their relation to body composition: A review. *Human Biology*, **53**, 181-225.

Lohman, T.G. (1984). Research in progress in the validation of laboratory methods of assessing body composition. *Medicine and Science in Sports and Exercise*, **16**, 596-603.

Lohman, T.G., Boileau, R.A., & Slaughter, M.H. (1984). Body composition in children and youth. In R.A. Boileau (Ed.), *Advances in pediatric sports sciences: Vol. 1. Biological issues* (pp. 29-57). Champaign, IL: Human Kinetics.

Lohman, T.G., Slaughter, M.H., Boileau, R.A., Bunt, J., & Lussier, L. (1984). Bone mineral measurements and their relation to body density in children, youth and adults. *Human Biology*, **56**, 667-680.

Moulton, C.R. (1923). Age and chemical development in mammals. *Journal of Biological Sciences*, **57**, 79-97.

Osserman, E.F., Pitts, G.C., Welham, W.C., & Behnke, A.R. (1950). In vivo measurement of body fat and water in a group of normal men. *Journal of Applied Physiology*, **2**, 633-639.

Pařízková, J. (1961). Total body fat and skinfold thickness in children. *Metabolism*, **10**, 794-809.

Pate, R.R., Ross, J.G., Dotson, C.O., & Gilbert, G.G. (1985). The National Children and Youth Fitness Study: The new norms a comparison with the 1980 AAHPERD norms. *Journal of Physical Education, Recreation and Dance*, **56**, 70-72.

Riendeau, R.P., Welch, B.E., Crisp, C.E., Crowley, L.V., Griffin, P.E., & Brockett, J.E. (1958). Relationships of body fat to motor fitness test scores. *Research Quarterly*, **29**, 200-203.

Siri, W.E. (1961). Body composition from fluid spaces and density: Analysis of methods. In J. Brozek & A. Henschel (Eds.), *Techniques for measuring body composition* (pp. 223-244). Washington, DC: National Academy of Sciences.

Slaughter, M.H., Lohman, T.G., Boileau, R.A., Going, S.B., & Horswill, C.A. (1984). Anthropometric equations for estimation of body fatness in children and youth. *AAHPERD Research Abstracts*, 51.

Slaughter, M.H., Lohman, T.G., Boileau, R.A., Stillman, R.J., Van Loan, M., Horswill, C.A., & Wilmore, J.H. (1984). Influence of maturation on relationship of skinfolds to body density: A cross-sectional study. *Human Biology*, **56**, 681-689.

Tanner, J.M. (1962). *Growth at adolescence* (2nd ed.). Oxford: Blackwell Scientific.

Tcheng, T-K., & Tipton, C.M. (1973). Iowa wrestling study: Anthropometric measurements and prediction of a "minimal" body weight for high school wrestlers. *Medicine and Science in Sports, 5,* 1-10.

Wilmore, J.H., & McNamara, J.J. (1974). Prevalence of coronary heart disease risk factors in boys 8-12 years of age. *Journal of Pediatrics, 84,* 527-533.

Ylitalo, V. (1981). Treatment of obese school children. *Acta Paediatrica Scandinavica* (Suppl. 290), 1-108.

Young, C.M., Bogan, A.D., Roe, D.A., & Lutwak, L. (1968). Body composition of pre-adolescent and adolescent girls. IV. Body water and creatinine. *Journal of the American Dietetic Association, 53,* 579-587.

Young, C.M., Sipin, S.S., & Roe, D.A. (1968). Body composition of pre-adolescent and adolescent girls. I. Density and skinfold measurements. *Journal of the American Dietetic Association, 53,* 25-31.

Body Composition
of Young Runners and Young Wrestlers

Chester J. Zelasko
Wayne D. Van Huss
Sharon A. Evans
Robert L. Wells
David J. Anderson

The body composition of young athletes is of great interest for two reasons: The first reason is related to performance. The prevailing thought is that excess body fat is detrimental to an athlete's performance. Long-distance running and wrestling are sports that have the lowest percentage body fat associated with the adult participants. Whether an optimal amount of body fat for maximal performance exists in young athletes is not known for certain. The second is related to expected exercise-induced differences in body composition. Young athletes would be expected to carry less body fat and possibly more fat-free mass than young nonathletes as a result of strenuous exercise.

It may be difficult to discriminate between the potential causes for changes in body composition in young athletes. There is little question that body composition changes as children mature. As the athletes progress through puberty into adolescence, body fat tends to be more variable than the fat-free mass. Females tend to accumulate more body fat than males. Both males and females gain body fat early in adolescence. However, the difference becomes striking in adolescence, stopping, and even regressing in males, whereas females continue to put on body fat as adolescence continues (Forbes, 1978).

Genetics may also play an important role in changes in the body composition of young athletes. Body size, physique, and biological maturation rate are genetically determined and interrelated. The location of fat deposition in humans is also genetically determined (Bouchard & Malina, 1983). However, the quantity of body fat is dependent on environmental factors as well as a genetic predisposition to accumulate body fat.

The body composition of the adult responds to exercise by increasing the fat-free mass while decreasing the percentage body fat. Fat weight may decrease or remain stable. Exercise also appears to affect the body composition of the young. In a review of the role of exercise in weight control, Oscai (1973) stated that exercise can affect the body composition of growing children by decreasing or preventing an increase (associated with the growth spurt) in body fat and by increasing lean tissue.

The last consideration posed is the most perturbing: Does a particular sport like long-distance running or wrestling attract a certain type of young athlete or does the athlete seek out the particular sport? Many physiological as well as psychological and environmental reasons for sport selection could exist. Children may attempt involvement in sports that are appropriate to their body composition. Malina (1975) found negative effects of excess body weight, fatness, and endomorphy on motor items involving movements of the entire body. Thorland, Johnson, Fagot, Tharp, and Hammer (1981), in a study of Junior Olympic athletes, found that particular body composition and somatotype characteristics tended to distinguish between elite and nonelite adolescent competitors in the different activities they sampled. No conclusions can be made about why the young people chose to participate in running or wrestling. However, it must be recognized that the body composition of the young athletes, or their perception of their bodies, may have biased them toward a particular sport.

Body composition measurements of young athletes are one of many variables that are being examined during the longitudinal study of the effects of strenuous exercise on young athletes. This study is part of an interdisciplinary effort taking place at Michigan State University under the auspices of the Youth Sports Institute. The chronic effects of strenuous exercise on the body composition of young athletes, both within group and between groups, are the purpose of this portion of the overall study. This chapter will present some of the data collected on the body composition of young runners and young wrestlers.

Methods

The hydrostatic weighing system in the Center for the Study of Human Performance at Michigan State University used in the longitudinal studies of young runners and wrestlers incorporates two critical elements: First, the underwater lung volume is determined at the same time as the underwater weight, and second, there is a graphic recording of the underwater weight, as first recommended by Akers and Buskirk (1969). The water container is a 1,000 gal polyurethane tank. The weighing assembly is hung from a temperature compensated strain gauge (Model SR-4 Load Cell Type U1-B, Balwin-Lima Hamilton Corporation). The signal is sent to a wheatstone bridge, modified and then sent to the pen recorder (Model 2115M-Allen Datagraph Corporation). The scale is accurate to 0.05 kg with the subject seated anywhere on the weighing bench. The underwater weight of the subject is adjusted according to the depth in the water to compensate for the buoyancy of the air in the rebreathing valve and tubing.

The rebreathing apparatus incorporates a pneumatic driven Geesman valve. One tube leads to room air, whereas the other is attached by tubing to a 2-l capacity rebreathing bag. The valve is controlled by the operator with a toggle switch located on the control panel. Oxygen is bubbled through a water vessel and then into a storage spirometer. Saturating the oxygen with water eliminates the need to dry the sample before it is analyzed. Oxygen is withdrawn from the storage spirometer through a hand operated 1-l syringe (Jaeger). One or 2 l of oxygen are used, depending on the vital lung capacity of the subject. The method of Rahn, Fenn, and Otis (1949) is used to determine underwater lung volume with one modification: Four breaths are used in rebreathing instead of three. A Med-Science Nitralizer with a digital readout is used to analyze the gas in the rebreathing bag.

Calculations of body density are done with a Hewlett-Packard 67 programmable calculator. For this study three trials were used, and the mean of the three trials was used for body composition determinations. The Brozek, Grande, Anderson, and Keys (1963) formula was used for calculating body density, and the Siri (1961) formula was used for calculating percentage body fat. The hardware and methods used in the study ensure the integrity of the data; that is, data collected from one test period to another are reliable.

The data for the body composition analysis of the young runners consist of each subject's most recent measurement. Due to the low numbers of subjects in each age category, the data for the last 2 years were pooled. Multivariate analysis was used in a 2 × 2 design, runners-controls and male-female, with weight, percentage fat, and fat-free mass serving as dependent variables.

The data for the body composition analysis of the young wrestlers were selected differently. There were 55 wrestlers that were tested both in the fall of 1984 and the spring of 1985. This was defined loosely as preseason and postseason. The wrestlers were divided into seven age groups, and a repeated measures multivariate analysis of variance was used to determine what differences, if any, occurred between the two testing sessions. Weight, percentage body fat, fat-free mass, and height served as dependent variables.

Results

Young Runners

Table 1 gives the mean values and standard deviations for weight, percentage body fat, and fat-free mass. There were fewer controls than desired, but a completely balanced research design with equal numbers of subjects in each possible category in a longitudinal study of this magnitude is not possible. Comparing the means, it is apparent that across the variables, the magnitude of the differences between the means of the control group is greater than that of the runner group. There was a 1.3-kg difference in weight between male runners-female runners versus a 5.9-kg difference for male controls-female controls. In percentage body fat, there was a 2.6% difference between male runners-female runners versus a 4.8% difference in male controls-female controls. Finally, there was a 4.5-kg difference in fat-free mass in male runners-female runners versus an 8.0-kg difference between male controls-female controls.

Table 1 Runners Versus Controls: Mean Values for Weight, Percentage Fat, and Fat-Free Mass

Group	N	Weight (kg)	Fat (%)	Fat-free mass (kg)
Male runners	21	43.5 ± 11.1$_a$	13.6 ± 5.2	37.9 ± 10.9
Female runners	16	42.2 ± 7.4$_b$	16.2 ± 3.4$_b$	35.4 ± 6.4
Male controls	10	57.3 ± 9.0$_a$	17.1 ± 5.4$_c$	47.6 ± 8.9
Female controls	12	51.4 ± 7.2$_b$	22.9 ± 4.0$_{bc}$	39.6 ± 5.4

Note. Means having the same subscript are significantly different at $p < .01$.

All multivariate comparisons of runners versus controls were significant at the .01 level. The univariate comparisons of male runners versus male controls found only weight was significantly different ($p < .01$) among the dependent variables. The univariate comparison of female runners and female controls showed there were statistically significant differences in weight and percentage body fat ($p < .01$) but not in fat-free mass.

The multivariate analysis of male runners versus female runners was not significant ($p = .33$). The multivariate analysis of the comparison of male controls versus female controls was significant overall ($p < .01$). In the univariate comparisons, only percentage body fat was significant ($p < .01$).

Young Wrestlers

The analyses of the data of the young wrestlers are represented in Figures 1, 2, 3, and 4. Each subject was placed in an age group for the fall testing session and remained in that group for all data analysis.

No statistically significant differences were evident in percentage body fat, weight, fat-free mass, or height between the testing sessions. However, there were changes in each dependent variable across each age group. Each age group, except the last, experienced a decrease in percentage body fat. The mean decrease in percentage body fat was 1.3%. Each age group experienced an increase in body weight from fall to spring. The mean increase in weight was 1.5 kg. Each age group demonstrated an increase in fat-free mass. The mean increase in fat-free mass was 2.2 kg. Each age group underwent an increase in height with the mean increase of 1.7 cm.

Although there were no statistically significant differences between percentage body fat, weight, fat-free mass, and height from fall to spring, a statistically significant effect of age in all four variables was observed. The effect of age was expected. It is reasonable to expect that as young persons get older they will gain weight and grow taller.

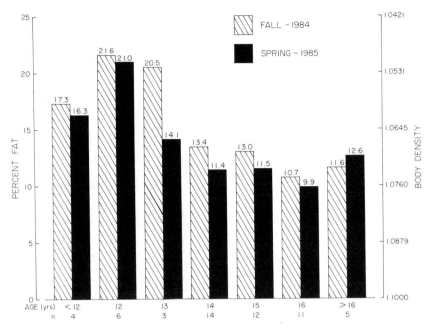

Figure 1 Young wrestlers' percentage body fat—body density, fall 1984-spring 1985, by age group.

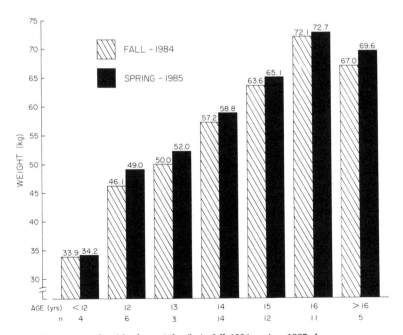

Figure 2 Young wrestlers' body weight (kg), fall 1984-spring 1985, by age group.

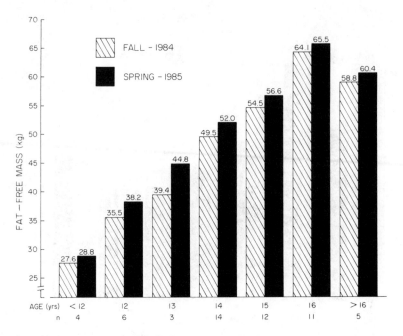

Figure 3 Young wrestlers' fat-free mass (kg), fall 1984-spring 1985, by age group.

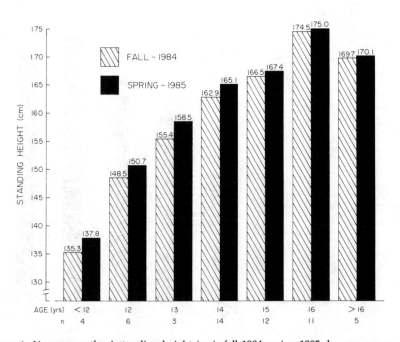

Figure 4 Young wrestlers' standing height (cm), fall 1984-spring 1985, by age group.

Discussion

The data on the young runners (Table 1) reveal no surprises. Differences between runners and controls were expected. Studies on young runners are limited. Mayers and Gutin (1979), in a study of prepubertal male cross-country runners, found that the runners tended to be leaner (less body fat) than did the controls. This preliminary analysis tends to support that conclusion.

Differences between males and females were also expected. The male controls-female controls conformed to expected differences in percentage body fat and fat-free mass. The male runners-female runners comparisons for percentage fat were in the expected direction. Male runners were leaner by 2.6% body fat. This difference in percentage body fat from female runners can be explained by the increased fat-free mass of the male runners.

The data on the young wrestlers (Figures 1 to 4) proved interesting. One of the primary concerns of strenuous exercise in young wrestlers is that growth may be inhibited. We would expect a decrease in percentage body fat. Although not statistically significant, there was a decrease in percentage body fat in each age group except the over-16 age group. The overall mean for all wrestlers (12.6%) was less than that for male runners. Sady, Thomson, Savage, and Petratis (1982) found that wrestlers 9 to 12 years of age were significantly leaner than control subjects.

Pařizková (1976) reported that in a longitudinal study of a group of normal young males, rapid increases in weight, fat-free mass, and standing height occurred between the ages of 12.7 to 15.7 years. The activity levels of that study reported 25% of the subjects were involved in vigorous activity whereas 25% were sedentary. The remaining 50% were considered to be moderately active. The mean increases in weight, fat-free mass, and standing height were greatest for the 13- through 16-year-old age groups in the present study.

The mean increases in weight, fat-free mass, and standing height that each age group experienced between testing sessions in the current study are encouraging. The data suggest that, at least in this preliminary analysis, growth may not have been impaired by their strenuous participation in wrestling.

The data require further analysis. Although all subjects in the study of young wrestlers were wrestlers, they were not all at the same level of competition. The level of competition may affect or may be affected by the body composition of the participants. The data must also be analyzed taking into consideration the age at which the subjects began competitive wrestling. The results of this preliminary analysis of the data, however, are very encouraging.

There is a final consideration. The biological variability of young persons may have an effect on body composition estimations. Lohman, Slaughter, Boileau, Bunt, and Lussier (1984) reported that the bone mineral content of children is less than in adults. Boileau et al. (1984) reported that the total body water of children is a greater percentage of the lean body mass than in adults. The combined effect of less bone mineral and greater total body water would yield overestimations of percentage body fat in children. Studies have yet to be completed on the bone mineral, total body water, and protein mass of young athletes. It will be important to examine the exercise effects on each compartment (bone mineral, body water, and protein mass) and their possible implications in body composition estimations.

References

Akers, R., & Buskirk, E.R. (1969). An underwater weighing system utilizing force cube transducers. *Journal of Applied Physiology*, **26**, 649-652.

Boileau, R.A., Lohman, T.G., Slaughter, M.H., Ball, T.E., Going, S.B., & Hendrix, M.K. (1984). Hydration of the fat free body in children during maturation. *Human Biology*, **56**, 651-656.

Bouchard, C., & Malina, R.M. (1983). Genetics of physiological fitness and motor performance. In R.L. Terjung (Ed.), *Exercise and sport sciences reviews* (Vol. 11, pp. 306-339). Philadelphia: Franklin Press.

Brozek, J., Grande, F., Anderson, J.T., & Keys, A. (1963). Densitometric analysis of body composition: Revision of quantitative assumptions. *Annals of the New York Academy*, **110**, 113-140.

Forbes, G.S. (1978). Body composition in adolescence. In F. Falkner & J.M. Tanner (Eds.), *Human growth* (Vol. 2, pp. 239-272). New York: Plenum Press.

Lohman, T.G., Slaughter, M.H., Boileau, R.A., Bunt, J., & Lussier, L. (1984). Bone mineral measurements and their relation to body density in children, youth and adults. *Human Biology*, **56**, 667-679.

Malina, R.M. (1975). Anthropometric correlates of performance. In J.H. Wilmore & J.F. Keogh (Eds.), *Exercise and sport sciences reviews* (Vol. 3, pp. 249-274). New York: Plenum Press.

Mayers, N., & Gutin, B. (1979). Physiological characteristics of elite prepubertal cross country runners. *Medicine and Science in Sports and Exercise*, **11**, 172-176.

Oscai, L.B. (1973). The role of exercise in weight control. In J.H. Wilmore (Ed.), *Exercise and sport sciences reviews* (Vol. 1, pp. 103-125). New York: Academic Press.

Pařízková, J. (1976). Growth and growth velocity of lean body mass and fat in adolescent boys. *Pediatric Research*, **10**, 647-650.

Rahn, H., Fenn, W.O., & Otis, A.B. (1949). Daily variations of vital capacity, residual air and expiratory reserve including a study of the residual air method. *Journal of Applied Physiology*, **1**, 725-736.

Sady, S.P., Thomson, W., Savage, M., & Petratis, M. (1982). The body composition and physiological dimensions of 9 – 12 year old experienced wrestlers. *Medicine and Science in Sports and Exercise*, **14**, 210-213.

Siri, W.E. (1961). Body composition from fluid spaces and density: Analysis of methods. In *Techniques for measuring body composition* (pp. 223-244). Washington, DC: National Academy of Sciences.

Thorland, W.G., Johnson, G.O., Fagot, T.G., Tharp, G.D., & Hammer, R.W. (1981). Body composition and somatotype characteristics of Junior Olympic athletes. *Medicine and Science in Sports and Exercise, 13*, 332-338.

Comparison of Nutrient Intakes Between Elite Wrestlers and Runners

Rachel A. Schemmel

Elaina Ryder

Jane A. Moeggenberg

Carole A. Conn

Interest and participation in organized athletic activities have increased in the United States. This may be related to several factors, one of which is an overall concern for health. Thus, health professionals are frequently asked to provide information on appropriate diets for athletes. However, little is known about the food practices of high school athletes or their knowledge about nutrition. In a study designed to assess high school athletes' knowledge about nutrition and food behavior, Douglas and Douglas (1984) reported that from among participants in 18 different sports, participants in track and field had significantly more knowledge about nutrition and significantly better food practices than the average for all other athletes. On the other hand, the study suggested that wrestlers knew less about nutrition than all other athletes. Even so, as was true for runners, there was a trend for wrestlers to have better food practices than the average for all other participants in the study. In a different study, wrestlers' food practices, based on whether or not they ate all of the foods recommended in the four food groups (United States Department of Agriculture [USDA], 1977), were similar to track and field high school athletes.

Even though there have been several government supported studies (Carrol, Abraham, & Dresser, 1983; USDA, 1980; United States Department of Health, Education, and Welfare [US Dept. HEW], 1977) carried out to determine the nutrient intakes of people in the United States, little is known about what young athletes eat. The purpose of this study was to determine what young runners and wrestlers ate and to compare their nutrient intakes to each other as well as with the Recommended Dietary Allowances (RDA) (Food and Nutrition Board, 1980). Because nutrient intakes of males and females in the general population differ (Bailey, Wagner, Davis, & Dinning, 1984), nutrient intakes for male runners only were compared to nutrient intakes of male wrestlers.

Method

Seventy-four elite young male wrestlers and 22 elite young male runners participated in the study. The wrestlers were the winners in their specific age/weight classifications at state wrestling matches in Michigan. The runners were winners in cross-country races held in Michigan. Subjects ranged in age from 8 years, 6 months to 15 years, 8 months.

Subjects were requested to keep a 3-day record of all foods eaten. The 3 days included 2 weekdays and 1 weekend day. Parents and subjects were provided written instructions regarding proper completion of food records. Subjects were urged to include such information as brand names, recipe ingredients, and methods of preparation on the food records. They were also asked to indicate on the food record any intake of vitamin supplements, the amount ingested, and the brand name. The food records were brought to the Youth Sports Institute on the day of testing. At that time a trained interviewer evaluated the food records with the subject. Parents, when present, also participated in the interview. Various sized glasses, bowls, plates, and models representative of meat serving sizes were available to help subjects estimate the amount of food eaten. During the interview, records were checked for possible omissions such as butter or margarine on bread or sugar added to cereal.

The information obtained from the food records was coded for computer analyses using the MSU Nutrient Data Bank (Morgan & Zabik, 1984). The Nutrient Data Bank contains over 5,000 food items, many of which are listed by brand name. Nutrient intakes were evaluated based on RDA (Food and Nutrition Board, 1980).

Subjects were grouped according to the age classifications used for the RDA. Subjects classified as ≤ 10 included runners 8 years, 6 months to 10 years, 5 months and wrestlers 10 years, 0 months to 10 years, 5 months. Eleven- to 14-year-old subjects for both wrestlers and runners included subjects who ranged in age from 10 years, 6 months to 14 years, 5 months. Subjects classified as ≥ 15 included subjects 14 years, 6 months to 15 years, 8 months for both wrestlers and runners.

To determine relative weights of the subjects, the actual height per age was plotted on the NCHS growth charts for males (Hamill et al., 1979), and the weight that fell in the same percentile as height per age was used as a reasonable weight. The actual weight divided by the reasonable weight multiplied by 100 equaled the relative weight. To evaluate energy intakes relative to body weight, three relative weight classifications were used: ≤ 90%, 95 to 105%, and ≥ 120%. Energy intakes of wrestlers and runners who fell within these classifications were compared. Other subjects, who had relative weights ranging from 91 to 94% and 106 to 119% were dropped from the comparisons. The Bonferroni t test (Games, 1977) was used to determine significant differences between nutrient intakes of wrestlers and runners.

Table 1 Energy Intakes of Wrestlers and Runners

Sport	Age (years/months)	N	Total kcal	Energy intakes RDA (%)	BW (kcal/kg)
All subjects					
Wrestlers	10/0 - 15/8	74	2479 ± 112^a	95 ± 5^b	52 ± 3^b
Runners	8/5 - 15/8	22	2469 ± 123	99 ± 6^b	63 ± 3^b
Age classifications					
⩽ 10					
Wrestlers	10/0 - 10/5	4	1892 ± 205^c	77 ± 16^c	64 ± 14^c
Runners	8/5 - 10/5	4	1952 ± 229^c	77 ± 2^c	65 ± 1
11 - 14					
Wrestlers	10/6 - 14/5	50	2459 ± 124^{b,c,d}	92 ± 5^{b,c,d}	53 ± 3^{b,c,d}
Runners	10/6 - 14/5	14	2541 ± 159^{b,c,d}	105 ± 7^{b,c}	66 ± 5^{b,d}
⩾ 15					
Wrestlers	14/6 - 15/8	20	2703 ± 270^d	105 ± 11^d	44 ± 5^d
Runners	14/6 - 15/8	4	2736 ± 185^d	102 ± 14	50 ± 2^d

^{a}Means ± SEM. ^{b}Significant difference ($p < .01$) between all wrestlers and runners or between wrestlers and runners in the same age classification. ^{c}Significant difference ($p < .01$) between subjects ⩽ 10 vs. 11 to 14 years old who participated in the same sport. ^{d}Significant difference ($p < .01$) between subjects 11 to 14 vs. ⩾ 15 years old who participated in the same sport.

Results

Energy

Mean intakes of energy for both wrestlers and runners were close to 100% of the RDA, even though wrestlers consumed a slightly lower percentage of the recommended dietary allowance for kilocalories ($p < .01$) than did runners (Table 1). The mean intake of total kilocalories per day was the same for wrestlers and runners. This observation was surprising but meaningless due to diverse ages and weights of subjects within the groups. Nevertheless, it does provide a common basis for intake comparisons of other nutrients. In general, younger subjects consumed fewer total kilocalories, a lower percentage of the RDA for energy, but more kilocalories per kilogram body weight than older subjects. Runners consumed 21% more energy per kilogram body weight than did wrestlers (Table 1). However, the difference in energy intake of wrestlers compared to runners was related to body weight differences. When body weight differences were eliminated by expressing body weight as relative body weight, kilocalorie intakes of runners and wrestlers per kilogram

Table 2 Energy Intakes of Wrestlers and Runners Based on Relative Body Weights

Sport	Relative weight (%)	Subjects N	%	Energy intake RDA (kcal, %)	BW (kcal/kg)
Wrestlers	≤ 90	4	6	133 ± 27^{a,b}	74 ± 10^b
Runners	≤ 90	8	35	107 ± 12^b	68 ± 8^b
Wrestlers	95 to 105	27	38	98 ± 6^{b,c}	58 ± 4^{b,c}
Runners	95 to 105	8	35	94 ± 7^b	58 ± 3^b
Wrestlers	≥ 120	15	21	79 ± 10^c	38 ± 5^c
Runners	≥ 120	1	4	62	37

^{a}Means ± SEM. ^{b}Significant difference ($p < .01$) between subjects with a relative weight of ≤ 90% vs. 95 to 105% who participated in the same sport. ^{c}Significant difference ($p < .01$) between subjects with a relative weight of 95 to 105% vs. ≥ 120% who participated in the same sport.

body weight (Table 2) were similar. The data in Table 2 also clearly show that lighter weight subjects consumed more energy per kilogram of body weight than did heavier subjects.

Thirty-five percent (8 out of 22) of the runners had a relative weight of ≤ 90% compared to only 6% (4 out of 74) of the wrestlers. However, 21% of the wrestlers had a relative weight of ≥ 120%, whereas only 1 of 22 runners (4%) was included in that classification.

Runners consumed a higher percentage of energy from carbohydrates than did wrestlers (Table 3). To compensate for the lower percentage of energy intake from carbohydrates, wrestlers consumed a higher percentage of energy from fat than did runners.

Protein

About 13 to 14% of dietary energy was derived from protein (Table 3). Mean intakes of protein were nearly twice the RDA for both wrestlers and runners (Table 4). The mean intake of protein expressed as percentage of the RDA was highest for subjects between 11 and 14 years of age when compared with younger or older subjects ($p < .01$). Generally, wrestlers consumed slightly more animal protein than did runners, whereas runners consumed slightly more plant protein than did wrestlers. However, this was not true for subjects ≤ 10 years of age.

Fat and Carbohydrate

Runners consumed less dietary fat than wrestlers. This finding was less evident in the ≤ 10-year-old group (Table 5) than in the other two groups.

Table 3 Sources of Energy in the Diets of Wrestlers and Runners

Source	Percentage of energy (kcal)		
	Wrestlers	Runners	Sig
Protein	13.0 ± 0.4^a	13.9 ± 0.5	NS
Carbohydrate	48.1 ± 0.8	51.3 ± 1.2	$p < .01$
Fat	40.7 ± 1.7	36.7 ± 1.0	$p < .01$

[a]Means $\pm$ SEM.

Table 4 Quantity and Sources of Protein in Diets of Wrestlers and Runners

Sport		Protein intakes[a]	
	RDA (%)	Animal (% of total)	Plant (% of total)
All subjects			
Wrestlers	$196 \pm 10^{b,c}$	60 ± 2^c	23 ± 1^c
Runners	214 ± 15^c	55 ± 4^c	28 ± 2^c
Age classifications (years)			
$\leqslant 10$			
Wrestlers	186 ± 38^d	59 ± 11	36 ± 7^d
Runners	201 ± 30^d	66 ± 6^d	24 ± 4
11 - 14			
Wrestlers	$202 \pm 12^{c,d,e}$	60 ± 2^c	$23 \pm 2^{c,d}$
Runners	$222 \pm 22^{c,d,e}$	$52 \pm 6^{c,d}$	29 ± 3^c
$\geqslant 15$			
Wrestlers	$181 \pm 18^{c,e}$	58 ± 4	25 ± 2
Runners	$200 \pm 21^{c,e}$	59 ± 4	30 ± 2

[a]Values for percentage of animal and plant protein do not add up to 100% because the protein source in some food mixtures is not identified. [b]Means $\pm$ SEM. [c]Significant difference ($p < .01$) between all wrestlers and runners or wrestlers and runners in the same age classifications. [d]Significant difference ($p < .01$) between subjects $\leqslant 10$ vs. 11 to 14 years old who participated in the same sport. [e]Significant difference ($p < .01$) between subjects 11 to 14 vs. $\geqslant 15$ years old who participated in the same sport.

However, the polyunsaturated to saturated fat ratio was similar for all groups. Wrestlers consumed 9% (a mean of 29 mg) more cholesterol than did runners. Greater quantities of dietary fat and cholesterol were consumed by older than by younger subjects. It should be pointed out,

Table 5   Fat, Cholesterol, and Dietary Fiber Intakes of Wrestlers and Runners

Sport	Fat (g)	P:S[a] ratio	Cholesterol (mg)	Dietary fiber (g)
All subjects				
Wrestlers	114 ± 6[b,c]	1:2.9	335 ± 24[d]	9 ± 1[c]
Runners	101 ± 6[c]	1:3.3	306 ± 53[d]	12 ± 1[c]
Age classifications (years)				
≤ 10				
Wrestlers	79 ± 9[e]	1:3.4	243 ± 37[c,e]	11 ± 3
Runners	76 ± 6[e]	1:3.1	213 ± 67[c,e]	10 ± 4
11 - 14				
Wrestlers	114 ± 7[c,e,f]	1:2.7	343 ± 30[d,e,f]	8 ± 1[c]
Runners	106 ± 7[c,e]	1:3.3	332 ± 69[d,e]	11 ± 2[c,f]
≥ 15				
Wrestlers	127 ± 14[c,f]	1:3.3	326 ± 46[f]	9 ± 1[c]
Runners	107 ± 12[c]	1:3.2	327 ± 94	16 ± 3[c,f]

[a]Polyunsaturated to saturated fat ratio. [b]Means ± SEM. [c,d]Significant difference ([c] = $p <$ .01; [d] = $p <$ .05) between all wrestlers and runners or between wrestlers and runners in the same age classifications. [e]Significant difference ($p < .01$) between subjects ≤ 10 vs. 11 to 14 years old who participated in the same sport. [f]Significant difference ($p < .01$) between subjects 11 to 14 vs. ≥ 15 years old who participated in the same sport.

however, that older subjects also ate more food than younger subjects (Table 5).

In general, runners consumed 34% more dietary fiber than wrestlers (Table 5). However, there was no difference in intakes in subjects 10 years old or less. Runners 15 years and older tended to have higher intakes of dietary fiber than younger runners.

Minerals and Vitamins

Mean intakes expressed as percentage of RDA for calcium, phosphorus, iron, zinc, and iodine were the same for wrestlers and runners (Table 6). However, runners consumed significantly more magnesium than did wrestlers.

Except for wrestlers 15 years and older, mean intakes of all minerals were over 67% of the RDA. Even though mean calcium intakes were over 100% of the RDA, 18% of the subjects did not receive 67% of the RDA

Table 6 Mineral Intakes of Wrestlers (W) and Runners (R) Expressed as Percentage of RDA

			Percentage RDA			
	Calcium	Phosphorus	Magnesium	Iron	Zinc	Iodine
All subjects						
W	102 ± 5[a]	128 ± 6	72 ± 5[b]	88 ± 4	74 ± 4	91 ± 10
R	103 ± 9	140 ± 12	101 ± 10[b]	91 ± 28	77 ± 7	88 ± 13
Age classifications (years)						
≤ 10						
W	115 ± 23[c]	143 ± 21	73 ± 15[b]	113 ± 44[c]	72 ± 15	70 ± 34[c]
R	98 ± 22	142 ± 34	99 ± 28[b]	124 ± 20[c]	85 ± 11[c]	79 ± 33
11 - 14						
W	97 ± 6[c,d]	125 ± 7[c,d]	75 ± 8[b,d]	86 ± 5[c]	74 ± 5	87 ± 12[c,d]
R	101 ± 10	131 ± 12[d]	98 ± 14[b,d]	80 ± 6[c,d]	70 ± 7[c,d]	80 ± 14[d]
≥ 15						
W	109 ± 12[d]	135 ± 14[b,d]	64 ± 5[b,d]	86 ± 8	75 ± 9	101 ± 21[d]
R	115 ± 38	167 ± 46[b,d]	118 ± 30[b,d]	97 ± 10[d]	94 ± 28[d]	128 ± 55[d]

[a]Means ± SEM. [b]Significant difference ($p < .01$) between all wrestlers and runners or between wrestlers and runners in the same age classification. [c]Significant difference ($p < .01$) between subjects ≤ 10 vs. 11 to 14 years old who participated in the same sport. [d]Significant difference ($p < .01$) between subjects 11 to 14 vs. ≥ 15 years old who participated in the same sport.

Table 7 Percentage of Athletes Who Ingested 200% or Over, Between 68 to 99%, and 67% or Less of the RDA for Minerals

Minerals	Percentage of athletes					
	> 200% of RDA		68-99% of RDA		< 67% of RDA	
	Wrestlers	Runners	Wrestlers	Runners	Wrestlers	Runners
Calcium (%)	1	5	31	32	18	18
Phosphorus (%)	10	18	22	23	5	5
Magnesium (%)	1	5	37	55	53	23
Iron (%)	0	0	43	46	30	23
Zinc (%)	0	0	28	27	51	50
Iodine (%)	7	5	15	23	39	41

Table 8 Vitamin Intake of Wrestlers (W) and Runners (R) Expressed as Percentage of the RDA

	Vitamin A	Vitamin C	Thiamin	Preformed niacin	Riboflavin	Vitamin B-6	Vitamin B-12	Folic acid
				Percentage RDA				
All subjects								
W	105 ± 7[a,b]	249 ± 28[b]	122 ± 4[b]	128 ± 6	140 ± 4[b]	84 ± 5[b]	161 ± 9[b]	66 ± 5[b]
R	146 ± 20[b]	351 ± 62[b]	144 ± 19[b]	129 ± 8	146 ± 7[b]	101 ± 9[b]	176 ± 15[b]	81 ± 10[b]
Age classifications (years)								
≤ 10								
W	128 ± 53[c]	207 ± 20[c]	128 ± 9	116 ± 11	136 ± 22	89 ± 11	116 ± 22[b,c]	87 ± 15[c]
R	128 ± 19	181 ± 69[c]	125 ± 14	154 ± 32[c]	144 ± 22	110 ± 28	169 ± 24[b]	96 ± 22[b]
11 - 14								
W	105 ± 9[b,c]	240 ± 37[b,c,d]	120 ± 5[b,d]	132 ± 8[d]	144 ± 5[d]	86 ± 7[d]	163 ± 11[c]	60 ± 5[c,d]
R	127 ± 22[b,d]	334 ± 66[b,c,d]	141 ± 30[b,d]	114 ± 8[c,d]	141 ± 7	88 ± 10[d]	165 ± 19[d]	62 ± 7[c]
≥ 15								
W	101 ± 9[b]	279 ± 51[b,d]	128 ± 9[b,d]	117 ± 9[d]	132 ± 10[b,d]	80 ± 8[b,d]	166 ± 20[b]	80 ± 8[b]
R	229 ± 82[b,d]	579 ± 254[b,d]	171 ± 17[b,d]	154 ± 12[d]	163 ± 29[b]	135 ± 24[b,d]	227 ± 47[b,d]	116 ± 32[b,d]

[a]Means ± SEM. [b]Significant difference ($p < .01$) between all wrestlers and runners or between wrestlers and runners in the same age classification. [c]Significant difference ($p < .01$) between subjects ≤ 10 vs. 11 to 14 years old who participated in the same sport. [d]Significant difference ($p < .01$) between subjects 11 to 14 vs. ≥ 15 years old who participated in the same sport.

Table 9   Percentage of Athletes Who Ingested 200% or Over, Between 68 to 99%, and 67% or Less of the RDA for Vitamins

| Vitamins | Percentage of athletes | | | | | |
| | > 200% of RDA | | 68-99% of RDA | | < 67% of RDA | |
	Wrestlers	Runners	Wrestlers	Runners	Wrestlers	Runners
A (%)	7	9	32	14	18	14
C (%)	57	68	12	9	7	5
Thiamin (%)	3	5	20	23	0	0
Niacin (%)	8	5	26	14	0	0
Riboflavin (%)	4	5	10	5	1	0
B-6 (%)	1	0	20	32	46	27
B-12 (%)	23	32	7	14	14	0
Folic acid (%)	0	0	22	41	60	46

for calcium (Table 7). Subjects within the 11- to 14-year-old age group, compared to the other age groups, consumed the lowest percentage of the RDA for calcium. Fifty-three percent of the wrestlers and 23% of the runners consumed less than 67% of the RDA for magnesium. Thirty percent of wrestlers and 23% of runners consumed less than 67% of the RDA for iron. Ten and 18% of wrestlers and runners, respectively, consumed over 200% of the RDA for phosphorus.

Data related to vitamin intake presented in Tables 8 and 9 refer to that present in food only. However, 43% of wrestlers and 27% of runners ingested multivitamin supplements either with or without iron. Mean intakes of all vitamins were over 100% of the RDA except for vitamin B-6 and folic acid. Mean food intakes of each vitamin expressed as percentage of RDA were significantly higher for all runners than for all wrestlers except for preformed niacin (Table 8). However, when classified according to age, this was not always true.

Even though mean intakes were 100% or more of the RDA, several subjects had low intakes of vitamins A, C, B-6, and folic acid (Table 9). Fifty-seven and 68% of wrestlers and runners, respectively, consumed over 200% of the RDA for vitamin C from the diet alone. In addition to this, 27% of runners and 22% of wrestlers ingested vitamin C supplements (generally 500 mg) on a regular basis, usually daily. Twenty-three and 32% of wrestlers and runners, respectively, received over 200% of the RDA for vitamin B-12.

Discussion

Energy needs of children and adolescents are difficult to assess because of differences in body size, stage of physical development, and intensity and duration of physical activity. For these reasons recommendations for kilocalories are necessarily broad, ranging from 45 to 60 kcal/kg body weight for males 11 to 14 years old as well as 15 to 18 years old (Alford & Bogle, 1983; Food and Agriculture Organization/World Health Organization [FAO/WHO] Joint ad hoc Committee, 1973; Food and Nutrition Board, 1980). The recommended energy intake (Food and Nutrition Board, 1980) for children 7 to 10 years old is 80 kcal/kg body weight. Based on kilocalories per kilogram body weight, younger children have higher energy needs than older children. Because the children in this study were closer to 10 years old than to 7 years old, the energy intake per kilogram of body weight was lower than the recommended levels. On the surface, it seems that runners consumed more kilocalories per kilogram per body weight than wrestlers. However, when body weights were standardized by use of relative weight, energy intakes were the same for wrestlers and runners. The study sample reflected a higher percentage of heavier wrestlers than runners. Energy needs of lean body mass are greater than for body fat.

In general, wrestlers consumed more dietary fat and cholesterol and less dietary fiber, plant protein, and vitamins than runners, whereas mineral intakes were similar between wrestlers and runners. For minerals such as iron and calcium, subjects 11 to 14 years old usually consumed a lower percentage of the RDA than subjects 10 years or younger. This is related to the changing standards of the RDA (Food and Nutrition Board, 1980) from 800 to 1,200 mg calcium per day and from 10 to 18 mg iron per day for subjects 7 to 10 years old versus subjects 11 to 14 years old, respectively. The RDA for subjects 15 years and older is the same as the RDA for subjects 11 to 14 years old. Subjects 15 years and older consumed more total kilocalories each day than subjects 11 to 14 years old, and as kilocalories increase, sources of other nutrients also increase (Morgan, Zabik, Cole, & Leveille, 1980). Although intakes of vitamin B-6, folic acid, zinc, and magnesium appear to be low for the subjects in this study, the data should be interpreted with restraint because at this time many foods have not yet been analyzed for these nutrients.

The intake of fat and cholesterol for wrestlers in this study was similar to the intake of fat and cholesterol reported in a previous study (Schemmel, Stone, & Conn, 1986) for male runners and controls. Compared with male runners in that study (Schemmel et al., 1986), male runners in this study consumed approximately 10% less fat, cholesterol, and iron.

Several authors (Frank, Hollatz, Webber, & Berenson, 1984; Guthrie, 1984) have raised questions about the validity of reported food and nutrient intake data obtained from diet records. However, use of food models to assist in quantifying food intake and a 3-day food diary, as obtained in this study, are effective in reducing experimental error. Even so, the slight but frequently significant differences in nutrient intakes between wrestlers and runners could fall within the experimental error of the method. Yet, the error would apply equally across both groups of subjects, thereby suggesting that the differences reported in this study are true differences.

Acknowledgments

The authors express thanks to Dr. Vern Seefeldt, Youth Sports Institute, Michigan State University, for inviting them to participate in this comprehensive study of elite young runners and wrestlers. This study was supported in part by an MSU Foundation Research Initiation Grant from the College of Human Ecology.

References

Alford, B.B., & Bogle, M.L. (1983). *Nutrition during the life cycle.* Englewood Cliffs, NJ: Prentice-Hall.

Bailey, L.B., Wagner, P.A., Davis, C.G., & Dinning, J.S. (1984). Food frequency related to folacin status in adolescents. *Journal of the American Dietetic Association,* **84**, 801-804.

Carrol, M.D., Abraham, S., & Dresser, C.M. (1983). *Dietary intake source data: United States, 1976-1980* (Vital and Health Statistics, Series 11-No. 231, DHHS Publication No. [PHS] 83-1681). Hyattsville, MD: National Center for Health Statistics.

Douglas, P.D., & Douglas, J.G. (1984). Nutrition knowledge and food practices of high school athletes. *Journal of the American Dietetic Association,* **84**, 1198-1202.

Food and Agriculture Organization/World Health Organization (FAO/WHO) Joint ad hoc Expert Committee. (1973). *Energy and protein requirements* (FAO of the United Nations Nutrition Meetings Report Series No. 52 and WHO Technical Report Series No. 522). Rome: Food and Agriculture Organization of the United Nations.

Food and Nutrition Board. (1980). *Recommended dietary allowances* (9th ed.). Washington, DC: National Research Council, National Academy of Sciences.

Frank, G.C., Hollatz, A.T., Webber, L.S., & Berenson, G.S. (1984). Effect of interviewer recording practices on nutrient intake—Bogalusa Heart Study. *Journal of the American Dietetic Association,* **84**, 1432-1439.

Games, P.A. (1977). An improved *t*-table for simultaneous control on g contrasts. *American Statisticians Association Journal,* **72**, 531-534.

Guthrie, H.A. (1984). Selection and quantification of typical food portions for young adults. *Journal of the American Dietetic Association,* **84**, 1440-1444.

Hamill, P.V.V., Drizd, T.A., Johnson, C.L., Reed, R.B., Roche, A.F., & Moore, W.M. (1979). Physical growth: National Center for Health Statistics percentiles. *American Journal of Clinical Nutrition,* **32**, 607-629.

Morgan, K.J., & Zabik, M.E. (1984). *Coding manual for Michigan State University Data Bank.* East Lansing: Michigan State University.

Morgan, K.J., Zabik, M.E., Cole, R., & Leveille, G.A. (1980). *Nutrient intake patterns of children ages 3 to 12 years based on seven-day food diaries* (Research Report 406). East Lansing: Michigan State University Agricultural Experiment Station.

Schemmel, R.A., Stone, M., & Conn, C. (1986). Comparison of dietary habits and nutrient intakes of competitive runners with age/gender matched controls. In M. Weiss & D. Gould (Eds.), *Sport for children and youths* (pp. 231-238). Champaign, IL: Human Kinetics.

United States Department of Agriculture. (1977). *Food for fitness—A daily food guide* (3rd rev. ed.) (Leaflet No. 424). Washington, DC: U.S. Government Printing Office.

United States Department of Agriculture. (1980). *Food and nutrient intakes of individuals in 1 day in the United States, spring, 1977.* USDA Nationwide Food Consumption Survey, 1977-1978 (Prelim. Rep. No. 2, Consumer Nutrition Center). Washington, DC: U.S. Government Printing Office.

United States Department of Health, Education, and Welfare. (1977). Dietary Intake Findings, United States, 1971-1974. Data from the National Health and Nutrition Examination Survey (Series 11, No. 202. DHEW Publ. No. [HRA] 77-1647). Hyattsville, MD: National Center for Health Statistics.

PART II

Psychological Aspects

From Stress to Enjoyment: Parental and Coach Influences on Young Participants

Tara K. Scanlan
Rebecca Lewthwaite

If there were one principle regarding youth sports that we could all agree upon as medical personnel, practitioners, parents, and scientists, it would probably be this one: Most youths do not spend their time wrestling, swimming, or playing baseball and soccer in the closet, by themselves, day after day, season after season. Instead, or at least more commonly, they engage in sports in the presence of other people, with other people, against other people, and sometimes just for other people.

Competitive youth sport is a social experience, and the cast of characters is enormous. Involved are peers in the form of both teammates and opponents and a myriad of adults, including coaches, parents, officials, spectators, record and score keepers, and sometimes judges. And yet, we have been reasonably remiss in sport psychology in that we are just beginning to study the impact that these people have on the young athlete's sport experience. The focus of this article, therefore, is on some of our recent research at UCLA that focuses on the influence that some of these people have on young athletes' experience of precompetition stress (which is a negative emotion—the "bad news") and on their sport enjoyment (which is a positive emotion—the "good news").

We will focus on those people who we are beginning to refer to as the "primary family of sport" which includes the athlete and his or her mother, father, and coach. The athlete's parents and coach are individuals who typically (a) are the most significant or important to the youth and (b) are the most personally involved in the athlete's sport experience. In fact, if they are not involved, as in the case of parents who do not attend events, they are often sorely missed. Hence, we might expect that parents' and coaches' performance evaluations of the athlete, and their interactions with the athlete, typically count a great deal. Moreover, we might suspect that the young athlete's sport experience is important to these adults. After all, parents and coaches are putting their time, money, energy, and sometimes more than a little ego into the activity.

The information that we will present in this article is from a multifaceted study in which we examined a variety of predictors of several interrelated variables important to the youth sport experience. These variables include

41

competitive stress (Scanlan & Lewthwaite, 1984), competitive trait anxiety (Lewthwaite & Scanlan, 1986), performance outcomes (Scanlan, Lewthwaite, & Jackson, 1984), performance expectancies (Scanlan & Lewthwaite, 1985), and sport enjoyment (Scanlan & Lewthwaite, 1986). We will return to competitive stress and sport enjoyment shortly. Competitive trait anxiety refers to a personality disposition that reflects the tendency to perceive competitive sport situations as threatening and may be thought of as an individual's customary or chronic level of competitive stress. We defined performance outcome as winning or losing a competitive contest—specifically, a wrestling match. Performance expectancies represent children's precompetition perceptions or expectations of how well they will perform in their upcoming contest.

We will focus on the relationships between participants' characteristic worries and perceptions of their mothers, fathers, and coaches and their personal feelings of precompetition stress and sport enjoyment. We will examine these relationships in two ways: (a) simple correlations between the various adult influences and stress and enjoyment will be presented, and (b) the results of regression analyses will be discussed. These regression results will provide a feel for the relative importance of the adult influences in the prediction of stress and enjoyment, in light of other individual difference factors that we also found were related to these variables.

Method

Participants

The participants in this field study were 76 boys between the ages of 9 and 14 years. These boys were participants in the season's final tournament of the California Age Group Wrestling Association (CAGWA). The competitors reflected a wide range of wrestling abilities and experience and were members of 16 CAGWA teams that represented many different regions of the state. Parental involvement in CAGWA was extensive; 80% of the wrestlers in our sample had one or both parents in attendance at the final tournament. Further details about this sample are provided in Scanlan and Lewthwaite (1984).

Testing

Data collection for the overall study took place in six different time periods. Questionnaires were administered to the wrestlers (a) 2 weeks prior to the final tournament (Pretournament Questionnaire), (b) following the morning weigh-in, about 2 hours before competition started at the final tournament (Postweigh-in Questionnaire), (c) before each of the first two rounds of the tournament (Prematch 1 and 2 Questionnaires), and (d) immediately after each of these first two matches (Postmatch 1 and 2 Questionnaires). The majority of the data that we will present here were gathered during the postweigh-in period, where adult influences and sport enjoyment were assessed, and approximately 10 to 20 minutes before the first tournament match, where children's prematch competitive stress was measured.

Adult Influences

We measured adult influences from the participants' perspective in two ways. First, we assessed the typical frequency with which various thoughts and worries were experienced before competition. Included in this set of prematch cognitions were worries about parents' and coaches' actions and reactions. Second, we measured participants' perceptions of a wide range of adult influences, including the characteristic thoughts, feelings, and reactions of their mothers, fathers, and coaches.

We then ran two factor analyses—one for the prematch worries questions and the other for the characteristic adult influences—to determine the various items clustered or grouped together into common themes or factors. Three factors emerged for the prematch thoughts and worries items. Eight factors resulted from the characteristic adult influences factor analysis. Details of these analyses are available in Scanlan and Lewthwaite (1984). Here, we will further discuss only those factors that related significantly to the stress and enjoyment variables. These factors will be examined as we move on to consider the relationship of adults to children's competitive stress and sport enjoyment.

Results

Competitive Stress

Competitive stress is a process that occurs when competitive situations are perceived as threatening to self-esteem. Stress is triggered when an imbalance is perceived between competitive demands and resources to meet those demands, in situations where negative consequences are believed to follow such an imbalance (Martens, 1977). State anxiety is a negative emotional response that reflects stress and is defined as feelings of apprehension, tension, and elevated autonomic arousal (Spielberger, 1966). Competitive stress or state anxiety was measured in this study by the children's form of the Competitive State Anxiety Inventory (CSAI-C) (Martens, Burton, Rivkin, & Simon, 1980).

Table 1 reports the adult factors and their items that were significantly correlated with competitive stress. The factor, parental pressure to wrestle, arose from the characteristic adult influences factor analysis and correlated $-.30$ ($p < .05$) with prematch stress. The factor, worries about adult expectations and social evaluation, emerged from the prematch worries factor analysis and correlated $-.32$ ($p < .05$) with precompetition stress.

These two adult factors were included in a stepwise regression analysis, along with the individual difference variables of baseline stress or state anxiety (CSAI-C) (r with competitive stress = .47), competitive trait anxiety ($r = .57$), self-esteem ($r = -.39$), prematch expectancies ($r = .51$),

Table 1 Significant Adult Factors Related to Precompetition Stress

---

Parental Pressure to Wrestle
"I wrestle because I feel that I have to wrestle to please my mom (dad)."[a]

Worries About Adult Expectations and Social Evaluation
"I worry about letting my mom (dad, coach) down."[b]
"I worry about what my mom (dad, coach) will say if I don't wrestle well in the tournament."[b]

---

[a]1 = "a very important reason for why I wrestle" to 5 = "not an important reason at all for why I wrestle." [b]1 = "very often" to 5 = "never."

and worries about failure ($r = -.40$). Baseline stress, competitive trait anxiety, and self-esteem were assessed on the Pretournament Questionnaire with the CSAI-C, Martens' (1977) Sport Competition Anxiety Test (SCAT), and the Washington Self-Description Questionnaire (Smith & Smoll, 1982), respectively. Prematch expectancies were assessed on the Prematch 1 Questionnaire with the question, "How sure are you that you will win this first match?" This question was answered on a 5-point Likert scale where 1 = "very sure" and 5 = "not sure at all." Worries about failure were assessed on the Postweigh-in Questionnaire with a scale derived from the prematch worries factor analysis (Scanlan & Lewthwaite, 1984).

In the regression analysis, five predictors entered the regression equation for prematch stress (Model F (5, 70) = 23.88, $p < .0001$; adjusted $R^2 = .609$). These included baseline stress, which was entered mandatorily as a control variable (beta weight = .267), prematch expectancies (beta = .439), worries about failure (beta = -.306), competitive trait anxiety (beta = .198), and the adult factor, parental pressure to wrestle (beta = -.148), which entered at the $p < .06$ level. Thus, greater stress was experienced by boys who had (a) higher baseline stress and competitive trait anxiety levels, (b) lower prematch performance expectancies, and (c) more frequent worries about failure when compared with boys with the opposite attributes.

Important to our examination of adult influences, competitors who perceived greater parental pressure to participate in wrestling reported greater prematch stress ($p < .06$) than did those boys who perceived little parental pressure. Worries about adult expectations and social evaluation did not enter the regression, but this may have been due to its correlation with the parental pressure to wrestle factor ($r = .56$, $p < .0001$). Thus, in comparison or competition with other individual difference variables, the adult factors were weakly, or perhaps indirectly (cf. the relationship of adult influences to children's prematch performance expectancies [Scanlan & Lewthwaite, 1985]), related to the stress these children experienced prior to competition.

Table 2 Significant Adult Factors Related to Enjoyment

Negative Adult Affective Reactions
"My mom (dad, coach) is ashamed of me when I don't wrestle well."[a]
"My dad (coach) gets upset with me when I don't wrestle well."[a]

Positive Adult Involvement and Interactions
"I wrestle because my parents and I have fun going to the tournaments together."[b]
"I wrestle because my dad or mom helps me with my wrestling and I like this."[b]
"I wrestle because I like my coach."[b]
"My coach tries to make me feel good when I don't wrestle well."[a]

Negative Adult Evaluations and Interactions
"My dad (coach) makes me uptight and nervous about my wrestling."[c]
"No matter how well I wrestle, my mom (dad, coach) doesn't think it is good enough."[c]

Adult Satisfaction With Season's Performance
"How pleased do you think your mom (dad, coach) is with the way you wrestled this season?"[d]

Negative Maternal Interactions
"My mom makes me uptight and nervous about my wrestling."[c]
"My mom gets upset with me when I don't wrestle well."[a]

[a]1 = "usually" to 3 = "hardly ever." [b]1 = "a very important reason for why I wrestle" to 5 = "not an important reason at all for why I wrestle." [c]1 = "how I feel" to 3 = "not how I feel." [d]1 = "very pleased" to 5 = "not pleased at all."

Sport Enjoyment

Enjoyment, though a critical aspect of the youth sport experience, is a new concept or construct that has received relatively little research attention. Enjoyment or fun has been identified by children as a major reason for their sport participation, whereas the lack of enjoyment has been associated with children's decisions to drop out of organized sport (e.g., Gill, Gross, & Huddleston, 1985; Gould & Horn, 1984; Passer, 1982; Sapp & Haubenstricker, 1978, April). Our own data indicate that wrestlers' enjoyment and their desires for future wrestling participation are positively correlated .70 ($p < .01$). Further, situationally experienced or contest-specific enjoyment or fun has been consistently related to postcompetition stress; children who have more fun during their game or match, regardless of whether they win or lose, are less stressed after the contest than are children who experience less fun (Scanlan & Lewthwaite, 1984; Scanlan & Passer, 1978, 1979).

Sport enjoyment is defined here as a positive emotional response to one's sport experience that reflects feelings and/or perceptions such as pleasure, liking, and perceived fun. Adults may contribute to children's sport enjoyment by (a) providing positive social evaluation and recognition for children's achievements and (b) being positively involved, in general, in children's sport experiences without regard to the quality of children's performance achievements (Scanlan & Lewthwaite, 1986).

To measure enjoyment, a sport enjoyment scale was created by summing two highly correlated items on the Postweigh-in Questionnaire. These items concerned (a) the amount of fun the boys felt they had wrestling for the season and (b) how much they liked to wrestle. Both items were answered on 5-point Likert scales where 1 = "very much fun (very much)" and 5 = "no fun at all (not at all)."

Table 2 shows the five adult influence factors and their items that correlated significantly ($p < .05$) with sport enjoyment. Three adult factors were negatively correlated with enjoyment: (a) negative adult affective reactions (r with enjoyment = $-.27$), (b) negative adult evaluations and interactions ($r = -.23$), and (c) negative maternal interactions ($r = -.31$). Two adult factors were positively related to enjoyment: (a) positive adult involvement and interactions ($r = .24$) and (b) adult satisfaction with season's performance ($r = .47$).

These five adult influence factors were included in a stepwise regression analysis for sport enjoyment, along with two individual difference or intrapersonal variables: age (in years) and children's perceptions of their wrestling ability (relative to other boys of the same age and experience). This regression analysis identified five predictors of sport enjoyment (Model $F(5, 70) = 9.87$, $p < .0001$; adjusted $R^2 = .380$). In the order of their entry into the regression equation, these predictors included (a) adult satisfaction with season's performance (beta weight = .308), (b) negative maternal interactions (beta = $-.282$), (c) age (beta = .236), (d) perceived wrestling ability (beta = .224), and (e) positive adult involvement and interactions (beta = .161, $p < .10$). We report the last factor here, despite its relatively weak predictive power, because we feel it is important, given the early stage of our investigations into these influences, to consider all significant adult variables with potential relevance to this construct.

These results indicate that younger children, and those who perceive themselves as more able wrestlers, report greater enjoyment of their sport experience than do older boys and those with perceptions of lower ability. Importantly, with respect to our consideration of adult influences, boys (a) who felt their parents and coaches were more satisfied with their season's wrestling performance and (b) who perceived more positive adult involvement and interactions in the sport context ($p < .10$) experienced greater enjoyment than their counterparts with less positive perceptions. Further, less enjoyment was reported by those children who perceived pressure and negative performance interactions from their mothers.

Caution must be taken with regard to the determination of cause and effect among these variables. Although it is possible that perceived ability and the adult factors contribute in a causal sense to sport enjoyment, it is also possible that greater enjoyment produces more positive perceptions of the self and others. More complex bidirectional relationships may also exist between sport enjoyment and its predictors.

Discussion

The results presented here suggest the important role that parents and coaches play in children's negative and positive emotional responses to competitive sport involvement. Parents who pressure their children to participate in sport may contribute to the level of stress the children experience prior to competition and may be involved in other more indirect ways in this stress. Parents and coaches who express satisfaction with children's sport performance, who interact positively with the children, and who are generally positively involved and supportive in the children's sport experience may enhance the enjoyment youngsters derive from their sport participation. Importantly, this information can be used to educate parents and coaches as to their critical roles in children's sport experiences—perhaps the most direct, positive intervention that can take place in youth sport programs. By recognizing how adults relate to outcomes such as children's stress and enjoyment, parents and coaches can deal more effectively with the social, emotional, and psychological needs of their young athletes.

References

Gill, D.L., Gross, J.B., & Huddleston, S. (1985). Participation motivation in youth sports. *International Journal of Sports Psychology*, **14**, 1-14.

Gould, D., & Horn, T. (1984). Participation motivation in young athletes. In J.M. Silva III & R.S. Weinberg (Eds.), *Psychological foundations of sport* (pp. 359-370). Champaign, IL: Human Kinetics.

Lewthwaite, R., & Scanlan, T.K. (1986). *Psychosocial aspects of chronic competitive stress in male youth sport participants*. Manuscript submitted for publication.

Martens, R. (1977). *Sport Competition Anxiety Test*. Champaign, IL: Human Kinetics.

Martens, R., Burton, D., Rivkin, F., & Simon, J. (1980). Reliability and validity of the Competitive State Anxiety Inventory (CSAI). In C.H. Nadeau, W.R. Halliwell, K.M. Newell, & G.C. Roberts (Eds.), *Psychology of motor behavior and sport-1979* (pp. 91-99). Champaign, IL: Human Kinetics.

Passer, M.W. (1982). Children in sport: Participation motives and psychological stress. *Quest*, **33**, 231-244.

Sapp, M., & Haubenstricker, J. (1978). *Motivation for joining and reasons for not continuing youth sport programs in Michigan*. Paper presented at AAHPERD Conference, Kansas City, MO.

Scanlan, T.K., & Lewthwaite, R. (1984). Social psychological aspects of competition for male youth sport participants: I. Predictors of competitive stress. *Journal of Sport Psychology*, **6**, 208-226.

Scanlan, T.K., & Lewthwaite, R. (1985). Social psychological aspects of competition for male youth sport participants: III. Determinants of personal performance expectancies. *Journal of Sport Psychology, 7,* 389-399.

Scanlan, T.K., & Lewthwaite, R. (1986). Social psychological aspects of competition for male youth sport participants: IV. Predictors of enjoyment. *Journal of Sport Psychology,* **8,** 25-35.

Scanlan, T.K., Lewthwaite, R., & Jackson, B.L. (1984). Social psychological aspects of competition for male youth sport participants: II. Predictors of performance outcomes. *Journal of Sport Psychology, 6,* 422-429.

Scanlan, T.K., & Passer, M.W. (1978). Factors related to competitive stress in male youth sport participants. *Medicine and Science in Sports,* **10,** 103-108.

Scanlan, T.K., & Passer, M.W. (1979). Sources of competitive stress in young female athletes. *Journal of Sport Psychology,* **1,** 151-159.

Smith, R.E., & Smoll, F.L. (1982). *The development and correlates of a general self-esteem scale for children and adults.* Unpublished manuscript, University of Washington.

Spielberger, C.D. (1966). Theory and research on anxiety. In C.D. Spielberger (Ed.), *Anxiety and behavior.* New York: Academic Press.

Psychological Characteristics of Competitive Young Hockey Players

Martha E. Ewing
Deborah L. Feltz
Todd D. Schultz
Richard R. Albrecht

In recent years the number of studies investigating the psychological characteristics of various athletic populations has increased substantially (Fuchs & Zaichkowsky, 1983; LeUnes & Nation, 1982; Morgan & Pollock, 1977). Researchers have assumed that these characteristics or traits govern performance. Thus, some have argued that elite performers must possess different psychological characteristics than less elite performers. Various psychological instruments have been used to assess psychological characteristics in order to facilitate the understanding of what makes an elite performer elite. Without debating the merits or faults of this line of research, the practical implication of understanding the psychological characteristics of elite performers is that coaches could provide guidance regarding the psychological skills necessary for particular types of athletes to reach their potential.

One of the concerns in assessing psychological characteristics is the stability of these characteristics. Should we focus on trait characteristics, state characteristics within a carefully controlled competitive sport situation, or on the interaction of trait and state measures? Or, as has been suggested more recently, should we focus on the cognitions of individuals, assuming that the perceptions of individuals are better predictors of behavior than psychological traits (Roberts, 1982)?

Past research in the area of psychological characteristics of athletes has spanned a wide range of sports, ranging from youth to professional, as well as a variety of characteristics. More recently, the most frequently assessed characteristics include perceived anxiety, self-confidence, perceived ability, achievement motives, and personality traits. Assessment of these characteristics reflects a cognitive approach to understanding the psychological characteristics of athletes.

Scanlan and Passer (1978, 1979) reported that most children do not find competition to be very stressful, although some children who were classified as high competitive trait anxious perceived sport competition as an anxiety-inducing experience. At the high school level, competitive athletics have been found to produce no more anxiety than physical education classes, band competitions, or academic tests (Simon & Martens, 1979; Skubic, 1955). However, Simon and Martens (1979) reported that children who competed in individual sports (swimming and wrestling) experienced greater state anxiety than children who competed in team sports.

Vealey (1985) investigated trait and state sport confidence of elite world class gymnasts. She reported that trait sport confidence (trait-SC) interacted with the gymnast's competitive achievement orientation (i.e., outcome or performance orientation) to influence precompetitive or state sport confidence (state-SC). Specifically, she reported that high trait-SC performance-oriented athletes were higher in state-SC than high trait-SC outcome-oriented athletes, low trait-SC outcome-oriented athletes, or low trait-SC performance-oriented athletes. This research represents an interactive approach to understanding elite performers by assessing both trait and state characteristics and cognitions of the athletes.

Other researchers investigating the achievement goals or motives of athletes and sport dropouts have utilized a cognitive approach. For example, Ewing (1981) found that high school athletes were more likely to participate in sport for social approval goals, that is to please others, than either nonsport participants or sport dropouts. Gould, Feltz, Weiss, and Petlichkoff (1982) reported that the reason young athletes participated in sport was to "improve skills" and to "have fun." Burton (1985) reported that perceived ability differed significantly between youth wrestler participants and dropouts. Specifically, Burton reported that participants had higher perceived wrestling ability than dropouts.

The research indicated may be characterized as investigating the influence of various cognitive correlates of performance. Additional correlates such as future expectancy, attributions, and performance satisfaction could be added to the list. These correlates represent cognitions of the athlete at a specific time in very specific situations.

In addition to the cognitive and interactive approaches, some researchers describe athletes in terms of personality characteristics. For example, Morgan and Johnson (1978) described the personality features of elite oarsmen using the Profile of Mood States (POMS). This test typically has been used to measure the feelings that a person has had "during the past week," although occasionally it has been used to assess more enduring psychological moods. Six mood factors are measured: tension, depression, anger, vigor, fatigue, and confusion. An interesting finding on the POMS scale from Morgan's research is the portrayal of an "iceberg profile."

When analyzing data from elite runners, wrestlers, and oarsmen, Morgan and his colleagues (1977, 1978) found that athletes scored lower than the general population on the first three factors of tension, depression, and anger; lower on the last two factors of fatigue and confusion; but much higher on the middle factor of vigor—thus the so-called iceberg profile. This profile has also been found with male and female bodybuilders (Fuchs & Zaichkowsky, 1983) and college football players (Nation & LeUnes, 1983).

Several problems exist in trying to synthesize the many approaches to investigating the psychological characteristics of elite performers. First, the use of trait versus state measures results in confusion and concern about stability of the characteristics. Second, very few research studies report the use of more than one or two measures, which provides an incomplete and biased view of the psychological characteristics of the population investigated. Third, confusion exists that is brought about through the use of personality versus cognitive based measures.

The purpose of our research was threefold: First, our goal was to assess the psychological characteristics of elite hockey players using a multiplistic approach (Shadish, 1986) that included a wide array of psychological tests. Second, we wanted to investigate differences in psychological characteristics of varying levels of elite performers. Finally, we wanted to identify those variables that best discriminated among the most elite performers.

Method

Subjects

Subjects for this study were 337 male, elite hockey players from across the country who had been selected by their regions to attend a week-long Amateur Hockey Association of the United States (AHAUS) Development Camp at either the Lake Placid or Colorado Springs Olympic Training Centers. Three camps representing different skill levels were held: midget, midget elite, and junior national. Two hundred and sixteen attended the midget camp, 81 attended the midget elite camp, and 40 attended the junior national camp. Twenty players were selected from the junior national camp to represent the United States in international competition. Thus, the junior nationals could be delineated further by qualifiers and nonqualifiers. Subjects ranged in age from 15 to 19 years with mean ages of 16.65, 16.65, and 17.8 for the midget, midget elite, and junior nationals, respectively.

Instruments

A variety of instruments was used to assess the psychological characteristics of the hockey players. Specifically, questionnaires included the Competitive State Anxiety Inventory (CSAI-2), the Sport Confidence Trait Inventory, the POMS, the achievement orientation, and the participation motivation questionnaires. Assessments of perceived hockey ability, perceived sport ability, and satisfaction with one's hockey ability were obtained along with demographic information.

Procedures

Data were collected during each 1-week development camp. Precamp state anxiety and demographic data were collected on Sunday evening, the first day at camp, and before any on-ice activities were scheduled. In addition, perceived hockey and sport ability and satisfaction with hockey ability were assessed. The achievement orientation questionnaire was given on the second full day of camp with the participant motivation questionnaire, and the trait sport confidence measures were given on the third day of camp. The POMS data were collected only at the junior national camp on the next to the last day of the camp with directions to respond for the week of camp. One hour was set aside per day for psychological testing. Athletes were taken to a classroom where two trained assistants distributed the assessment instruments, explained the directions, and collected the instruments. The assistants monitored all test sessions to ensure that responses were derived independently.

Results and Discussion

The results of this study will be presented by camp, which correspond to a designated level of skill, and then as a composite profile of the junior national players. In particular, attention will be given to those psychological characteristics that discriminate qualifiers and nonqualifiers for international competition as selected from the junior national team.

Camp

AHAUS has organized many age levels of play for young hockey players. However, the AHAUS camps were organized to reflect both age and ability. For example, the distinction between midget and midget elite camps was based on the regional coaches' ratings of the ability of players who were the same age. Does the athlete's perception of his ability match that of the coaches' as reflected by camp differences? In other words, do the junior nationals perceive themselves higher in ability than the midget elites who perceive themselves higher in ability than the midget regionals?

Partial support was found for this question. A one-way analysis of variance on perceived hockey ability by camp was highly significant, $F(2,334) = 7.83$, $p < .001$. Scheffé post hoc analysis confirmed that the players at the junior national camp rated their ability higher on a 9-point scale than both the midget and midget elite players who did not differ significantly in their ratings. Thus, for the younger athletes, the distinction between midget and midget elite abilities was arbitrary as they perceived it. Means and standard deviations are reported in Table 1.

Related to perceived hockey ability was the question of how satisfied hockey players were with their ability. No significant difference among athletes on a 5-point scale was found, $F(2,300) = 0.88$, $p > .05$. Interestingly, all these elite players were only "somewhat satisfied" to "satisfied" with their ability (see Table 1).

Because these elite hockey players differed in their perceived ability, it could be argued that they should also differ in their perceived ability to meet game demands (trait sport confidence) and in their level of anxiety

Table 1 Perceived Ability of Hockey Players by Camp

| | Hockey ability | | Satisfaction with ability | |
	M	SD	M	SD
Midget (N = 216)	7.4	0.7	3.6	0.8
Midget elite (N = 81)	7.5	0.8	3.8	0.9
Junior national (N = 40)	8.0	0.4	3.9	1.0

Table 2 Trait Sport Confidence of Hockey Players by Camp

	M	SD
Midget (N = 216)	93.5	12.3
Midget elite (N = 81)	93.9	13.2
Junior national (N = 40)	94.5	9.6

about demonstrating their ability in a game (state sport anxiety). As can be seen in Table 2, this was not the case. There was no significant difference in trait-SC, $F(2,321) = 0.45$, $p > .05$. Indeed, regardless of camp, all of these hockey players were highly confident of their ability to handle almost any hockey situation. Likewise, no significant difference was apparent among these hockey players in either cognitive anxiety, somatic anxiety, or confidence as assessed prior to the start of camp, $F(9,884) = 1.25$, $p > .05$ (see Table 3 for means and standard deviations). However, these are strong findings considering the large sample size, which usually biases tests toward significant findings. These results suggest that hockey players experience a moderate level of doubt or concern about their performance (cognitive anxiety), a low level of physical anxiety in reaction to competition (somatic anxiety), and a moderately high degree of self-confidence about performance.

Do elite hockey players have different reasons for participating in hockey? Athletes at all camps identified "the desire to go to a higher level" as the most important reason for participating (28%, 30%, 33% for midget, midget elite, and junior national, respectively). However, the midget and midget elite players rated "to improve skills" as their second most important reason. Interestingly, the junior nationals rated "to win" as their second reason.

These reasons are not surprising given the fact that these athletes knew they had been selected because of their skill to attend camp. In addition, college coaches and professional scouts were observing the intracamp

Table 3 Precamp Anxiety of Hockey Players by Camp

	Cognitive anxiety		Somatic anxiety		Confidence	
	M	SD	M	SD	M	SD
Midget (N = 216)	20.0	5.6	15.4	4.6	26.1	5.3
Midget elite (N = 81)	20.3	5.8	15.4	4.6	26.3	5.3
Junior national (N = 40)	20.8	5.1	15.4	4.8	27.1	4.9

games. Obviously, the opportunity was there for these athletes to move to higher levels of competition. Many of the athletes indicated informally that they had dreamed of playing on a college or professional team.

Related to the reasons for participating are the achievement goals of elite hockey players. Achievement goals were assessed by asking the hockey players to identify an experience in hockey in which they felt successful. Using this experience as a referent, players identified why they felt successful. Achievement goals range from feeling successful because of demonstrating ability to others to enjoying the challenge or risk to wanting to please others. Discriminant function analysis revealed a significant difference among camp athletes, $\chi^2(6) = 16.06$, $p < .05$. Specifically, midget camp athletes were discriminated from both the midget elite and junior national camp athletes. Midgets scored lower on both social approval (desire to please others) and sport competence (desire to demonstrate ability). There was no difference among the groups on sport mastery and sport venture goals.

Because achievement behaviors such as persistence and striving to achieve at higher levels are believed to be associated with these achievement goals, we were interested in examining the distribution of athletes with varying goals across camps. There was a distinct shift from a rather even distribution of athletes across all four achievement goals at the midget camp level to an increase in social approval oriented athletes at the midget elite camp to a large majority of junior national athletes participating in order to please others (social approval). Above the midget level, there was almost a complete loss of players who competed because they enjoyed the challenge of the task (sport mastery). These data suggest that either higher levels of competition do not allow athletes to attain certain achievement goals (e.g., sport mastery) or that pleasing the coach and others is the best way to survive in sport. Athletes apparently were motivated to engage in hockey for many reasons, but participating for fun or to enjoy the game seems the least fulfilled at higher levels of hockey participation. This is not to say that elite athletes do not have fun, because they do. Rather, if this is the motivation behind an athlete's involvement, it may not be fulfilled or it may not provide the necessary impetus to strive for higher levels of competition.

In summary, prior to the start of camp, these elite hockey players could be characterized as differing only in their perception of ability, where the junior national camp athletes rated themselves as having higher hockey ability than either the midget or midget elite athletes. All of these elite players reported little precamp cognitive or somatic anxiety and were moderately high in self-confidence and sport confidence. Although these results are consistent with earlier studies of older elite athletes, they provide only partial support for coaches' ratings of these athletes. Both coaches and junior national athletes rated the junior national players' ability as highest. However, the midget and midget elite athletes did not differ in perceived ability even though coaches had rated the midget elite athletes higher in ability. If these younger athletes perceive their ability to be similar, what accounts for the difference in ratings between the coaches and athletes? There are many possible explanations. For example, coaches may be rating athletes on the potential use of their ability rather than on the execution of skills alone. Or coaches may include in their rating of an athlete's ability such psychological characteristics as sport confidence and ability to control anxiety. If this is indeed the case, it would seem appropriate to determine whether athletes who rate themselves as high in ability differ in self-reported measures of psychological characteristics from those who rate themselves lower in ability.

Perceived Ability

In an attempt to understand better the psychological characteristics of these hockey players, the athletes were recategorized by level of their own perceived ability (average, very good, exceptional). The analyses of data for these groups revealed a slightly different view of the psychological characteristics of elite hockey players.

Similar to the results obtained by camp, there was no significant difference in the player's satisfaction with their hockey ability, $F(2,296) = 2.56$, $p > .08$. On a 5-point scale, means reported by the groups were 3.5, 3.8, and 3.6 for the average, above average, and exceptional groups, respectively. Each perceived ability group perceives there to be room for improvement.

There was a significant difference in trait sport confidence among athletes of differing perceived ability, $F(2,316) = 13.01$, $p < .001$. As might be expected, trait sport confidence was lower for the lowest ability level. The highest levels of confidence were reported by those who rated themselves "very good." (See Table 4 for the means and standard deviations.)

In addition, there was a significant difference among these athletes on precamp anxiety about their performance, $F(6,582) = 5.86$, $p < .001$. Specifically, athletes did not differ on reported cognitive and somatic trait anxiety, but the greater one's perceived ability, the greater the concern expressed with performing poorly (less self-confidence). Means and standard deviations are reported in Table 5. Perhaps what we have here is a relatively large group of "egotistical dudes" who perceive themselves to be great but are not as confident that they will be.

Table 4 Trait Sport Confidence of Hockey Players by Perceived Ability

	M	SD
Average to above (N = 19)	86.8	12.1
Very good (N= 164)	95.9	11.2
Exceptional (N = 138)	90.9	12.5

Table 5 Precamp Anxiety of Hockey Players by Perceived Ability

	Cognitive anxiety		Somatic anxiety		Confidence	
	M	SD	M	SD	M	SD
Average to above (N = 14)	17.8	6.5	12.5	6.2	31.6	6.8
Very good (N = 164)	19.7	5.7	15.0	4.5	27.3	5.1
Exceptional (N = 138)	20.7	5.1	15.9	4.4	24.6	4.8

With respect to achievement goals, no significant difference was noted among the perceived ability groups, $F(8,648) = 1.26, p > .05$. All achievement goals were represented. However, there was a dramatic shift in the reasons for participating. The most important reason for participating for the average skilled group was "to have fun," followed by "to go to a higher level" and "to improve skills." The very good and exceptional groups rated "to go to a higher level" as most important, followed by "to improve skills" and "like to compete."

In summary, perceived ability does appear to be a critical factor in understanding the psychological characteristics of elite hockey players. These data suggest that competitive hockey can be more stressful for those athletes who perceive themselves to be lower in hockey ability and whose reasons for participating are to have fun rather than improve skill. This may be a result of their lower confidence in their ability to succeed. Those athletes who rated their own ability as "exceptional" also find hockey more stressful both generally and in the precamp situation. They worry that they will not do as well in competition as they believe their ability suggests that they should do.

Achievement Orientations

Because these athletes had demonstrated persistence in hockey and had expressed a desire to play hockey at a higher level (both are achievement

Table 6 Perceived Ability of Hockey Players With Differing Achievement Goals

	Hockey ability		Satisfaction with ability	
	M	SD	M	SD
Social approval (N = 50)	7.5	0.8	3.8	1.2
Sport venture (N = 41)	7.5	1.0	3.9	1.0
Sport mastery (N = 4)	7.0	1.4	4.0	1.0
Sport competence (N = 40)	7.7	0.7	4.2	0.7

Table 7 Trait Anxiety of Hockey Players With Differing Achievement Goals

	Cognitive anxiety		Somatic anxiety		Confidence	
	M	SD	M	SD	M	SD
Social approval (N = 50)	21.3	5.5	16.4	5.5	26.3	5.3
Sport venture (N = 41)	19.5	5.4	14.8	4.9	27.2	5.0
Sport mastery (N = 4)	21.3	4.7	16.0	4.7	27.0	5.0
Sport competence (N = 40)	19.4	5.7	15.3	5.8	28.1	5.6

behaviors), it seemed reasonable to examine psychological characteristics from differing achievement orientations (i.e., sport competence, sport venture, sport mastery, social approval). It should be noted that only four athletes classified themselves as having sport mastery as a goal. There were no significant differences in ratings of perceived ability among the four orientation groups, $F(3,102) = 0.81$, $p > .05$. Likewise, there were no significant differences in precamp anxiety among the four groups, $F(9,248) = 1.02$, $p > .05$ (see Tables 6 and 7).

There was a trend toward significance on satisfaction with hockey ability, $F(3,90) = 2.43$, $p > .07$ (see Table 8 for means and standard deviations). Social approval-oriented athletes tended to be least satisfied with their ability, whereas sport competence-oriented athletes tended to be most satisfied. These results might suggest that because coaches are seldom satisfied with a player's performance, their feedback may impact more on social approval-oriented athletes who look to please others.

Similarly, a trend toward significance existed among the four orientations for trait sport confidence, $F(3,94) = 1.98$, $p > .12$. Sport competence athletes tended to be the most confident and social approval athletes tended to be the least confident in their ability to perform successfully. Means were 98.6, 96.5, 95.9, and 94.7 for sport competence, sport mastery,

Table 8   Trait Sport Confidence of Hockey Players With Differing Achievement Goals

	M	SD
Social approval (N = 50)	94.7	13.8
Sport venture (N = 41)	95.9	11.5
Sport mastery (N = 4)	96.5	10.6
Sport competence (N = 40)	98.6	10.1

sport venture, and social approval, respectively. Again, there is perhaps a dependence tendency on the coach by social approval athletes to determine if they are playing well rather than through making their own assessment.

Results of the participation motivation questionnaire resulted in a form of validation of the assumption that achievement orientations influence achievement behavior. Most athletes in this elite sample indicated that "to go to a higher level" was the most important reason for participating.

In summary, the psychological characteristics of elite hockey players appear relatively stable across achievement orientations. Sport competition appears to interact positively with all of the achievement orientations with the possible exception of sport mastery. Because of the small number one can only speculate, but these may be the athletes who have dropped out of hockey. Further research is needed with this group.

Profile of Mood States

To this point, we have reported psychological characteristics that reflect psychological traits or cognitions of elite hockey players. It seemed appropriate to include in our investigation a personality measure, namely, the POMS. Only the junior national camp athletes were asked to complete the questionnaire because of the reading level required. The questionnaire was completed at the end of the camp with the instructions to respond with how they felt during their week at camp.

In contrast to the results reported by Morgan and Pollock (1977) and Morgan and Johnson (1978), only partial support for the iceberg profile was found. Means and standard deviations from our data and others are reported in Table 9.

As can be seen from Table 9, the hockey scores were higher on all factors except vigor. The most notable deviation from the iceberg profile for these hockey players was not a lack of vigor but rather the high levels of tension, depression, and anger reported by both the qualifiers and nonqualifiers. These results may reflect the pressure experienced by these young athletes during the week of camp knowing that their performance was critical to their being selected for the junior national team. Similar to results reported for world-class runners and elite speed skaters, the

Table 9 Comparison of Raw Score Means and Standard Deviations on the POMS for Hockey Players, Runners, and Speed Skaters

	Hockey nonqualifiers (N = 24)		Hockey qualifiers (N = 16)		Runners[a] (N = 27)		Speed skaters[b] pretrial (N = 11)	
	M	SD	M	SD	M	SD	M	SD
Tension	15.79	4.5	20.06	10.3	10.46	5.57	10.7	5.2
Depression	8.58	7.9	12.13	15.2	6.82	7.93	1.9	2.1
Anger	13.32	7.2	17.06	14.1	7.89	6.03	2.6	2.8
Vigor	18.49	4.7	19.63	4.4	21.07	5.60	19.9	3.4
Fatigue	9.91	6.6	9.05	7.3	6.89	5.30	6.9	5.4
Confusion	7.96	4.4	10.50	6.2	7.43	4.12	3.7	2.0

[a]From "Psychological Characterization of the Elite Distance Runner" by W.P. Morgan and M.L. Pollock, 1977, *Annals of the New York Academy of Sciences*, **301**, 382-403. [b]From "Training Stress in Olympic Speed Skaters: A Psychological Perspective" by M.C. Gutmann, M.L. Pollock, C. Foster, and D. Schmidt, 1984, *The Physician and Sportsmedicine*, **12**(12), 45-57.

hockey players reported a higher level of vigor and lower levels of fatigue and confusion. For purposes of analysis, the junior national athletes were divided into two groups: qualifiers and nonqualifiers for international competition. There were no significant differences between the groups on the six POMS subscales, $F(6,33) = 1.05$, $p > .05$.

One of the reasons for these results might be that for most of these hockey players, the hockey season had been over for several months prior to the training camp. This long layoff may have caused additional stress for these hockey players. Not being at one's competitive best may result in an increase in tension, anger, and depression. Additionally, very few teammates were at camp. Consequently, these hockey players may have felt that they were not always able to give their best performance because the timing on plays was often not synchronous. These missed opportunities could also result in increased tension, anger, and depression. Certainly, much more research is needed to understand how the situation affects an athlete's mood states.

Composite Analysis

In a further attempt to distinguish between these two levels of elite hockey players, a discriminant function analysis was performed. Discriminating variables included perceived ability, precamp anxiety, four achievement goals, trait sport confidence, and the six POMS subscales. A significant function emerged, $\chi^2(7) = 19.16$, $p < .01$. This function correctly classified 81% of the cases, a healthy increase over the 50% expected by chance alone.

The most discriminating variables were precamp cognitive anxiety, sport venture, sport mastery, precamp self-confidence, perceived sport ability, vigor rating, and fatigue rating. Variables favoring the qualifiers were sport venture, overall sport ability, and vigor. Based on the results of the discriminant function for the most elite hockey players, a combination of cognitive, trait, and personality assessments was needed to describe fully the psychological characteristics of elite athletes.

Conclusions

Although it is tempting to conclude that participation in hockey results in very positive psychological characteristics, this may be the case only for those who perceive themselves to be highly skilled. Perhaps the most significant finding from these data is that we are dealing with a very complex set of interactions among athletes' cognitions, sport-specific traits, sport situation states, and personality correlates. To understand fully the psychological characteristics of elite athletes, a variety of variables must be assessed. These data suggest that future researchers should be aware of the impact of perceived ability of the athletes and should not use coaches' ratings of athletes' ability or intact groups to reflect level of ability. In addition, these data suggest the need to begin looking at more within-subject analyses if the interaction of psychological characteristics and specific sport situations on performance is to be understood.

References

Burton, D. (1985). *Evaluation of goal setting training on selected cognitions and performance of collegiate swimmers*. Unpublished dissertation, University of Illinois, Urbana.

Ewing, M.E. (1981). *Achievement orientations and sport behavior of males and females*. Unpublished dissertation, University of Illinois, Urbana.

Fuchs, C.Z., & Zaichkowsky, L.D. (1983). Psychological characteristics of male and female bodybuilders: The iceberg profile. *Journal of Sport Behavior*, 6(3), 137-145.

Gould, D., Feltz, D., Weiss, M., & Petlichkoff, L. (1982). Participation motives in competitive youth swimmers. In T. Orlick, J.T. Partington, & J.H. Salmela (Eds.), *Mental training for coaches and athletes* (pp. 57-59). Ottawa: Coaching Association of Canada.

LeUnes, A.D., & Nation, J.R. (1982). Saturday's heros: A psychological portrait of college players. *Journal of Sport Behavior*, 5(2), 139-149.

Morgan, W.P., & Johnson, R.W. (1978). Personality characteristics of successful and unsuccessful oarsmen. *International Journal of Sport Psychology*, 9, 119-133.

Morgan, W.P., & Pollock, M.L. (1977). Psychological characterization of the elite distance runner. *Annals of the New York Academy of Sciences, 301*, 382-403.

Nation, J.R., & LeUnes, A.D. (1983). Personality characteristics of intercollegiate football players as determined by position, classification, and redshirt status. *Journal of Sport Behavior, 6*(2), 93-102.

Roberts, G.C. (1982). Achievement motivation in sport. In R. Terjung (Ed.), *Exercise and sport science reviews* (Vol. 10). Philadelphia: Franklin Institute Press.

Scanlan, T.K., & Passer, M.W. (1978). Factors related to competitive stress among male youth sport participants. *Medicine and Science in Sports, 10*, 103-108.

Scanlan, T.K., & Passer, M.W. (1979). Sources of competitive stress in young female athletes. *Journal of Sport Psychology, 1*, 151-159.

Shadish, W.R. Jr. (1986). Planned critical multiplism: Some elaborations. *Behavioral Assessment, 8*, 75-103.

Simon, J.A., & Martens, R. (1979). Children's anxiety in sport and non-sport evaluative activities. *Journal of Sport Psychology, 1*, 160-169.

Skubic, E. (1955). Emotional responses of boys to Little League and Middle League competitive baseball. *Research Quarterly, 26*, 342-352.

Vealey, R. (1985). *The conceptualization and measurement of sport-confidence.* Unpublished dissertation, University of Illinois, Urbana.

Psychological Stress and the Age-Group Wrestler

Daniel Gould
Linda Petlichkoff

Wrestling is one of the oldest recorded sports, dating back to antiquity. It has remained popular throughout history, as evidenced by the 44 countries represented in the wrestling competition of the 1984 Olympic Games. Recent statistics also show that wrestling is popular in the United States with over 16,000 participants taking part in collegiate wrestling every year. The popularity of wrestling in this country is not limited to collegiate competitors, however. Over 281,000 athletes participate in high school programs each season, and approximately 500,000 children between the ages of 8 and 14 compete in nonschool youth programs. The number of children participating in wrestling has also been found to be increasing.[1] Thus, all available evidence reveals that age-group wrestling is becoming an increasingly popular children's sport.

Not only is the popularity of youth wrestling growing in this country, but so too is the debate about its desirability. The National Kids Council of USA Wrestling, for example, has debated such issues as the desirability of national championships for young wrestlers, the optimal length of seasons, the emphasis on competition, and rule modifications needed to protect the health and safety of young competitors. At the core of many of these issues are psychological concerns, particularly the amount of competitive stress experienced by young wrestlers and their ability to cope with it.

Understanding psychological stress in young wrestlers is important for several reasons: First, wrestling is an individual sport where success and failure, as well as the potential for social evaluation, is highly visible. For example, although a wrestler can lose to an opponent on points earned for executing various maneuvers, success or failure is often determined by the pin—where one competitor completely dominates the other, exposing and holding his back to the mat. Failure resulting from this type of total dominance may cause higher levels of stress in young wrestlers than defeat in other sports where outcome is less visible. Second, wrestling is a contact sport and has a higher rate of injury than noncontact sports. Therefore, a fear of injury may create stress in some children. Finally, experienced wrestling coaches have voiced concern about the chronic effects of psychological stress on young wrestlers. It has been argued that beginning wrestling competition at an early age predisposes children to "burnout" later in their competitive careers.

Although many of the above concerns have not been substantiated by research, some empirical evidence supports those who express these notions. In a study of competitive stress in children participating in a variety of youth sports, for example, Simon and Martens (1979) found that, although not excessive, youth wrestlers between the ages of 9 and 14 years had the highest precompetitive stress levels. More recently, Gould, Horn, and Spreemann (1983a) reported that of the 458 junior elite wrestlers surveyed, 58% indicated they had trouble sleeping the night before a wrestling competition. For these reasons, studying stress in youth wrestlers has been a primary objective of the USA Wrestling Science and Medicine Research Unit.[2]

This manuscript is designed to examine psychological stress in youth wrestling. In particular, we will study the amounts of stress experienced, sources of stress, and the consequences of stress on performance. To accomplish these objectives the stress nomenclature will be examined, a model of stress presented, and selected youth wrestling stress studies reviewed. In addition, implications for adult leaders involved in youth wrestling programs will be forwarded as well as future research directions.

The Stress Nomenclature

There is little doubt that those involved in children's wrestling are concerned with the competitive stress placed on the young wrestler. Problems arise when attempting to discuss this issue, however, because stress is defined differently by different individuals. At times stress is defined as an environmental variable (e.g., the crowd stress was excessive), whereas at other times it is viewed as an emotional response to a specific situation (e.g., losing places too much stress on the young wrestler). Smith and Smoll (1982) have indicated that these two definitions of stress are not synonymous. Young athletes will vary greatly in their interpretations of how "stressful" they perceive certain environments. Specifically, one young wrestler may perceive competing in front of a large crowd as very stressful, whereas another may not. A distinction must therefore be made between potential stressors in the environment and the young athlete's perception of stress.

Not only has stress been defined both as an environmental variable affecting the young athlete and as a psychological reaction to environmental events, but it has often been automatically labeled as having positive or negative effects. Youth wrestling critics suggest that stress is always bad for the young wrestler, whereas proponents of youth wrestling look on stress more favorably. These value-ladened definitions are inappropriate because stress researchers have shown that stress can have both positive and negative effects (Selye, 1974).

Because of the previous difficulties that have arisen in defining stress, youth sports researchers have adopted a process definition. One of the

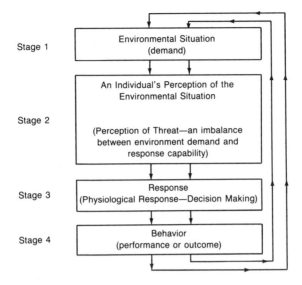

Figure 1 McGrath's (1970) stress process.

most widely accepted process definitions of stress is that of social psychologist, Joseph McGrath (1970). McGrath defines stress as a process or sequence of steps whereby "a substantial imbalance [occurs] between [environmental] demand and response capability, under conditions where failure to meet the demand has important consequences" (p. 20). Moreover, the stress process is subdivided into four interrelated stages (see Figure 1).

First, an individual encounters a set of environmental circumstances that places a demand on him or her (e.g., a young wrestler must compete in front of a large crowd). However, the environmental circumstances are not perceived as a demand by all children. Therefore, Stage 2 of the process focuses on the individual's perception of the situation and if it is appraised as threatening. Moreover, Martens (1977) indicates that threat occurs when individuals perceive an imbalance between the perceived demand and their response capabilities (e.g., the young wrestler feels threatened because he or she has doubts about winning).

The third stage in McGrath's model focuses on the individual's physiological response, actual decision making, and response selection to the perceived demand placed on him or her (e.g., he or she becomes nervous, tightens up, and gets taken down). Lastly, the fourth stage focuses on the actual behavior or outcome of the process (e.g., the wrestler loses).

Viewing stress in this fashion has several advantages: First, stress is viewed as a cycle made up of interrelated stages that can be individually examined. Second, McGrath's definition of stress places emphasis on the individual's perception of the objective environment and not the environment alone. This is necessary because all events are not perceived in an identical way by all individuals. Finally, this process definition of stress eliminates viewing stress in an emotional context, automatically assuming that it is good or bad. Rather, stress is defined as a sequence of events that lead to certain reactions and behaviors that may at times be positive, negative, or neutral.

In addition to defining stress itself, several other terms must be defined before the stress process and its ramifications can be fully understood. These include state and trait anxiety. State anxiety is often a by-product of the stress process. Specifically, it is defined as "an existing or current emotional state characterized by feelings of apprehension and tension and associated with activation of the organism" (Martens, 1977, p. 9).

In essence, state anxiety is a negative feeling experienced at a particular moment in time. It is a feeling everyone at some time in his or her life has noticed, whether it be the butterflies felt a few minutes before an athletic competition or that queasy feeling in one's stomach before giving a public speech for the first time. Closely associated with state anxiety is trait anxiety. Unlike state anxiety, trait anxiety is considered to be an enduring attribute, part of one's personality. Trait anxiety is defined as "a predisposition to perceive certain environmental stimuli as threatening or nonthreatening and to respond to these stimuli with varying levels of state anxiety" (Martens, 1977, p. 9).

Trait anxiety is important because it has been consistently shown to influence one's level of state anxiety. Specifically, a high trait anxious child tends to perceive evaluative environments, like competition, as very threatening and in so doing experiences increases in state anxiety. In contrast, when a low trait anxious child is placed in the same competitive environment, he or she does not perceive the environment to be as threatening and does not experience marked increases in state anxiety. Thus, the level of state anxiety a child experiences in evaluative environments is directly related to his or her level of trait anxiety.

In summary, a child's level of trait anxiety affects Stage 2 of McGrath's stress process by influencing his or her perception of the demands of the environment (see Figure 1). High, as compared to low, trait anxious children tend to perceive competition as threatening and this results in an increased state anxiety response (see Stage 3, Figure 1). Moreover, increases in state anxiety have been found to be associated with performance variations (Stage 4).

Stress Research in Youth Wrestling

Using the McGrath (1970) process definition of stress, a number of investigators have begun to examine stress in children's wrestling. Three major questions have received the greatest attention in this line of research. These include (a) an examination of the levels of state anxiety experienced by young wrestlers in competitive settings; (b) the identification of the sources or antecedents of state anxiety in young wrestlers; and (c) the effects of stress responses on the performance of young wrestlers. The research examining each of these questions will now be discussed.

Levels of State Anxiety Experienced by Young Wrestlers

Simon and Martens (1979) conducted the first extensive investigation examining the levels of state anxiety experienced by young athletes in competitive settings. The state anxiety levels of boys 9 to 14 years old were assessed in practice settings and just before competitions using the Competitive State Anxiety Inventory for Children (CSAI-C) (Martens, 1977). Differences between practice and competitive state anxiety levels were examined, and comparisons were made between band solo performers, band group performers, boys taking an academic test, boys taking part in a physical education competition, and boys competing in baseball, basketball, tackle football, gymnastics, ice hockey, swimming, and wrestling competitions. The results revealed that state anxiety was elevated over practice levels, although the overall change in state anxiety occurring prior to competition was not excessive. For example, the mean precompetitive state anxiety score for the entire sample was 16.87. Given that the scoring of the Competitive State Anxiety Inventory for Children ranges from 10 to 30, the precompetitive state anxiety levels did not seem excessive. It was noted, however, that substantial individual differences existed, with some boys exhibiting extremely high state anxiety levels.

Of particular interest in the Simon and Martens (1979) study was the comparison of state anxiety levels of boys participating in wrestling to boys participating in other competitive activities. Comparisons across the specific activities revealed that participants in band solos exhibited the greatest state anxiety ($M = 21.48$), followed by individual sport participants (M wrestling $= 19.52$, M gymnastics $= 18.52$), with the physical education participants showing the lowest levels of anxiety ($M = 14.47$). Of all sport participants, wrestlers exhibited the highest precompetitive state anxiety levels. Once again, however, these levels were not excessive.

In a recent investigation, Bump, Gould, Petlichkoff, Peterson, and Levin (1985) also examined state anxiety levels of children involved in wrestling competitions. Specifically, the Competitive State Anxiety Inventory for Children was administered prior to competitive tournament matches to boys 13 and 14 years old. The findings revealed that for the 112 participants, prematch state anxiety levels averaged 18.9. Once again, these state anxiety levels were not judged as being excessive. It should be recognized, however, that although the average level of precompetitive state anxiety for these young wrestlers was not excessive, substantial individual differences did exist. For instance, state anxiety scores ranged from 10 to 29 in the 112 wrestlers, and 9% of the sample recorded precompetitive state anxiety levels in the upper quarter of the scale (M CSAI-C > 25). Some of these children, then, experienced high levels of competitive stress.

In summary, the results of the research examining levels of precompetitive stress experienced by age-group wrestlers are consistent with that conducted on other young athletes (Scanlan & Passer, 1978, 1979). That is, as a group most young wrestlers are not experiencing excessive levels of precompetitive state anxiety. It must be recognized, however, that certain children in certain situations experience excessive levels of stress. It is of critical importance for those involved in youth wrestling to identify these children and the situations in which they perceive high levels of stress.

Personal and Situational Sources of Stress in Young Wrestlers

Because it has been found that certain children experience high levels of stress in certain athletic situations, investigators have begun to identify personal and situational factors associated with heightened stress in young wrestlers. Gould, Horn, and Spreemann (1983), for example, conducted one of the first of these investigations. In particular, 458 junior elite wrestlers, ranging in age from 13 to 19 years, rated the frequency with which they typically experienced 33 sources of stress before competitions. Descriptive statistics revealed that 53% of the sample rated performing up to his or her level of ability, 47% improving on his or her last performance, 44% participating in championship meets, 44% losing, 43% not making weight, 42% not wrestling well, and 41% being able to get mentally ready to wrestle as frequent stress or worry sources. It was also found that high, as compared to low, trait anxious wrestlers worried more about fear of failure—feelings of inadequacy items as well as items reflecting social evaluation. Similarly, inexperienced wrestlers worried more about fear of failure items than more experienced wrestlers. It was concluded that the fear of failure is a major stress source for these young wrestlers and that those children characterized by high trait anxiety and little experience are most susceptible to heightened stress.

Two recent investigations took slightly different approaches in identifying antecedents of state anxiety in young wrestlers (Bump et al., 1985; Scanlan & Lewthwaite, 1984). Both these investigations employed similar methodological approaches. In particular, the Competitive State Anxiety Inventory for Children was administered to young wrestlers immediately before and after competing in several tournament matches. In addition, measures such as self-esteem, trait anxiety, performance expectancies, parental pressure to participate, various worries, match outcome, achievement orientations, and years of wrestling experience were assessed. Relationships between these variables were then examined.

Table 1 contains a summary of those variables found in these studies to be related to heightened pre- and postmatch state anxiety in these young wrestlers. Wrestlers experiencing heightened prematch state anxiety were higher in trait anxiety, had lower prematch performance expectancies, perceived greater parental pressure to wrestle, were lower in self-esteem, worried more about failure, and worried more about adult expectations and social evaluation. Predictors of postmatch state anxiety included match outcome, with losing wrestlers experiencing higher levels of state anxiety than winning wrestlers. Level of prematch state anxiety, amount of perceived fun, performance expectancies, years of experience, and performance satisfaction were also found to be significant predictors of postmatch state anxiety. Finally, young wrestlers who were characterized by a sport mastery orientation—those who desire to perform as well

Table 1 Antecedents of Pre- and Postmatch State Anxiety in Youth Wrestlers

Antecedents of prematch state anxiety	Antecedents of postmatch state anxiety
[a]Trait anxiety	[a]Match outcome (win-lose)
[a]Prematch performance expectancies	[a]Prematch state anxiety
[a]Parental pressure to wrestle	Perceived fun
Self-esteem	Performance expectancies
Worries about failure	Years of experience
Worries about adult expectations and social	Performance satisfaction
evaluation	Task orientation

[a]Variables found to predict pre- and postmatch state anxiety across the Scanlan and Lewthwaite (1984) and Bump et al. (1985) investigations.

as possible regardless of outcome—tended to experience less postmatch state anxiety.

Further inspection of Table 1 shows that level of trait anxiety, prematch performance expectancies, and parental pressure to wrestle were the variables found to predict prematch state anxiety across both the Scanlan and Lewthwaite (1984) and Bump et al. (1985) studies. Consistent predictors of postmatch state anxiety across studies included match outcome and level of prematch state anxiety.

In summary, these studies show that those young wrestlers who experience heightened levels of competitive anxiety are characterized by a particular personality profile that includes high trait anxiety and low self-esteem. These personality dispositions predispose these children to view competitive environments as threatening (Stage 2 of the stress process) and respond with increased worries about failure, social evaluation, and low performance expectations. These children also report that they are less satisfied with their performance, and that the competitive experience is less fun for them. Losing wrestlers are also found to experience more postmatch state anxiety than winning wrestlers and inexperienced wrestlers more anxiety than experienced wrestlers.

The Effects of State Anxiety and Stress-Related Cognitions on the Performance of Age-Group Wrestlers

Until recently, most of the attention of youth wrestling researchers has focused on examining the first three stages of the stress process (see Figure 1). That is, attention has been focused on identifying environments or situations (Stage 1) that are perceived as stressful by young wrestlers (Stage 2) and assessing the child's physiological and psychological response to these perceived sources of stress (Stage 3). Two recent studies (Gould, Bump, Petlichkoff, & Peterson, 1985; Scanlan, Lewthwaite, & Jackson, 1984), however, have examined the relationship between state

anxiety, stress-related cognitions (e.g., worries), and wrestling performance (Stage 4 of the stress process).

Both of these studies employed the same samples described earlier in
this review and utilized similar methodological approaches. Specifically,
the relationship between state anxiety, expectancies, and various worries
were compared between winning and losing wrestlers across two tournament matches.

The results of Scanlan et al. (1984) revealed that competitive experience
and prematch performance expectancies were the most stable and influen-
tial predictors of match outcome in their sample of 76 9- to 14-year-old
wrestlers. Additionally, failure worries significantly predicted performance
in the first match of the tournament.

The Gould et al. (1985) investigation also showed that competitive experience and prematch performance expectancies were consistent predictors of match outcome. Moreover, perception of wrestling ability and level
of prematch state anxiety were also found to be significant but less stable
predictors of performance. No support was found for the significant
relationship between failure cognitions and performance reported by
Scanlan et al. (1984).

Although it is premature to derive definitive statements about causal
relationships between particular stress response variables and performance from these initial studies, several general conclusions can be made.
In particular, these studies show that relationships exist between state
anxiety, stress-related cognitions, and performance, with prematch expectancies being the most stable predictor of performance. Moreover,
failure worries, state anxiety, and ability perceptions have at times been
found to be related to match outcome and warrant further investigation.

Interpretations and Future Research Directions

The initial studies examining stress in children's wrestling have proven
to be very fruitful. The evidence has shown that as a group most young
wrestlers are not experiencing excessive levels of competitive stress. Thus,
children can and should compete in youth wrestling. This conclusion
should not be misinterpreted to mean that excessive stress is not a problem
in age-group wrestling, however. The results clearly show that some children experience extremely high levels of stress in competitive wrestling
environments. For example, if the Bump et al. (1985) finding that 9% of
age-group wrestlers score in the upper quarter of the prematch state
anxiety scale is generalized to all 500,000 participants nationwide, this
would mean that 45,000 children experience high levels of stress in youth
wrestling. Efforts must therefore be made to identify these children and
help them develop strategies to cope with the stress of competition.

Unfortunately, recognizing those young wrestlers who have difficulty
coping with stress is no easy task. Research by Martens and Simon (1976)
and Martens, Rivkin, and Burton (1980), for example, has shown that
coaches are ineffective in identifying young athletes with these problems.
An important area of future research, then, would be studying ways in

which youth wrestling coaches could be taught to recognize children with low self-esteem, high trait anxiety, and low performance expectancies—the characteristic profile of the age group wrestler who experiences high levels of stress. Of special significance would be an assessment of the utility of coaching education programs in accomplishing this objective.

A number of stress management procedures for helping children cope with stress have also been suggested (Gould, 1987; Smoll, 1985). These range from manipulating the physical environment (e.g., reducing event importance by eliminating publicity and pageantry associated with children's sports events) to teaching young athletes self-control strategies (e.g., systematic desensitization). A need exists to compare and evaluate the effectiveness of these techniques in helping young wrestlers cope with stress.

Further research on identifying antecedents and sources of stress must also be conducted. Of special interest would be an examination of the influence of parental and coach behaviors on the young wrestler's perception of stress. A continuation of the work of Scanlan and Lewthwaite (1984) in this area would be especially appropriate. In addition, a need exists to assess the effects of match and meet importance on the stress experienced by young wrestlers because most of the previous research has taken place in the early rounds of tournaments. Assessing levels of stress experienced by young wrestlers in the final rounds of local, regional, and national tournaments would be invaluable as would examining changes in levels of perceived stress occurring from the early to final rounds of a tournament.

Lastly, future investigations should more clearly examine the stress-performance relationship in the young wrestler. This will require different methodological procedures, however. Multiple measures of both state anxiety and performance will need to be taken because Sonstroem and Bernardo (1982) have shown that intraindividual, as opposed to interindividual, analyses will be needed. Similarly, attempts must be made to obtain more precise measures of wrestling performance than merely match outcome.

Notes

1. These estimates were taken from unpublished statistics compiled by USA Wrestling.
2. Much of the original research carried out by the authors and cited in this review was conducted as part of the USA Wrestling Science and Medicine Research Program. The authors are indebted to USA Wrestling for their continued support for this research.

References

Bump, L., Gould, D., Petlichkoff, L., Peterson, K., & Levin, R. (1985, May). *The relationship between achievement orientations and state anxiety in youth wrestlers.* Paper presented at the North American Society for the Psychology of Sport and Physical Activity Conference, Gulfpark, MS.

Gould, D. (1987). Promoting positive sport experiences for children. In J.R. May & M.J. Asken (Eds.), *Sport psychology: The psychological health of the athlete.* Elmsford, NY: Pergamon.

Gould, D., Bump, L., Petlichkoff, L., & Peterson, K. (1985, May). *Psychological predictors of age group wrestling performance.* Paper presented at the North American Society for the Psychology of Sport and Physical Activity Conference, Gulfpark, MS.

Gould, D., Horn, T.S., & Spreemann, J. (1983a). Competitive anxiety in junior elite wrestlers. *Journal of Sport Psychology, 5,* 58-71.

Gould, D., Horn, T.S., & Spreemann, J. (1983b). Sources of stress in junior elite wrestlers. *Journal of Sport Psychology, 5,* 159-171.

Martens, R. (1977). *Sports competition anxiety test.* Champaign, IL: Human Kinetics.

Martens, R., Rivkin, F., & Burton, D. (1980). Who predicts anxiety better: Coaches or athletes? In C.H. Nadeau, W.R. Halliwell, K.M. Newell, & G.C. Roberts (Eds.), *Psychology of motor behavior and sport—1979* (pp. 84-90). Champaign, IL: Human Kinetics.

Martens, R., & Simon, J.A. (1976). Comparison of three predictors of state anxiety in competitive situations. *Research Quarterly, 47,* 381-387.

McGrath, J.E. (1970). A conceptual formulation for research on stress. In J.E. McGrath (Ed.), *Social and psychological factors in stress* (pp. 10-21). New York: Holt, Rinehart & Winston.

Scanlan, T.K., & Lewthwaite, R. (1984). Social psychological aspects of competition for male youth sport participants: I. Predictors of competitive stress. *Journal of Sport Psychology, 6,* 208-226.

Scanlan, T.K., Lewthwaite, R., & Jackson, B.L. (1984). Social psychological aspects of competition for male youth sport participants: II. Predictors of performance outcomes. *Journal of Sport Psychology, 6,* 422-429.

Scanlan, T.K., & Passer, M. (1978). Factors related to competitive stress among male youth sports participants. *Medicine and Science in Sports, 10,* 103-108.

Scanlan, T.K., & Passer, M. (1979). Sources of competitive stress in young female athletes. *Journal of Sport Psychology, 1,* 151-159.

Selye, H. (1974). *Stress without distress.* New York: New American Library.

Simon, J., & Martens, R. (1979). Children's anxiety in sport and nonsport evaluative activities. *Journal of Sport Psychology, 1,* 160-169.

Smith, R.E., & Smoll, F.L. (1982). Psychological stress: A conceptual model and some intervention strategies in youth sports. In R.A. MaGill, M.J. Ash, & F.L. Smoll (Eds.), *Children in sport* (pp. 178-195). Champaign, IL: Human Kinetics.

Smoll, F.L. (1985). Stress reduction strategies in youth sport. In M.R. Weiss & D. Gould (Eds.), *Sport for children and youths* (pp. 127-136). Champaign, IL: Human Kinetics.

Sonstroem, R.J., & Bernardo, P. (1982). Intraindividual pregame state anxiety and basketball performance: A re-examination of the inverted-v curve. *Journal of Sport Psychology*, **4**, 235-245.

PART III

Training and Injuries

Biochemical Scan Reports:
A Tool for Evaluating Athletes
and Their Training Program

Jon J. Kabara
Lisa Morris

Not many years ago, the number of blood samples that could be analyzed in the clinical laboratory was limited principally by the speed of the analytical technique employed. However, with the advent of automatic instruments in 1957, the number of analyses able to be performed has increased greatly. Today, because of the low cost of tests done by automated analyzers, it is more economical to order batteries of tests than individual analyses.

Although performance during competition is the ultimate test of an athlete's ability, little is known in a quantitative way about the biochemical effects of training and exercise. At Michigan State University (MSU) we have designed a unique biochemical screen based on blood constituents that can help evaluate an athlete's health status. In addition to choosing those blood markers that would be most useful in providing information on organ systems of the body, a computer software package has been designed to interpret the values. This evaluation system is not only useful in stating the training condition of the subject but also is valuable in detecting any abnormal condition(s). The blood chemistry screen (biochemical scan) provides a health profile from over 31 biochemical/ enzyme/isoenzyme markers (see Table 1).

Most attempts to evaluate the effect of training/exercise are limited to a few biochemical parameters: lactic acid, lipids, enzyme levels, etc. The translation of changes in these parameter levels to specific effects of conditioning is seldom made. Therefore, a need exists to measure biochemical marks that will give a more global picture of exercise effects. The ability to pinpoint biochemical changes in a specific organ or organ system will give us objective measures for designing exercise/training programs. To be able to measure changes in organs prior to clinical manifestation is a goal to be desired. It is in this area of athletic training where we wish to provide greater information to people responsible for athletic programs.

The particular focus of our program is the young elite athlete. The project is designed to assess the effects of training on growth and development of young adults (9- to 18-year-olds).

Table 1 Biochemical Scan Report Computerized Interpretation of Biochemical Data on Sample as Received

Sample No. _____

Normal Values

15	Age (0-135) years
1	Sex (0-1) 0-Female 1-Male
140	NA (136-145) meq/l
4.3	K (3.6-5) meq/l
105	CL (96-105) meq/l
30	C02 (22-30) meq/l
18	BUN (7-22) mg/100 ml
1	CR (.7-1.5) mg/100 ml
10	CA (8.5-10.5) mg/100 ml
3.5	P (2.5-4.5) mg/100 ml
100	GLU (70-115) mg/100 ml
4.5	ALB (3.5-5) mg/100 ml
7.4	TP (6-8) mg/100 ml
4	U.A. (3-8) mg/100 ml
.2	BILI (0-1.2) mg/100 ml
250	CHOL (150-280) mg/100 ml
190	LDH (100-220) U/ml
35	SGOT (AST) (1-040) U/ml
60	ALK P (30-100) U/ml
110	CPK (30-110) MU/ml
1	ESR (0-16) mm/hr
300	TIBC (210-450) UG/100 ml
100	FE (65-175) UG/100 ml
28	T3 (23-32) & uptake
7.5	T4 (5-13) UG/100 ml
30	SGPT (ALT) (2-54) U/ml
32	CUP (30-50) MGS %
40	GGT (0-45) U/ml
0	HEMOLYSIS (0-1) 0-no 1-yes
18	BUN/CR ratio (7-25)

Abnormal Values

180 (.181)	TRIG (50-160) mg/100 ml
10 (9.25)	MG (1.8-2.6) mg/100 ml
5 (−1)	ANION GAP (8-16)

Interpretation

—MG/CA this high suggests renal or pulmonary disease
—AN anion gap less than six may be due to dilution, hypoalbuminemia, CA, MG, NA, hyperviscosity bromides, or paraproteinemias

Interpretation

—high triglycerides
familial hyperlipidemia
liver disease
nephrotic syndrome

(Cont.)

Table 1 (Cont.)

Sample No. _____

hypothyroidism
diabetes mellitus
pancreatitis

Disclaimer:
This program is designed to be used by physicians, and the final judgment concerning medical problems *must always rest with the physician* based on the total clinical picture.

All subjects were tested under standardized protocols in the Center for the Study of Human Performance. Eleven tests of physical characteristics related to performance (blood chemistry, echocardiography, electrocardiography, orthopedic examination, work capacity on the treadmill, cinematography, anthropometry, strength-torque, motor skills, reaction-movement time, and biological age) and five assessments of contemporary and historical involvement in activity (competitive stress, activity history, nutritional history, perceived exertion, and medical history) constituted the test battery. Pilot testing of this comprehensive battery was conducted in the fall of 1982. Fifteen faculty members from various disciplines on the Michigan State campus were involved in the testing and supervision of the data collection at designated stations. This report is only one aspect of the total evaluation program sponsored by the Youth Sports Institute at Michigan State University.

This report focuses on the blood chemistry program from these subjects and attempts to show the value of our approach not only for training purposes but also for detecting the health status of the individual.

Biochemical Scan Report

Over the years a blood chemistry screening program has evolved. Tests have been added and subtracted as technology was developed and experience gained. Although the program is still in dynamic flux, we have enough confidence in our present stage of development to pick up many clinical and preclinical conditions. Over 35 individual biochemical parameters were identified. These tests are from two groups. The first group consists of those multiphasic blood tests found in most clinical laboratories and do not represent exotic or unavailable procedures. The first 31 tests used in our screen are given in Table 1. The second group of blood tests are electrophoresis tests: protein (SPE), lipoprotein (LP), isoenzymes of lactic acid dehydrogenase (LDH), creatine kinase (CK) (in older literature this enzyme is referred to as creatine phosphokinase [CPK]), and alkaline phosphatase (Alk P). The latter electrophoretic tests are the apogee of our screening systems. The information from these two groups of tests can be used together to reinforce the interpretation of any abnormal result(s) with greater confidence.

Because electrophoretic patterns are used in a limited way by most physicians, it may be instructive to review briefly what kind of information these blood tests can yield.

Protein Electrophoresis

Migration of proteins in an electrical field was first perfected in 1937 by Tiselius. His original interest was to develop a procedure that would measure normal and abnormal proteins in human sera. Fifty years later updated technology has finally solved some of the technical problem reproducibility to make this idea a feasible approach. The field has moved beyond the simple five-zone electrophoresis—albumin, and alpha-1, alpha-2, beta, and gamma globulin—to greater resolution (see Figure 1). Therefore, more clinically significant information is available from a simple electrophoretic test than could be obtained previously.

The following list summarizes some of the more common qualitative abnormalities seen in electrophorograms of serum along with some associated disease entities:

1. Hypoalbuminemia (marked reduction in the staining of the albumin band)
   - Spruce (gluten intolerance)
   - Lipoid nephrosis (also associated with high alpha-2 and low gamma globulin)
   - Meningitis
   - Starvation
   - Hepatitis (less marked)
2. Decrease in Albumin and Globulin. Fulminating virus hepatitis.
3. Polyclonal Hypergammaglobulinemia (marked diffuse increase in staining of gamma globulin zone)
   - Advanced tuberculosis
   - Sarcoidosis
   - Waldenstrom's benign hypergammaglobulinemic purpura
   - Lymphogranuloma venereum
   - Disseminated lupus erythematosus
   - Serum sickness
   - Schonlein-Henoch purpura
   - Sjorgren's syndrome
   - Acquired hemolytic anemia
   - Allergic reactions
   - Rheumatoid arthritis
   - Cirrhosis of liver

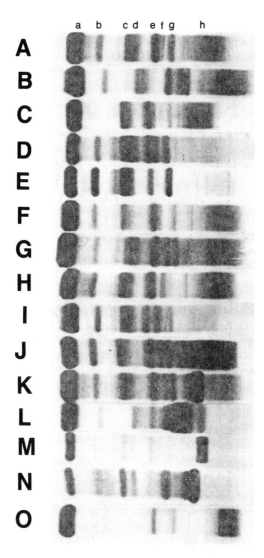

Figure 1 By using Agrose gel instead of paper or even cellulose acetate, 12 rather than 5 protein zones can be observed. These 12 proteins make up 95% of the total protein mass in healthy individuals (data taken from Sun, Lien, and Gross [1978]). Normal and specific clinical patterns are shown.

4. Beta-Gamma Bridging with polyclonal gammopathy indicates diffusion, increase, and overlapping of gamma and beta globulin areas so that a separation between the two is not clear. The phenomenon occurs most commonly with cirrhosis of the liver and hepatitis but also in rheumatoid arthritis and in severe, chronic infections.

5. Hypogammaglobulinemia (decrease in staining of gamma globulin zone)
6. Aggammaglobulinemia (very rare: total absence of gamma globulins)
7. Bisalbuminemia. Two albumin bands are present. One migrates normally, the other more slowly.
   - Familial
   - Transient *artifact* occurring with penicillin therapy
8. Decreased or Absent Alpha-1 Globulin. A "fast" alpha-1 globulin variant also occurs.
   - Cirrhosis of the liver in children
   - Hereditary emphysema in adults
9. Increased Alpha-2 Globulin
   - Myocardial infarction
   - Severe trauma

Lipoprotein Phenotyping

Hyperlipoproteinemias are produced by abnormalities in the metabolism of triglycerides and cholesterol. With few exceptions, the lipids in the blood are attached to proteins—lipoproteins. Four major lipoprotein bands can be separated by electrophoresis: chylomicrons, beta (LDL), pre-beta (VLDL), and alpha (HDL). In the fasting normal subject, cholesterol is carried predominantly by beta lipoproteins, triglycerides by the pre-beta lipoproteins, and phospholipids by the alpha fraction. The five main types of hyperlipoproteinemia and their principal clinical findings are outlined (see Table 2).

Isoenzymes

The term *isoenzymes* refers to enzymes that have similar substrate specificity and catalyze the same reaction but have certain different physical properties, particularly in electrophoretic migration rates. This makes it possible to resolve them.

Lactic dehydrogenase (LDH). The total serum LDH represents the sum of five fractions. The concentration of the individual fraction is determined by its electrophoretic ratio (percentage of total) multiplied by the total serum LDH concentration, determined chemically.

When an LDH isoenzyme pattern is abnormal, it is useful to classify the abnormality into one of three overlapping zones:

$$LDH_{1,2} = \text{first zone pattern}$$
$$LDH_{2,3,4} = \text{midzone or second zone pattern}$$
$$LDH_{4,5} = \text{third zone pattern}$$

Elevation of $LDH_{1,2}$, usually associated with myocardial infarction, is due to the destruction of cardiac muscle. The same pattern, however, is

Table 2   Summary of Lipoprotein Characteristics

Type of hyperlipoproteinemia	Symptomatology	Rule out (secondary type)	Usual age of detection
Normal Type I	Cream-of-tomato-soup blood; lipemia retinalis; hepatosplenomegaly; xanthomas, abdominal pain	Pancreatitis Diabetes	Early childhood
Type II	Tendinous and tuberous xanthomas; corneal arcus; accelerated atherosclerosia	Hypothyroidism Obstructive liver disease Nephrotic syndrome	Early childhood (in severe cases)
Type III	Eruptive xanthomas especially plantar; diabetes; hyperuricemia; accelerated atheromatosis	Hepatic disease Dysglobulinemia Uncontrolled diabetes	Adulthood (over age 20)
Type IV	Coronary disease in young adults; accelerated vascular disease; diabetes; hyperuricemia; lipemia retinalis; eruptive xanthomas; hepatosplenomegaly	Hypothyroidism Diabetes Pancreatitis Glycogen storage disease Nephrotic syndrome Pregnancy Multiple myelonia	Adulthood
Type V	Abdominal pain; milky peritoneal fluid; lipemia retinalis; eruptive xanthomas; hepatosplenomegaly	Insulin-dependent diabetes Pancreatitis alcoholism	Early adulthood

produced by myocarditis, cardiac tumors (either primary or metastatic), and surgical trauma to the heart. Myocarditis, due to rheumatic fever or to a known virus (e.g., Coxsackie), produces in children an LDH isoenzyme pattern identical to myocardial infarction in the adult. Such a pattern in a child is suggestive of myocarditis when hemolytic anemia or renal disease is excluded. With suspected myocardial infarction, a blood specimen should be drawn as soon as possible and followed by specimens 24 and 48 hours later to demonstrate the characteristic changes.

Some abnormal LDH isoenzyme patterns occurring in certain disease states are given first in a diagrammatic and then in summary form (Figure 2 and Table 3). These patterns represent composite patterns resulting from the mixing of normal serum patterns with isoenzymes leaking from the damaged organ(s). For example, in infectious hepatitis, the serum LDH fraction (the predominant enzyme in normal liver) is markedly elevated. It is readily apparent that serum isoenzyme patterns are of great practi-

Table 3   Summary of Serum LDH Isoenzyme Patterns in Some Important Clinical Conditions

Myocardial infarction	Moderate elevation of LDH_1; slight elevation of LDH_2
Pulmonary infarction	Moderate elevation of LDH_2; LDH_3; slight elevation of LDH_4
Acute hepatitis	Marked elevation of LDH_5; moderate elevation of LDH_4
Arthritis and joint effusions	Elevation of LDH_5
Muscular dystrophy	Elevation of LDH_1, LDH_2, LDH_3
Dermatomyositis	Elevation of LDH_5
Sickle cell anemia	Moderate elevation of LDH_1, LDH_2
Megaloblastic anemia	Marked elevation of LDH_1
Agnogenic myeloid metaplasia	Elevation of LDH_2, LDH_3; mild elevation of LDH_4
Granulocytic leukemia	Elevation of LDH_2; slight elevation of LDH_3
Essential myoglobinuria	Moderate to severe elevation of LDH_5; moderately elevated LDH_3, LDH_2
Intravascular hemolysis	Marked elevation of LDH_1; moderate elevation of LDH_2, LDH_3
Muscular dystrophy—muscle biopsy	LDH_5 markedly decreased compared to normal muscle
Arthritis with joint effusions synovial fluid	Elevation of LDH_5
Hemolyseal RBC	Elevation of LDH_1, LDH_2
Destruction of lymphocytes	Elevation of LDH_3, LDH_4, LDH_5
Aplastic anemia	LDH_1, LDH_2, LDH_3, LDH_4, LDH_5, all elevated due to destruction of both RBC and WBC

cal clinical importance for the diagnosis of myocardial damage; the LDH isoenzyme pattern remains abnormal for periods up to 3 weeks, reverting to normal more slowly than total levels of SGOT.

Sometimes additional tests aid in interpreting abnormal isoenzyme patterns. For instance, cases of hemolytic anemia mimic the LDH isoenzyme pattern of myocardial infarction. A concomitantly reduced or absent haptoglobin level would suggest a hemolytic process and militate against a diagnosis of myocardial infarction. Artifactual hemolysis can be detected by the presence of complexed Hp-Hb in the serum without the addition of Hb, whereas in true hemolytic anemias the haptoglobin is decreased or absent.

Creative kinase isoenzymes (CK).   The value of CK-isoenzyme determinations in diagnosis of myocardial infarction has been documented (Galen, 1975; Roe, 1977), creating strong interest in this procedure among clinical laboratories. CK-MM is the slow moving band and represents skeletal muscle band; CK-MB is the heart band; CK-BB is an indication of brain involvement. An elevation of total CK may be caused by a number of disorders. Separating total CK into its isoenzymes by electrophoresis provides useful information in identifying the cause. Total CPK and CK-MB, for instance, are elevated over normal levels 24 hours following a myocardial infarction. Other conditions characterized by abnormal CK levels include muscular dystrophy, skeletal muscle disease, neurologic disorders, etc. These facts make CK determinations a critically important addition to clinical laboratory electrophoresis programs.

Of particular interest to the physician examining athletes is the change in CK-isoenzyme. The presence of CK-MB ($> 5\%$) and elevated CK-MM is an indication of an abnormal pattern. Ordinarily this pattern is interpreted as being due to myocardial infarction (MI). In a patient who has been vigorously training, this pattern suggests abnormal breakdown of cardiac/skeletal muscle. This CK pattern along with an LDH_1/LDH_2 slip ($LDH_1 > LDH_2$) is cause for concern because this pattern also suggests cardiac muscle leakage.

The CK isoenzyme is also a good measure of blows to the head. In a number of reports it has been found that there is an increase in the BB fraction of the CK isoenzyme. In fact, these observations could be used to screen boxers for their fitness to return to the ring.

Alkaline phosphatase. Alkaline phosphatase is a microsomal isoenzyme that hydrolyzes phosphoric esters. There are five isoenzymes that fractionate upon cellulose acetate electrophoresis. However, not all of them will be present in a given sample. These isoenzymes come from the liver, intestine, bone, and placenta. The liver may produce two isoenzymes or a single alkaline phosphatase isoenzyme, or a mixture of the isoenzyme may be found in both normal and pathologic serum. Precise identification of the organ's specific isoenzyme is a valuable diagnostic aid.

In the young adult, alkaline phosphatase is an important measurement because it gives an indication of bone growth. Normally, two alkaline phosphatase isoenzyme bands appear in actively growing children—a liver band and a bone band migrating slightly behind in juxtaposition to the liver band. In some diseases of the kidney, an abnormal rapidly migrating band appears just ahead of the normal liver band. High values are seen in a growing population. Thus, the effect of exercise, conditioning, and so forth on bone development and kidney function can be determined.

Results on Blood Samples Taken From Elite Athletes

Young athletes between 9 to 17 years old and who had won several major competitions were used in this study. The control group consisted of 16 individuals, the runner group had 33, and the wrestlers 57. Samples were taken over a period of 18 to 24 months.

Creatine Kinase

CK enzyme (total concentration) and isoenzyme activity, for the most part, measures skeletal and cardiac muscle. Higher than normal values

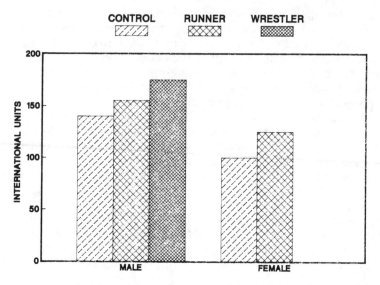

Figure 2 Total CK values for control (n = 16), runners (n = 33), and wrestlers (n = 57).

are due to increased leakage/breakdown of muscle cells. If the CK-MM fraction is increased, the source of the enzyme is believed to be due to skeletal muscle. An increase in CK-MM and CK-MB suggests massive breakdown of skeletal muscle, cardiac tissue, or both. In only a few cases was CK-MB, the so-called cardiac fraction, present.

The CK data are presented graphically in Figure 2. CK male values ranged between 32 to 157 IU/l and female values ranged between 17 to 119 IU/l. Our data showed differences between mean male values (138 ± 43 IU/l) and female values (98 ± 35 IU/l). The difference may be due to a more active male population than a sex difference. This conclusion was perceived because both male and female runners had similar values: 157 ± 52 IU/l and 139 ± 54 IU/l, respectively. There was a slight but significant difference between female control values (98 ± 35 IU/l) and runner values (139 ± 54 IU/l). Male runners showed a slight but not significant elevation over control values. All wrestlers were male and had mean CK values of 178 ± 54 IU/l, which were higher than control CK values (138 ± 43 IU/l).

From total enzyme values alone, only slightly higher values were measured between the exercised groups and the controls. Only in those individuals where CK-MB (cardiac tissue) was present could the individuals be differentiated as being overtrained or in poor condition in their particular sport.

Lactic Dehydrogenase (LDH)

Total LDH enzyme values for both sexes are similar and are presented in Figure 3. Clinical control values for ages 9 to 14 range between 170

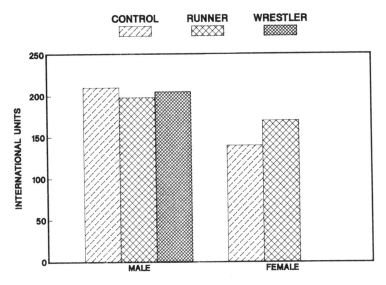

Figure 3 LDH mean values for male and female elite athletes.

to 328 IU/l and for 15 to 19 years old, 149 to 265 IU/l. In this study, control LDH values for females (146 ± 19 IU/l) were lower than male (208 ± 48 IU/l) values. Female runners had total LDH mean values higher (190 ± 41 IU/l) than control numbers. For the male all three groups—control, runner, and wrestler—had similar values.

Again, total LDH enzyme, as with total CK data values, had poor descriptive power to differentiate activity groups and would be a poor parameter to indicate the effects of conditioning.

CK and LDH Isoenzyme Data

As previously stated for CK isoenzyme data, only a few of the runners and/or wrestlers indicated abnormal CK patterns. The abnormal pattern was due to the presence of CK-MB and a marked elevation of CK-MM fraction.

The LDH isoenzyme data were more remarkable because it clearly established specific patterns between control, runners, and wrestlers. Although the observed isoenzyme profiles were not always observed on all athletes in each group, a group pattern seemed to emerge.

Total LDH is composed of five isoenzymes: LDH_1 to LDH_5. As a generalization, LDH_1 represents LDH from cardiac tissue; LDH_5 is measured in greater concentration in liver and muscle. A normal pattern consists of LDH_1 (25%), LDH_2 (35%), LDH_3 (25%), LDH_4 (10%), and LDH_5 (5%).

A usual increase in LDH_1 in the group of male and female runners was seen, followed by decreases in LDH_4 and LDH_5 (Figure 4). This increase in the most forward (LDH_1) band was emphasized in aerobic exercise,

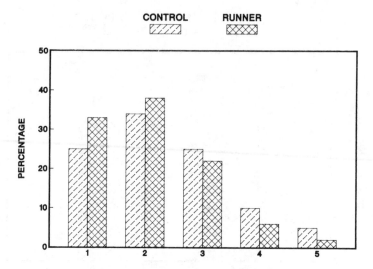

Figure 4 LDH isoenzyme profile of control and runner values.

whereas in the wrestlers group the slower bands appear more prominent. In the wrestlers group, LDH_3 was more prominent than LDH_1 (see Figure 5). This type of pattern is seen in posttraumatic states, thrombocytosis, or with thromboplastin release into peripheral blood.

Discussion

All the blood data from our biochemical scan on these young athletes are presented. Despite focusing on only two enzymes, CK and LDH, an important principle was noted: Even though total enzyme values were "normal," "abnormal" isoenzyme patterns could be measured. This is a very important statement because clinically most hospital laboratories will not carry out isoenzyme studies if the total enzyme value is normal. Data presented here conclusively show abnormal patterns even where the total enzyme value is between normal limits.

Effect of Running on Biochemical Parameters

Early reports showed the elevation of serum enzyme levels in man after strenuous exercise (Cantone & Cerretelli, 1960; Henley, Schmidt, & Schmidt, 1960; Lindemann, Exanger, Opstand, Nummestad, & Ljosland, 1978). It has been stated that the serum enzyme elevation after exercise is associated with alterations in cell membrane, short of necrosis (Altland & Highman, 1961, and references therein). After prolonged exercise, rat samples revealed changes in muscle fibers, heart, liver, kidney, and adrenal cortex. Some animals showed a few foci of inflammation and

CONTROL **WRESTLER**

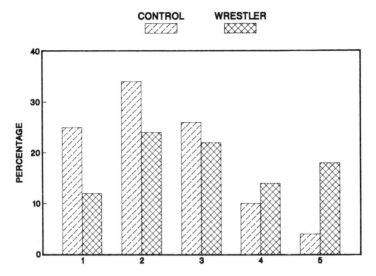

Figure 5 LDH isoenzyme profile of male control and male wrestlers.

necrosis in the muscles. These findings suggest a causal relationship between pathology and serum enzyme elevations. The sole exception was a decline in serum alkaline phosphatase. The reason for the decline is uncertain (Altland & Highman).

A small group of conditioned male joggers (27 to 36 years) had blood samples taken pre- and post-near-maximum exercise (6 to 10 miles) (Kamen, Goheen, Patton, & Raven, 1977). The data showed that CK, LDH, and SGOT were increased. The greatest increase was for CK, and all of the increase was for CK.MM. Although the change in LDH was less than the change in total CK levels, there was a definite "flip," that is, $LDH_1 > LDH_2$.

Many workers have reported a general increase in serum enzymes following submaximal (Forssell, Nordlander, Nyquist, & Styrelius, 1975; Laurell & Nyman, 1957) and near-maximal exercise (Karlsson & Salton, 1970; Misner, Massey, & Williams, 1973). Although there is some confusion with respect to the patterns seen in studies limited to immediate (1 hour) postexercise analyses, those few studies that have monitored CPK and LDH for extended periods postexercise agree that (a) both are elevated and (b) both the fitness of the individual (Sanders & Bloor, 1975) and the type, duration, and intensity of exercise involved (Shapiro, Magazanik, Sohar, & Reich, 1973) will cause changes in the total enzymes produced. In both humans (Critz & Cunningham, 1972) and rats (Highman & Altland, 1965; Nuttall & Jones, 1968), the effect of training is to diminish the release of enzymes into the serum after exercise. Participants considered to be well-trained individuals, yet near maximum exercise, still produce levels of serum enzymes far above those considered normal. Clearly, total enzyme levels may be elevated to greater than normal levels even in trained individuals who participate in intensive running efforts.

The presence of MB isoenzyme in highly stressed athletes presents an interesting situation because the CK.MB is widely held to be a sensitive and specific indicator of myocardial infarction (Galen, 1975). However, reports are available that question the specificity of the MB isoenzyme (Mohiuddin et al., 1976; Olivier et al., 1978; Smith, Radford, Wong, & Oliver, 1976). Evidence exists that MB may be isolated from normal skeletal muscle, probably Type II fibers (Galen, 1974; Roe, 1977; Roe, Limbird, Wagner, & Nerenberg, 1978).

In an attempt to resolve these conflicting views, Kielblock, Manjoo, Booyens, and Katzeff (1979) reported the effect of a 160-km marathon on LDH and CK isoenzymes. Blood samples were obtained from 20 runners in the age group 27 to 63. Total CK rose about tenfold, and 65% of the runners had detectable MB-isoenzymes. The BB isoenzyme was seen in 12 runners (60%). Total LDH values rose to nearly four times upper limit values. General elevation was mainly in LDH_3 and LDH_4. A flipped pattern ($LDH_1 > LDH_2$) was present in five runners. As a group, the faster runners exhibited greater elevation in enzyme levels than did slower runners (Noakes & Carter, 1976). In the 1976 Comrades Marathon, Olivier et al. (1978) reported earlier that 50% of the runners exhibited CK.MB isoenzyme.

Although inapparent intravascular hemolysis incident to sustained physical exertion may contribute significantly to elevated LDH_1 and LDH_2, the criteria of $LDH_1 > LDH_2$ and the presence of CK.MB in conjunction with one another are highly indicative of myocardial infarction. The implication of such changes to apparently healthy individuals warrants careful consideration. In studies (Davies, Daggett, & Watt, 1982) carried out on veteran class runners, enzyme profiles similar to patients with myocardial infarction were reported. Studies where CK-MB is present raise the question regarding the advisability of participating in prolonged, intensive exercise under competitive conditions for even veteran class runners. The question for young elite athletes is particularly apropos because there is controversy relating the incidence of myocardial events (Noakes, Opie, Rose, & Kleynham, 1979) to prolonged intensive exercise events that have previously been associated with immunity (Bassler, 1977).

Several authors (Fowler, Gardner, Kazerunian, & Lauvstad, 1962; Garbus, Highman, & Altland, 1964; Papadopoulos, Leon, & Bloor, 1968) have studied the effects of muscular work on plasma enzyme activity both in untrained and trained subjects. It has been shown that the plasma enzyme response to a given amount of exercise might be useful as a biochemical estimate of physical fitness (Nuttal & Jones, 1968): Plasma enzyme activities may well serve as sensitive indexes of exercise stress and/or physical fitness in the laboratory investigation of athletes (Berg & Haralambie, 1978; Hunter & Critz, 1971; Sanders & Bloor, 1975). Our results suggest that isoenzymes as well as total activity should be measured.

This issue was investigated by some Japanese researchers (Ohkuwa, Saito, & Miyamura, 1984). In their study of 13 male sprint runners (400 m), they found that CK and LDH isoenzymes were better indicators of physical training and/or physical performance than peak blood lactate or plasma LDH activities. They noted, however, that LDH levels do not appear to be useful indexes of physical training or physical performance in anaerobic work.

Maximal aerobic capacity (MAC), as determined by maximal oxygen uptake, has been universally accepted as a primary indicator of cardiovascular fitness. MAC, however, describes only a limited aspect of physical condition and response. The release of enzymes from skeletal muscles following exercise may occur as a result of muscle hypoxia (Bratton, Chowdhury, Fowler, Gardner, & Pearson, 1962; Critz & Cunningham, 1972) ischemia or necrosis (Critz & Cunningham), or other conditions that cause a change in all membrane permeability (Maxwell & Bloor, 1981; Shapiro, Magazanik, Sohar, & Reich, 1973). Shapiro et al. have proposed that the release of enzymes after high-intensity training can be minimized by regular physical training.

Another cellular response to exercise is the haptoglobin (Hapt.) level that could reflect hemolysis caused by compression of the muscles during physical activity. Levels of free-circularly Hapt. decrease as the Hapt. molecules combine with free hemoglobin to conserve iron. Because the measurement of free-Hapt. in the serum has been used extensively to evaluate hemolytic activity, posttrauma, and disease (Brus & Lewis, 1959; Marchand, Galen, & VanLente, 1980), measurement postexercise could provide evidence of acute hemolytis condition. Lower resting Hapt. levels might indicate a greater degree of physical activity.

The above hypothesis has received support from a recent report (Spitler, Alexander, Hoffler, Dolic, & Buchanan, 1984). Although the results indicated that one progressive test to maximal aerobic capacity is not sufficient to induce significant CK, LDH, or hemolytic stress response, they do suggest that a chronic hemolytic condition exists as a result of conditioning activity (aerobic).

Exercise-induced hemolysis has been described after marching (Stahl, 1957), running (Hunding, Jordal, & Paulev, 1981; Siegel, Hennekens, Solomon, & VanBoeckel, 1979), and extensive physical activity of other forms. The mechanisms proposed for such hemolysis are mechanical intravascular after strenuous exercise among persons with differing aerobic capacity.

We did not find such a gradation of response in this study. The slight increase in serum concentration of Hapt. evident after exercise in all groups can be explained by the exercise-induced hemoconcentration as evidenced by calculated decreases in plasma volumes of 15.9 to 18.5%. The lack of differences in Hapt. response between the men and women or between fitness levels indicates that one brief bout of progressive physical activity to individual maximal intensity does not produce sufficient trauma to differentiate states of hemolysis.

Myhre, Rasmussen, and Andersen (1970) suggested that LDH activity in the serum may be a better indication of intravascular hemolysis than Hapt. Increased LDH activity has been observed in patients with coronary heart disease (Wolfson et al., 1972) and in normal individuals following exercise (Murray, Connell, & Pert, 1961; Siegel et al., 1979). The 16% increase in LDH postexercise appears to be accounted for by hemo-

Table 4 Enzyme Activity of Control and Wrestlers (55)

| | CK | LDH | LDH isoenzymes | | | | |
			1	2	3	4	5
Control	21 + 14	110 + 18	24 + 5	36 + 4	26 + 3	8 + 2	7 + 2
Wrestlers							
(pre)	31 + 9	145 + 21	36 + 6	52 + 6	52 + 12	15 + 4	10 + 3
(post)	33 + 9	157 + 15	37 + 7	57 + 7	57 + 16	17 + 6	14 + 5

concentrations, and therefore, one needs to be careful in assigning increases to exercise alone.

Effect of Wrestling on Biochemical Parameters

Thirteen members of a high school team were examined before and after a league meet (Rasch & Schwartz, 1972). Total CK and LDH as well as isoenzymes of the latter group were measured. Untrained laboratory personnel (n = 20) served as control for the study. The preexercise activity of both enzymes was substantially higher than that of the untrained group. Wrestling matches of longer than 5 min brought about a significant rise in CK and LDH levels. Rises in LDH fractions 2, 3, 4, and 5 account for almost all of the LDH increases (see Table 4).

The LDH pattern found in the Rasch and Schwartz (1972) and our own study with wrestlers strongly suggests some type of thromboplastin or thromboplastin-like substance release into peripheral blood. An exact interpretation will be possible only when a more definitive study of peripheral blood is made. The effect of LDH leakage from blood also has to be considered.

Leakage of myoglobin into serum was measured after the completion of three different types of exercise: dynamic, isometric, and isokinetic (Pette, 1980). The maximal rises in serum-myoglobin could be reduced by training.

It has been reported previously that physical conditioning significantly reduces myoglobin release from muscle cells after exercise (Ledwich, 1973; Maxwell & Bloor, 1981; Ritter, Stone, & Willerson, 1979; Roxin, PerVenge, & Friman, 1984). Untrained or sedentary individuals also have been shown to react with higher serum myoglobin levels after exercise (Norregaard-Hansen, Bjerre-Knudsen, Brodthagen, Jordal, & Paulev, 1982; Ross, Attwood, Atkin, & Villar, 1983; Sabria, Ruibal, Rey, Fox, & Domenech, 1983). Although all of these reports deal with severe or prolonged exercise, mechanisms similar to those observed in this study may be involved after short time exercise. Ritter et al. proposed that an altered metabolic situation after training may improve aerobic metabolism and muscle cell welfare during exercise. Norregaard-Hansen et al. concluded that training might reduce muscle cell sarcolemma permeability and therefore decrease the efflux of muscle protein, whereas Maxwell and Bloor and Roti et al. (1981) favor the idea that physical conditioning prevents muscle cell rhabdomyolysis.

H-subunits of LDH-isoenzyme predominate in tissues exhibiting aerobic metabolism. In tissues functioning under more anaerobic conditions, more M-units are evident. An increase in the proportion of M- to H-subunits of LDH-isoenzyme has been reported in the heart muscles of patients with ischemic heart disease (Hayashi & Tanaka, 1984). The regulation of the LDH-isoenzyme pattern may in some way be dependent on oxygen tension (Hammond, Nadal-Ginard, Talner, & Markert, 1976).

A study on the effect of hypoxia on LDH isoenzyme was carried out by inducing a hypoxic state with thyroxine (Roti et al., 1981). In rats, a decrease in the LDH_1 fraction and an increase in LDH_2 and LDH_3 fractions of heart muscle were observed. Little change was observed in the liver (LDH_5). In mice, a decrease in LDH_1 and LDH_2 and an increase in LDH_3 and LDH_4 were measured. During low oxygen loading, plasma LDH isoenzymes did not show marked changes. Therefore, although LDH isoenzyme is not always a useful indicator of myocardial damage in the hypoxic state, it would seem to indicate hypoxia. From the studies reported in the literature as well as our own experience, CK and LDH isoenzymes are valuable parameters to measure effects of exercise and give a profile of body conditioning.

Conclusion

A thorough biochemical scan is being proposed to evaluate the training program of athletes. The program is not only a useful barometer of training intensity but also can be used to detect early or possible health problems. The research presented in this chapter led to the following conclusions:

- CK and LDH total enzyme activity is a good measure of exercise activity per se.
- CK and LDH isoenzymes are good discriminators of exercise programs (i.e., runners vs. wrestlers).
- Runners present a unique biochemical profile mimicking myocardial infarction. This isoenzyme profile is not seen in wrestlers, who have their own profile.
- Wrestlers have an LDH pattern that seems to be associated with thromboembolic lesions/muscle injury or trauma.

References

Altland, P.D., & Highman, B. (1961). Effects of exercise on serum enzymes values and tissue of rats. *American Journal Physical, 90*, 393-395.

Bassler, T.J. (1977). Marathon running and immunity to atherosclerosis. *American New York Academy of Science*, **301**, 579-592.

Berg, A., & Haralambie, G. (1978). Changes in serum creatine kinase and hexose phosphate isomerase activity with exercise duration. *European Journal of Applied Physiology*, **39**, 191-201.

Bratton, R.D., Chowdhury, S.R., Fowler, W.M., Jr., Gardner, G.W., & Pearson, C.M. (1962). Effects of exercise on serum enzyme levels in untrained males. *Research Quarterly of American Association of Health & Physical Education*, **33**, 182-193.

Brus, I., & Lewis, S.M. (1959). The haptoglobin content of serum in haemolytic anemia. *British Journal of Haematology*, **5**, 348-355.

Cantone, A., & Cerretelli, P. (1960). The effect of muscular work on serum aldolase activity in trained and untrained men. *International Zeitschrift für Angewandte Physiologie*, **28**, 107-111.

Critz, J.B., & Cunningham, D.A. (1972). Plasma enzyme levels in man after different physical activities. *Journal of Sports Medicine and Physical Fitness*, **12**, 143-149.

Davidson, R.J.L. (1969). March or exertional haemoglobinuria. *Semin. Hematol.*, **6** (Suppl. 2), 150-161.

Davies, B., Daggett, A., & Watt, D.A.L. (1982). Serum creative kinase and isoenzyml responses of veteran class fell runners. *European Journal of Applied Physical*, **48**, 345-354.

Forssell, G., Nordlander, R., Nyquist, O., & Styrelius, I. (1975). Creatine phosphokinase after submaximal physical exercise in untrained individuals. *Acta Medica Scandinavica*, **197**, 503-505.

Fowler, W.M., Gardner, G.W., Kazerunian, H.H., & Lauvstad, W.A. (1962). The effect of exercise on serum enzymes. *Archives of Physical Medicine*, **49**, 554-565.

Galen, R.S. (1974). *Iso-enzymes and myocardial infarction* (Advanced Clinical Chemistry Monograph No. ACC-11). New York: American Society of Clinical Pathologists.

Galen, R.S. (1975). The enzyme diagnosis of myocardial infarction. *Human Pathology*, **6** (Suppl. 2), 141-155.

Garbus, J., Highman, B., & Altland, P.D. (1964). Serum enzymes and lactic dehydrogenase isoenzymes after exercise and training in rats. *American Journal of Physiology*, **207**, 467-472.

Hammond, G.L., Nadal-Ginard, B., Talner, N.S., & Markert, C.L. (1976). Myocardial LDH isoenzyme distribution in the ischemic and hypoxic heart. *Circulation*, **53**, 637-643.

Hayashi, T., & Tanaka, T. (1984). Studies of a shift of LDH-isoenzyme during hypoxia. In H. Hirari (Ed.), *Electraphoresis '83* (pp. 453-455). Berlin: Walter de Gruyter.

Henley, K.S., Schmidt, E., & Schmidt, F.W. (1960). Serum enzymes. *Journal of the American Medical Association*, **119**, v. 174 (Suppl. 8), 977-981.

Highman, B., & Altland, P.D. (1963). Effects of exercise and training on serum enzyme and tissue changes in rats. *American Journal of Physiology*, **205**, 162-166.

Hunding, A., Jordal, R., & Paulev, P. (1981). Runner's anemia and iron deficiency. *Acta Medica Scandinavica*, **209**, 315-318.

Hunter, J.B., & Critz, J.B. (1971). Effect of training on plasma enzyme levels in man. *Journal of Applied Physiology*, **31**, 20-23.

Kamen, R.L., Goheen, B., Patton, R., & Raven, P. (1977). The effects of near maximum exercise on serum enzymes: The exercise profile vs the cardiac profile. *Clinica Chimica Acta*, **81**, 145-149.

Karlsson, J., & Salton, G. (1970). Lactate, AIP, and CP in working muscles during exhaustive exercise in man. *Journal of Applied Physiology*, **29** (Suppl. 5), 598-602.

Kielblock, A.J., Manjoo, M., Booyens, J., & Katzeff, I.E. (1979). Creative phosphokinacl and lactate dehydrogenase levels after ultra long-distance running. *South African Medical Journal*, **55**, 1061-1064.

Laurell, C., & Nyman, M. (1957). Studies on the serum haptoglobin level in hemoglobinemia and its influence on renal excretion of hemoglobin. *Hematology*, **12**, 493-506.

Ledwich, J.R. (1973). Changes in serum creatine phosphokinase during submaximal exercise testing. *Canadian Medical Association Journal*, **109**, 273-278.

Lindemann, R., Exanger, R., Opstand, P.K., Nummestad, M., & Ljosland, R. (1978). Hematological changes in normal men during prolonged severe exercise. *American Correctional Therapy Journal*, **32**, 107-111.

Marchand, A., Galen, R.S., & VanLente, F. (1980). The predictive value of serum haptoglobin in hemolytic disease. *Journal of the American Medical Association*, **243**, 1909-1911.

Maxwell, J., & Bloor, C.M. (1981). Effects of conditioning on exertional rhabdomyolysis and serum creatine kinase after severe exercise. *Enzyme*, **26**, 177-181.

Misner, J.E., Massey, B.H., & Williams, B.T. (1973). The effect of physical training on the response of serum enzymes to exercise stress. *Medicine and Science in Sports*, **5** (Suppl. 2), 86-88.

Mohiuddin, S.M., Rafetto, J., Sketch, M.H., Lynch, J.D., Schultz, R.D., & Runco, V. (1976). LDH isoenzymes and myocardial infarction in patients undergoing coronary bypass surgery: An excellent correlation. *American Heart Journal*, **92** (Suppl. 5), 584-588.

Murray, R.K., Connell, G.E., & Pert, J.H. (1961). The role of haptoglobin in the clearances and distribution of extracorpuscular hemoglobin. *Blood*, **17**, 45-53.

Myhre, E., Rasmussen, K., & Andersen, A. (1970). Serum lactic dehydrogenase activity in patients with prosthetic heart valves: A parameter of intravascular hemolysis. *American Heart Journal, 80*, 463-468.

Noakes, T.D., & Carter, J.W. (1976). Biochemical parameters in athletes before and after having run 160 kilometres. *South African Medical Journal, 50*, 1562-1566.

Noakes, T.D., Opie, L., Rose, A.G., & Kleynham, P.H.T. (1979). Autopsy-proved coronary atherosclerosis in marathon runners. *New England Journal of Medicine, 301*, 86-89.

Norregaard-Hansen, K., Bjerre-Knudsen, J., Brodthagen, U., Jordal, R., & Paulev, P.E. (1982). Muscle cell leakage due to long distance training. *European Journal of Applied Physiology, 48*, 177-188.

Nuttall, F.Q., & Jones, B. (1968). Creatine kinase and glutamic oxalacetic transaminase activity in serum: Kinetics of change with exercise and effect of physical conditioning. *Journal of Laboratory & Clinical Medicine, 71*, 847-853.

Ohkuwa, T., Saito, M., & Miyamura, M. (1984). Plasma LDH and CK activities after 400 m sprinting by well-trained sprint runners. *European Journal of Applied Physiology, 52*, 296-299.

Olivier, L.R., Dewaal, A., Retief, F.J., Marx, J.D., Kriel, J.R., Human, G.P., & Potgieter, G.M. (1978). Electrocardiographic and biochemical studies on marathon runners. *South African Medical Journal, 53* (Suppl. 20), 783-787.

Papadopoulos, N.M., Leon, A.S., & Bloor, C.M. (1968). Effects of exercise on plasma lactate dehydrogenase and isoenzyme activities in trained and untrained rats. *Proc. Soc. Exp. Biol. Med., 129*, 232-234.

Pette, D. (1979, September). *Plasticity of muscle.* Paper presented at a symposium at the University of Konstanz, Germany.

Rasch, P.J., & Schwartz, P.L. (1972). Effect of amateur wrestling on selected serum enzymes. *Journal of Sports Medicine & Physical Fitness, 122*, 82-86.

Refsum, H.E., Jordfald, J., & Stromme, S.B. (1976). Hematological changes following prolonged heavy exercise. *Medicine & Science in Sports, 9*, 91-99.

Ritter, W.S., Stone, M.J., & Willerson, J.T. (1979). Reduction in exertional myoglobinemia after physical conditioning. *Archives of International Medicine, 139*, 644-647.

Roe, C.R. (1977). Diagnosis of myocardial infarction by serum isoenzyme analysis. *Annals of Clinical and Laboratory Science, 7* (Suppl. 3), 201-209.

Roe, C.R., Limbird, L.E., Wagner, G.S., & Nerenberg, S.T. (1978). *Journal of Laboratory & Clinical Medicine, 80*, 577-590.

Rose, L.I., Lowe, S.L., Carroll, D.R., Wolfson, S., & Cooper, K.H. (1970). Serum lactate dehydrogenase isoenzyme changes after muscular exertion. *Journal of Applied Physiology, 28*, 279-281.

Ross, J.H., Attwood, E.C., Atkin, G.E., & Villar, R.N. (1983). A study on the effects of severe repetitive exercise on serum myoglobin, creatine kinase, transaminases and lactate dehydrogenase. *Quarterly Journal of Medicine* (New Series), **52**, 268-279.

Roti, S., Iori, E., Guiducci, U., Emanuele, R., Robuschi, G., Bandini, P., Gnudi, A., & Roti, E.L. (1981). Serum concentrations of myoglobin, creatine phosphokinase and lactic dehydrogenase after exercise in trained and untrained athletes. *Journal of Sport Medicine and Physical Fitness*, **21**, 113-118.

Roxin, L.E., PerVenge, D., & Friman, G. (1984). Variation in serum myo globin after a 2-min. isokinetic exercise test and the effects of training. *European Journal of Applied Physiology*, **53**, 43-47.

Sabria, M., Ruibal, A., Rey, C., Fox, M., & Domenech, F.M. (1983). Influence of exercise on serum levels of myoglobin measured by radioimmunoassay. *European Journal of Nucleic Medicine*, **8**, 159-161.

Sanders, T.M., & Bloor, C.M. (1975). Effects of repeated endurance exercise on serum enzyme activities in well-conditioned males. *Medicine & Science in Sports*, **7** (Suppl. 1), 44-47.

Shapiro, Y., Magazanik, A., Sohar, E., & Reich, C.B. (1973). Serum enzyme changes in untrained subjects following a prolonged march. *Canadian Journal of Physiology & Pharmacology*, **51**, 271-276.

Siegel, A.J., Hennekens, C.H., Solomon, H.S., & VanBoeckel, B. (1979). Exercise-related hematuria. *Journal of the American Medical Association*, **241**, 391-392.

Smith, A.F., Radford, D., Wong, C.P., & Oliver, M.F. (1976). Creatine kinase MB isoenzyme studies in diagnosis of myocardial infarction. *British Heart Journal*, **38**, 225-232.

Spitler, D.L., Alexander, W., Hoffler, G.W., Dolic, D.F., & Buchanan, P. (1984). Haptoglobin and serum enzymatic response to maximal exercise. *Medicine and Science in Sports & Exercise*, **16**, 366-370.

Stahl, W.C. (1957). March hemoglobinuria. *Journal of the American Medical Association*, **164**, 1458-1460.

Sun, T., Lien, Y.Y., & Gross, S. (1978). Clinical application of a high-resolution electrophoresis system. *Annals of Clinical and Laboratory Science*, **8**, 219-227.

Wolfson, S., Rose, L.I., Bousser, J.E., Parisi, A., Acosta, A.E., Cooper, K.H., & Schechter, E. (1972). Serum enzyme levels during exercise in patients with coronary heart disease: Effects of training. *American Heart Journal*, **84**, 478-483.

Strength Training in the Young Athlete

Lyle J. Micheli

The growth of sport science, a relatively new area of exercise science, has resulted in a systematic approach to studying not only the performance of athletes but also the factors, such as the athletic training regimen, responsible for this performance. The determinants of athletic performance and the components of the training regimen include cardiovascular, musculoskeletal, nutritional, psychological, and of course, skill factors.

An effective training regimen incorporates these factors into a program that is able to enhance athletic performance without increasing the chance of injury. A careful matching of the demands of a given sport with the capacities of the individual athlete is essential to develop an effective and safe training program.

All sports place demands on the musculoskeletal system. Although the demands on the different characteristics of the musculoskeletal system (strength, power, endurance, or flexibility) may vary from sport to sport, there is general agreement that increasing the strength of the athlete, in particular, can enhance performance and decrease the chance of injury.

Strength training incorporates the use of progressive resistance to increase the ability to exert or resist force. This progressive resistance force or load may take the form of free weights, constrained weight machines, hydraulic or pneumatic devices, or the athlete's own body weight (Knuttgen, 1978).

Observations that increased strength benefits adult athletes, both male and female, by enhancing sport performance and decreasing susceptibility to injury have resulted in the use of strength training in sports as varied as distance running, gridiron football, and gymnastics (Asmussen, 1973; Wilmore, 1974).

The use of strength training for young athletes, however, has been a matter of much controversy. The concerns are focused on three major areas: (a) the safety of strength training in this age group, (b) whether strength gains are actually attainable, and (c) whether increased strength benefits the young athlete. In order to more effectively study each of these questions, it is useful to divide young athletes into prepubescent, or child athletes, and postpubescent, or adolescent athletes.

Pubescence, the onset of adolescence and the final growth spurt, is a time of rapid hormonal changes in the growing child. At this time, development of the sexual organs takes place as well as changes in body habitus and genital hair—the "secondary sexual characteristics." The determination of the degree of sexual maturation can be done in a number of ways: (a) measurement of hormone levels in blood or urine, (b) measurement of relative bone age via X ray, or (c) physical examination of the child for the presence or absence of body changes. Of the three, physical examination and the grading of the child's development by the classification developed by Professor J.M. Tanner is the easiest and least expensive (Falkner & Tanner, 1978). Relative maturation through pubescence from Tanner's Stage-I through Tanner's Stage-IV is based on graphs and charts developed by Professor Tanner and his colleagues in London. It is generally agreed that the prepubescent is Tanner-I or Tanner-II level of maturation, whereas adolescents are Tanner-III and Tanner-IV. The closure of the growth plates of the bones occurs in a sequential fashion through adolescence, with the closure of the last plates, at the knee, signaling the onset of adulthood.

Although some studies of strengthening have been done without reference to maturation level of the child (Carron & Bailey, 1974), most have wisely separated prepubescents from pubescents in studying responses to strength training (Vrijens, 1978).

There is good evidence that the adolescent male makes strength gains in much the same pattern as the adult male when placed on a properly designed progressive resistive strengthening program (Asmussen, 1973; Croucher, 1984; Jackson, Wiltse, & Dingerman, 1982). It must be remembered, of course, that a proper strengthening program incorporates progressive resistance, terminating in a final overload repetition where the resistance can just barely be lifted or moved. Some confusion has resulted from studies of strength training in adolescents that employed submaximal resistance (Fleck & Schutt, 1983; Gillman, 1981). Adolescent girls will also gain strength in response to progressive resistive training, although the response is less dramatic than that seen in boys (Blanksby & Gregor, 1981).

Of greater concern have been reports of serious injuries, including growth plate injuries, in adolescents performing weight training (Benton, 1983; Brady, Cahill, & Bodnar, 1982). In most cases of reported injury, improperly done lifts or power-type training with heavy weights and a small number of repetitions can be indicated as factors. In particular, overhead lifts such as the military press have been associated with upper arm and back injuries. Brady et al. reviewed 80 weight training-related injuries in adolescents and condemned heavy lifting and the military press in particular. Gumbs (1982) and Ryan and Salciccioli (1976) have reported fractures through the growth plates of the wrists, again associated with excessive lifts.

Back injuries have been the other area of concern in adolescent weight training. Once again, however, a review of the reported injuries shows that most were due to poor training techniques and heavy lifts (Jackson, 1979; Mason, 1970). Additionally, Jesse (1977, 1979) has suggested that Olympic lifting techniques should also be contraindicated for the young athlete.

Of equal concern is the potential for cardiovascular and neurologic injuries such as "black out" in young weight trainers. Hypertension has been an additional concern (Allen, Byrd, & Smith, 1973; Brown & Kimball, 1983; Compton, Hill, & Sinclair, 1973). Once again, most reported cases have occurred in association with improper training programs.

In the care of young athletes, this author has often recommended a progressive resistive strength training program that has been named the "7-11 Program." In this program, the young athlete is taught proper posture and technique for the lift in question. He or she lifts an amount of weight that can just barely be lifted for seven repetitions. They complete all lifts in series, performing two or sometimes three complete sets of lifts. They train three or sometimes four times per week. They increase the number of repetitions with the same resistance, as strength increases, until they are able to perform 11 repetitions. Then they increase the resistance so that they can just perform seven repetitions again. This increase is generally in the range of 5 to 10%. No standing lifts are performed. Curls and presses are performed in the sitting position. Full squats are not allowed.

The benefits of strength training in enhancing performance in adolescent athletes appear well accepted in the coaching ranks (Hatfield, 1980). In addition, reports by Cahill (1977) and Hejna (1982) suggest that proper strength training programs increase the safety of sport participation—particularly for contact sports—in adolescents.

Until quite recently, the question of the safety and indications for weight training in the prepubescent were even more controversial than that of adolescent weight training. Opposition to strength training for prepubescent children has been based on three contentions: (a) the prepubescent child, lacking adequate levels of circulating androgens, is incapable of significant strength gains in response to progressive resistive exercise; (b) resistive weight training is dangerous for children, having in and of itself an unacceptable risk of injury; and (c) strength gains, if attainable, would not benefit performance or reduce the risk of injury in children's sports.

The American Academy of Pediatrics (1983), in a position stand on weight training and lifting, gave guarded support to the concept of weight training for adolescents, condemned weight lifting competitions for adolescents, and opinioned that weight training for the prepubescent was not useful or indicated.

As noted above, opinion has varied widely as to whether the prepubescent child can actually gain in strength when compared to age-matched controls. It has been only very recently that information has become available from several studies (Sewall & Micheli, 1984; Rians, Wettson, Cahill et al., 1985) investigating this question. One of the reasons for this difference of opinion is that the prepubescent child increases in strength simply by growing. This, of course, is not true with the adult. Studies of strength gains in response to resistive training in children, therefore, have had to be very carefully controlled with age-matched controls not on training programs. Historically, certain clinical observations have supported the view that prepubescents can increase in strength. Physicians caring for handicapped children or children being rehabilitated following injury or illness with strengthening exercises have noted that even the prepubescent child is capable of relatively dramatic strength gains in response to such progressive rehabilitative strengthening programs.

As a result of several recent studies (Sewall & Micheli, 1984; Rians et al., 1985), it is now possible to conclude that the prepubescent is indeed capable of significant strength gains when placed on a progressive resistive exercise program. Sewall and Micheli studied a group of children with Tanner-I and Tanner-II levels of maturation placed on a strengthening program. These children were on progressive resistive programs utilizing the CAM-II and Nautilus exercise machines. Strength gains in each child were compared to age-matched controls over a training period of 9 weeks. Results showed statistically significant increased strength at the shoulder and positive trends in both upper and lower extremity for the other movements studied. Knee flexion, which was not specifically strengthened in the exercise program, showed no change when compared to the age-matched controls.

More recently, studies by Rians et al. (1985) as well as one by Servidio, Bartels, Hamlin et al. (1985), have demonstrated statistically significant strength gains in prepubescent children in response to training. The study by Rians et al. utilized circuit training on eight hydraulic resistance machines, whereas the study by Servidio et al. used Olympic-style lifts with free weights. Each demonstrated significant gains in strength in the test subjects when compared to age-matched control groups.

Although the basic physiological question regarding strength training in the prepubescent appears to be satisfactorily answered by these recent studies, other physiologic questions regarding strength training in this age group remain unanswered and are very much in need of additional research. These include questions on how progressive resistance strength training affects flexibility; cardiovascular parameters such as blood pressure, aerobic fitness, and anaerobic fitness; and body composition. There are, as yet, inadequate scientific studies on which to base any valid conclusions regarding these questions.

The second major area of concern, that of the potential for acute or long-term injury to the prepubescent child who is engaged in strength training, also is a matter of much debate, very little of which is based upon fact or careful scientific observation. At the present time, there have been no epidemiological studies on the rate of injury occurring with resistance weight training in prepubescents. Therefore, the rate of injury in this activity cannot be compared to any other activity of prepubescence. As with the adult weight trainer, the potential for musculoskeletal injuries such as muscle strains or joint sprains is, of course, present. In addition, the prepubescent shares with the pubescent, or adolescent, the potential for growth plate injuries. This potential for growth plate injury may actually be less in the prepubescent than in the pubescent, however, because the growth plate is actually much stronger and more resistant to sheer stress in younger children than in adolescents. In actuality, acute growth plate injuries are rare, even in the adolescent (Brady et al., 1982; Gumbs, 1982; Ryan & Salciccioli, 1976). As of yet, there have been no reports of growth plate injuries in prepubescents doing weight training. In the studies conducted by Sewall (1984) and Rians et al. (1985), no serious injuries were reported in the course of these carefully supervised weight training programs.

The potential for low-grade repetitive microtrauma injuries to the growth tissue in the prepubescent, although theoretically present, is most probably extremely unlikely. The only reports of children sustaining apparent growth arrests from excessive lifting or loading activities have come from a few isolated reports. Kato and Ishiko (1964) reported that some children doing heavy manual labor in lower economic groups in certain parts of Japan experienced a significant decrease in stature, due presumably to repetitive growth plate injury. Their study did not control for other possible etiologic factors such as nutrition, toxicology, and so forth.

Ironically, this author has more concern about repetitive impact activities, such as running, causing long-term growth problems in this age group than I do with resistive weight training because weight training may be performed in a much more controlled environment and actually results in much less shearing-type load of the joints when properly done. Shear stress appears to be the culprit in many growth tissue overuse injuries in children and adolescents (Mueller & Blyth, 1981).

In conclusion, a review of the present scientific literature on weight training in both the adolescent and prepubescent suggests that, under proper conditions with the use of appropriate equipment and the proper supervision, it is a relatively safe activity when compared to other childhood activities. Secondly, there is now good evidence that progressive resistive strength training or weight training results in increased strength in both adolescent and preadolescent when properly done. In the adolescent, there appears to be reasonable evidence that this increased strength serves to enhance motor performance and may increase the resistance to injury in certain sport activities. Similar specific advantages or benefits from weight training in the prepubescent have not yet been demonstrated, but it is this author's opinion that this will also prove to be the case.

References

Allen, T.E., Byrd, R., & Smith, D. (1973). Hemodynamic consequences of circuit weight training. *Quarterly, 47*, 299-306.

American Academy of Pediatrics. (1983). Committee on Sports Medicine: Weight Training and Weight Lifting: Information for the pediatrician. *Physician and Sportsmedicine, 11*, 157-161.

Asmussen, E. (1973). Growth in muscular strength and power. In L.G. Rarick (Ed.), *Physical activity, human growth and development* (pp. 60-79). New York: Academic Press.

Benton, J.W. (1983). Epiphyseal fractures in sports. *Physician and Sportsmedicine, 10*, 63-71.

Blanksby, B., & Gregor, J. (1981). Anthropometric, strength and physiological changes in male and female swimmers with progressive resistance training. *Australian Journal of Sports Sciences, 1*, 3-6.

Brady, T.A., Cahill, B., & Bodnar, L. (1982). Weight training related injuries. *American Journal of Sports Medicine, 10,* 1-5.

Brown, E.W., & Kimball, R. (1983). Medical history association with adolescent powerlifting. *Pediatrics, 72,* 636-644.

Cahill, B.R. (1977). Stress fracture of the proximal tibial epiphysis: A case report. *American Journal of Sports Medicine, 5,* 186-187.

Carron, A.V., & Bailey, D.A. (1974). Strength development in boys from 10 through 16 years. *Monographs of the Society for Research in Child Development, 39,* 1-37.

Compton, D., Hill, P.M., & Sinclair, H. (1973). Weight lifters black out. *Lancet, 2,* 1234-1237.

Croucher, J. (1984). An analysis of world weight lifting records. *Research Quarterly for Exercise and Sport, 55,* 285-288.

Falkner, F., & Tanner, J.M. (1978). *Human growth II—Postnatal growth.* New York: Plenum Press.

Fleck, S.J., & Schutt, R.C.L., Jr. (1983). Types of strength training. *Orthopedic Clinics of North America, 14,* 449-457.

Gillman, G.M. (1981). Effects of frequency of weight training on muscle strength enhancement. *Journal of Sports Medicine, 21,* 432-435.

Gumbs, V.L. (1982). Bilateral distal radius and ulnar fracture in weightlifters. *American Journal of Sports Medicine, 10,* 375-379.

Hatfield, F.C. (1980). *Weight training for the young athlete* (IX, 118). New York: Atheneum.

Hejna, W. (1982). Weight training for high school football. Prevention of sports injuries in high school students through strength training. *Journal of NSCA,* **Feb,** 28-31.

Jackson, D.W. (1979). Low back pain in young athletes: Evaluations of stress reaction and discogenic problems. *American Journal of Sports Medicine, 7,* 364-366.

Jackson, D.W., Wiltse, H., Dingerman, R.D., et al. (1982). Stress reactions involving the pars interarticularis in young athletes. *American Journal of Sports Medicine, 9,* 304-312.

Jesse, J.P. (1977). Olympic lifting movements endanger adolescents. *Physician and Sportsmedicine, 5,* 60-67.

Jesse, J.P. (1979). Misuse of strength development programs. *Athletic Training Physicians and Sportsmedicine, 7,* 46-52.

Kato, S., & Ishiko, T. (1964). Obstructed growth of children's bones due to excessive labor in remote corners. In S. Kato (Ed.), *Proceedings of International Congress of Sports Sciences, Japanese Union of Sports Sciences* (p. 476). Tokyo.

Knuttgen, H.G. (1978). Force, work, power and exercise. *Medicine and Science in Sports, 10,* 227-228.

Mason, T.A. (1970). Is weight lifting deleterious to the spines of young people? *British Journal of Sports Medicine, 5*, 54-56.

Mueller, F., & Blyth, C. (1981). Epidemiology of sports injuries in children. *Clinical Sports Medicine, 15*, 229-233.

Rians, C.B., Wettson, A., Cahill, B.R., et al. (1985). *Strength training in pre-pubescent males: Is it safe?* Presented at the Annual Meeting, American Orthopaedic Society for Sports Medicine, Nashville, TN.

Ryan, J.R., & Salciccioli, G.G. (1976). Fracture of the distal radial epiphysis in adolescent weight lifters. *American Journal of Sports Medicine, 4*, 26-27.

Servidio, F., Bartels, R., Hamlin, R., et al. (1985). The effects of weight training, using Olympic style lifts, on various physiological variables in pre-pubescent boys. *Medicine and Science in Sports and Exercise, 17*, 238.

Sewall, L., & Micheli, L.J. (1984). Strength development in children. *Medicine and Science in Sports and Exercise, 16*, 158.

Vrijens, J. (1978). Muscle strength development in the pre- and post-pubescent age. *Medicine and Sports, 11*, 152-158.

Wilmore, J.H. (1974). Alterations in strength, body composition, and anthropometric measurements consequent to a 10-week training program. *Medicine and Science in Sports, 6*, 133-138.

Study of Injury Mechanisms in Youth Sports

Eugene W. Brown

According to Martens (1978), there are an estimated 17 million children between the ages of 6 and 16 years participating in over 30 non-school-sponsored sports programs each year. In another survey, conducted by the Athletic Institute (Parker, 1975), 20 million children were estimated to participate in nonschool sports. Vogel and Seefeldt (1981) have also reported that over 5 million children annually participate in a variety of school-sponsored youth sports programs. Thus, a substantial proportion of the youth population of the United States participates in sports.

In the past, the National Education Association and the American Medical Association expressed opposition to highly organized sports activities for youth below the ninth grade because of concerns for psychological and physical stress imposed upon children and youth (Seefeldt, 1982). Other researchers (Kozar & Lord, 1983; Rarick, 1978; Thornton, 1974) have expressed similar concerns. In spite of these admonitions, youth sports programs have continued to grow. Therefore, there is a need for research to document the condition under which youth sports occur and the outcomes of these sport activities. Because of concern for physical stress, epidemiological study of youth sports injuries is also warranted.

Need for Injury Data in Youth Sports

Several groups and individuals could utilize and benefit from valid injury data in youth sports, including the following:

- *Single sport agency leaders.* Single sport agencies are organizing bodies, often national in scope, that establish rules and conditions of play and sanction competition. Examples of single sport agencies include Pop Warner Football, Little League Baseball, and United States Youth Soccer Association. Rules established at the single sport agency level are often adopted with minor modification by independent community sports organizations. Therefore, the influence of single sport agencies often extends beyond their youth sports registrants. Valid data on the mechanisms of injury, specific to the youth sports governed by single sport agencies, could provide valuable input into decisions made by agency leaders establishing rules and conditions of play in order to reduce the potential for future injuries.

- *Community recreation leaders.* The need of recreation leaders, who run local youth sports programs, to have access to and understand the etiology and epidemiology of sports injuries is similar to the need of single sport agency leaders. However, the need of recreation leaders may be broader because they usually administer several different sports programs.
- *Participants and parents.* The decision of a parent or guardian to permit a child to participate in sport should be based on a careful evaluation of the risks and benefits of sport involvement. Lack of valid information on injury mechanisms and epidemiology associated with sport participation at different competitive levels may result in tenuous decisions.
- *Coaches.* Some of the many responsibilities assumed by the youth sports coach relate directly to sports injuries. These responsibilities include informing parents and participants of the potential for injury, providing proper instruction on the performance of sport skills and techniques, conducting practices and contests under appropriate conditions, monitoring participants to insure that suitable protective equipment is worn, and immediate and appropriate care of injuries. Valid injury information can assist coaches in carrying out their responsibilities, reducing negligence, and reducing injuries in youth sports participants.
- *Manufacturers of sporting goods.* In order to design and manufacture protective equipment for sport, basic information on injury mechanisms specific to each sport and condition under which it is practiced and contested is needed.

Study of Youth Sports Injuries

Research data on the occurrence of injury in many different sports have been provided by surveillance techniques. The Consumer Product Safety Commission (1984) is a United States Government regulatory agency that functions to reduce the risk of injury to consumers. One way in which it attempts to accomplish this function is through its National Electronic Injury Surveillance System (NEISS). Through a sampling of injuries seen in hospital emergency rooms, NEISS is able to project a national incidence of injuries associated with the use of consumer products. This data collection process also includes sports injuries, in 5- to 14- and 15- to 24-year age groups, associated with "activity, equipment, and apparel." Another surveillance system specific to sports injuries was the National Athletic Injury Reporting System (NAIRS). Congress' concern for the impact of athletic injuries led to the formation of NAIRS. This reporting system was designed for the collection of injury data on high school and college varsity sports participants, upon which detailed information could be kept (Calvert, 1979).

Surveillance techniques, however, have been superficial. According to Damron (1981), surveillance reporting systems for sports accidents leaves "much to be desired." These systems focus on "after the incidence

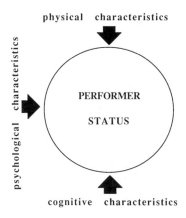

Figure 1   Characteristics that determine the status of the performer.

events'' and injuries requiring medical attention. In youth sports, most injuries do not receive medical attention. One can only conjecture as to the effect of repeated microtraumas, as well as serious injuries, on the future activities of youth sports participants.

In addition to surveillance studies, there are several studies that have focused on sports injuries associated with (a) the status of physical development of youth athletes (Chambers, 1979; Harvey, 1982; Micheli, 1983; Walter & Wolf, 1977; Wilkins, 1980), (b) children of specific age groups (Chandy & Grana, 1985; Garrick & Requa, 1978; Shively, Grana, & Ellis, 1981; Zaricznyj, Shattuck, Mast, Robertson, & D'Elia, 1980), and (c) specific youth sports (Brown & Kimball, 1983; McCarroll, Meaney, & Sieber, 1984). Generalization of results of each of these studies, however, is limited by population, sport, data collection techniques, and/or types of injuries studied.

Injury Mechanism Model

The mechanisms of injury in sport are the processes by which sports injuries occur. These processes involve interactions of many factors associated with the participant and the sport performance. By studying the mechanisms of injuries in sports, the incidence and severity of injuries may be able to be reduced through rational decisions regarding the (a) modification of sports rules; (b) design and use of sports equipment and personal protective supplies, devices, and clothing; (c) equation of competition; and (d) establishment of age requirements.

Status of the Performer

There are three categories of characteristics that determine the status of the sport participant (see Figure 1). These are the participant's physi-

Figure 2 Injury mechanisms associated with physical participation in sport.

cal, psychological, and cognitive characteristics. These characteristics are internal to the performer. Examples of these characteristics are as follows: (a) physical characteristics—strength, somatotype, weight, sex, skeletal maturation; (b) psychological characteristics—trait anxiety, self-confidence, risk taking, state anxiety; and (c) cognitive characteristics—knowledge of rules, knowledge of proper performance, knowledge about opponent, strategy. Each specific characteristic may have an influence on a sport participant's potential for injury. Therefore, in studying injuries associated with youth involvement in sport, it is important to consider these and other specific characteristics even though the large number of specific characteristics, the interaction among characteristics, and the dynamic nature of the youth sport participant make evaluation of performer status a difficult task.

Sport Performance

Injury mechanisms associated with the physical participation in sport (see Figure 2) may be thought of as environmental (external to the performer). Some of these factors are condition of the field, characteristics of implements used in sport, properties of protective equipment, and force and torque applied to the performer. These environmental factors associated with performance are often influenced by the level of competition. For example, the magnitude of contact forces in a youth flag football game will generally be less than those experienced in a highly competitive tackle football game.

Interaction Between Performer and Performance

A schematic model to study injury mechanisms in youth sports is presented in Figure 3. This approach suggests that sports injuries result

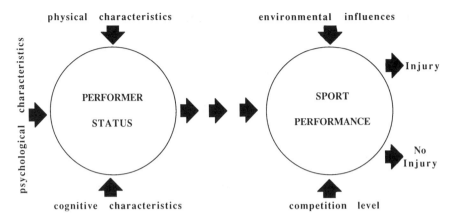

Figure 3 Schematic model to study injury mechanisms.

from interactions, on an individual level, between the sport participant and specific physical activity associated with performance in sport. The suggested relationship between performer and performance are in accord with Lysens et al. (1984) who stated that "sports injuries result from a complex interaction of identifiable risk factors at a given point in time."

Recommendation

Should we encourage our 10-year-old, who is small for his age, to participate in a competitive ice hockey program? Is participation in an organized youth soccer program less likely to result in a severe injury than participation in an organized youth football program? Are there coaching and training techniques that will help to reduce the potential for shoulder pain and injury on my youth swimming team? Can a face mask be designed to prevent facial, dental, and eye injuries from occurring in youth baseball?

These questions and many more are being asked by physical educators, sports agency leaders, recreation leaders, parents, coaches, participants, and sporting goods manufacturers. Some of these specific questions may be answered by specific epidemiological surveys. However, according to Milner (1981), injury studies that have addressed specific issues are limited in utility and frequently lead to misinterpretation. He suggests that there is a need for an ongoing system to study sports injuries. In order to answer the many questions about youth sports injuries, it is the recommendation of this report that (a) etiological factors involving the interaction between the performer and the sport environment should be studied on a longitudinal basis and (b) a broad base of data on many sports and levels of participation should be collected in order to make valid comparisons between sports. This type of study is needed to make rational decisions about participation, rule changes, coaching techniques, and the design of equipment in order to potentially reduce the level and severity of youth sports injuries and to provide parents with basic information needed to make decisions about the likely risks and benefits of sport as it relates to their child.

References

Brown, E.W., & Kimball, R.G. (1983). Medical history associated with adolescent powerlifting. *Pediatrics, 72*(5), 636-644.

Calvert, R. (1979). *Athletic injuries and deaths in secondary schools and colleges.* Washington, DC: U.S. Department of Health, Education, and Welfare.

Chambers, R.B. (1979). Orthopaedic injuries in athletes (ages 6 to 17). *The American Journal of Sports Medicine, 7*(3), 195-197.

Chandy, T.A., & Grana, W.A. (1985). Secondary school athletic injuries in boys and girls: A three-year comparison. *The Physician and Sportsmedicine, 13*(3), 106, 108, 110-111.

Consumer Product Safety Commission. (1984). *Product summary report and NEISS estimates of national injury incidents.* Washington, DC: National Injury Information Clearinghouse.

Damron, C.F. (1981). Injury surveillance systems for sport. In P.F. Vinger & E.R. Hoerner (Eds.), *Sports injuries: The unthwarted epidemic* (pp. 2-25). Littleton, MA: PSG.

Garrick, J.G., & Requa, R.K. (1978). Injuries in high school sports. *Pediatrics, 61*(3), 465-469.

Harvey, J.S. (1982). Overuse syndromes in young athletes. *Pediatric Clinics of North America, 29*(6), 1369-1381.

Kozar, B., & Lord, R.M. (1983). Overuse injuries in the young athlete: Reasons for concern. *The Physician and Sportsmedicine, 11*(7), 116-122.

Lysens, R., Steverlynck, A., Auweele, Y. van den, Lefevre, J., Renson, L., Claessens, A., & Ostyn, M. (1984). The predictability of sports injuries. *Sports Medicine, 1*(1), 6-10.

Martens, R. (1978). *Joy and sadness in children's sports.* Champaign, IL: Human Kinetics.

McCarroll, J.R., Meaney, C., & Sieber, J.M. (1984). Profile of youth soccer injuries. *The Physician and Sportsmedicine, 12*(2), 113-117.

Micheli, L.J. (1983). Overuse injuries in children's sports: The growth factor. *Orthopedic Clinics of North America, 14*(2), 337-360.

Milner, E.M. (1981). Proposals for improvement. In P.F. Vinger & E.R. Hoerner (Eds.), *Sports injuries: The unthwarted epidemic* (pp. 36-39). Littleton, MA: PSG.

Parker, T. (1975). Establishing communication, leadership, and motivation in youth sports. *The National Youth Sports Directors' Conference Proceedings Report*. Chicago, IL: The Athletic Institute.

Rarick, G.L. (1978). Competitive sports in childhood and early adolescence. In R.A. Magill, M.J. Ash, & F.L. Smoll (Eds.), *Children in sports: A contemporary anthology* (pp. 113-128). Champaign, IL: Human Kinetics.

Seefeldt, V. (1982). The changing image of youth sports in the 1980s. In R.A. Magill, M.J. Ash, & F.L. Smoll (Eds.), *Children in sport* (pp. 16-26). Champaign, IL: Human Kinetics.

Shively, R.A., Grana, W.A., & Ellis, D. (1981). High school sports injuries. *The Physician and Sportsmedicine, 9*(8), 46-50.

Thornton, M.L. (1974). Pediatric concerns about competitive preadolescent sports. *Journal of the American Medical Association, 227*(4), 418-419.

Vogel, P., & Seefeldt, V. (1981, November). *Criteria for adding, retaining, or eliminating sports from the interscholastic program*. Paper presented at the Michigan Association for Health, Physical Education, Recreation and Dance Annual Conference, Grand Rapids, MI.

Walter, N.E., & Wolf, M.D. (1977). Stress fractures in young athletes. *The American Journal of Sports Medicine, 5*(4), 165-170.

Wilkins, K.E. (1980). The uniqueness of the young athlete: Musculoskeletal injuries. *The American Journal of Sports Medicine, 8*(5), 377-382.

Zaricznyj, B., Shattuck, L.J.M., Mast, T.A., Robertson, R.V., & D'Elia, G. (1980). Sports-related injuries in school-aged children. *The American Journal of Sports Medicine, 8*(5), 318-323.

PART IV

Physiological Aspects

Physiologic and Echocardiographic Studies of Age-Group Runners

Bernard Gutin
Nancy Mayers
James A. Levy
Michael V. Herman

As part of a series of investigations of cardiorespiratory factors related to endurance performance in children and adults, we conducted two studies of some outstanding age-group runners in the New York metropolitan area. We compared them with nonrunners on several indices of aerobic, anaerobic, and cardiac function. The first study was the first to describe physiological characteristics of elite prepubertal cross-country runners, and the second was undertaken when there were no published data on cardiac dimensions of such children.

Physiological Characteristics of Elite Prepubertal Cross-Country Runners

Methods

Two groups of boys between 8.3 and 11.8 years old were studied (Mayers & Gutin, 1979). The 8 runners (R) had been competing for 2 to 4 years and were among the best in their events at the regional or national level in events ranging from 1 mile to 15 km. Testing was done during the spring when training mileage was 20 to 55 miles per week. Most training was continuous, but some interval training was used. The R were usually also involved in other sports including soccer, basketball, swimming, and baseball.

The 8 nonrunners (NR) were normally active children from a local elementary school who in addition to regular physical education classes engaged in activities such as swimming, soccer, basketball, baseball, and touch football. However, none had trained for running.

All children ran on a treadmill at zero grade for 4 min at 5 mph (134 m/min), 6 mph (161 m/min), and 7 mph (187 m/min), with a 4-min rest between runs. For the NR the treadmill was then raised in elevation by 2.5% every 2 min up to exhaustion. The R rested for 4 min after the 7 mph run and then ran for 4 min at 8 mph (213 m/min) before the grade was progressively increased in 2-min stages as for the NR. Oxygen con-

Table 1 Best Mile Run Times by Age

Subject	Club	Age	7 years	8 years	9 years	10 years	11 years
MC	A	10.2	5:51.9[a]	5:45[b]	5:38[c]	5.30	5.33
TG	A	11.3	n.a.[e]	5:57	5:43	5:28.2	5:33
JO	A	11.2	n.a.[e]	5:42[d]	5:38.8	2:22[a]	5:16.4
ER	B	8.3	6:40	6:33			
GP	B	9.8	6:30	6:21	6:02		
CB	B	11.0	6:14	6:01	5:51	5:41	5:23.4
MF	C	11.2	d.n.r.[f]	6:17	5:51	5:48	5:35.5
MH	C	11.5	d.n.r.[f]	d.n.r.	d.n.r.	6:05	5:46

[a]Best mile time in U.S. for age group for that year. [b]Second best mile time in U.S. for age group for that year. [c]Third best mile time in U.S. for age group for that year. [d]Best mile time in U.S. for age group for that year and fourth best mile time ever recorded for that age group. [e]Not available. [f]Did not run.

sumption ($\dot{V}O_2$) was measured during the last 2 min of each 4-min work bout and the last 1 min of each 2-min work bout. Heart rate was measured during the last 15 s of each work bout.

The following criteria were used to assure that $\dot{V}O_2max$ was reached: (a) an increase of less than 2 ml/kg in $\dot{V}O_2$ at the last work level, (b) HR greater than 195 beats per minute or leveling of the HR over the last two loads, and (c) a respiratory exchange ratio (R) greater than 1.0. When the child first indicated that he was exhausted, he was allowed to rest for about 20 s while he was asked to try one higher work level. All children agreed. The children then ran for 30 s holding the treadmill rail and at least 30 s without holding the rail before another 30-s measurement was made. Utilizing these criteria and procedures, it was concluded that all but one subject had attained a $\dot{V}O_2max$.

Anaerobic capacity (AC) was assessed using a modification of the Wingate anaerobic test (Bar-Or & Inbar, 1976). This test was performed on a Monark Junior Bicycle 30 min after the maximal treadmill test. The seat height was adjusted, and a practice period of 2 min at 300 kpm/min was completed. At the command "go," the subject pedaled as fast as possible. The resistance was quickly increased to 1.5 kg within 3 to 4 s, and the counting of pedal revolutions was begun. AC was expressed as the number of revolutions completed in 30 s.

All of the runners competed in the National Postal Mile Championships during the spring track season in which they were tested. Six of them ran in the seeded heat in the 10- to 11-year-old age group, whereas the other 2 ran in the seeded heat in the 8- to 9-year-old race. The times for this mile run (MR) were used in the statistical comparisons with the control subjects. Because some of the top runners did not perform well in this race, the best career mile time (BCM) for the runners was used for intragroup statistical comparison (Table 1).

Results

The mean ages of the runners and nonrunners were very similar (10.2 and 10.3 years, respectively) as were the mean weights (32.0 and 32.4 kg). The runners tended to be taller (144 cm vs. 138 cm), but this difference did not reach significance.

Owing to mechanical failures, the AC bicycle test was not completed on two subjects: one runner and one nonrunner. There was a significant difference between the means of the two groups on this test, with the runners completing a mean of 54 revolutions/30 s versus a mean of 44 revolutions/30 s for the nonrunners.

One of the runners did not reach his $\dot{V}O_2$max according to our criteria, and in comparisons of $\dot{V}O_2$max and HRmax this subject has not been included. There was a significant difference between the means of the runners (56.6 ml/kg/min) and the nonrunners (45.6 ml/kg/min) for $\dot{V}O_2$max. These characteristics are summarized in Table 2.

Comparisons were made between the two groups for respiratory exchange ratio (R), HR, and $\dot{V}O_2$ across the three submaximal work loads of 5, 6, and 7 mph using a two-way ANOVA with repeated measures on the running speed variable. For all measures the values for runners were significantly lower than the values for nonrunners with no significant interactions between group and work load (Table 3).

Because the runners were slightly, though not significantly, taller than the nonrunners, an analysis of the covariance was done on the submax $\dot{V}O_2$ values at 5, 6, and 7 mph using height as the covariate. This resulted in a nonsignificant F ratio for the differences between the groups.

For the best career mile run time (BCM), when comparisons were made within the running groups, the variables related to performance were very different from those variables of importance for the two groups combined. Most noticeable within the running groups was the lack of correlation of $\dot{V}O_2$max with BCM (.06). Variables that were most closely related to BCM were AC (−.89), percentage $\dot{V}O_2$max at 8 mph (−.87), and age (−.85). The AC bicycle test and percentage $\dot{V}O_2$max at 8 mph are indicators of the anaerobic and aerobic energy pathways, respectively. Both pathways contribute substantially to the mile performance of approximately 5.5 min run by these elite athletes.

Among the runners, height was highly correlated with submax $\dot{V}O_2$. When considered as a percentage of $\dot{V}O_2$max, the correlations were −.81, −.88, −.91, and −.83 at 5, 6, 7, and 8 mph, respectively.

Physiologic and Echocardiographic Characteristics of Young Runners

This study extended our previous work by using echocardiography (echo) to examine cardiac structure and function and by including measures of the ventilatory breakpoint (VB) and respiratory compensation threshold (RCT).

Table 2 Cardiovascular, Anthropometric, and Performance Characteristics

Subject (club)	Age	Height (cm)	Weight (kg)	Body fat (%)	$\dot{V}O_2$ at 6 mph	HR at 6 mph	Max $\dot{V}O_2$	Max HR	AC[a] BT	MR[b]	BCM[c]
Runners											
MC (A)	10.2	149.9	38.1	18.6	31.9	131	58.7	195	61	6:02	5:28.5
TG (A)	11.3	147.3	33.9	14.5	31.7	153	57.7	200	57	5:35	5:28.2
JO (A)	11.2	149.9	33.1	17.5	28.2	133	53.0	208	56	5:44	5:16.4
ER (B)	8.3	139.7	30.3	16.9	32.2	143	—	—	43	6:33	6:33
GP (B)	9.8	134.1	26.5	14.0	34.9	148	54.8	205	46	6:03	6:02
CB (B)	10.8	143.0	30.3	15.6	32.8	148	57.2	205	58	5:23	5:23
MR (C)	11.2	139.7	29.0	13.5	31.8	152	58.3	210	57	5:35	5:35
MH (C)	11.5	150.6	34.2	16.0	30.1	143	56.7	200	—	5:46	5:46
M	10.5	144.3	31.9	15.8	31.7	144	56.6	203	54	5:50	5:41.6
SD	1.1	6.1	3.6	1.8	2.14	8.2	2.04	5	7	0:22	
Nonrunners											
JL	10.3	142.2	35.4	17.5	34.8	171	42.9	208	37	7:13	
PS	9.4	128.3	27.2	18.0	—	165	45.3	200	31	7:43	
EV	10.1	141.7	32.0	17.0	33.5	171	45.6	197	49	—	
CT	9.8	143.5	29.7	14.5	32.6	188	47.3	209	46	7:12	
PH	8.8	120.1	24.6	16.8	38.0	190	43.4	212	36	—	
SS	11.8	143.5	42.1	21.8	34.0	185	44.8	210	—	8:35	
MM	11.3	142.2	32.6	19.9	35.9	180	47.5	203	53	7:36	
DH	11.4	145.5	35.8	16.8	35.5	183	50.9	203	53	7:23	
M	10.4	138.4	32.4	17.8	34.3[d]	179[d]	45.9[d]	205	44[d]	7:37.0[d]	
SD	1.1	9.1	5.5	2.2	2.33	9.1	2.56	5	9	0:31	

[a]AC—anaerobic capacity bicycle test, revolutions/30 s. [b]MR—mile run time. [c]BCM—best career mile run time. [d]Significant difference between groups ($p < .05$).

Table 3 Submaximal Cardiovascular and Metabolic Responses for Runners (n = 8) and Nonrunners (n = 8)[a]

Variable	Group	5 mph	6 mph	7 mph
$\dot{V}O_2$	Runners	27.96 (1.96)	31.68 (2.14)	36.20 (2.63)
	Nonrunners	30.36 (1.80)	34.34 (2.33)	38.35 (2.56)
R	Runners	0.82 (0.06)	0.83 (0.06)	0.84 (0.04)
	Nonrunners	0.88 (0.05)	0.91 (0.05)	0.90 (0.07)
HR	Runners	131 (8)	144 (8)	158 (10)
	Nonrunners	165 (8)	179 (9)	191 (10)

[a]Values are means (*SD*). For all variables the values for the runners are significantly lower than values for nonrunners.

Table 4 General Characteristics of Children in the Second Study[a]

Group	N	Age (years)	Weight (kg)	Height (cm)	Training mileage (per week)
ER	11	11.1 ±1.0	36.18 ±3.39	146.46 ±5.46	29.6 ±1.96
TR	10	11.4 ±0.6	35.42 ±2.40	146.61 ±3.73	26.4 ±1.26
NR	10	11.1 ±0.85	36.09 ±2.32	140.72 ±4.14	

[a]*M* ± SEM.

The subjects were three groups of boys 6 to 14 years of age. Two of the groups were cross-country runners who had been competing for at least 2 years at distances from 1 mile to the marathon (26.2 miles).

In order to categorize the runners as elite runners (ER) or trained runners (TR), a point system was devised that took into account training mileage, success in regional and national competition during the past year, and a best 1- or 2-mi time for the past year. This resulted in 11 ER and 10 TR. One of the TR had an extreme pectus excavatum, and his echo data were not used.

The third group (NR) were 20 children similar to the NR of the first study; only 9 NR agreed to have echo measurements made. Table 4 describes the groups.

All children performed a progressive treadmill test starting at 4 mph with speed increased by 0.5 mph every 2 min until 6 mph was reached.

Table 5   Submaximal Physiological Measurements at 6 mph[a]

Group	N	$\dot{V}O_2$ at 6 mph (ml/kg/min)		HR (bpm)		V_E (l/min)		R
		$\bar{x}$	$a\bar{x}$	$\bar{x}$	$a\bar{x}$	$\bar{x}$	$a\bar{x}$	$\bar{x}$
ER	11	40.89 ±1.08	41.93 ±0.96	158.2 ±3.9	158.9 ±3.1	41.72 ±3.97	40.65 ±1.93	0.886 ±0.02
TR	9	40.82 ±1.13	41.03 ±1.06	154.9 ±4.2	155.6 ±3.4	39.39 ±2.40	38.43 ±2.13	0.893 ±0.02
NR	10	43.07 ±1.17	42.61 ±1.02	179.2[b,c] ±2.7	177.8[b] ±3.0	45.83 ±2.62	47.87[b,c] ±2.04	0.974[b,c] ±0.02

[a]Means ($\bar{x}$) and means adjusted ($a\bar{x}$) for height by analysis of covariance (ANCOVA) (±SEM).
[b]Significantly different from ER. [c]Significantly different from TR.

Then, depending on age and training, either speed or grade was increased by 0.5 mph or 2%, respectively, up to exhaustion. In order to prevent termination of the test due to leg fatigue on a severe grade, loads were increased by speed rather than grade once a 6% grade was reached. $\dot{V}O_2$ and HR were measured during the 2nd min at each work rate, and criteria for determining $\dot{V}O_2$max were similar to those in the first study. VB was taken as the upturn in the $VE/\dot{V}O_2$ ratio plotted against work rate, and the RCT was taken as the sharp break in $VE/\dot{V}O_2$ plotted against work rate.

Cardiac evaluation included a 12 lead ECG and an M-mode echo. The echoes were obtained in the resting supine and 30° left lateral positions using a 2.25 or 3.5 mHz unfocused transducer in the third or fourth left intercostal space at end-expiration, with a V5 ECG lead recorded simultaneously. Techniques and measurements were administered as recommended by the American Society for Echocardiography (Sahn, De Maria, Kisslo, & Weyman, 1978).

Each recording was read independently by two cardiologists without knowledge of the child's training status. Several dimensions of the heart were measured and several functions calculated using established regression equations (Teicholz, Kreulen, Herman, & Gorlin, 1976).

The .05 level of significance was used for statistical comparisons.

Results

Submaximal physiological responses were compared at 6 mph (Table 5). Means for $\dot{V}O_2$, HR, and VE were adjusted for height by covariance in

Table 6   Physiological Measurements at the Ventilatory Breakpoint[a]

Group	N	$\dot{V}O_2$ at VB (ml/kg/min)	$\dot{V}O_2$max (%)	HR (bpm)	R	HRmax (%)
ER	11	45.95[c] ±1.92	71.19 ±1.47	169 ±4.7	0.90 ±0.02	84.9 ±1.36
TR	9	38.92[b] ±1.87	66.62 ±1.81	147[b] ±5.3	0.87 ±0.02	75.4[b] ±2.30
NR	10	31.37[b,c] ±2.14	61.02[b] ±3.21	145[b] ±5.2	0.92 ±0.01	74.8[b] ±2.27

[a]Means ± SEM. [b]Significantly different from ER. [c]Significantly different from TR.

Table 7   Physiological Measurements at the Respiratory Compensation Threshold[a]

Group	N	$\dot{V}O_2$ (ml/kg/min)	HR (bpm)	$\dot{V}O_2$max (%)	R	HRmax (%)
ER	11	57.28[c] ±2.21	189 ±3.3	88.39 ±5.51	0.95 ±0.03	94.43 ±0.84
TR	9	49.33[b] ±1.32	177 ±1.2	84.90 ±5.49	0.92 ±0.02	90.5 ±1.25
NR	10	43.33[b,c] ±1.58	180 ±1.8	85.27 ±3.68	0.98 ±0.01	91.95 ±1.36

[a]Means ± SEM. [b]Significantly different from ER. [c]Significantly different from TR.

Table 8   Physiological Measurements at Maximal Capacity[a]

Group	N	$\dot{V}O_2$ (ml/kg/min)	$\dot{V}O_2$ (l/min)	HR (bpm)	R	VE (l/kg/min)
ER	10	64.31[c] ±2.34	2.36 ±0.29	199 ±3.5	1.03 ±0.03	1.00 ±0.05
TR	9	58.34[b] ±2.08	1.92 ±0.22	195 ±2.3	0.99 ±0.02	0.87 ±0.04
NR	10	51.17[b,c] ±1.50	1.80[b] ±0.15	196 ±3.5	1.03 ±0.01	0.79[b] ±0.03

[a]Means ± SEM. [b]Significantly different from ER. [c]Significantly different from TR.

Table 9 Echocardiographic Measurements[a]

Group	N	LVDd (mm)		LVDs (mm)		SWd (mm)	
		$\bar{x}$	a$\bar{x}$	$\bar{x}$	a$\bar{x}$	$\bar{x}$	a$\bar{x}$
ER	11	42.87 ±1.12	43.16 ±0.62	27.71 ±0.78	27.89 ±0.70	6.57 ±0.40	6.64 ±0.30
TR	9	42.58 ±1.43	42.39 ±0.68	26.67 ±1.24	26.60 ±0.78	6.37 ±0.46	6.33 ±0.33
NR	9	41.16 ±0.92	40.98[c] ±0.68	25.61 ±1.10	25.44[c] ±0.78	6.86 ±0.35	6.80 ±0.33

Group	PWd (mm)		LAts[b] (mm)	AoR (mm)		FS[b] (%)	HRE[b] (bpm)
	$\bar{x}$	a$\bar{x}$	$\bar{x}$	$\bar{x}$	a$\bar{x}$	$\bar{x}$	a$\bar{x}$
ER	6.25 ±0.42	6.32 ±0.26	24.67 ±0.51	22.73 ±0.58	22.89 ±0.61	35.29 ±1.27	71.73 ±3.28
TR	6.41 ±0.46	6.40 ±0.29	26.91 ±1.84	22.68 ±0.99	22.55 ±0.67	37.40 ±2.01	64.33 ±3.17
NR	6.74 ±0.29	6.67 ±0.29	21.84 ±3.68	22.33 ±0.90	22.25 ±0.67	37.90 ±1.83	80.11[d] ±4.67

Note. LVDd—left ventricular dimension at end-diastole; LVDs—LVD at end-systole; SWd—interventricular septal wall thickness at end-diastole; PWd—LV posterior wall thickness at end-diastole; LAts—left atrial dimension during systole; AoR—aortic root; FS—fractional shortening of left ventricular cavity dimension; HRE—heart rate taken during echocardiography.
[a]Values are means ($\bar{x}$) and means adjusted for weight and age by ANCOVA (a$\bar{x}$), ± SEM.
[b]Not influenced by weight or age; analysis by ANOVA. [c]Significantly different from ER.
[d]Significantly different from TR.

light of the results of the first study and the fact that the NR were slightly shorter. $\dot{V}O_2$ values were similar, whereas HR, ventilation, and the R were reliably lower in both running groups; the ER and TR did not differ reliably on these measures.

The VB was reliably higher in the ER than the TR and NR regardless of how expressed (Table 6). The VB was significantly higher in the TR than the NR when expressed as $\dot{V}O_2$ or as percentage of $\dot{V}O_2$max.

The RCT could not be accurately detected in one ER and one NR. Only when expressed as a $\dot{V}O_2$ were there reliable differences among groups (Table 7).

$\dot{V}O_2$max progressed reliably from the NR to the TR to the ER (Table 8), whereas HRmax and R were similar across groups. VEmax was reliably higher in the ER than in the NR.

Table 10   Derived Volumes From Echocardiographic Measurements[a]

Group	LVDV (mm)		LVSV (mm)		SV (ml)		EF[b] (%)
	$\bar{x}$	a$\bar{x}$	$\bar{x}$	a$\bar{x}$	$\bar{x}$	a$\bar{x}$	$\bar{x}$
ER	80.4	82.1	21.8	22.2	48.6	49.6	0.60
		±3.5		±1.45		±3.0	±0.02
TR	79.3	78.3	19.9	19.8	50.3	49.5	0.64
		±3.9		±1.6		±3.35	±0.03
NR	70.5	69.5[c]	17.6	17.2[c]	45.0	44.5	0.64
		±3.86		±1.60		±3.34	±0.03

Note. LVDV—LV end-diastolic volume; LVSV—LV end-systolic volume; SV—stroke volume; EF—ejection fraction.
[a]Values are means ($\bar{x}$) and means adjusted for weight and age by ANCOVA (a$\bar{x}$), ± SEM.
[b]EF not influenced by weight or age; analysis by ANOVA. [c]Significantly different from ER.

Most echo comparisons used weight and age as covariates (Table 9). Left ventricular end-diastolic dimension (LVDd) and left ventricular end-systolic dimension (LVDs) were both reliably larger in the ER than NR, with the TR falling between and not reliably different from the ER and NR. Wall thicknesses did not differ reliably. Derived values for stroke volume and ejection fraction did not differ reliably even though end-diastolic and end-systolic volumes were significantly lower in the NR (Table 10).

Across all boys, $\dot{V}O_2$max expressed in liters per minute was highly correlated with LVDd (.87) and LVDs (.66). When weight was partialed out, the correlation with LVDd remained moderate (.51), and when resting HR was also partialed out, the correlation was still moderate (.48). After accounting for weight, the correlation of $\dot{V}O_2$max and LVDs was not significant.

Based on age and weight, LVDd and LVDs were predicted (Henry, Gardin, & Ware, 1980), and these values were compared to our measured values using paired t tests. The measured values of the running groups were significantly higher than the predicted values, whereas the measured values for the NR were similar to the predicted values.

Discussion

Considering both studies together, what conclusions can be drawn about the cardiorespiratory characteristics of young male runners?

Clearly, the maximal aerobic power of these boys is impressive, especially the value of 64 ml/kg/min for the ER of the second study. Their anaerobic capacities are also impressive. This is consistent with other studies that showed anaerobic and aerobic abilities to be correlated in children (Palgi, Gutin, Young, & Alejandro, 1984; Gutin et al., 1978). Because this was not true in a college-age group (Gutin, Torrey, Welles, & Vytvytsky, 1975), it seems that these qualities are not so well differentiated in children but become so during the teen years.

The submaximal responses of the children were particularly noteworthy. Although their lower submaximal $\dot{V}O_2$ was largely accounted for by their tendency to be taller, their respiratory exchange ratios and HR were quite low compared to the NR. For example, in the first study the mean difference between groups in submaximal HR was a substantial 35 bpm. This agrees with the idea that submaximal HR is more sensitive to endurance run training than is $\dot{V}O_2$max (Stewart & Gutin, 1976).

The VB proved quite valuable in distinguishing the ER from the NR because it occurred at a higher percentage of $\dot{V}O_2$max and HRmax. The RCT also tended to occur at a higher relative load in the ER than the TR (even though the among-groups F for percentage HRmax was not significant, a t test comparing the ER and TR showed that the difference was reliable). Thus, the superior performance of the ER over the TR despite similar training regimens is apparently related to superior maximal and submaximal characteristics that probably allow them to work at higher relative work rates before lactate accumulation rises to substantial levels, possibly hampering performance (Simon, Young, Gutin, Blood, & Case, 1983).

The resting echo measurements revealed that the left ventricular volumes were large in the runners, whereas the wall thicknesses were similar. This is in agreement with the larger LV cavities found in adult endurance athletes (Morganroth, Maron, Henry, & Epstein, 1975), sometimes with increased wall thickness as well (Gilbert et al., 1977), but in contrast to one study of child swimmers (Allen, Goldberg, Sahn, Schy, & Wojcik, 1977) that showed only enlarged wall thickness. A study of changes due to an 8-month aerobic games and dance program in 6- to 7-year-old boys and girls showed increased left posterior wall thickness and left ventricular mass but no significant change in left ventricular end-diastolic dimension (Geenen, Gilliam, Crowley, Moorehead-Steffens, & Rosenthal, 1982). Therefore, it is possible that in the early stages of training, especially in children as young as 6 to 7 years of age, increases in dimensions do result, whereas in longer term training of slightly older children and adults, increased cavity size is more likely. Of course, because our study was cross-sectional rather than longitudinal, it is possible that the greater cavity size of our runners was a preexisting reason for their success in running rather than a result of their training. Because $\dot{V}O_2$max expressed in liters per minute was the best predictor of LVDd, even after adjustments for body size, it seems that these qualities are fairly well matched. The large cavity size should provide a greater reserve that can be called on during exercise to increase the stroke volume. The resulting increase in cardiac output would contribute somewhat to the greater $\dot{V}O_2$max in these children. However, the difference between the ER and NR in left ventricular end-diastolic volume, as predicted from LVDd, was 14%, whereas the difference in $\dot{V}O_2$max was 26%, suggesting that peripheral oxidative capacity accounts for some of the maximal as well as submaximal qualities of the runners.

It is worth emphasizing the value of submaximal measures such as the VB in describing the aerobic fitness of children as shown in the second study. $\dot{V}O_2$max testing demands a great and often unpleasant effort from the child, one we might hesitate to impose repeatedly. Furthermore, peak values are usually obtained at peak work rates, suggesting that $\dot{V}O_2$max is as much a measure of performance as of physiology. On the other hand, VB, and perhaps other submaximal measures like lactate breakpoint, provide a physiological value that tells of the child's ability to work for long periods at a given submaximal rate. Expressed as $\dot{V}O_2$, it provides information about both the $\dot{V}O_2$max and the percentage of $\dot{V}O_2$max at which he can work. That is, it provides more information than is provided by $\dot{V}O_2$max alone. Thus, it seems sensible to focus more of our efforts on refining our measurement and use of submaximal rather than maximal measures.

In summary, young boys who engage in distance running exhibit excellent resting, submaximal, and maximal metabolic and cardiovascular qualities, as has been shown in adult endurance athletes. We produced no evidence that the intensive training and competition engaged in by these children were associated with any negative adaptation in their resting cardiac structure or function.

Acknowledgment

Supported by a grant from the American Heart Association, Orange-Rockland-Sullivan Chapter and Dutchess County Chapter.

References

Allen, H., Goldberg, S., Sahn, D., Schy, N., & Wojcik, R. (1977). Quantitative echocardiographic study of championship child swimmers. *Circulation, 55*, 142-145.

Bar-Or, O., & Inbar, O. (1976). *Relationships among aerobic capacity, sprint and middle distance running of school children.* Paper presented at the pre-Olympic meeting of the International Committee of Physical Fitness Research, Trois Rivières, Canada.

Geenen, D., Gilliam, T., Crowley, D., Moorehead-Steffens, C., & Rosenthal, A. (1982). Echocardiographic measures in 6 to 7 year old children after an 8 month exercise program. *American Journal of Cardiology, 49*, 1990-1995.

Gilbert, C., Nutter, D., Felner, J., Perkins, J., Heymsfield, S., & Schlant, R. (1977). Echocardiographic study of cardiac dimensions and function in the endurance trained athlete. *American Journal of Cardiology, 40*, 529-533.

Gutin, B., Torrey, K., Welles, R., & Vytvytsky, M. (1975). Physiological parameters related to running performance in college trackmen. *Journal of Human Ergology*, **4**, 27-34.

Gutin, B., Trinidad, A., Norton, C., Giles, E., Giles, A., & Stewart, K. (1978). Morphological and physiological factors related to endurance performance of 11- to 12-year-old girls. *Research Quarterly*, **49**, 44-52.

Henry, W., Gardin, J., & Ware, J. (1980). Echocardiographic measurements in normal subjects from infancy to old age. *Circulation*, **62**, 1054-1061.

Mayers, N., & Gutin, B. (1979). Physiological characteristics of elite prepubertal cross-country runners. *Medicine and Science in Sports*, **11**, 172-176.

Morganroth, J., Maron, B., Henry, W., & Epstein, S. (1975). Comparative left ventricular dimensions in trained athletes. *Annals of Internal Medicine*, **82**, 521-524.

Palgi, Y., Gutin, B., Young, J., & Alejandro, D. (1984). Physiological and anthropometric factors underlying endurance performance in boys and girls. *International Journal of Sports Medicine*, **5**, 67-73.

Sahn, D., De Maria, A., Kisslo, J., & Weyman, A. (1978). Recommendations regarding quantitation in M-mode echocardiography. *Circulation*, **58**, 1072-1083.

Simon, J., Young, J., Gutin, B., Blood, D., & Case, R. (1983). Lactate accumulation relative to the anaerobic and respiratory compensation thresholds. *Journal of Applied Physiology*, **54**, 13-17.

Stewart, K., & Gutin, B. (1976). Effects of physical training on cardiorespiratory fitness in children. *Research Quarterly*, **47**, 110-120.

Teicholz, L., Kreulen, T., Herman, M., & Gorlin, R. (1976). Problems in echocardiographic determinations: Echocardiographic-angiographic correlations in the presence or absence of asynergy. *American Journal of Cardiology*, **37**, 7-11.

Comparative Characteristics
of Elite Junior- and Senior-Level Athletes

William G. Thorland
Glen O. Johnson
Gerald D. Tharp
Terry J. Housh

Although many studies have described various anatomical and functional qualities of highly proficient young adult athletes, until recently there have been considerably fewer such investigations concerning child or adolescent competitors. Heightened investigative interest in the effects of youth sports competition has paralleled the greatly increased opportunities for participation in organized athletic programs currently available to the young. An important outcome of such research would be the recognition of age-related factors potentially limiting the level of peak performance achievable in well-trained, preadult populations. Therefore, this chapter will focus on a few of the structural and physiological characteristics that potentially contribute to athletic performance. An attempt will be made to characterize some of these qualities and, when possible, compare peak performance levels between child and adolescent (junior-level) competitors, nonathletic peers, and elite young adult (senior-level) performers. Such profiles can help to identify some of the characteristics that are consistent with mature top-level performance, as well as indicate what might typically be observed in younger top-level junior competitors within different age groups. However, these profiles will not necessarily imply that the younger individuals with characteristics at the high levels of performance shown for their age groups will mature to the top levels shown for young adults. Instead, these results may serve more appropriately to reveal factors that could explain some of the basis for the athletic performance standards unique to different age groups.

Method

Between 1978 and 1983 at the University of Nebraska Center for Youth Fitness and Sports Research, data were collected on 325 male and 326 female elite junior-level athletes ranging in age from 11 to 18 years. These volunteers were either competitors in Junior Olympic National Championships or were scholarship athletes invited to Olympic development training camps. Of these subjects, 172 males and 212 females are represented in the body composition and somatotype results, another 66 males and 31 females are profiled in the isokinetic peak torque results, and an additional 26 males and 21 females are described in the anaerobic capacity test results.

Body composition was determined by underwater weighing with corrections for residual lung volume based on oxygen dilution or nitrogen washout techniques. Additional details of these procedures have been previously described (Thorland, Johnson, Fagot, Tharp, & Hammer, 1981; Thorland, Johnson, Housh, & Refsell, 1983). Somatotype was determined utilizing the anthropometric rating methods of Heath and Carter (1967). Skinfold thicknesses were measured utilizing Lange calipers, diameters were determined with a broad blade metal anthropometer, and circumferences were taken with a Lufkin metal tape fitted with a Gulick handle.

Isokinetic torque was determined with a Cybex II dynamometer. The dominant leg, based on kicking preference, was measured for torque output during extension at 180°/s. Following three to four submaximal warm-up trials, three maximal-effort leg extensions were performed with peak torque reported as the highest observed value with the recorder dampening set at 2. A further description of these procedures has been presented previously by Housh, Thorland, Tharp, Johnson, and Cisar (1984).

Maximal, high-intensity, short-term work response was determined on a Monark bicycle ergometer, utilizing the Wingate Anaerobic Test procedures of Bar-Or (1978). A 2-min warm-up trial at low resistance (0.5 kg) preceded the actual test. To determine anaerobic capacity, the subject completed as many pedal revolutions as possible in a 30-s period throughout which resistance was set at 75 g/kg of body weight. Strong verbal encouragement was provided, and pedal revolutions were monitored by means of a microswitch connected to a Physiograph recorder. Tharp, Johnson, and Thorland (1984) have previously reported a more complete description of these procedures.

To allow for comparisons with young adult athletes or with nonathletic peers, data from a variety of sources are presented. Table 1 summarizes these sources. Comparisons of body composition or somatotype between junior-level athletes and either age-group peers or senior-level athletes were based on visual inspection. Similar types of contrasts of either the peak torque or the anaerobic capacity results utilized ANOVA and Scheffe post hoc techniques ($p < .05$).

Results and Discussion

Assessment of body composition provides data on the amounts of fat (adipose tissue) and fat-free body weight (muscle, bone, vital organs, etc.) in a subject, as well as the proportion (relative fat) to which they constitute body weight. Somatotype is an expression of the interrelation of three qualities that characterize an individual's body build. The first of these qualities—endomorphy—reflects fatness, the second—mesomorphy—reflects musculoskeletal development, and the third—ectomorphy—reflects the linearity of the build.

Table 1   Sources of Data on Young Adult Athletes and on Reference Subjects

Source	Body composition		Peak torque		Anaerobic capacity	
	Male	Female	Male	Female	Male	Female
Barnes (1981)	SH					
Behnke & Wilmore (1974)	TH					
Bloomfield & Sigerseth (1965)	SW	GD,SW				
Conger & Macnab (1967)	DR					
Costill (1970)	TH,WR					
Fahey et al. (1975)	RF	RF				
Forbes (1972)	WR					
Gale & Flynn (1974)						
Hagerman et al. (1980)			RF	DR		
Holmes & Alderink (1984)			DR	RF	DR,RF	
Housh et al. (1984)						RF
Jacobs et al. (1982)		SW				
Katch et al. (1969)			RF			
Larsson et al. (1979)		DR,JU,SH,TH				
Malina et al. (1971)	GD,SW					
Novak et al. (1968)	RF	RF				
Novak et al. (1973)		DR,GD,SW				
Novak et al. (1977)					RF	RF
Palgi et al. (1984)	DR,GD,SW,WR	GD				
Parizkova (1977)	SH,TH,JV	DR,JU,SH,TH				
Pipes (1977)	DR					
Pollock et al. (1977)	DR					
Rusko et al. (1978)	WR					
Sinning (1974)						
Sinning & Lindberg (1972)		GD				
Sprynarova & Parizkova (1969)	DR,SW	GD,SW				
Sprynarova & Parizkova (1971)						
Thorstensson et al. (1977)			SH,RF			
Wilmore & Brown (1974)	TH	DR				
Wilmore et al. (1977)		DR,SH,SW,TH				
Young et al. (1968)		RF				

Note.   Group codes are as follows: DR, distance runners; GD, gymnasts or divers; JV, jumpers or vaulters; JU, jumpers; SH, sprinters or hurdlers; SW, swimmers; TH, weight throwers; WR, wrestlers; and RF, nonathletic reference group.

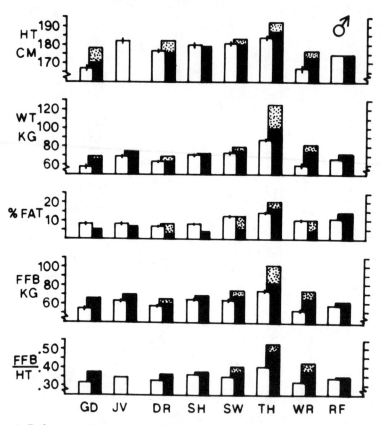

Figure 1 Body composition of male athletes and nonathletic reference samples. Values are $\bar{x} \pm$ SEM. Adolescent subjects are shown as open bars, and young adults are shown as solid bars with speckled areas indicating the range of means from various studies.

A number of studies have been conducted to assess the body composition and/or body build characteristics of athletes in various sports. Most typically, these studies have appraised such characteristics in senior-level performers, many of whom engaged in national or international level competition. As a result of such investigations, it has become apparent that particular compositional or build traits are often associated with high-level performance in certain athletic events. However, although the extent to which such factors contribute to athletic performance is not totally clear, in many cases they are secondary to factors such as metabolic response traits, strength levels, and so forth (Housh, 1984; Pollock, Jackson, & Pate, 1980). Nonetheless, it is reasonable to assume that, to varying degrees, body composition and build characteristics can be of some significant influence on the level of performance that may be achieved. Therefore, description of the structural qualities that distinguish the elite young adult competitor can provide insight into additional aspects of developmental objectives that may be desirable for an aspiring younger performer.

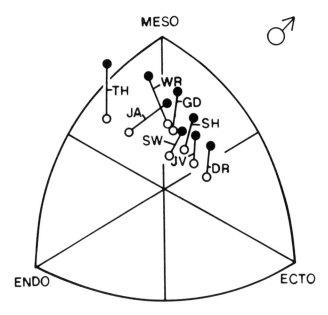

Figure 2 Mean somatotypes of Olympic (solid circles) and Junior Olympic (open circles) male athletes. Data for Olympic athletes are from DeGaray, Levine, and Carter (1974). Event codes are defined in Table 1.

Figures 1 and 2 present physical characteristics of male Junior Olympians grouped by categories of events. In addition, data are presented for young adult athletes (intercollegiate, international, or Olympic level performers) as well as for adolescent and young adult nonathletic reference groups. Among these males, similar sport-specific trends were noted when either the junior-level or the senior-level athletes were compared to their respective age-group reference samples. In this regard, jumpers, sprinters and hurdlers, swimmers, and in particular, weight throwers tended to be taller than their nonathletic peers. Only the younger gymnasts and divers or the younger wrestlers were notably short in stature. Body weight, fat-free body weight (FFB), and the ratio of fat-free body weight to height (FFB/HT) were generally similar in the trends that resulted from comparisons between athletes and nonathletes. Within either age group, throwers were remarkably more massive overall, whereas jumpers and vaulters, sprinters and hurdlers, and swimmers differed only in FFB-related characteristics when contrasted with nonathletes. Among all groups, with the exception of the throwers and some samples of swimmers or wrestlers, male athletes were slightly less fat than were the reference groups.

When comparisons were made between junior-level and senior-level athletes, several general trends were evident. Among the throwers, senior-level competitors were greater in all characteristics. However, when differences appeared among the other sports, most were attributable to

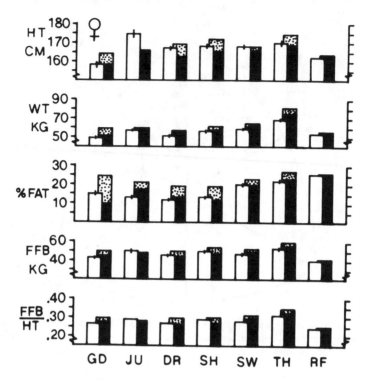

Figure 3 Body composition of female athletes and nonathletic reference samples. Values are $\bar{x} \pm$ SEM. Adolescent subjects are shown as open bars, and young adults are shown as solid bars with speckled areas indicating the range of means from various studies.

greater FFB and lower relative fat levels in the senior-level competitors. These trends toward greater FFB development in senior-level competitors paralleled the nature of differences also seen in somatotypes between the two age groups of competitors. As Figure 2 reveals, junior-level competitors were primarily characterized as being less mesomorphic than their senior-level counterparts among all sports.

Figures 3 and 4 summarize the physical characteristics of female athletes as well as nonathletes. Primarily, with the exception of gymnasts and divers, athletes in either age group tended to be taller than their nonathletic peers. Although body weight was lower in gymnasts and divers and greater in throwers, athletes in other sports were similar in weight when compared to their age-group peers. However, the body composition differed markedly, with athletes in all of the sports tending to have less fat and greater FFB and FFB/HT levels than nonathletes.

Junior- and senior-level female athletes in the same events tended to have smaller differences in physical characteristics than was the case among the males. Differences of note included the senior-level jumpers being taller and the senior-level throwers being slightly greater in both fat and FFB-related characteristics when compared to junior-level com-

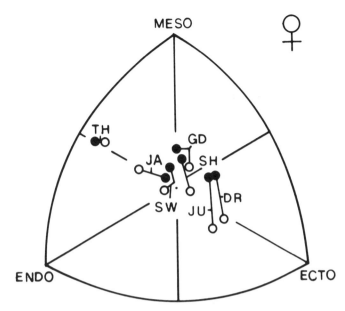

Figure 4 Mean somatotypes of Olympic (solid circles) and Junior Olympic (open circles) female athletes. Data for Olympic athletes are from DeGaray et al. (1974). Event codes are defined in Table 1.

petitors. Somatotype characteristics, as shown in Figure 4, also indicated fewer large differences in mesomorphy between the two age groups of competitors. Such trends most likely reflect the lower anabolic stimuli available to promote training-induced fat-free mass development in women (Fox & Mathews, 1981, p. 371).

The production of high-force outputs can be consistent with success in many sport activities. Competitive-level performance may further require that high forces be generated rapidly in order to achieve sufficiently high velocity in movements such as throwing, jumping, kicking, or sprinting. Therefore, although great strength, per se, may be important to a weight lifter, the ability to produce forces of a somewhat lower magnitude, but achieved at higher limb velocities, may be a particularly crucial characteristic for other athletes (Thorstensson, Larsson, Tesch, & Karlsson, 1977). Isokinetic testing provides a means for measuring peak torque production at any of a variety of low to moderate limb velocities. Figure 5 provides mean peak torque values for leg extension at 180°/s for different groups of male senior-level athletes. Among the groups shown, peak torque levels were higher for jumpers, sprinters, alpine skiers, and weight throwers, which are sports requiring particularly rapid accelerations of body mass.

Peak torque values for leg extensions at moderate velocities under isokinetic loading are shown for different age groups of male and female athletes, respectively, in Figures 6 and 7. Also included are results for

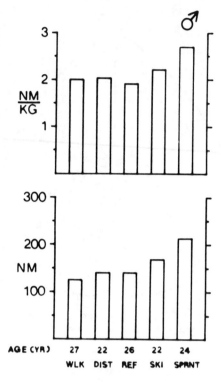

Figure 5   Mean peak torque levels for male subjects performing isokinetic leg extensions at 180°/s. Data are adapted from Thorstensson et al. (1977).

nonathletic reference samples. Age-related differences were evident in peak torque within all of the groups (distance runners, sprinters, or reference subjects). These differences persisted when values were corrected for body weight (or FFB) by the use of either ratio scores or covariate adjustments. This indicated that strength increases exceeded the ratio of growth in body mass. Among the males, sport-related differences were shown only among the young adult subjects, with the sprinters having significantly higher peak torque levels (both unadjusted and adjusted for body weight) than either distance runners or the nonathletes. Within the sample of females, only the youngest subjects displayed sport-related differences, with the sprinters being stronger. However, it should be noted that data were lacking to allow comparisons with female young-adult sprinters or with female reference subjects in most age groups. Therefore, further research is needed to determine if relatively high torque-generating abilities distinguish the more mature female sprinters from their peers or from younger competitors in a manner similar to that seen among the males.

Rapid bursts of effort requiring high energy production rates are primarily supported anaerobically by phosphagen and glycolytic metabolism.

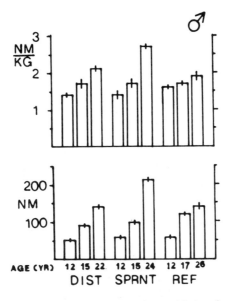

Figure 6 Peak torque levels for male runners and nonathletic reference subjects. Values are $\bar{x} \pm$ SEM for leg extension at 180°/s.

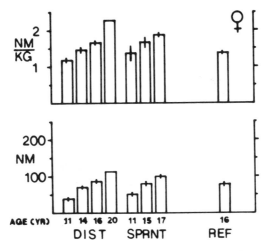

Figure 7 Peak torque levels for female runners and nonathletic reference subjects. Values are $\bar{x} \pm$ SEM for leg extension at 180°/s.

Anaerobic energy response characteristics are related to muscle fiber type, generally being greater in fast twitch fiber (Bar-Or, 1978). However, such metabolic characteristics are also subject to growth and training influences. Specific enzyme activities may serve as rate-limiting factors. Phospho-

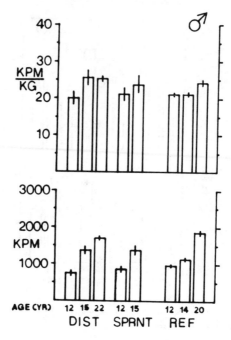

Figure 8 Anaerobic capacity levels for male runners and nonathletic reference subjects. Values are $\bar{x} \pm$ SEM.

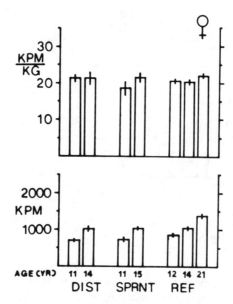

Figure 9 Anaerobic capacity levels for female runners and nonathletic reference subjects. Values are $\bar{x} \pm$ SEM.

fructokinase (PFK) activity is typically considered as rate limiting to glycolysis, and Ericksson (1972) has shown that this quality is lower in children than in adults, regardless of training status. Therefore, prior to adolescence, younger athletes will have a lower metabolic ability for "sprint-type" activities.

Figures 8 and 9, respectively, display the anaerobic capacity (AC) characteristics of male and female athletes and nonathletes. Among either sex, age-related differences in AC were shown within each of the sport or reference groups. However, when similar comparisons were made using values adjusted for body weight, only the adult male reference subjects had significantly higher values than their younger counterparts. In addition, no sport-specific differences in AC were found. But in this regard it is important to note that data on young adult sprinters were absent from these comparisons. Therefore, although younger sprinters do not differ in anaerobic capacity when compared to their peers, it remains unknown as to the degree to which this quality must be developed to characterize responses consistent with high sprint ability at adult levels.

In summary, these results collectively indicate maturation differences that distinguish elite junior-level athletes from young adult competitors. In a number of sports, greater FFB development clearly characterizes the more mature performers. Related to this may be enhanced capabilities for strength and anaerobic responses that, conceivably, are of high importance to peak performance in some activities.

References

Bar-Or, O. (1978). *A new anaerobic test—Characteristics and applications.* Paper presented at the 21st World Congress in Sports Medicine, Brasilia.

Barnes, W.S. (1981). Selected physiological characteristics of elite male sprint athletes. *Journal of Sports Medicine and Physical Fitness, 21,* 49-54.

Behnke, A.R., & Wilmore, J.H. (1974). *Evaluation and regulation of body build and composition* (pp. 169-171). Englewood Cliffs: Prentice-Hall.

Bloomfield, J., & Sigerseth, P.O. (1965). Anatomical and physiological differences between sprint and middle-distance swimmers at the university level. *Journal of Sports Medicine and Physical Fitness, 5,* 76-81.

Conger, P.R., & Macnab, R.B.J. (1967). Strength, body composition and work capacity of participants and nonparticipants in women's intercollegiate sports. *Research Quarterly, 38,* 184-192.

Costill, D.L. (1970). Metabolic responses during distance running. *Journal of Applied Physiology, 28,* 251-255.

DeGaray, A.L., Levine, L., & Carter, J.E.L. (1974). *Genetic and anthropological studies of Olympic athletes.* New York: Academic Press.

Ericksson, B.O. (1972). Physical training, oxygen supply and muscle metabolism in 11-13 year old boys. *Acta Physiologica Scandinavica* (Suppl. 384).

Fahey, T.D., Akka, L., & Rolph, R. (1975). Body composition and VO_2max of exceptional weight-trained athletes. *Journal of Applied Physiology, 39,* 550-561.

Forbes, G.B. (1972). Growth of lean body mass in man. *Growth, 36,* 325-335.

Fox, E.L., & Mathews, D.K. (1981). *The physiological basis of physical education and athletics.* Philadelphia: Saunders.

Gale, J.B., & Flynn, K.W. (1974). Maximal oxygen consumption and relative body fat of high-ability wrestlers. *Medicine and Science in Sports, 6,* 232-234.

Hagerman, F.D., Hagerman, G.R., Rozenek, R., Burke, E.F., Kirkendall, D.T., & Nagell, S.H. (1980, Fall). Baseline physiological data compiled on women distance runners. *Track and Field Quarterly Review,* pp. 60-61.

Heath, B.H., & Carter, J.E.L. (1967). A modified somatotype method. *American Journal of Physical Anthropology, 27,* 57-74.

Holmes, J.R., & Alderink, G.J. (1984). Isokinetic strength characteristics of the quadriceps femoris and hamstring muscles in high school students. *Physical Therapy, 64,* 914-918.

Housh, T.J. (1984). *The contribution of selected physiological variables in the discrimination of middle distance running performance.* Unpublished doctoral dissertation, University of Nebraska, Lincoln.

Housh, T.J., Thorland, W.G., Tharp, G.D., Johnson, G.O., & Cisar, C.J. (1984). Isokinetic leg flexion and extension strength of elite adolescent female track and field athletes. *Research Quarterly for Exercise and Sport, 55,* 347-350.

Jacobs, I., Bar-Or, O., Karlsson, J., Dotan, R., Tesch, P., Kaiser, P., & Inbar, O. (1982). Changes in muscle metabolites in females with 30-s exhaustive exercise. *Medicine and Science in Sports and Exercise, 14,* 457-460.

Katch, F.I., Michael, E.D., & Jones, E.M. (1969). Effect of physical training on the body composition and diet of females. *Research Quarterly, 40,* 99-104.

Larsson, L., Grimby, G., & Karlsson, J. (1979). Muscle strength and speed of movement in relation to age and muscle morphology. *Journal of Applied Physiology: Respiratory, Environmental and Exercise Physiology, 46,* 451-456.

Malina, R.M., Harper, A.B., Avent, H.H., & Campbell, D.E. (1971). Physique of female track and field athletes. *Medicine and Science in Sports, 3,* 32-38.

Novak, L.P., Hyatt, R.E., & Alexander, J.F. (1968). Body composition and physiologic function of athletes. *Journal of the American Medical Association, 205,* 764-770.

Novak, L.P., Tauxe, W.N., & Orvis, A.L. (1973). Estimation of total body potassium in normal adolescents by whole-body counting: Age and sex differences. *Medicine and Science in Sports*, **5**, 147-155.

Novak, L.P., Woodward, W.A., Bestit, C., & Mellerowicz, H. (1977). Working capacity, body composition, and anthropometry of Olympic athletes. *Journal of Sports Medicine and Physical Fitness*, **17**, 275-283.

Palgi, Y., Gutin, B., Young, J., & Alejandro, D. (1984). Physiologic and anthropometric factors underlying endurance performance in children. *International Journal of Sports Medicine*, **5**, 67-73.

Parizkova, J. (1977). *Body fat and physical fitness*. The Hague: Martinus Nihoff.

Pipes, T.V. (1977). Body composition characteristics of male and female track and field athletes. *Research Quarterly*, **48**, 244-247.

Pollock, M.L., Gettman, L.R., Jackson, A., Ayres, J., Ward, A., & Linnerud, A.C. (1977). Body composition of elite class distance runners. *Annals of the New York Academy of Sciences*, **301**, 361-370.

Pollock, M.L., Jackson, A.S., & Pate, R.R. (1980). Discriminant analysis of physiological differences between good and elite distance runners. *Research Quarterly for Exercise and Sport*, **51**, 521-532.

Rusko, H., Havu, M., & Karvinen, E. (1978). Aerobic performance capacity in athletes. *European Journal of Applied Physiology*, **38**, 151-159.

Sinning, W.E. (1974). Body composition assessment of college wrestlers. *Medicine and Science in Sports*, **6**, 139-145.

Sinning, W.E., & Lindberg, G.D. (1972). Physical characteristics of college age women gymnasts. *Research Quarterly*, **43**, 226-234.

Sprynarova, S., & Parizkova, J. (1969). Comparison of the functional, circulatory, and respiratory capacity in girl gymnasts and swimmers. *Journal of Sports Medicine and Physical Fitness*, **9**, 165-172.

Sprynarova, S., & Parizkova, J. (1971). Functional capacity and body composition in top weight-lifters, swimmers, runners, and skiers. *Internationale Zeitschrift fur Angewandte Physiologie*, **29**, 184-194.

Tharp, G.D., Johnson, G.O., & Thorland, W.G. (1984). Measurement of anaerobic power and capacity in elite young track athletes using the Wingate test. *Journal of Sports Medicine and Physical Fitness*, **24**, 100-106.

Thorland, W.G., Johnson, G.O., Fagot, T.G., Tharp, G.D., & Hammer, R.W. (1981). Body composition and somatotype characteristics of Junior Olympic athletes. *Medicine and Science in Sports and Exercise*, **13**, 332-338.

Thorland, W.G., Johnson, G.O., Housh, T.J., & Refsell, M.J. (1983). Anthropometric characteristics of elite adolescent competitive swimmers. *Human Biology*, **55**, 735-748.

Thorstensson, A., Larsson, L., Tesch, P., & Karlsson, J. (1977). Muscle strength and fiber composition in athletes and sedentary men. *Medicine and Science in Sports*, **9**, 26-30.

Wilmore, J.H., & Brown, C.H. (1974). Physiological profiles of women distance runners. *Medicine and Science in Sports*, **6**, 178-181.

Wilmore, J.H., Brown, C.H., & Davis, J.A. (1977). Body physique and composition of the female distance runner. *Annals of the New York Academy of Sciences*, **301**, 764-776.

Young, C.M., Sipin, S.S., & Roe, D.A. (1968). Body composition of preadolescent and adolescent girls. *Journal of the American Dietetic Association*, **53**, 25-31.

Physiological Characteristics
of Male and Female Age-Group Runners

Wayne Van Huss
Sharon A. Evans
Theodore Kurowski
David J. Anderson
Ray Allen
Kenneth Stephens

The factors that limit endurance performance in children and adolescents have not been established. In adult athletes it is clear that endurance performance is closely related to aerobic capacity. In children and adolescents, however, less support exists for this position. In elite prepubertal cross-country runners, Mayers and Gutin (1979) found no correlation between running performance and aerobic capacity. In the study of untrained children the same group of investigators (Palgi, Gutin, Young, & Wejandro, 1984) found aerobic capacity to be related to endurance performance. In the latter study of the untrained children, anaerobic performance was as closely related to the endurance criteria as aerobic capacity.

It is a matter of controversy as to the extent endurance training during the growth years can increase aerobic capacity. Increases of about 10% have been observed as a result of endurance training (Ekblom, 1969; Eriksson, 1972; Lussier & Buskirk, 1977). On the other hand, Daniels, Oldridge, Nagle, and White (1978) and Stewart and Gutin (1976) were unable to demonstrate any training effects. The difference in results may be related to when the initial testing was done (i.e., very early in their running careers or after their training patterns have been established). Daniels and Oldridge (1971) and Daniels et al. (1978) noted that changes in oxygen consumption during growth were matched by equal changes in weight, resulting in no change in $\dot{V}O_2$ ml • min^{-1} • kg^{-1}. The aerobic demand of a standard submaximal running speed was also shown to diminish over time (Daniels & Oldridge, 1971).

The aerobic capacities of endurance-trained 12-year-old boys and 17-year-old adolescent runners were compared by Lehmann, Keul, and Hesse (1982). The $\dot{V}O_2$max values of 60.3 and 65.0 ml • min^{-1} • kg^{-1}, respectively, were not significantly different. The $\dot{V}O_2$max values observed in this study were similar to the values obtained by Sundberg and Elovainio (1982) for endurance runners of 12 and 16 years of age (59.3

and 66.0 ml • min^{-1} • kg^{-1}). When elite male endurance runners 12 to 14 years of age were compared with control subjects of the same age (Lehmann et al., 1982), the runners weighed less, were leaner, and had higher $\dot{V}O_2$max values (59.3 and 63.7 as compared to 51.1 and 56.0 ml • min^{-1} • kg^{-1}, respectively). Although Lehmann et al. (1982) concluded that the young boys showed no disadvantage to the adolescents, the difference in means of the two groups across both studies was in the range of 10%.

Rutenfranz et al. (1982) studied the development of aerobic power in selected population groups. They observed that the increase during the prepubertal years was mainly an effect of growth in body size. A slightly higher level of maximal aerobic power was observed at the end of adolescence. The study showed, however, that the maximum aerobic power varied considerably from year to year. This instability has been observed in other longitudinal studies by Parizkova (1977) and Kobayashi et al. (1978). It was the view of Rutenfranz et al. that maximum aerobic power reacts rather quickly to changes in the external and internal environment.

No previous studies were found that reported aerobic capacity in endurance-trained female runners in the age range of 8 to 14 years. Older female runners have been found to have higher $\dot{V}O_2$max values than nonendurance-trained controls (Bransford & Howley, 1977; Daniels, Krahenbuhl, Foster, Gilbert, & Daniels, 1977; Wilmore & Brown, 1974). Burke and Brush (1979) studied elite teenage female distance runners (mean age x = 16.2 years) and found their mean $\dot{V}O_2$max to be 63.2 ml • min^{-1} • kg^{-1}. In a large sample of female cross-country runners the mean $\dot{V}O_2$max was 50.8 ml • min^{-1} • kg^{-1} (Butts, 1982). Minimal data are available on young untrained female subjects. Chausow, Riner, and Boileau (1984), in a study of three children with an average age of 10.1 years, observed a $\dot{V}O_2$max of 49.1 ml • min^{-1} • kg^{-1}. Palgi et al. (1984) reported mean $\dot{V}O_2$max values of 42.9 ml • min^{-1} • kg^{-1} for young trained females (mean age x = 11.9 years). Nagle, Hagberg, and Kamei (1977) measured samples of girls (n = 120) and boys (n = 120) aged 14 to 17 years from a northern midwest U.S. high school. The mean $\dot{V}O_2$max values were 40.8 and 54.7 ml • min^{-1} • kg^{-1} for the girls and boys, respectively. In this investigation, no differences across age were observed in either sex.

The present study was undertaken to further examine the levels of aerobic capacity in elite young runners, ages 9 to 15 years, by (a) comparing performance, aerobic capacities, and work economy with control subjects of the same ages, (b) comparing performance and physiological characteristics of young male and female distance runners, and (c) examining the relationship of selected physiological parameters with work performance.

Method

The subjects consisted of 42 elite runners aged 9 to 15 (22 female, 20 male) and 26 control subjects (11 female, 15 male) of the same ages. The control subjects were healthy and physically active but untrained as runners. An intermittent treadmill protocol was utilized that consisted of progressively more intense 3-min work intervals with intervening 3-min rest intervals until the subject was exhausted. A 15-min recovery period followed. The work intensity progression was Level 1—6 mph, 0% grade; Level 2—6 mph, 5% grade; Level 3—7 mph, 6% grade; Level 4—8 mph, 7% grade, and so forth. The increase was 1 mph and 1% grade for each additional level.

The oxygen uptake was measured using the traditional Douglas bag method as described by Consolazio, Johnson, and Pecora (1963). Throughout work and rest intervals and during the first 5 min of recovery the gas collections were fractionated into 1-min bags. The electrocardiogram was monitored continuously using the CM-5 lead. Minute values were recorded for the heart rate from strip counts. The blood pressure was measured by sphygmomanometer immediately following each work level and at 5, 10, and 15 min of recovery. Blood lactate was measured by taking 20 l-arterialized blood samples at the same time the blood pressure was being measured. The blood samples were taken from the prewarmed fingertip, and the whole blood samples were analyzed in the Roche 640 Analyzer.

Runner versus control group and male runner versus female runner group comparisons were analyzed using the Sign Test (Siegel, 1956) and MANOVA procedure (Hull & Nie, 1981). For the work economy analysis of Levels 2 to 4, the repeated measures MANOVA procedure (Hull & Nie) was used. Relationships and contributions to performance capacity were examined using step-wise multiple regression procedures (Nie, Hull, Jenkins, Steinbrenner, & Bent, 1975). A probability level of 0.05 was used to determine significant differences.

Results and Discussion

The pooled experimental versus control subjects data for the maximum oxygen consumption ($\dot{V}O_2$max), heart rate (HR), systolic blood pressure (SBP), and blood lactate (Lact) for all points are shown in Figures 1 to 4. The patterns observed in the pooled data graphs are consistent with the differences observed between the male or the female runners and their respective control groups. The oxygen uptake during the work intervals was consistently higher in the runners ($p < .01$), and the runners, as expected, worked longer and attained higher $\dot{V}O_2$max values. During the rest intervals, the $\dot{V}O_2$ values were consistently lower for the runners ($p < .01$). It is evident from the graphs that the responses of the runners were significantly more aerobic.

These data must be interpreted with care. Study of the exercise $\dot{V}O_2$ values in Figure 1 shows that neither the runners nor the control subjects have attained steady state in the work interval. The runners responded faster by attaining a higher $\dot{V}O_2$ sooner than the control subjects, therefore, the runners' oxygen deficit was lower. The lower $\dot{V}O_2$ values in recovery and the lower HR, SBP, and Lact values of the runners during the work interval support this position. If the work had continued

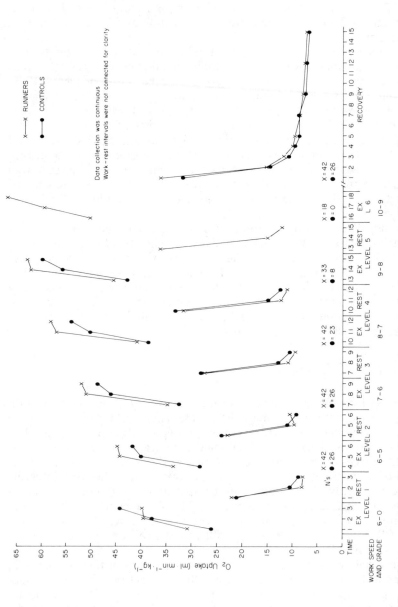

Figure 1 Pooled runners versus controls: Mean oxygen uptake values during work, rest intervals, and recovery.

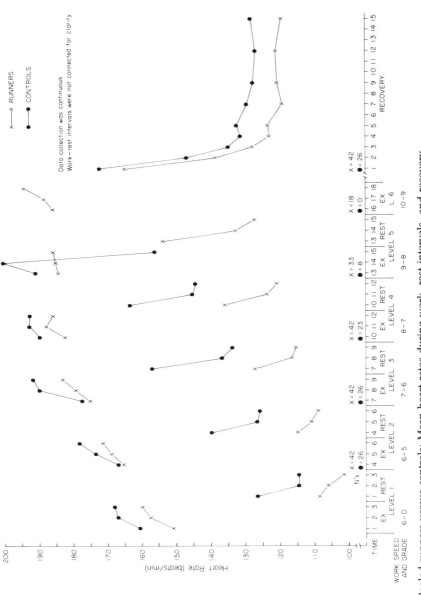

Figure 2 Pooled runners versus controls: Mean heart rates during work, rest intervals, and recovery.

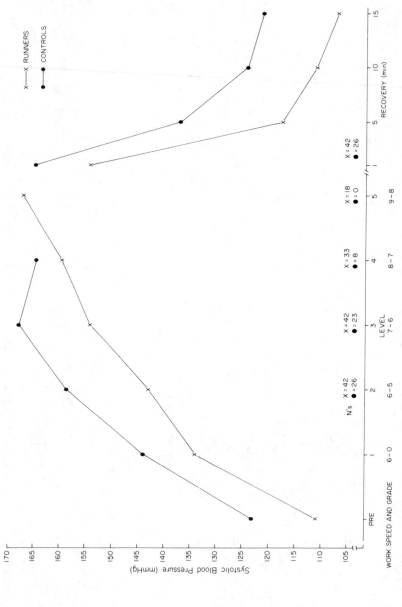

Figure 3 Pooled runners versus controls: Mean systolic blood pressures during rest intervals and recovery.

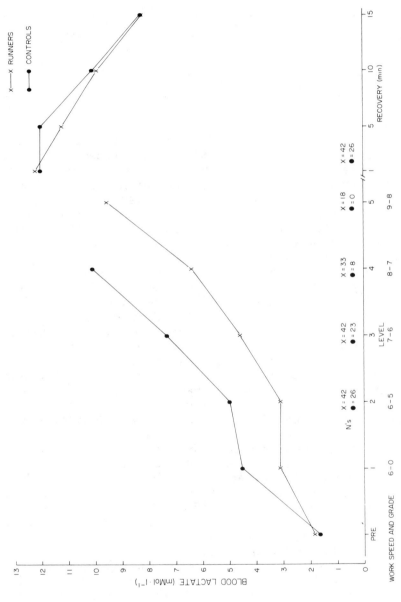

Figure 4 Pooled runners versus controls: Mean lactate values during rest intervals and recovery.

Table 1   Runners Versus Controls—Mean Peak Values

Group	N	PT	$\dot{V}O_2$max	HR	SBP	Lact
Male runners	20	15.3	65.9	197	166	12.8
Male controls	13	12.3	56.7	201	174	11.7
Female runners	21	13.7	59.9	199	166	11.8
Female controls	11	10.5	47.2	199	173	12.5

at these submaximal levels, the $\dot{V}O_2$ values of the control subjects would surpass those of the runners. It is important to place in perspective when these data were collected during and following the work interval, because it is well known that with continued training the work is performed more economically (Bransford & Hawley, 1977; Daniels, 1985). The present data are not in contradiction but rather are supportive of the greater aerobic capacity of the trained subjects. These data do, however, draw attention to the early portion of the work-response curve, which has not received a great deal of research attention.

The HR, SBP, and Lact results are supportive of the $\dot{V}O_2$ data with greater differences evident between the runner and control groups. The results are in the expected directions with the heart rates of the runners consistently lower throughout exercise (Sign Test $p < .01$), rest intervals ($p < .01$), and recovery ($p < .01$). The SBP values were consistently lower across levels and during recovery ($p < .01$). Likewise, the postexercise and recovery Lact values of the runners were consistently lower ($p < .01$).

As mentioned, the pooled results shown are representative of the male and female runners versus control comparisons. The male data were similar in direction and magnitude to previous studies (Sundberg & Elovainio, 1982). The unique comparison of the female runners with female controls was identical in direction with the male comparison.

The mean peak values for all groups and all parameters being reported—performance time (PT), $\dot{V}O_2$, HR, SBP, and Lact—are shown in Table 1. The probability values obtained from the statistical analysis (MANOVA) are shown in Table 2. For the three comparisons shown of runners versus control subjects, the PT and $\dot{V}O_2$max were significantly different. No differences in peak HR or Lact were observed. The pooled data for the SBP difference in runners versus control subjects were not significantly different ($p = .06$). In the male comparison and the female comparison, the SBP was not significantly different even though the magnitude of the difference was about 7 mmHg. Clearly, the trained runners were capable of running for longer times and were able to achieve higher levels of oxygen uptake. Whether these greater values are attained at lower max BP values is still open to question. It is quite evident that the max HR and Lact values are not different between the groups.

Table 2 Runners Versus Controls—Probability Values From Statistical Comparison of Peak Values

Comparison	PT	$\dot{V}O_2$max	HR	SBP	Lact
Pooled: runners vs. controls	< .01	< .01	.48	.06	.70
Male runners vs. male controls	< .01	< .01	.30	.13	.13
Female runners vs. female controls	< .01	< .01	.99	.26	.56

Table 3 Males Versus Females—Probability Values From Statistical Comparison of Peak Values

Comparison	PT	$\dot{V}O_2$max	HR	SBP	Lact
Pooled: males vs. females	< .01	< .01	.79	.86	.63
Male runners vs. female runners	< .01	< .01	.45	.93	.27

In Table 3 the probability values are presented from the statistical comparison of the peak measures of the males versus females. In the pooled male versus female data (male and female runners), the PT and $\dot{V}O_2$max values were significantly greater for the males. The magnitude of the respective differences was 2.5 min and 8.2 ml • min^{-1} • kg^{-1}. When the male runners were compared with the female runners, the peak values of PT and $\dot{V}O_2$max were significantly greater for male runners.

A subsample from the total sample available was analyzed primarily to compare the difference in $\dot{V}O_2$max values when divided by kilograms of total body weight and when divided by kilograms of the fat-free mass (FFM). It was hypothesized that the differences in $\dot{V}O_2$ between male and female runners would disappear when divided by kilograms of the FFM. The mean values for the subsample are shown in Table 4 with the probability values from the MANOVA analysis in Table 5. Consistent with the total group results, the PT and $\dot{V}O_2$ • ml • min^{-1} • kg^{-1} are significantly greater ($p < .01$) for the pooled runners, pooled males, and for the male runners. Likewise, the HR and Lact results are not different. In the runner versus control comparison, however, the BP differences are significantly different ($p < .01$) with the lower peak blood pressures in the running group. There were no differences in the analysis by gender of HR, SB, or Lact, whether the data were pooled or only the runners were compared.

The hypothesized change in the $\dot{V}O_2$ results when divided by kilograms of FFM did not materialize. The difference in $\dot{V}O_2$ ml • min^{-1} • kg • FFM^{-1} was 9.4, which was exactly the same difference observed when dividing

Table 4   Male-Female Mean Peak Values: Subsample to Compare the Maximum Oxygen Consumption Divided by Kilograms Total Body Weight Versus Divided by Kilograms of the Fat-Free Mass

Group	N	PT	$\dot{V}O_2$/kg	$\dot{V}O_2$/FFM	HR	BP	Lact
Male runners	11	14.7	67.7	79.0	200	165	12.3
Female runners	11	12.6	58.3	69.6	201	161	11.6
Male controls	13	12.3	56.7	70.7	201	174	11.6
Female controls	11	12.5	47.2	62.2	199	173	12.5

Table 5   Subsample Comparisons: Probability Values From Statistical Analysis of Peak Values

Comparison	PT	$\dot{V}O_2$/kg	$\dot{V}O_2$/FFM	HR	SBP	Lact
Pooled: males vs. females	< .01	< .01	< .01	.88	.52	.89
Pooled: runners vs. controls	< .01	< .01	< .01	.93	< .01	.90
Male runners vs. female runners	< .01	< .01	< .01	.85	.50	.54

by kilogram of total body weight. Statistically, it made no difference which denominator was used for the $\dot{V}O_2$ (Table 5).

The $\dot{V}O_2$ and HR for the 3rd min of work and the 2nd min of the rest interval were compared across work Levels 2, 3, and 4. This analysis was performed because the work loads in these levels are standard, thus some indication of work economy could be obtained. In Table 6 the mean values for SBP and Lact obtained immediately following the respective work intervals are also shown. In Table 7 the statistical results from a repeated measures MANOVA are presented comparing pooled data, male runners versus male controls, female runners versus female controls, and male runners versus female runners. The pooled data show that the groups are significantly different in all measures except HR in the 3rd min of the work intervals. Significant differences between males and females were found only in the $\dot{V}O_2$. In the males, the $\dot{V}O_2$ values were consistently higher.

The male runners versus male control results mirror the pooled data except that HR in the 2nd min of the rest interval was not statistically significant, even though the mean differences in each of the levels was 10 beats per minute or greater. The female runner-control comparison was slightly different in that both HR values were statistically significant whereas the SBP was not. $\dot{V}O_2$ and Lact were similar to the pooled data comparison.

Table 6 Mean Values by Group for Work Levels 2, 3, and 4[a]

Group	N	3rd min of work $\dot{V}O_2$	HR	2nd min of rest $\dot{V}O_2$	HR	Postwork[b] SBP	Lact
Level 2							
Male runners	20	45.6	170	9.9	109	144	3.0
Male controls	14	43.9	174	10.7	119	159	4.4
Female runners	22	43.8	173	9.4	112	143	2.9
Female controls	12	39.2	184	11.1	136	158	5.9
Level 3							
Male runners	20	53.1	182	11.0	114	152	4.2
Male controls	14	50.5	189	13.2	131	167	7.1
Female runners	22	51.0	184	10.8	119	156	4.9
Female controls	11	44.8	196	12.6	147	167	7.8
Level 4							
Male runners	20	60.5	188	12.4	123	156	6.0
Male controls	9	56.3	185	15.0	136	165	9.9
Female runners	17	56.0	183	12.2	125	162	6.9
Female controls	6	50.6	204	14.6	172	163	10.4

[a]3 min work at each level. [b]Immediately in the rest interval.

In the comparison of male versus female runners, only the $\dot{V}O_2$ was significantly different. The female runners were slightly but not significantly fatter than male runners. Because each of the three work levels was standard in intensity and time, the body fatness was not significantly different and none of the other parameters measured (i.e., HR, SBP, and Lact) were significantly different. It appears that the female runners were performing the work more economically. These results are in contradiction to the data of Bransford and Howley (1977) and Howley and Glover (1974) on adults. Wells, Hecht, and Krahenbuhl (1981), however, found no differences in the work economy of male and female marathon runners.

The $\dot{V}O_2$max for all subjects separated according to gender and age is shown in Figure 5. This analysis was undertaken to determine if an age-associated level of $\dot{V}O_2$max existed for either males or females. The male data are similar in magnitude and indicate no significant effect of age, supporting the results of Daniels et al. (1978). The $\dot{V}O_2$max values of the females also show no effect of age, although the values are slightly less in magnitude. In Table 8 the mean $\dot{V}O_2$max values are shown for the same subjects across 3 years. Although the numbers of subjects are small, no trends have emerged by gender.

The data for the total sample of experimental and control subjects ($N = 68$) were pooled irrespective of gender, group, or age, and a multiple regression analysis was run using PT as the criterion variable to determine the relative contribution of the parameters under study to the PT.

Table 7 Probability Values: Comparison of Groups Over Levels 2, 3, and 4

Comparison and times	Measure	Group differences	Sex differences
Pooled data			
3rd min of work	$\dot{V}O_2$	< .01	< .01
	HR	NS	NS
Immediately in rest interval	SBP	< .01	NS
	Lact	< .01	NS
2nd min of rest interval	$\dot{V}O_2$	< .01	NS
	HR	< .01	NS
Male runners vs. male controls			
3rd min of work	$\dot{V}O_2$	< .02	—
	HR	NS	—
Immediately in rest interval	SBP	< .03	—
	Lact	< .01	—
2nd min of rest interval	$\dot{V}O_2$	< .02	—
	HR	NS	—
Female runners vs. female controls			
3rd min of work	$\dot{V}O_2$	< .01	—
	HR	< .04	—
Immediately in rest interval	SBP	NS	—
	Lact	< .01	—
2nd min of rest interval	$\dot{V}O_2$	< .02	—
	HR	< .01	—
Male runners vs. female runners			
3rd min of work	$\dot{V}O_2$	—	.02
	HR	—	NS
Immediately in rest interval	SBP	—	NS
	Lact	—	NS
2nd min of rest interval	$\dot{V}O_2$	—	NS
	HR	—	NS

The multiple R was 0.78, with $\dot{V}O_2$max making the greatest contribution to the explained variance (57%). This might be expected due to the results of the runner versus control subject comparison. The 41% contribution of lactate, however, was not expected. With these limited data, it is not possible to conclude what the lactate reflects.

In summary the runners, irrespective of gender, differ from the control subjects in performance times and the $\dot{V}O_2$max. HR and Lact were not significantly different. Although the difference in SBP was not significant ($p < .06$) between runners and controls, it is possible that significance would have been noted using a larger sample. Only in $\dot{V}O_2$max and PT were the male results significantly different from the females. Also, it made no difference in this sample whether the $\dot{V}O_2$ was divided by

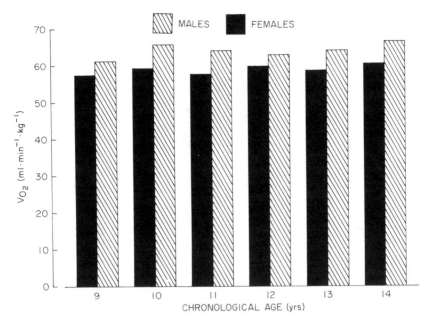

Figure 5 The mean maximal oxygen consumption of all runners by chronological age.

Table 8 Longitudinal Changes in Maximum Oxygen Consumption

Subject		$\dot{V}O_2$ml • min^{-1} • kg^{-1}		
	N	1982	1983	1984
Pooled				
Males	9	65.5	64.7	64.1
Females	6	53.3	58.2	59.1
10- and 11-year-olds[a]				
Males	4	65.3	63.9	61.5
Females	2	59.5	59.0	59.4
12- and 13-year-olds[a]				
Males	5	65.7	65.4	66.3
Females	4	62.5	60.2	59.9

[a]Age at initiation of the study in 1982.

kilogram of total body weight or by the FFM. The results were the same. The $\dot{V}O_2$max in young runners did not appear to change with age in males or females. When the repeated measure results for Levels 2, 3, and 4 were compared, the $\dot{V}O_2$ values were consistently higher during work in the

Table 9   Multiple Regression Analysis Using Performance Time as the Criterion Variable: Total Sample (N = 65, R = 0.78)

Variable	B	B^2	Percent contribution
$\dot{V}O_2$max	13.9	193.2	57
Lactate max	11.7	136.9	41
HR max	2.6	6.8	2
BP max	1.0	1.0	0
		337.9	100

runners, both male and female, and consistently lower during recovery, indicating that the runners were performing more aerobically. Female runners appeared to perform more economically because their $\dot{V}O_2$ during work was less, whereas their $\dot{V}O_2$ in the rest interval was also less but not significantly. The aerobic capacity contributed most of the explained variance related to PT. The Lact, which contributed 41% of the variance reflected in the R of 0.78, is not interpretable from these data.

References

Bransford, D.R., & Howley, E.T. (1977). Oxygen cost of running in trained and untrained men and women. *Medicine and Science in Sports,* **9**, 41-44.

Burke, E.Y., & Brush, F.C. (1979). Physiological and anthropometric assessment of successful teenage female distance runners. *Research Quarterly,* **50**, 180-187.

Butts, N.K. (1982). Physiological profiles of high school female cross-country runners. *Research Quarterly for Exercise and Sports,* **53**, 8-14.

Chausow, S.A., Riner, W.F., & Boileau, K. (1984). Metabolic and cardiovascular responses of children during prolonged physical activity. *Research Quarterly for Exercise and Sports,* **55**, 1-7.

Consolazio, C.F., Johnson, R.E., & Pecora, L.J. (1963). *Physiological measurements of metabolic functions in man.* New York: McGraw-Hill.

Daniels, J.T. (1985). A physiologist's view of running economy. *Medicine and Science in Sports and Exercise,* **17**, 332-338.

Daniels, J., Krahenbuhl, G., Foster, C., Gilbert, J., & Daniels, S. (1977). Aerobic responses of female distance runners to submaximal and maximal exercise. *Annals New York Academy of Science,* **301**, 726-733.

Daniels, J., & Oldridge, N. (1971). Changes in oxygen consumption in young boys during growth and running training. *Medicine and Science in Sports,* **3**, 161-165.

Daniels, J., Oldridge, N., Nagle, F., & White, B. (1978). Differences and changes in VO_2 among young runners 10 to 18 years of age. *Medicine and Science in Sports*, **10**, 200-203.

Ekblom, B. (1969). Effect on physical training in adolescent boys. *Journal of Applied Physiology*, **27**, 350-355.

Eriksson, B.O. (1972). Physical training, oxygen supply and muscle metabolism in 11-12 year old boys. *Acta Physiologica Scandinavica* (Suppl. 290).

Howley, E.T., & Glover, M.E. (1974). The caloric costs of running and walking one mile for men and women. *Medicine and Science in Sports*, **6**, 235-237.

Hull, C.H., & Nie, N.H. (Eds.). (1981). *SPSS Update 7-9*. New York: McGraw-Hill.

Kobayashi, K., Kitamura, K., Miura, M., Sodeyama, H., Murase, Y., Miyashita, M., & Matsui, H. (1978). Aerobic power as related to body growth and training in Japanese boys: A longitudinal study. *Journal of Applied Physiology*, **44**, 666-672.

Lehmann, M., Keul, J., & Hesse, A. (1982). Zur aeroben und anaeroben Kapazitat sowie catecholaminexkretion von Kindern und Jugendlichen während langdauernder submaximaler Korperarbeit [On the aerobic and anaerobic capacity as well as catecholamine excretion of children and youth during long-duration submaximal physical activity]. *European Journal of Applied Physiology*, **48**, 135-145.

Lussier, L., & Buskirk, E.R. (1977). Effects of an endurance training regimen on assessment of work capacity in prepubertal children. *Annals New York Academy of Science*, **301**, 734-747.

Mayers, M., & Gutin, B. (1979). Physiological characteristics of elite prepubertal cross-country runners. *Medicine and Science in Sports*, **11**, 172-176.

Nagle, F., Hagberg, J., & Kamei, S. (1977). Maximal oxygen uptake of boys and girls—ages 14-17. *European Journal of Applied Physiology*, **36**, 75-80.

Nie, N.H., Hull, C.H., Jenkins, J.G., Steinbrenner, K., & Bent, D.H. (1975). *Statistical package for the social sciences*. New York: McGraw-Hill.

Palgi, Y., Gutin, B., Young, J., & Wejandro, D. (1984). Physiologic and anthropometric factors underlying endurance performance in children. *International Journal of Sports Medicine*, **5**, 67-73.

Parizkova, J. (1977). *Body fat and physical fitness*. The Hague: Martinus Nijoff.

Rutenfranz, J., Andersen, K.L., Seliger, V., Ilmarin, J., Klimmer, F., Kylian, H., Rutenfranz, M., & Ruppel, M. (1982). Maximal aerobic power affected by maturation and body growth during childhood and adolescence. *European Journal of Pediatrics*, **139**, 106-112.

Siegel, S. (1956). *Nonparametric statistics*. New York: McGraw-Hill.

Stewart, K.J., & Gutin, B. (1976). Effects of physical training on cardio-respiratory fitness in children. *Research Quarterly, 47,* 110-120.

Sundberg, S., & Elovainio, R. (1982). Cardiorespiratory function in competitive endurance runners aged 12-16 years compared with ordinary boys. *Acta Paediatrica Scandinavica, 71,* 987-992.

Wells, C.L., Hecht, L.H., & Krahenbuhl, G.S. (1981). Physical characteristics and oxygen utilization of male and female marathon runners. *Research Quarterly for Exercise and Sport, 52,* 281-285.

Wilmore, J.H., & Brown, C.H. (1974). Physiological profiles of women distance runners. *Medicine and Science in Sports, 6,* 178-181.

Physiological Characteristics of Young Active Boys

David A. Cunningham
Donald H. Paterson

The growth and development of the cardiorespiratory and metabolic capacities of children are associated with several markers of maturational development. Children experience several periods of growth as they mature, and during the pubescent growth spurt a significant portion of their adult size is reached. Large variation in the age and magnitude of this growth spurt imposes problems on the study of physiological characteristics of children. Chronologically age-based data, therefore, may not be representative of true growth-related changes. If changes in functional characteristics are also to be related to patterns of physical activity during this period of rapid growth, intercorrelations between separate factors make the interpretation difficult or impossible. Problems such as this require that studies that involve children be designed to account for the many interactions of the multiple variables involved in the growth phase.

Maximal Oxygen Uptake

Maximal oxygen uptake ($\dot{V}O_2$max) in children has been described in several cross-sectional studies (Andrew, Becklake, Guleria, & Bates, 1972; Boileau, Bonen, Heyward, & Massey, 1977; Cunningham, Stapleton, MacDonald, & Paterson, 1981; Hamilton & Andrew, 1976; Yamaji & Miyashita, 1977) in which chronological age rather than the level of maturation was used as the reference factor. In such studies, differences attributed to age or body size may be confounded by the wide variation in maturation. Longitudinal studies, however, have been reported in which the influence of growth and maturation on the cardiorespiratory system has been accounted for (Cunningham, Paterson, Blimkie, & Donner, 1984; Kobayashi et al., 1978; Mirwald, Bailey, Cameron, & Rasmussen, 1981; Sprynarova, 1974).

Maximal oxygen uptake ($1 \cdot min^{-1}$) is greater in older and bigger children, but this difference may disappear when weight is used as a reference factor. Results are not consistent, however, and reports indicate no change, a slight increase, or a decline with age. These discrepancies may be the result of the cross-sectional nature of the data, and therefore, the differences in the samples of children studied. Such variations in results,

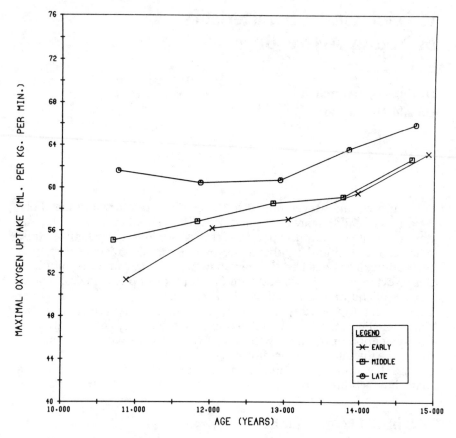

Figure 1 Comparison of $\dot{V}O_2$max with chronological age in early, middle, and late maturing groups.

however, have also been found in longitudinal studies (Cunningham, Paterson, & Blimkie, 1984). The levels of habitual physical activity among the studies might be one of the contributive factors to the variability of results. In addition, weight per se, as a reference factor for the growth of the cardiorespiratory system in this age (10 to 15 years) range, has been shown to have a very different level of association with $\dot{V}O_2$max at each age. The explained variance in $\dot{V}O_2$max due to weight ranged from 55 to 75% in ages 9 to 15 years (Cunningham & Paterson, 1985); however, it remained the best factor when compared to height and fatness.

As part of this study of young active boys, the importance of body size and early or late maturation was related to the longitudinal changes in $\dot{V}O_2$max (Cunningham, Paterson, Blimkie, & Donner, 1984). Eighty-one boys were recruited into the study over a 4-year intake period. They were approximately 10 years of age at entry into the study and were participants in an organized ice hockey program (Cunningham, Van Waterschoot, Paterson, Lefcoe, & Sangal, 1977), although few (< 20%) of the boys re-

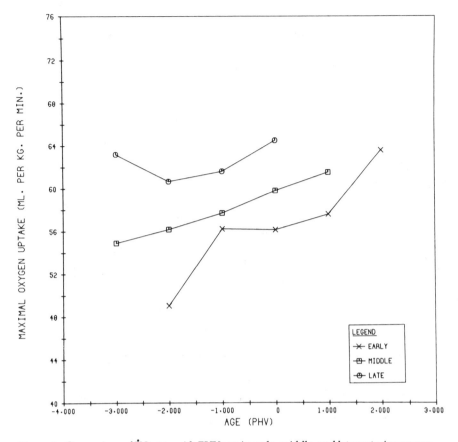

Figure 2   Comparison of V̇O₂max with PHV age in early, middle, and late maturing groups.

mained in active participation beyond age 12 years. The boys were involved in many sport activities, ice hockey being only one of these. The boys completed annual tests over a 5-year period from mean age 10.7 to 14.7 years.

Maximum oxygen uptake was determined annually on a treadmill test. Maturation level was found by a hand-wrist X ray at ages 10 and 14 years. The group was divided into early and late maturers. The data for V̇O₂max were presented relative to both chronological age and peak height velocity (PHV).

The results demonstrated a steady increase in V̇O₂max each year from 1.95 l • min⁻¹ or 55.4 ml • kg⁻¹ • min⁻¹ at 10.8 years to 3.66 or 63.2 ml • kg⁻¹ • min⁻¹ at 14.8 years (Figure 1). Mean height and weight increased over this age range by 22.8 cm and 25.8 kg, respectively, and body fatness changed little. Level of recreational activity (determined from a questionnaire in which a total score was derived based on sports and recreational participation) remained similar throughout this period. Maximal heart rate was consistent at about 198 bpm, whereas postexercise

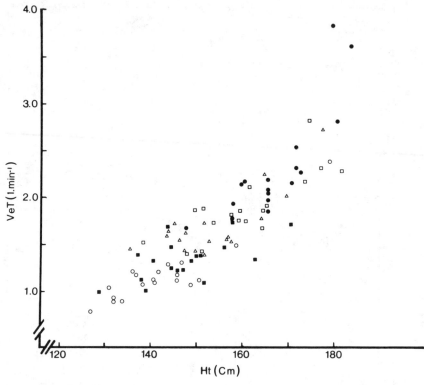

Figure 3 Ventilation threshold with height in boys studied longitudinally from age 10.8 to 14.8 years. The symbols represent ages 10.8 (O), 11.8 (■), 12.8 (△), 13.8 (□), and 14.8 (●).

blood lactate increased by 54%. Plotted against chronological age, late maturers had a higher $\dot{V}O_2$max (ml • kg^{-1} • min^{-1}, Figure 1).

When the data of $\dot{V}O_2$max were compared at similar points of growth (PHV) (Figure 2), the differences in $\dot{V}O_2$max that were large before or at the age of PHV appeared to be reduced as the early maturers showed a large gain in $\dot{V}O_2$max. These differences appeared to be due to unequal stages of weight gain among the groups. It appears that the capacity for oxygen delivery will catch up to this weight gain resulting in a similar $\dot{V}O_2$max among groups at full growth (Figure 2). The $\dot{V}O_2$max of the early maturers reached the level of the $\dot{V}O_2$max of the late maturers by +2 years PHV, and the $\dot{V}O_2$max of the late maturers was expected to plateau as peak weight gain will be reached in this 2-year period.

The relative importance of growth factors, including height, weight, and body fatness, and of maturative group and activity level as contributors to the level of $\dot{V}O_2$max were analyzed by multiple regression. The $\dot{V}O_2$max was explained by the body size factors of weight and skinfold at all ages. The level of sport or recreational activity and maturative group

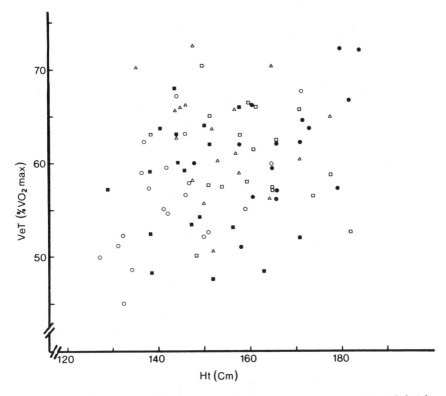

Figure 4 Ventilation threshold as a percentage of maximum oxygen uptake with height in boys studied longitudinally from age 10.8 to 14.8 years. The symbols represent ages 10.8 (O), 11.8 (■), 12.8 (△), 13.8 (□), and 14.8 (●).

was not associated with $\dot{V}O_2$max (Cunningham, Paterson, Blimkie, & Donner, 1984).

Ventilation Threshold and Growth

Ventilation threshold ($\dot{V}_ET$) as well as $\dot{V}O_2$max were determined each year in 18 of the most active boys in the group (unpublished observations). The V_ET and $\dot{V}O_2$max were determined on a continuous treadmill test. The V_ET was the first disproportionate increase in the plot of V_E (BTPS) versus $\dot{V}O_2$ (STPD) using lines of best fit drawn by eye.

The $\dot{V}O_2$max and $\dot{V}_ET$ increased significantly from year to year from ages 10.8 through 14.8 years. $\dot{V}O_2$max and $\dot{V}_ET$ relative to body height (Figure 3) or weight also increased significantly. $\dot{V}_ET$ was significantly correlated with body height ($r = .86$) and weight ($r = .90$) across this age span. The log-log transformations of $\dot{V}_ET$ and $\dot{V}O_2$ versus body weight

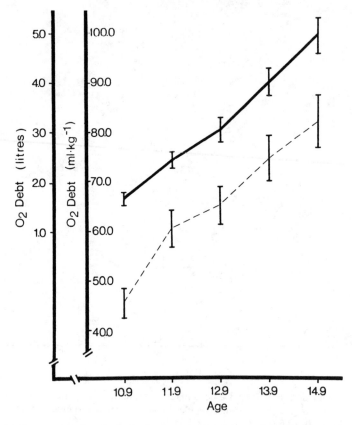

Figure 5   Oxygen debt (l and ml • kg⁻¹) at standardized chronological ages. Data are means ± SEM. Solid line is O_2 debt in l; dashed line is O_2 debt in ml • kg⁻¹.

yielded scaling factors of 1.13 and 1.02, respectively. These factors were not significantly different. $\dot{V}_ET$ occurred at a significantly higher proportion of $\dot{V}O_2$max as the boys grew older. The mean value ranged from 56 to 62%. The range of values is shown in Figure 4 of $\dot{V}_ET$ as a percentage of $\dot{V}O_2$max versus height for all 5 years of study. The relationship between $\dot{V}O_2$max and $\dot{V}_ET$ increased with age ($r = .71$ at 10.8 years; $r = .95$ at 14.8 years).

In this study of very active boys the $\dot{V}O_2$max was high (> 60 ml • kg⁻¹ • min⁻¹) over the 5 years, and boys were taller and heavier than found in the general population. Increases in $\dot{V}O_2$max (relative to body weight) with age have been reported in other studies of active boys (Andersen & Froberg, 1980; Kobayashi et al., 1978). This is in contrast to studies of less active boys where stable or slightly declining values have been found (see Cunningham, Paterson, & Blimkie, 1984). Similarly, a stable or declining $\dot{V}_ET/\dot{V}O_2$max has been found previously (Cooper, Weiler-Ravell,

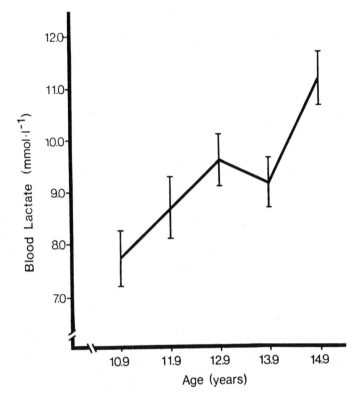

Figure 6   Blood lactate (mmol • l⁻¹) at standardized chronological ages. Data are means ± SEM.

Whipp, & Wasserman, 1984; Gaisl & Buchberger, 1984), whereas in this study the active boys showed an increase in $\dot{V}_E T/\dot{V}O_2$max.

On the basis of evidence in the literature a high relative threshold ($\dot{V}_E T/\dot{V}O_2$max) might be expected for boys. Generally, circulatory systems of small animals can deliver oxygen to muscle fast enough to avoid using muscle glycogen anaerobically. In children compared to adults, factors of O_2 transport (a greater blood flow per kilogram of muscle; Koch, 1980) and greater O_2 utilization (more oxidative enzymatic profile of muscle, Eriksson et al., 1972) would be expected to delay the onset of exercise-induced metabolic acidosis. At a given relative physiologic strain in the child compared to the adult the reliance on anaerobic pathways is not as great. The result is a lower blood lactate concentration and [H⁺]. The mean relative $V_E T$ for boys throughout this study (56 to 62%) and data from the literature were slightly higher than reported for young adults (50 to 55%, Davis, 1985; McLellan & Skinner, 1981). On the other hand, the boys of this study and others (Gaisl & Buchberger, 1984) were active, but the $\dot{V}_E T$ was lower than in active adults (70%, Davis, 1985).

Although, as described, both $\dot{V}O_2max$ and $\dot{V}_ET$ were highly correlated with height and weight across the age span, the scaling factors with weight were greater than expected for muscle mass gain alone (0.75), wherein they were of the magnitude corresponding to the expected gain for muscle force change (1.0). Thus, the increases in $\dot{V}O_2max$ and $\dot{V}_ET$ appeared greater than that attributable to gains of muscle mass, but $\dot{V}_ET$ did not show a growth function curve coincident with greater growth at age of PHV, unlike that for $\dot{V}O_2max$. These longitudinal data suggest that although the relation with size is a determinant of $\dot{V}_ET$ during growth, other factors of physical activity, hormonal influences, or other physiological changes with growth have important influence on $\dot{V}_ET$. The findings also suggest that growth and training influences alter $\dot{V}_ET$ independently of the alterations in $\dot{V}O_2max$.

Anaerobic Capacity

The measurement of anaerobic capacity (AnC) is not without problems. The concept of oxygen debt and postexercise blood lactate representing the level of oxygen not paid for during the exercise has been challenged. Blood lactate measures are subject to question regarding production versus removal, equilibration between muscle and blood, and uneven distribution in body fluid compartments. Blood lactate also may be elevated without "anaerobic glycolysis" (Brooks & Gaesser, 1980; Gaesser & Brooks, 1984). The relationship of recovery O_2 to previous use of anaerobic sources or an oxygen deficit also has been questioned (Brooks & Gaesser; Gaesser & Brooks). Recovery O_2 also includes demands for restoration of myoglobin O_2 stores, dissolved O_2 in tissues, venous oxyhemoglobin, and for increased metabolic levels associated with catecholamine production, higher body temperature, and increased ventilation and circulation. The measures of recovery O_2 and blood lactate can provide a qualitative estimate of AnC.

Notwithstanding these very important problems, information can be extracted from these measures taken in a longitudinal study. A recent study (Paterson, Cunningham, & Bumstead, 1986) has described the rate of development of anaerobic capacity during adolescence and the relationship to chronological or maturative age.

As part of the larger longitudinal study on 81 boys, recovery O_2 (or O_2 debt) and blood lactate (La, mmol • l^{-1}) were measured on 19 boys following supramaximal treadmill tests (20% grade) designed to stress the anaerobic energy systems maximally. AnC improved from age 11 to 15 years as indicated by a tripling of recovery O_2 (l), an 80% increase in recovery O_2 per kg (Figure 5), and a 45% rise in [La] (Figure 6). Changes were similar from year to year with average yearly increments in recovery O_2 of 0.8 l or 9 ml • kg^{-1} and in [La] of 0.9 mmol • l^{-1}. Individual data were plotted in relation to age of peak height velocity (PHV, 12.9 ± 1.2 years). Changes in the measures of AnC were not significantly different when related to biological rather than chronological age. Development of AnC did not show a growth function curve and was not closely correlated with size. The development of AnC was not changed immediately following maturation. Thus, in this longitudinal study, recovery O_2 and [La] as measures of AnC showed large increases from age 11 to 15 years, but the gains were similar year to year and, unlike the changes in $\dot{V}O_2$max, were not related to growth per se. Similar findings have been published in a cross-sectional study (Blimkie, Cunningham, & Leung, 1978). Hormonal influences at maturation could not account for the observed changes.

Summary

These longitudinal growth studies have provided a unique means to investigate the changes in functional characteristics of the gas transport systems. In particular, the influences of periods of rapid growth can be analyzed rather than relationships with size alone (as in cross-sectional studies). In the studies of active boys, maximal oxygen uptake was observed to increase across age, whereas studies of very sedentary children demonstrate a decrease in this function during adolescence. In addition, $\dot{V}O_2$max in early and late maturing active boys reached a similar value at maturity. Ventilation threshold in very active boys increased with growth, similar to that of $\dot{V}O_2$max. The rate of change, however, was significantly greater in $\dot{V}_ET$. The ratio of $\dot{V}_ET/\dot{V}O_2$max increased with age (11 to 15 years). Measures of anaerobic capacity (O_2 debt and [La]) indicated very large changes across age in addition to that associated with size alone.

References

Andersen, B., & Froberg, K. (1980). Maximal oxygen uptake and lactate concentration in highly trained and normal boys during puberty. *Acta Physiologica Scandinavica*, **108**, 37A.

Andrew, G.M., Becklake, M.R., Guleria, J.S., & Bates, D.V. (1972). Heart and lung functions in swimmers and non-athletes during growth. *Journal of Applied Physiology*, **32**, 245-251.

Blimkie, C.J.R., Cunningham, D.A., & Leung, F. (1978). Urinary catecholamine excretion during competition in 11 to 23 year old hockey players. *Medicine and Science in Sports and Exercise*, **10**, 183-193.

Boileau, R.A., Bonen, A., Heyward, V.H., & Massey, B.H. (1977). Maximal aerobic capacity on the treadmill and bicycle ergometer of boys 11-14 years of age. *Journal of Sports Medicine and Physical Fitness*, **7**, 153-162.

Brooks, G.A., & Gaesser, G.A. (1980). End points of lactic acid and glucose metabolism after exhausting exercise. *Journal of Applied Physiology*, **49**, 1057-1069.

Cooper, D.M., Weiler-Ravell, D., Whipp, B.J., & Wasserman, K. (1984). Aerobic parameters of exercise as a function of body size during growth in children. *Journal of Applied Physiology: Respiratory, Environmental and Exercise Physiology,* **56**, 628-634.

Cunningham, D.A., & Paterson, D.H. (1985). Age specific prediction of maximal oxygen uptake in boys. *Canadian Journal of Applied Sport Sciences,* **10**, 75-80.

Cunningham, D.A., Paterson, D.H., & Blimkie, C.J.R. (1984). The development of the cardiorespiratory system with growth and physical activity. In R.A. Boileau (Ed.), *Advances in pediatric sport sciences: Vol 1. Biological issues* (pp. 85-116). Champaign, IL: Human Kinetics.

Cunningham, D.A., Paterson, D.H., Blimkie, C.J.R., & Donner, A.P. (1984). Development of cardiorespiratory function in circumpubertal boys: A longitudinal study. *Journal of Applied Physiology: Respiratory, Environmental and Exercise Physiology,* **56**, 302-307.

Cunningham, D.A., Stapleton, J.J., MacDonald, I.C., & Paterson, D.H. (1981). Daily energy expenditure of young boys as related to maximal aerobic power. *Canadian Journal of Applied Sport Sciences,* **6**, 207-211.

Cunningham, D.A., Van Waterschoot, B.M., Paterson, D.H., Lefcoe, M., & Sangal, S.P. (1977). Reliability and reproducibility of maximal oxygen uptake measurements in children. *Medicine and Science in Sports and Exercise,* **9**, 104-108.

Davis, J.A. (1985). Anaerobic threshold: Review of the concept and directions for future research. *Medicine and Science in Sports and Exercise,* **17**, 6-18.

Eriksson, B.O. (1972). Physical training, oxygen supply and muscle metabolism in 11-13 year old boys. *Acta Physiologica Scandinavica* (Suppl. 384), 1-48.

Gaesser, G.A., & Brooks, G.A. (1984). Metabolic bases of excess post-exercise oxygen consumption: A review. *Medicine and Science in Sports and Exercise,* **16**, 29-43.

Gaisl, G., & Buchberger, J. (1984). Changes in the aerobic-anaerobic transition in boys after 3 years in special education. In J. Ilmarinen & I. Valimaki (Eds.), *Children and sport* (pp. 156-161). New York: Springer-Verlag.

Hamilton, P., & Andrew, G.M. (1976). Influence of growth and athletic training on heart and lung functions. *European Journal of Applied Physiology and Occupational Physiology,* **36**, 27-28.

Kobayashi, K., Kitamura, K., Miura, M., Sodeyama, H., Murase, Y., Miyashita, M., & Matsui, H. (1978). Aerobic power as related to body growth and training in Japanese boys: A longitudinal study. *Journal of Applied Physiology: Respiratory, Environmental and Exercise Physiology,* **44**(5), 666-672.

Koch, G. (1980). Aerobic power, lung dimensions, ventilatory capacity and muscle blood flow in 12-16 year old boys with high physical activity. In K. Berg & B.O. Eriksson (Eds.), *Children and exercise IX* (pp. 99-108). Baltimore: University Park Press.

McLellan, T.M., & Skinner, J.S. (1981). The use of the aerobic threshold as a basis for training. *Canadian Journal of Applied Sport Sciences, 6,* 197-201.

Mirwald, R.L., Bailey, D.A., Cameron, N., & Rasmussen, R.L. (1981). Longitudinal comparison of aerobic power in active and inactive boys aged 7.0 to 17.0 years. *Annals of Human Biology, 8*(5), 405-414.

Paterson, D.H., Cunningham, D.A., & Bumstead, L.A. (1986). Recovery O_2 and blood lactic acid: Longitudinal analysis in boys aged 11 to 15 years. *European Journal of Applied Physiology and Occupational Physiology, 55,* 93-99.

Sprynarova, S. (1974). Longitudinal study of the influence of different physical activity programs on functional capacity of the boys from 11 to 18 years. *Acta Paediatrica Belgica, 28,* 204-213.

Yamaji, K., & Miyashita, M. (1977). Oxygen transport system during exhaustive exercise in Japanese boys. *European Journal of Applied Physiology and Occupational Physiology, 36,* 93-99.

PART V

Sport and the Female Athlete

Pubertal Development in Endurance-Trained Female Athletes

Alan D. Rogol

Although recreational sports have been available to young women for a number of years, competitive athletics and other strenuous training routines are relatively new. With these large numbers of girls, female adolescents, and adult women participating in sports activities, a new series of issues relating to the effects of such training on the reproductive cycle has been raised. These may be summarized by the following questions:

1. What are the effects of preadolescent endurance-type training on pubertal progression?
   - Is menarche delayed by endurance-type training?
   - Are physically active, later maturing girls more suited for, and thus, more successful in endurance-type events?
2. What are the effects of endurance-type training on the reproductive function of postmenarchal adolescent women?

Before I attempt to provide answers to these questions, I shall review the normal pubertal process in the female, paying particular attention to the broad range of timing of the individual pubertal stages.

Adolescent development has been extensively reviewed by Tanner and his colleagues (Marshall & Tanner, 1969, 1970; Tanner, 1962). This group of investigators has described a staging system that defines the normal progression of adolescent sexual development for boys and girls, as well as defining some of the variations (particularly in onset) that are considered to represent the range of normal. This method simply relies on a careful physical examination of the child or adolescent and does not require any endocrine laboratory or radiological studies. Children of both sexes are categorized by pubic hair development. In addition, girls are evaluated for breast changes and boys for testicular and phallic development.

The pubertal process is usually an orderly one that has a high degree of variability in its onset and completion. Once entrained, however, the variability between stages, although present, is much less. Given this basic format, one can then describe how adolescents mature and have a firm basis for accurately pinpointing aberrations in puberty development.

Table 1   Pubic Hair Development in the Female

Stage	Characteristics	Age (years) Mean [95% confidence limits]
I	Prepubertal; no sexual hair	
II	Sparse growth of long, slightly pigmented hair over mons veneris or labia majora	11.7 [9.2-14.1]
III	Further darkening and coarsening of hair with spread over the symphysis pubis	12.4 [10.2-14.6]
IV	Hair is adult in character but not in distribution; has not spread to medial surface of the thighs	13.0 [10.8-15.1]
V	Hair is adult with extension to the medial thighs	14.4 [12.2-16.7]

Table 2   Breast Development

Stage	Characteristics	Age (years) Mean [95% confidence limits]
I	Prepubertal	
II	Breast budding, widening of areola with elevation of the breast and papilla as a small mound	11.1 [9.0-13.3]
III	Continued enlargement of both breast and areola but without separation of their contours	12.2 [10.0-14.3]
IV	Formation of the areola and papilla as a secondary mound projecting above the contour of the breast	13.1 [10.8-15.3]
V	Adult; project of the papilla only with the areola recessed to the contour of the breast. Not all girls pass through Stage V; others may maintain Stage IV development	15.3 [11.9-18.8]

Adolescent Sexual Development

Pubic hair and breast development are divided into five stages of maturation, which are listed in Tables 1 and 2.

The greatest variation is in the age of onset of pubertal development—usually heralded as breast budding—although in 10 to 20% pubic hair will precede breast development (see Tables 1, 2, and 3). Once puberty has

Table 3   Typical Age Ranges for Normal Female Pubertal Development

Breast budding
Mean 11.2 years
95% confidence limits 9.0-13.3 years

Pubic and axillary hair (adrenarche)
Mean 11.7 years
95% confidence limits 9.3-14.1 years

Menarche
Mean 12.8 years
95% confidence limits 10.8-14.8 years

begun, most girls will experience menarche between 2 and 2-1/2 years after the onset of breast budding. In the United States the average age at menarche is 12.8 ± 1.2 (SD) years. A summary is provided in Figure 1.

These structural changes are the outward manifestations of the pubertal neuroendocrine developmental process and are roughly coordinated with the rising levels of circulating sex steroid hormones. The height spurt occurs relatively early for girls, and menarche is a relatively late development of the pubertal process attained well after the maximal growth velocity.

Puberty may be considered delayed in girls if they have not achieved breast budding by 13 years or if more than 5 years has elapsed between breast budding and menarche. If a girl has not begun breast development by 13 years, one should be suspicious of an abnormality in pubertal development. Any girl over 15 years who has not begun pubertal development should have further medical evaluation.

In addition to the impact of the physiological processes of puberty on athletic performance, one must also be cognizant of sociological factors. Malina and coworkers have substantially broadened the framework of the analysis of the interaction between training and puberty by formulating a two-part hypothesis (Malina, Spirduso, Tate, & Baylor, 1978). The available data suggest that delayed adolescent development is common in endurance-trained girls. The hypothesis developed suggests that the physical characteristics associated with delayed adolescent maturation in females are perhaps more suitable for successful athletic performance in selected sports activities. The later maturing adolescent girl is characteristically longer legged (lesser upper-segment-to-lower-segment ratio) and narrow hipped, has a more linear physique, less weight for height, and has less relative fatness than her early maturing peers. The second part of the hypothesis relates to the socialization process. The early maturing girl is perhaps socialized away from sports competition for a number of reasons. However, the later maturing adolescent may not experience these social pressures and may have increased motivation to compete based on success in her athletic competition.

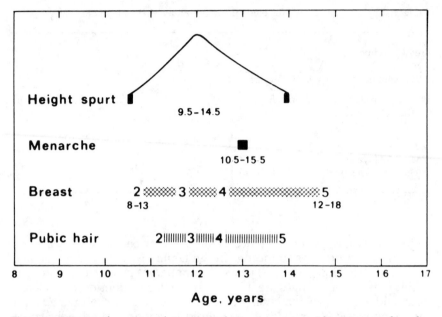

Figure 1 Diagram of sequence of events at puberty. An average girl is represented in relation to the scale of ages: The range of ages within which some of the changes occur is indicated by the figures below them. (Reproduced with permission from *Archives of Disease in Childhood*, **45**, 13-23.)

Physiology of the Menstrual Cycle

The function of the reproductive system results from the coordinated interaction of a number of structures: the cerebral cortex, hypothalamus, pituitary, and ovary. The focus of this section will be on the maturing neuroendocrine apparatus of child and adolescent. Those changes that are pertinent to this orderly process will be highlighted (Fitz & Speroff, 1983; Winter, Hughes, Reyes, & Faiman, 1976).

The cell bodies for the major collections of gonadotropin-releasing hormone (GnRH) neurons reside in the hypothalamus. Axons from these peptidergic neurons project into the median eminence to terminate upon the primary capillaries of the portal circulation. Axosomatic and axo-dendritic synapses from many ascending and descending neural tracts (bioaminergic and opiate neurons) impinge upon the GnRH neurons and tracts to modulate the delivery of the releasing hormone to the sinusoids of the anterior pituitary where it may interact with specific cell surface receptors on the gonadotrophs.

Fluctuations with time of luteinizing hormone (LH) concentrations in the circulation of GnRH in portal blood suggest intermittent pulsatile secretory discharges of GnRH from the hypothalamic neurons. The pulse generator is apparently located in the more anterior portions of the hypothalamus. The frequency and amplitude of the GnRH pulse may be dictated in part by the spontaneous activity of the pulse generator; however, the pattern of LH secretion is vitally dependent on the hormonal milieu as it affects the responsivity of the gonadotrophs. In the remaining portion of this section, the changes in responsivity of the hypothalamic-pituitary unit with maturation will be highlighted.

During the first 2 years the levels of LH are low and equivalent in boys and girls; however, the concentrations of follicle-stimulating hormone (FSH) are higher in girls than boys before the first 2 years. The levels of both hormones remain relatively constant until the pubertal rise as outlined below. The concentrations of the gonadal steroid hormones remain low throughout this period because of an operative and sensitive negative feedback effect on the hypothalamic pulse generator and/or on the gonadotrophs themselves.

As the onset of puberty approaches, the feedback sensitivity of the gonadal steroids on GnRH and the gonadotropins changes. No longer are the prepubertal gonadal steroid levels able to keep the GnRH neurons pulsing at a rate slow enough to allow FSH secretion to be greater than LH secretion. The pulse generator accelerates, the young adolescent has more secretory episodes of LH (and FSH), and greater amounts of the gonadotropins are secreted.

As the pubertal process continues, the gonads respond by increased steroid hormone production until a new "equilibrium" (set point) is reached and pulsatile gonadotropin secretion occurs at a frequency indicative of the adult. For men this rate is relatively constant, but for women the rate increases remarkably as ovulation is impending and slows substantially under the influence of progesterone in the luteal phase (Boyar et al., 1972; Jakacki et al., 1982; Kulin, 1974). The transition through puberty is not as simple as stated, however. The pulse generator begins its acceleration phase only at night so that the early prepubertal child has pulsatile gonadotropin secretion during sleep. Pulsations subsequently begin to appear during the day, but there are still day-night differences with a greater proportion of gonadotropin secreted at night. By late mid-puberty, the day-night differences disappear.

Nutrition and the Reproductive System

In lower animals, subhuman primates, and humans there is a very strong dependence of reproductive system function upon adequate nutrition. The timing of the onset of puberty is more closely related to the body weight (nutritional status) than to chronological age (Frisch & Revelle, 1970; Kennedy & Mitra, 1963). Studies in humans first implicated a threshold body weight and then a minimum percentage of body fat as important metabolic signals determining the onset of puberty in girls (Frisch & MacArthur, 1974). More recent reports suggest that this concept is too simple to explain the physiology of pubertal development, although there is a strikingly significant association between the onset of puberty and the attainment of a specific body weight or percentage body fat. If the attainment of a specific body weight or fat composition does not "explain" the physiology of adolescent development, what other signals might be implicated in the maturation of the reproductive axis?

Recent studies in the monkey have suggested that certain hormones or metabolic substrates such as insulin, glucose, amino acids, beta-hydroxybutyrate, or glycerol, acting as humoral derivatives of body mass, might serve as important cues to the reproductive axis to stimulate the onset of puberty. It has been suggested that changes in the concentrations of these metabolic fuels that occur during the transition from childhood to adult provide such a signal to the neuroendocrine centers that regulate reproduction function (Steiner, Cameron, McNeill, Clifton, & Bremner, 1983). The signal could be correlated with the decreasing sensitivity of the hypothalamic GnRH neurons to the feedback inhibition of gonadal steroid hormones.

In the human, puberty and the restoration of cyclic reproductive function can be negatively correlated with either decreased caloric intake or with increases in physical exertion. During starvation, the "nonessential" or potentially detrimental processes (e.g., gonadotropin secretion) are decreased, whereas those essential for survival (e.g., ACTH or thyroxine secretion) are retained. Delay in pubertal development during famine and the restriction of fertility to the few months of adequate nutrition have been noted for the nomadic Kung San hunter gatherers.

Energy expenditure itself or in concert with low body weight and low percentage body fat can delay pubertal development in adolescent female dancers and endurance-training athletes. The effects of exercise on pubertal development must be assessed with respect to the variations described within the nontraining majority of children. For boys this task is complicated by several factors. First, there is great variability in the onset of the puberty process with constitutional delay of growth and adolescence prevalent. Second, most athletic endeavors for male adolescents depend heavily on strength and power. The boy with delayed pubertal development is at a distinct disadvantage in this regard.

There are preliminary data to show that boys who purposefully reduce caloric intake (e.g., in the weight-related sports such as wrestling) have reduced growth during the competitive season. However, there are not any studies that show effects upon sexual maturation. It is not presently known whether there are long-term effects of reduced caloric intake on ultimate height and development; however, they must be minimal considering the number of participants in sports requiring rigid weight control or weight loss during the season. In the adult male, however, malnutrition can cause a decrease in gonadal function just as it does in the adolescent female with anorexia nervosa.

One can more readily assess the impact of exercise on the onset and progression of the pubertal process in girls because early pubertal development does not confer an advantage in many sports. Quite the contrary may be true for sports like gymnastics or ballet in which the prepubertal body configuration and flexibility may confer an advantage. A number of investigators have attempted to ascertain if prepubertal or peripubertal exercise and training affect the menarche. In the early 1970s, Malina et al. (1978) showed that track athletes had a later onset of menses than the more sedentary control women, and Olympic athletes, presumably more highly trained women, had later menarche than high school or college athletes.

Warren (1980) and Frisch, Wyshak, and Vincent (1980) have more intensively studied the onset and progression of pubertal development in groups of young women ballet dancers. There are unequivocal data that menarche is delayed by 1 to 3 years among these dancers, and secondary amenorrhea is quite prevalent. Warren has carefully distinguished between delayed puberty and adrenarche. She found that her group of dancers had delayed breast development and menarche (mediated by ovarian steroid hormones) but normal pubic hair development (mediated by adrenal androgenic steroids). This condition is one of several in which there is seen a dissociation of adrenarche from menarche. In addition, the young women had increased long bone growth, seemingly an asset for these performers. Although the data are not in question, the underlying mechanism is not clearly defined. Because some of these young women dancers rapidly progressed through puberty or attained menarche when forced to stop exercising (usually due to an injury) without change in body weight or body fat composition, Warren favors the hypothesis that it is the energy drain of training and competition rather than body weight or body fat composition as the proximate cause of delayed menarche.

Prepubertally training women swimmers and runners were also evaluated by Frisch and coworkers who noted delayed menarche when compared to women who began training after puberty. These investigators noted a 0.4-year delay in menarche for every 1 year of prepubertal training (Frisch, Gotz-Welbergen, & McArthur, 1982). The implication is that puberty was delayed in these athletes because of the early onset of training. However, it is also possible that the body habitus that is conducive to success at these athletic endeavors is also susceptible to delayed pubertal development.

Do these natural activities of young women have detrimental longer term reproductive consequences? There are anecdotal data that should reassure these young women that after they diminish their exercise load they are not at greater risk for reproductive system dysfunction than nonstrenuously exercising women. One should remember, however, that this self-selected group of women may be at greater risk for reproductive system dysfunction than the nonexercising group. Certainly, if fertility is not desired, it is prudent to employ some form of birth control since "athletic amenorrhea" is not absolute.

Cessation of menses is the most obvious effect of endurance training on the reproductive system; however, more subtle effects such as luteal phase defects and chronic anovulation can occur with regular or mildly irregular cyclic vaginal bleeding. A wide range for the prevalence of athletic amenorrhea has been reported: 1 to 43% compared to 2 to 5% in the general population (Abraham, Beaumont, Fraser, & Llewellyn-Jones, 1982; Dale, Gerlach, & Wilhite, 1979; Feicht, Johnson, Martin, Sparkes, & Wagner, 1978; Malina, Harper, Avent, & Campbell, 1973; Rebar & Cumming, 1981). This broad range is mainly due to methodological limitations; the definition of amenorrhea varies from 4 to 12 months, and there are wide variations in age, gynecological age, prior menstrual status, coincident health problems, ascertainment criteria, as well as training duration and intensity. Younger competitive athletes have noted a much higher incidence than older, recreational joggers.

Collectively, available cross-sectional studies indicate that the incidence of amenorrhea is considerably higher in young, intensively training competitive athletes than in the general population. Thus, some factor(s) during endurance training seems to disrupt the reproductive system in a significant number of young female athletes.

Specific Abnormalities in Reproduction Function Described in Female Athletes

Alterations in ovarian steroid hormone levels without changes in gonadotropin levels may occur acutely with exercise (Bonen et al., 1979; Jurkowski, Jones, Walker, Younglar, & Sutton, 1978). Increases in testosterone and prolactin have been noted (Boyden et al., 1982). Cumming and Rebar (1983) prospectively evaluated anterior pituitary and gonadal responses to graded bicycle exercise in five normally menstruating runners and six amenorrheic runners. Although these data described acute changes in hormonal levels, such changes are not necessarily pathogenetic to amenorrhea or directly pertinent to long-term cumulative effects of exercise on the reproductive system. Caspar, Wilkinson, and Cotterell (1984) have considered that endurance training chronically increases the metabolic clearance of gonadal steroids (but not gonadotropins).

Boyden et al. (1982) and Boyden, Pamenter, Stanforth, Rotkis, and Wilmore (1983, 1984) have shown that a running program results in frequent menstrual alteration (all but one of the subjects had menstrual changes; none was amenorrheic). These investigators did not address the issue of intensity of training.

Many have studied the relationship between exercise and amenorrhea. However, we believe that existing epidemiologic data are difficult and often impossible to compare because the definition of amenorrhea has ranged from 4 to 12 months, and timing, intensity, duration, and quantity of exercise have been highly variable. Although prevalence figures are difficult to interpret, some women experience no or slight alteration in cycle length, whereas others clearly develop prolonged intermenstrual intervals or become amenorrheic as they endurance train. Although several prospective studies of the effect of exercise on acute hormonal changes have been reported (Boyden et al., 1982), none has been designed to prospectively and quantitatively measure the effects of long-term, graded endurance training on the reproductive axis.

A more subtle abnormality is the defective (or inadequate) luteal phase (Sherman & Korenman, 1974a; Sherman & Korenman, 1974b). It may represent a proximate cause of infertility. Short luteal phase cycles have been suggested in marathon runners (Shangold & Levine, 1982), but methodologic limitations are severe (Bauman, 1981). In a single runner the luteal phase shortened as training mileage increased (Shangold, Freeman, Thysen, & Gotz, 1979). Histological confirmation with serum progesterone levels and reversibility of the abnormalities have been described in two runners (Prior, Yuen, Clement, Bowie, & Thomas, 1982). Sherman and Korenman (1974a, 1974b) have shown that the short luteal phase may be incorporated into normal cycles. Bonen and Keizer (1984) have shown severely abbreviated luteal phases (5.3 ± 2.1 days) in female athletes. However, the mechanisms for this type of menstrual abnormality in endurance-trained athletes are not known, nor has anyone documented the reversible emergence of this abnormality as a woman trains.

Are menstrual cycle changes reversible? In the studies to date, reversibility of the gonadal axis defects has been assumed, but not proven, except in two marathon runners (Prior et al., 1982). The following observations suggest that secondary amenorrhea related to exercise may be temporary (Baker, 1981): (a) When training is interrupted, long-distance runners and ballet dancers resume menses without change in weight; (b) when training intensity is decreased below a "critical level," menses returns; (c) resolution of amenorrhea occurs in rowers after the end of rowing season (Erdelyi, 1962); and (d) normal reproductive function is expressed in young female swimmers 10 years after training (Eriksson et al., 1978).

Reproductive System Function
in Amenorrheic Long-Distance Runners

Before attempting to study the changes in reproductive system function in prepubertal and peripubertal adolescent females, we undertook a cross-sectional study in highly endurance-trained adult female athletes (Veldhuis et al., 1985). We reasoned that if we could not define an alteration in the hypothalamic-pituitary-ovarian axis in this highly selected group, we would have great difficulty in defining alterations in less severely exercising girls and women.

To search for evidence of a measurable alteration in gonadotropin secretion in long-distance runners, we evaluated women with an unambiguously abnormal pattern of menstruation that developed in association with strenuous training. Strenuous training was defined as running at least 20 mi/week for the preceding 6 months on a regular basis. Abnormal menses included either secondary amenorrhea (0 to 1 spontaneous menses per year) or severe oligomenorrhea (2 to 3 menses per year). Seven women had a history of normal menstrual cycles prior to the onset of training. Two women began vigorous exercise before menarche and had delayed menarche (Table 4, Subjects VI and IX), but their menses resumed during periods of inactivity. Among all runners, the historically ascertained degree of weight loss after initiation of training was 3 to

Table 4   Clinical Characteristics of Women Runners

	Age at study	Age at menarche	Years of training	Training[a] mileage	Wt (kg)	Ht (cm)	Menses per year	Body mass index[b]	Body fat[c] (%)
Runners									
I	28	13	6	20-35	48	163	0-1	18.1	14.5
II	25	14	2	30-40	49	162	1-2	18.7	13.6
III	21	14	5	30-54	59	167	1-2	21.2	16.7
IV	18	14	5	30-45	56	169	2-3	19.6	17.4
V	19	13	4	30	64	166	0-1	23.2	—[d]
VI	21	17	10	40-70	62	163	0-1	23.3	11.2
VII	27	13	1.5	24-32	62	161	2-3	23.9	14.1
VIII	29	12	3	20-40	53	164	0-1	19.7	12.0
IX	27	16.5	15	40-60	55	162	2-3	21.0	16.7
Means	23.9	14.1	5.7	20-70	56.4	161	0-3	21.0	14.5
±SD	±4.2	±1.7	±4.2	(range)	±5.7	±9.6	(range)	±0.21	±2.4
Control women									
N = 10	27.1	12.8	NA	NA	63.0	168	11-13	22.4	24.0
(±SD)	±3.4	±0.60			±12.0	±6.9	(range)	±3.4	±4.7

Note. [a]Miles run per week on average in the 6 months preceding study. [b]Weight (kg)/height (m^2). [c]Estimated from skinfold thickness; see text. [d]Not available. NA = not applicable.

9 lb (range), but weight had been stable in each (± 3 lb) prior to study. Ten normally cycling women were studied in the early follicular phase (3 to 6 days after the onset of menses) to provide control subjects. The control women engaged in no strenuous activity or training routines exceeding 20 min three times per week. Oligomenorrheic runners also were studied days 3 to 6 after onset of their menses.

Clinical and Baseline Endocrine Characteristics of the Runners

The mean age of the women runners was 24 years (control women, 27 years), with a mean age at menarche in runners of 14 years (control, 12.8 years). The exercising women had trained for 6 years prior to entry in the study, with typical weekly training mileages of 20 to 70 (range). Their average body weight was 56 kg, and their height was 161 cm, compared to 63 kg and 168 cm in control women. The runners had 0 to 3 spontaneous menstrual cycles per year. The individual characteristics of each runner are shown in Table 4.

The body mass index, used as one indicator of relative obesity or leanness, averaged 21.0 in the women runners, compared to 22.4 in the normally cycling control women. Estimates of percentage body fat from skinfold thickness averaged 14.5 in running and 24.0 in control women. The percentage body fat did not correlate significantly with LH pulse frequency or amplitude or mean serum LH or estradiol concentrations. Serum concentrations of total and free testosterone were normal in each runner. As shown in Table 5, the runners had an average serum estradiol concentration of 52.3 pg/ml, which did not differ significantly from that of the control women: 80.9 pg/ml. In all women in both groups, the serum progesterone concentration was less than 1 ng/ml at the time of study.

The 24-hr mean serum LH concentrations in the running women averaged 6.61 mIU/ml, and the 24-hr integrated serum concentrations averaged 9,367 area units. These values were not significantly different from those in the normal women in the early follicular phase, in whom the respective 24-hr mean and integrated LH levels were 8.00 mIU/ml and 11,172 area units. Individual 24-hr mean and integrated LH concentrations for the runners are given in Table 5.

Six women runners had decreased LH pulse frequency, with individual values of 2, 3, 1, 5, 4, or 6 pulses/24 hr (Figure 2). None of the 10 control women studied in the early follicular phase, when serum estradiol and LH concentrations were similar to those in runners, had fewer than 8 pulses/24 hr. The control women had a mean LH pulse frequency of 10.5 (absolute pulse frequency range, 8 to 15 pulses/24 hr). Although 3 of the women runners had normal pulse frequencies of 12, 15, and 13 pulses/24 hr, we could not distinguish these individuals from those with decreased pulse frequency on the basis of serum estradiol concentrations or mean LH levels.

The patterns of LH pulses during the 24 hr of sampling in 4 long-distance runners are illustrated in Figure 3, A to D. In Panel A, a normal

Table 5   Properties of Pulsatile LH Secretion in Long-Distance Women Runners

Runners	Serum E$_2$ (pg/ml)	Mean LH[a] (mIU/ml)	LH area[b]	LH pulse frequency[c]	LH pulse (%)	Amplitude (mIU/ml)
I	74	8.22 ± 0.74	11,643	2	329	22
II	31	3.94 ± 0.09	5,615	3	75	2.9
III	48	5.43 ± 0.13	7,692	1	139	6.4
IV	71	7.90 ± 0.33	11,210	12	81	4.3
V	38	4.74 ± 0.32	6,668	15	122	5.3
VI	92	8.51 ± 0.26	12,007	13	81	5.0
VII	54	7.71 ± 0.27	10,989	5	97	4.9
VIII	38	6.38 ± 0.62	9,052	4	83	3.7
IX	25	6.64 ± 0.15	9,429	6	58	3.2
Means ± SEM	52.3 ± 7.5	6.61 ± 0.54	9,367 ± 770	(6.8 ± 1.7)	118 ± 28	6.4 ± 2.0
Control women	80.9 ± 11.0	8.00 ± 1.40	11,172 ± 2,030	10.5 ± 0.6	87 ± 7	4.3 ± 0.82

Note. [a]Mean (±SEM) of 72 individual LH values collected by sampling every 20 min for 24 hr. [b]mIU/ml × min. [c]Number of LH pulses/24 hr.

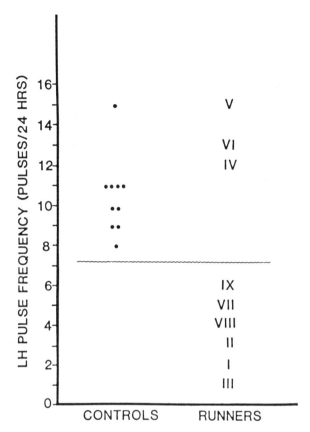

Figure 2 Distribution of LH pulse frequency in 10 control women and 9 severely oligomenor-rheic long-distance women runners. Control women were normally cycling individuals studied in the early follicular phase. Individual dots (left panel) denote LH pulse frequencies for the 10 control women. Roman numerals (right panel) denote LH pulse frequencies for the individual runners. LH pulse frequency (ordinate) is expressed as the number of LH pulses present per 24 hr. (Reproduced with permission from *Journal of Clinical Endocrinology and Metabolism, 61,* 557-563.)

LH pulse profile in Runner VI is depicted. In contrast, the striking patterns of reduced LH pulse frequency that characterized Runners III, II, and I are shown in Panels B, C, and D.

Spontaneous LH pulse amplitude was normal in all long-distance runners (Table 5), whether expressed as a fractional or absolute increment. For example, when LH pulse amplitude was calculated as a percentage increase above nadir, there was no significant difference between control and running women (87 and 118%, respectively) (see Table 5). Similarly, when spontaneous LH pulse amplitude was computed as a mIU/ml increment from the preceding nadir to peak, the control and running women also did not differ significantly (4.3 mIU/ml in control and 6.4 mIU/ml in running women, respectively).

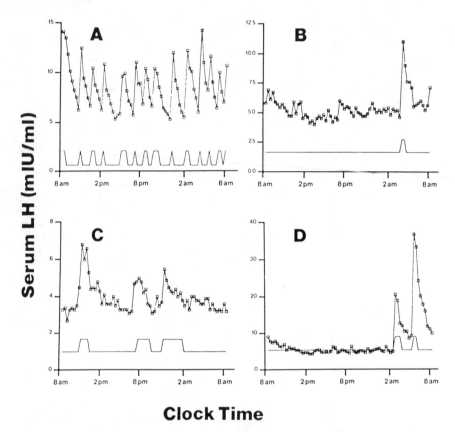

Figure 3   Individual LH pulse profiles in four representative long-distance runners. LH concentrations were measured in serum collected at 20-min intervals for 24 hr. The subsequent LH series were analyzed for LH pulses. The horizontal axis indicates time and the vertical axis the serum immunoactive LH concentration in mIU/ml. Panels A through D present the pulse patterns for Runners VI, III, II, and I, respectively. At the lower portion of each graph, the solid line schematizes the pulses detected by the computer program, indicating each pulse by an upward and subsequent downward deflection of the baseline. (Reproduced with permission from *Journal of Endocrinology and Metabolism, 61,* 557-563.)

Pituitary responsiveness to exogenous GnRH was assessed by infusing increasing graded doses (2.5, 5.0, 10, and 25 μg) of GnRH from submaximal to near-maximal doses as pulses every 2 hr. This schedule elicited a progressive increase in serum LH concentrations in control and in running women (see Figure 4). Peak serum LH levels, whether expressed as a percentage or as mIU/ml increase above basal, in response to the GnRH pulses were significantly higher in women runners than control women at the three lower (submaximal) doses of GnRH. This difference was found for each runner except Subjects VI and IX, who had normal but not accentuated responses. The two lowest GnRH doses also resulted in significantly greater responses in runners when the LH responses were

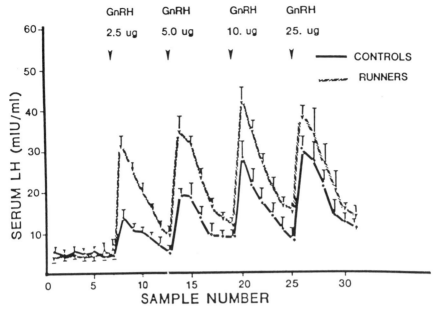

Figure 4 Mean (±SEM) serum LH before and after graded doses of gonadotropin-releasing hormone (GnRH). Control women (N = 10) and women runners (N = 9) were sampled at 20-min intervals for 10 hr before and after increasing doses of GnRH (2.5 μg, 5 μg, 10 μg, and 25 μg), given as bolus iv doses at 2-hr intervals. When the control women were compared with the long-distance runners with respect to peak serum LH concentrations attained after each pulse of GnRH, these groups differed significantly at GnRH doses of 2.5 μg ($p < .005$), 5 μg ($p < .01$), and 10 μg ($p < .03$). (Reproduced with permission from *Journal of Endocrinology and Metabolism*, **61**, 557-563.)

expressed as areas (or percentage increases in area) under the 2-hr time curves following each dose of GnRH and subjected to analysis of variance.

In the 6 runners with diminished spontaneous LH pulsatile release, sufficient serum was available from the exogenous GnRH infusion to assess ovarian estradiol secretion in response to pulsed increases in LH concentrations. These runners had normal progressive (fractional) elevations in serum estradiol concentrations during the infusion of graded pulses of GnRH. Absolute peak serum estradiol levels (pg/ml) attained after induced endogenous LH pulses were also normal in the runners.

The mean serum concentration of prolactin in the 6 runners with reduced LH pulse frequency was 10.1 g/ml when calculated from 24 hr of sampling (normal range, 3 to 18 ng/ml). In addition, the 24-hr mean FSH concentrations in these 6 runners averaged 8.68 mIU/ml (normal 3 to 12 mIU/ml).

This study was designed to test the hypothesis that pulsatile LH release is altered in long-distance running women with secondary amenorrhea or severe oligomenorrhea. LH pulse frequency was clearly decreased in certain long-distance runners with secondary amenorrhea or severe

Table 6   Possible Mechanisms for Hypogonadism in Endurance-Trained Athletes

---

Brain mechanisms
  Altered frequency or amplitude of basal pulsatile gonadotropic secretion
  Loss of estrogenic positive feedback
  Enhanced sensitivity to estrogenic negative feedback
Pituitary mechanisms
  Impaired synthesis/release of gonadotropins
  Biologically subactive gonadotropins
Gonadal mechanisms
  Diminished target-organ sensitivity
Other
  Hyperprolactinemia (multiple mechanisms)
  Beta-endorphin hypersecretion
  Altered aromatization of androgens
  Variable metabolic clearance rates of gonadal steroid hormones

---

oligomenorrhea. This attenuation of LH pulse frequency was not associated with any decline in spontaneous LH pulse amplitude or any decrease in pituitary responsiveness to exogenous GnRH. Rather, women distance runners had enhanced LH release in response to submaximally effective pulses of endogenous GnRH. Hence, we attribute reduced spontaneous LH pulse frequency in these women to an alteration in hypothalamic regulatory center(s) that control the episodic release of endogenous GnRH.

The proximate endocrine basis for diminished pulsatile release of LH in these severely oligomenorrheic long-distance women runners is not known. However, this neuroendocrine alteration seems to represent a feature of strenuous exercise, rather than the amenorrheic state per se, because Cumming et al. recently reported diminished LH pulsatility in regularly menstruating runners (Cumming, Vickovic, Wall, & Fluker, 1985). Based on the available literature, several pathophysiologic mechanisms may be considered (Table 6). First, endogenous opiate peptides suppress episodic LH secretion (Veldhuis, Rogol, Johnson, & Dufau, 1983), and exercise or physical conditioning increases circulating (but not necessarily hypothalamic) concentrations of opiates such as beta endorphin (Carr et al., 1981; Colt, Wardlaw, & Frantz, 1981). In addition, in one of 3 women runners, infusion of an opiate antagonist, naloxone, augmented serum LH concentrations (McArthur et al., 1980), but this accentuated response was not found in another study of 4 amenorrheic runners (Cumming et al., 1985) or 5 men who competed at marathon or greater distances (Rogol, Veldhuis, Williams, & Johnson, 1984). Second, increased concentrations of prolactin or sex steroid hormone, such as progesterone and testosterone, might suppress LH pulse frequency (Buckman, Peake, & Strivastava, 1981; Chang, Richards, Kim, & Malarkey, 1984; Goodman & Karsch, 1980; Loucks & Hovarth, 1984). However, the present runners had normal mean 24-hr serum prolactin concentrations and normal follicular phase progesterone and free testosterone concentrations. And third, epidemiological studies suggest that nutritional or psychological factors and the effects of energy drain may be implicated as causes of amenorrhea (Warren, 1980). The women studied here did have significantly decreased estimated percentage body fat. However, percentage body fat did not correlate significantly with any parameter of LH release, and the leanest runner (11.2% body fat vs. 24.0% in control women) had a normal pattern of LH pulsations (Panel A, Figure 4). Although lack of significant correlations could reflect the relatively small number of runners studied, the precise mechanism(s) by which altered body composition might influence the brain's regulation of pulsatile LH release is not known.

The present study documents mean serum immunoactive LH and FSH levels comparable to those of normally cycling women studied in the early follicular phase. These observations in runners differ from those in patients with anorexia nervosa or weight loss, in whom hypogonadotropism and hypoestrogenism occur. In contrast, basal serum estradiol concentrations were in the normal early to midfollicular phase range in this study and increased appropriately in response to GnRH-induced endogenous pulses of LH.

Sampling for 24-hr intervals also disclosed that LH pulses were restricted to the hours of sleep in two women runners. This pattern is reminiscent of that in puberty (Boyar, Katz et al., 1974; Judd, Parker, Siler, & Yen, 1974) and in some patients with anorexia nervosa (Boyar, Rosenfield et al., 1974). The importance of this observation in some runners is not known, and a common pathophysiological link, if any, among puberty, anorexia nervosa, and running has not been defined.

The present studies were conducted on a relatively small population of strenuously exercising young women with a history of normal menses when not actively training and with minimally reduced body weight. Endocrine results in these subjects would not necessarily typify those in other athletes who were of different ages, had significantly decreased body weight, lesser degrees of aerobic exercise, a history of menstrual irregularity before exercise, or preserved menstrual cyclicity despite physical training. Therefore, additional studies will ultimately be needed in larger groups of runners to assess the generality of our observations. Moreover, prospective studies using graded exercise regimens will be required to assess the exact "dose" effect of aerobic exercise on neuroendocrine function of the gonadal axis. The present results help to identify one discrete end point (i.e., the pulsatile mode of LH release) that would be pertinent to assess in such further investigations.

Summary

Certain long-distance women runners with secondary amenorrhea or severe oligomenorrhea have an unambiguous decrease in pulsatile LH secretion, despite normal mean serum gonadotropin, prolactin, and sex steroid levels. The reduction in LH pulse frequency in these runners was associated with normal or increased pituitary responsiveness to GnRH and intact acute ovarian estradiol secretion in response to GnRH-induced endogenous LH release. These observations point to an alteration in the brain's regulation of pulsatile LH secretion.

References

Abraham, S.F., Beaumont, F.J.V., Fraser, I.S., & Llewellyn-Jones, D.E. (1982). Body weight, exercise and menstrual status among ballet dancers in training. *British Journal of Obstetrics and Gynaecology,* **89,** 507-510.

Baker, E.R. (1981). Menstrual dysfunction and hormonal status in athletic women: A review. *Fertility and Sterility,* **36,** 691-696.

Bauman, J.E. (1981). Basal body temperature: Unreliable method of ovulation detection. *Fertility and Sterility,* **36,** 729-733.

Bonen, A., & Keizer, H.A. (1984). Athletic menstrual cycle irregularity: Endocrine response to exercise and training. *The Physician and Sportsmedicine,* **12,** 78-94.

Bonen, A., Ling, W.Y., MacIntire, K.P., Neil, R., McGrail, J.C., & Belcastro, A.N. (1979). Effects of exercise on serum concentrations of FSH, LH, progesterone and estradiol. *European Journal of Applied Physiology and Occupational Physiology,* **42,** 15-23.

Boyar, R., Finkelstein, J., Roffwarg, H., Kapen, S., Weitzman, E., & Hellman, L. (1972). Synchronization of augmented luteinizing hormone secretion with sleep during puberty. *New England Journal of Medicine,* **287,** 582-586.

Boyar, R.M., Katz, J., Finkelstein, J.W., Kapen, S., Weiner, H., Weitzman, E.D., & Hellman, L. (1974). Anorexia nervosa. Immaturity of the 24 hours luteinizing hormone secretory pattern. *New England Journal of Medicine,* **291,** 861-865.

Boyar, R.M., Rosenfield, R.S., Kapen, S., Finkelstein, J.W., Roffwarg, H.P., Weitzman, E.D., & Hellman, L. (1974). Simultaneous augmented secretion of luteinizing hormone and testosterone during sleep. *Journal of Clinical Investigation,* **54,** 609-618.

Boyden, T.W., Pamenter, R.W., Grosso, D., Stanforth, P., Rotkis, T., & Wilmore, J.H. (1982). Prolactin responses, menstrual cycles, and body composition of women runners. *Journal of Clinical Endocrinology & Metabolism,* **54,** 711-713.

Boyden, T.W., Pamenter, R.W., Stanforth, P., Rotkis, T.C., & Wilmore, J.H. (1983). Steroids and endurance running in women. *Fertility and Sterility,* **39,** 629-632.

Boyden, T.W., Pamenter, R.W., Stanforth, P., Rotkis, T.C., & Wilmore, J.H. (1984). Impaired gonadotropin responses to gonadotropin-releasing hormone stimulation in endurance-trained women. *Fertility and Sterility,* **41,** 359-363.

Buckman, M.T., Peake, G.T., & Srivastava, L. (1981). Patterns of spontaneous LH release in normo- and hyperprolactinaemic women. *Acta Endocrinologica*, **97**, 305-310.

Carr, D.B., Bullen, B.A., Skrinar, G.S., Arnold, M.A., Rosenblatt, M., Beitins, I.Z., Martin, J.B., & McArthur, J.W. (1981). Physical conditioning facilitates the exercise-induced secretion of beta-endorphin and beta-lipotropin in women. *New England Journal of Medicine*, **305**, 560-563.

Casper, R.F., Wilkinson, D., & Cotterell, M.A. (1984). The effect of increased cardiac output on luteal phase gonadal steroids: A hypothesis for runners amenorrhea. *Fertility and Sterility*, **41**, 364-368.

Chang, F.E., Richards, S.R., Kim, M.H., & Malarkey, W.B. (1984). Twenty-four hour prolactin profiles and prolactin response to dopamine in long-distance running women. *Journal of Clinical Endocrinology & Metabolism*, **59**, 631-635.

Colt, E.W.D., Wardlaw, S.L., & Frantz, A.F. (1981). The effect of running on plasma B-endorphin. *Life Sciences*, **28**, 1637-1640.

Cumming, D.C., & Rebar, R.W. (1983). Exercise and reproductive function in women. *American Journal of Industrial Medicine*, **4**, 113-125.

Cumming, D.C., Vickovic, M.M., Wall, S.R., & Fluker, M.R. (1985). Defects in pulsatile LH release in normally menstruating runners. *Journal of Clinical Endocrinology & Metabolism*, **60**, 810-812.

Dale, E., Gerlach, D.S., & Wilhite, A.L. (1979). Menstrual dysfunction in distance runners. *Obstetrics and Gynecology*, **54**, 47-53.

Erdelyi, G.J. (1962). Gynecological survey of female athletes. *Journal of Sports Medicine and Physical Fitness*, **2**, 174-179.

Eriksson, B.O., Engstrom, I., Karlberg, P., Lundin, A., Saltin, B., & Thoren, C. (1978). Long-term effect of previous swimtraining in girls. A 10-year follow-up of the "girl swimmers." *Acta Paediatrica Scandinavica*, **67**, 285-292.

Feicht, C.B., Johnson, T.S., Martin, B.J., Sparkes, K.E., & Wagner, W.W. (1978). Secondary amenorrhea in athletes. *Lancet*, **ii**, 1145-1146.

Fitz, M.A., & Speroff, L. (1983). Current concepts of the endocrine characteristics of normal menstrual function: The key to diagnosis and management of menstrual disorders. *Clinical Obstetrics and Gynecology*, **26**, 647-689.

Frisch, R.E., Gotz-Welbergen, A.V., & McArthur, J.W. (1982). Delayed menarche and amenorrhea in college athletes in relation to age of onset of training. *Journal of the American Medical Association*, **246**, 1559-1563.

Frisch, R.E., & MacArthur, J.W. (1974). Menstrual cycles: Fatness as a determinant of minimum weight for height necessary for their maintenance or onset. *Science*, **185**, 949-951.

Frisch, R.E., & Revelle, R. (1970). Height and weight at menarche and a hypothesis of critical body weights and adolescent events. *Science*, **169**, 397-399.

Frisch, R.E., Wyshak, G., & Vincent, L. (1980). Delayed menarche and amenorrhea in ballet dancers. *New England Journal of Medicine, 303,* 17-19.

Goodman, R.L., & Karsch, F.J. (1980). Pulsatile secretion of luteinizing hormone: Differential suppression by ovarian steroids. *Endocrinology, 107,* 1286-1290.

Jakacki, R.I., Kelch, R.P., Sauder, S.E., Lloyd, J.S., Hopwood, N.J., & Marshall, J.C. (1982). Pulsatile secretion of luteinizing hormone in children. *Journal of Clinical Endocrinology & Metabolism, 55,* 453-458.

Judd, H.L., Parker, D.C., Siler, T.M., & Yen, S.S.C. (1974). The nocturnal rise of plasma testosterone in pubertal boys. *Journal of Clinical Endocrinology & Metabolism, 38,* 710-713.

Jurkowski, J.E., Jones, J.L., Walker, W.C., Younglar, E.V., & Sutton, J.R. (1978). Ovarian hormonal responses to exercise. *Journal of Applied Physiology, 44,* 109-114.

Kennedy, G.C., & Mitra, J. (1963). Body weight and food intake as initiating factors for puberty in the rat. *Journal of Physiology, 166,* 408-418.

Kulin, H.E. (1974). The physiology of adolescence in man. *Human Biology, 46,* 133-144.

Loucks, A.B., & Hovarth, S.M. (1984). Exercise-induced stress responses of amenorrheic and eumenorrheic runners. *Journal of Clinical Endocrinology & Metabolism, 59,* 1109-1120.

Malina, R.M., Harper, A.B., Avent, H.H., & Campbell, D.E. (1973). Age at menarche of athletes and non-athletes. *Medicine and Science in Sports, 5,* 11-13.

Malina, R.M., Spirduso, W.W., Tate, C., & Baylor, A.M. (1978). Age at menarche and selected menstrual characteristics in athletes at different competitive levels and in different sports. *Medicine and Science in Sports, 10,* 218-222.

Marshall, W.A., & Tanner, J.M. (1969). Variation in pattern of pubertal changes in girls. *Archives of Disease in Childhood, 44,* 291-303.

Marshall, W.A., & Tanner, J.M. (1970). Variations in the pattern of pubertal changes in boys. *Archives of Disease in Childhood, 45,* 13-23.

McArthur, J.W., Bullen, B.A., Beitens, I.Z., Pagano, M., Badger, T.M., & Klibanski, A. (1980). Hypothalamic amenorrhea in runners of normal body composition. *Endocrine Research Communications, 7,* 13-25.

Prior, J.C., Yuen, B.H., Clement, P., Bowie, L., & Thomas, J. (1982). Reversible luteal phase changes and infertility associated with marathon training. *Lancet, I,* 269-270.

Rebar, R.S., & Cumming, D.C. (1981). Reproductive function in women athletes. *Journal of the American Medical Association, 246,* 1590.

Rogol, A.D., Veldhuis, J.D., Williams, F.T., & Johnson, M.L. (1984). Pulsatile secretion of gonadotropins and prolactin in endurance-trained men: Relation to the endogenous opiate system. *Journal of Andrology*, **5**, 21-27.

Shangold, M., Freeman, R., Thysen, F., & Gotz, M. (1979). The relationship between long distance running plasma progesterone and luteal phase length. *Fertility and Sterility*, **31**, 130-133.

Shangold, M.M., & Levine, H.S. (1982). The effect of marathon training upon menstrual function. *American Journal of Obstetrics and Gynecology*, **143**, 862-869.

Sherman, B.M., & Korenman, S.G. (1974a). Measurement of plasma LH, FSH, estradiol and progesterone in disorders of the human menstrual cycle: The short luteal phase. *Journal of Clinical Endocrinology & Metabolism*, **38**, 89-93.

Sherman, B.M., & Korenman, S.G. (1974b). Measurement of serum LH, FSH, estradiol and progesterone in disorders of the human menstrual cycle: The inadequate luteal phase. *Journal of Clinical Endocrinology & Metabolism*, **39**, 145-149.

Steiner, R.A., Cameron, J.L., McNeill, T.H., Clifton, D.K., & Bremner, W.J. (1983). Metabolic signals for the onset of puberty. In R. Norman (Ed.), *Neuroendocrine aspects of reproduction* (pp. 183-227). New York: Academic Press.

Tanner, J.M. (Ed.). (1962). *Growth at adolescence* (2nd ed.). Oxford, England: Blackwell Scientific Publications.

Veldhuis, J.D., Evans, W.S., Demers, L.M., Thorner, M.O., Wakat, D., & Rogol, A.D. (1985). Altered neuroendocrine regulation of gonadotropin secretion in women distance runners. *Journal of Clinical Endocrinology & Metabolism*, **61**, 557-563.

Veldhuis, J.D., Rogol, A.D., Johnson, M.L., & Dufau, M.L. (1983). Endogenous opiates modulate the pulsatile secretion of biologically active luteinizing hormone in man. *Journal of Clinical Investigation*, **72**, 2031-2040.

Warren, M.R. (1980). The effects of exercise on pubertal progression and reproductive function in girls. *Journal of Clinical Endocrinology & Metabolism*, **51**, 1150-1157.

Winter, J.S.D., Hughes, I.A., Reyes, F.I., & Faiman, C. (1976). Pituitary-gonadal relations in infancy. 2. Patterns of serum gonadal steroid concentrations in man from birth to two years of age. *Journal of Clinical Endocrinology & Metabolism*, **42**, 679-686.

Relationship Between Training, Menarche, and Amenorrhea

Christine L. Wells

Sharon A. Plowman

Many myths have been propagated regarding the interrelationships between physical training and menstrual function. Although there is considerable literature on the topic, there is little agreement among data sets or even the interpretation of similar data sets. Consequently, confusion remains. There is a particularly wide disparity between the scientific and popular press on certain aspects of the topic.

The female reproductive system is extremely complex. Control of the system involves several organs (including the hypothalamus, pituitary, adrenal glands, and ovaries) and numerous hormones and releasing factors (including gonadotropin-releasing hormone, GnRH; luteinizing hormone, LH; follicle-stimulating hormone, FSH; the estrogens, E; progesterone, P; prolactin, PRL; and the androgens, A). Considering the complexity of the system, it is not surprising that confusion exists regarding the influence of strenuous physical training on menstrual function.

When one considers the normal female life span, it is evident that there are several stages or physiological "states" involved. Each state has its own characteristic hormonal patterns that have been only partially described to date. Three states can be identified in the female reproductive system: Two of these are nonmenstruating, anovulatory states and are represented by State 1 (prepubertal state) and State 3 (postmenopausal state) in Figure 1. State 2 represents the menstrual or reproductive state, that period of life characterized by monthly menstrual flow, and usually, the regular ovulation of an ovum from the ovary. In this conceptual model (Loucks, 1981), the young girl switches from State 1 to State 2 at *menarche*. The middle-aged woman switches from State 2 to State 3 at *menopause*. Neither "switching event" has been described very thoroughly. Although the literature is gradually developing, much of it remains descriptive rather than mechanistic in nature and focuses primarily on the state and not the switching event or transition period.

The conceptual model presented above is useful in the discussion of the relationships between and among training, menarche (first menstrual flow), and amenorrhea (absence of menses). It provides a framework for questions such as the following: Does training affect these reproductive system states? Does training affect the state switching events? Is a young

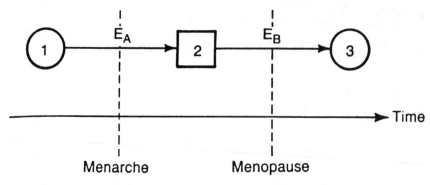

Figure 1   State diagram of the classical model of the reproductive system. Numbers indicate states: 1 = premenarcheal state, 2 = menstrual state, 3 = postmenopausal state. State switching events: E_A = menarche, E_B = menopause. From Loucks (1981).

athlete with primary amenorrhea (late or delayed menarche) being delayed in pubertal development because training retards the state switching event? Has an athlete with secondary amenorrhea (cessation of menstrual function without menopause) been switched from State 2 back to State 1 or ahead to State 3? There may be other possibilities as well. If the amenorrheic hormonal pattern does not fit either State 1 or State 3, then additional states as yet undescribed may exist.

Menarche and Sexual Maturation

Menarche is a single event that marks the beginning of menstrual function. Puberty, on the other hand, is the period of transition between childhood and adulthood. Menarche is a late event in puberty. The exact mechanism is unknown, but the most accepted theory is that the hypothalamus controls the onset of menstrual function. Apparently, the immature hypothalamus is extremely sensitive to very small amounts of estrogen produced by the ovaries of the prepubertal girl. The result is an inhibition of gonadotropins at the level of the central nervous system. Consequently, FSH and LH are not produced by the anterior pituitary, and the gonads remain undeveloped. As the hypothalamus gradually matures, however, the sensitivity of the organ decreases, requiring more estrogen to maintain inhibition of the gonadotropins from the pituitary. This decreased sensitivity is accompanied by increased GnRH, gonadotropic hormones, and in turn, gonadal steroid output that bring about sexual maturation. The gradually increasing production of estrogen and progesterone from the ovaries eventually results in menarche (Boyer, 1978; Root, 1973; Tepperman, 1980). The missing link in this explanation is what causes the brain to initiate the process (or, if the brain is not responsible for the initiation, determination of what else might be).

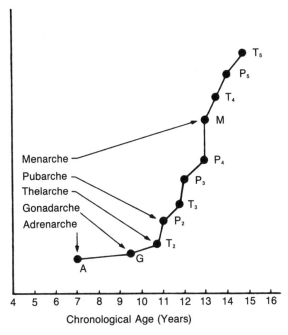

Figure 2 Figurative presentation of main pubertal events with chronological age as frame of reference (T_2 to T_5 = stages of breast development; P_2 to P_5 = stages of pubic hair development). From Brisson et al. (1982), p. 64.

The physical pattern of sexual maturation, however, is well character-ized, and again, is useful here in a discussion of the relationship between training and menarche (Brisson, Peronnet, Ledoux, & Dulac, 1982; Root, 1973; Tanner, 1962) (Figure 2). The onset of puberty is characterized by the main endocrine event called *adrenarche*. This corresponds to the acti-vation of the hypothalamus-pituitary-adrenal axis and brings about an increased release of the adrenal androgens: dehydroepiandrosterone (DHEA), dehydroepiandrosterone-sulfate (DHEAS), ^{4}-androstenedione, and ^{5}-androstenediol (Figure 3). This typically occurs between ages 6 and 8 years. This is followed at age 9 or 10 by *gonadarche*, the period when the hypothalamus-pituitary-ovarian axis is activated. This activates the increased secretion of gonadotropic hormones.

Following gonadarche comes a series of physical changes known as the *initial growth spurt* (IGS) and *thelarche* (the beginning of breast develop-ment) between 10 and 11 years of age, followed by *pubarche* (the appear-ance of pubic and axillary hair) at about age 11 and *peak height velocity* (PHV) (fastest growth period) at about age 12 years. The cortical androgens are causally associated with pubarche. Thelarche probably results from the estrogenic influence caused by activation of the hypothalamus-pituitary-ovarian axis. Eventually, *menarche* follows at approximately

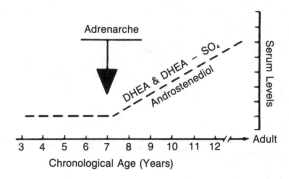

Figure 3 Increase in adrenal androgen (DHEA = dehydroepiandrosterone; DHEA − SO₄ = dehydroepiandrosterone-sulfate) secretory output occurs between the 6th and the 8th year of chronological age. From Brisson et al. (1982), p. 62.

12 years of age for American girls. This occurs when the gonadotropic hormones sufficiently stimulate the follicular estrogens to activate the ovarian-uterine axis. Complete sexual maturation may not be attained for another 3 years. As can be seen in Figure 2, both thelarche and pubarche have several separate stages.

Training and Menarche

Menarche occurs at a significantly later age in the young female athlete than in her nonathletic counterpart (Malina, Spirduso, Tate, & Baylor, 1978; Marker, 1981). Mean menarcheal age in the United States is between 12.3 to 12.8 years. Figures 4 and 5 indicate that the mean chronological age for menarche of athletic girls engaged in strenuous athletic training in a variety of sports is considerably later than that. Figure 4 provides mean ages, standard deviations, and ranges of menarcheal ages of European athletes. Here it is shown that divers, figure skaters, and gymnasts experienced the latest menarche in this large sample of subjects. Figure 5 provides data on American athletes from a number of sources. This figure shows essentially the same thing: Girls who engage in serious and strenuous physical training experience a later menarche than is the average for the relatively inactive population. This figure also indicates that the better performers (the more highly trained) have a later menarche than girls not so extensively trained. The high school and college athletes did not differ from each other in menarcheal age, but they did differ from the higher level athletes. The apparent association between a later age at menarche and more advanced competitive level also has been noted by Malina (1983) and Marker (1981).

Menarcheal age has not always been reported to be later in athletic groups. In their classic study on young Swedish swimmers, Åstrand et al. (1963) reported that menarche was achieved at an earlier age than

Prepuberal Training in Relation to Female Maturity

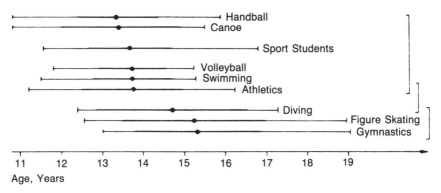

Figure 4 Mean values (●), standard deviations (heavy lines), and ranges of menarcheal ages of athletes for different sports. Markings at the right side indicate those groups, the mean menarcheal ages of which are not significantly different. From Marker (1981), p. 119.

the average Swedish girl. Another early study (Erdelyi, 1962) reported that Hungarian national athletes exhibited menarche at 13.6 years, the equivalent to the average for the Hungarian population at that time. These two studies, however, were completed when the scope and intensity of athletic training programs for women were not nearly so demanding as they are today. More recently, competitive swimmers from the midwestern United States were reported to have a significantly later menarcheal age than their nonathletic counterparts (Stager, Robertshaw, & Miescher, 1984).

Ballet dancers have been consistently cited as examples of girls with late menarche (primary amenorrhea). Warren (1980) studied 15 ballerinas beginning at ages 13 to 15 who maintained a consistently high level of activity throughout the 4-year study. Menarche did not occur until 15.4 years. While premenarcheal, all dancers had low to low-normal gonadotropin levels. Primary amenorrhea persisted in two of the dancers at age 18.

Another factor involving training and menarche appears to be the age at which training begins. Figure 6 indicates the number of years of training before menarche in the European athletes discussed above (Marker, 1981). The age at menarche appears to be associated with the number of years of training prior to menarche. This implies that the earlier a girl begins training, the later will be her menarche (Frisch et al., 1981). An observational artifact may be in operation here, however. In sports characterized by early entry (e.g., swimming, gymnastics, figure skating, and ballet), the later menarche occurs, the greater will be the number of years of training prior to menarche (Stager et al., 1984).

At least two explanations have been offered to explain the apparent association between strenuous physical training and late menarcheal age.

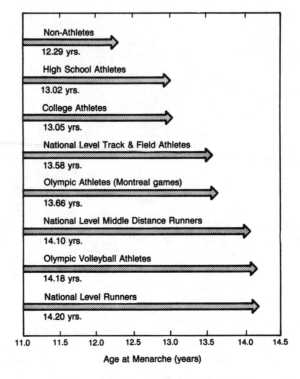

Figure 5 Age at menarche in nonathletes and athletes at different competitive levels. From Wells (1985), p. 81.

The critical weight-critical fat hypothesis proposed by Frisch and her colleagues (1971a, 1971b, 1971c, 1973) has generated the most interest and written text. The genetic disposition theory (Malina et al., 1978) has developed in opposition to Frisch's concept but is considerably less well developed.

Frisch sees physical training as causing a reduction in body weight or body fat, which, especially if combined with dietary restrictions, causes excessive thinness and, in turn, delays menarche. The hypothesis has been widely quoted and accepted in the popular press. The theory was first presented in 1971 when Frisch and Revelle (1971a) announced, "We have now found that . . . menarche . . . occurs at an unchanging mean weight" (p. 397). This conclusion was based on estimated height and weight values interpolated from growth data of 181 girls participating in three separate studies (file data). The mean age at menarche was found to be 12.9 years at a mean height of 158.5 cm and a mean weight of 47.8 kg. Those who matured later were taller but not heavier. The authors concluded that the attainment of the critical weight of 48 kg was essential for menarche. Additional papers reiterated the theory (Frisch &

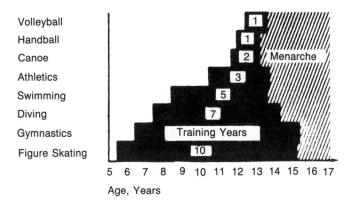

Figure 6   Number of years of training before menarche of female athletes. From Marker (1981), p. 121.

Revelle, 1971b, 1971c). In 1973, Frisch et al. expanded the analysis using the same file data to include total body water (TBW), lean body weight (LBW), and percentage body fat (%BF). TBW was calculated using the formula of Mellits and Cheek (1970):

$$TBW = -10.313 + 0.252 \text{ wt (kg)} + 0.154 \text{ ht (cm)}$$
$$\text{when ht exceeded 110.8 cm}$$

LBW was calculated by TBW/0.72 and fat by subtracting LBW from total body weight. These calculations resulted in an estimated mean TBW of 26.2 l, LBW of 36.3 kg, and fat weight of 11.5 kg. Mean %BF at menarche for late maturers was 21.9% and for early maturers, 24.6%. Frisch and McArthur (1974) extended the theory another step by emphasizing that both delayed menarche and secondary amenorrhea resulted from undernourishment and necessitated a critical percentage body fat—17% for primary and 22% for secondary amenorrhea.

A massive amount of literature regarding Frisch's work has since developed in the scientific press. This criticism can be grouped into three main areas: methodological, statistical, and experimental.

In terms of methodology, Frisch and coworkers obtained all their data indirectly. Percentage body fat was not measured by traditionally accepted methods such as densitometry or ⁴⁰K determination, but rather was estimated from the Mellits and Cheek (1970) estimation of total body water. Even height and weight were not obtained at the exact age of menarche. Although the interpolation of height and weight from data points approximately 6 months apart probably does not cause considerable error, the calculation of percentage body fat from the Mellits and Cheek estimation of total body water very likely does (Loucks, Horvath, & Freedson, 1984; Scott, 1984; Van't Hof & Roede, 1977). The appropriateness of the Mellits and Cheek formula has been questioned by numerous studies (Billewicz, Fellowes, & Hytten, 1976; Johnston, 1982; Johnston, Roche, Schell, & Wettenhall, 1975; Katch & Katch, 1980; Loucks et al., 1984; Scott & Johnson, 1982; Van't Hof & Roede, 1977). The use of height and weight has long been criticized for the failure of these variables to give an indication of body composition. In addition, the Mellits and Cheek methodology assumes that 72% is the biological constant for the water content of LBW or fat-free body (FFB). This is an assumption that most likely is not valid according to the recent evidence of Boileau et al. (1984). Utilizing a large sample of black and white males and females (ages 8 to 30 years), this group of researchers from the University of Illinois found that the percentage of water in the FFB progressively decreases from prepubescence to adulthood for both sexes at a rate of approximately 0.38% per year. Age group comparisons revealed that the pubertal age may be the critical stage at which a significant decrement in percentage of water in the FFB occurs. Actual values for white and black prepubescent girls were 76.0% and 75.4%, respectively; for postpubescent girls these values were 73.3% and 74.1%. These differences are sufficient to overestimate body fatness by at least 3 to 4%, certainly enough to lower the critical fat level, if such a factor actually exists.

From a statistical point of view, a major problem with Frisch's work is the interpretation of the descriptive measure of central tendency as a causative rather than merely an associated factor. Even if an "invariate" mean body weight or percentage body fat does coincide with the occurrence of menarche, this does not mean that a critical threshold value exists (Ellison, 1981a; Scott & Johnston, 1982). An outside variable (such as maturational age) indirectly related to the "invariate" variable may be the actual "causal" factor. Other statistical errors and points of disagreement have appeared in the literature as well (Billewicz et al., 1976; Johnston et al., 1975; Trussell, 1978, 1980).

Several studies designed to experimentally verify the critical weight or critical fat theory have failed. Johnston, Malina, and Galbraith (1971) studied American and Guatemalan girls and concluded that weight is not constant over age of menarche, and that the critical weight theory is an artifact arising from the failure to consider the expressed interrelationships of age, height, and weight. Utilizing additional data (including some cited by Frisch) Johnston et al. (1975) concluded that the evidence showed that mean weight at menarche is not invariant, and that partial correlations of age at menarche and weight at menarche at a constant height showed a tendency for early maturers to be heavier than late maturers. Other studies have also dealt experimentally with age at menarche and have concluded that menarche is not triggered by a set weight or body composition (Billewicz et al., 1976; Cameron, 1976; Crawford & Osler, 1975; Ellison, 1981a, 1981b).

Brisson et al. (1982) have integrated Frisch's critical body weight-fat thresholds into the pattern of pubertal development outlined above. Figure 7 indicates these critical thresholds in relation to the initiation of the adolescent growth spurt (IGS), peak height velocity (PHV), and

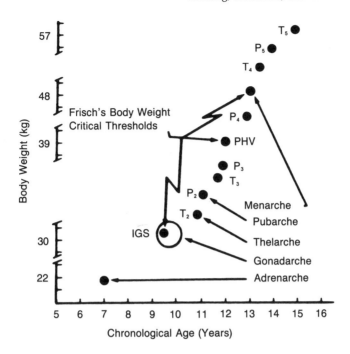

Figure 7 Same as Figure 2 but integrating Frisch's observations on critical body weights. IGS = initiation of growth spurt; PHV = peak height velocity; T_2 to T_5 = Tanner's stages for breast development; P_2 to P_5 = Tanner's stages for pubic hair development. From Brisson et al. (1982), p. 65.

menarche. They speculated that if Frisch's theory is correct, then the low body fat to lean body mass ratio of girls involved in strenuous exercise training "could influence gonadarche by significantly changing one or several characteristics of the steroid feedback to the hypothalamus-pituitary unit" (p. 65). Figure 8 suggests that athletes with late menarche could be late maturers with a generally slower maturation rate and with older ages for adrenarche, gonadarche, and consequently, menarche. This concept implies that a delay in menarche is not simply a delay in one event, but signifies a probable delay in many developmental events.

Figure 8 provides a nice introduction to the *genetic disposition theory* proposed in opposition to the concept of critical thresholds for the attainment of menarche (Malina et al., 1978). This theory is a belief that menarche is *not* delayed by strenuous training, but is simply later in some girls than in others, and that girls who tend to have a late menarche also tend to be girls who excel in athletic endeavors. This concept, then, is that girls genetically programmed for a late menarche are those also genetically favored in terms of "being good in sports." There is not much solid evidence to directly support this. However, proponents cite the fact that biological characteristics associated with later maturity in females are

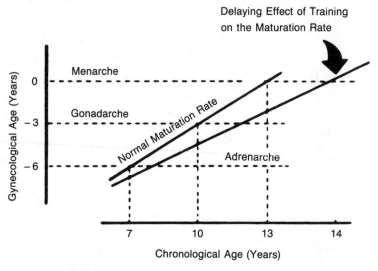

Figure 8 Diagram suggesting that athletes with delayed menarche could be late maturers, where a slower maturation rate implies delays in both adrenarche and gonadarche. From Brisson et al. (1982), p. 64.

generally those more suitable for athletic performance, and that those physical variables known to be associated with a decline in performance—gain in body fat, breast development, widening of the hips, for example—are also factors associated with maturation of the reproductive system. Factors known to be associated with excellence in athletic performance—slim hips, longer legs, low relative body fat, less weight per unit height, high lean body mass—are also associated with late maturers who experience menarche at an older age. Possibly there is a natural or self-selection process going on and no exercise effect at all. Are athletic girls those who would have had a late menarche even if they were not athletic? Do late maturers make better athletes? Or is there a true delay in menarche due to training?

So much space has been devoted here to the discussion of menarche for three reasons: One is that the topic of oligomenorrhea (irregular menses)/amenorrhea has been covered extensively elsewhere (the writings of Drinkwater, Shangold, and Wells—see Wells, 1985). The second is there is nothing really new on the topic. The third (and most important reason) is because we hypothesize that *if* there is a relationship between training and menstrual function, it is logical that the relationship is similar for the initiation of menstrual function (menarche) and for the temporary cessation of menstrual function (secondary amenorrhea). In other words, if training directly affects menstruation at all, the basic mechanism operationally influences both the onset of menarche and later interruptions in menstruation.

Training and Amenorrhea

There is a wide variety of definitions of amenorrhea found in the literature. Generally, amenorrhea has been used to mean the cessation of menstrual flow for more than 3 months. Oligomenorrhea is variously used for missing a few menstrual periods to menstruating once every 3 to 6 months. Obviously, the reported incidence of amenorrhea or oligomenorrhea varies with the stringency of the operational definition used. Generally, oligo/amenorrhea occurs in about 2 to 3% of the nonathletic, nonlactating, nonpregnant population. In the physically training population, the incidence of oligo/amenorrhea increases to between 12 and 45%, depending largely on the population studied (Drinkwater, 1984).

A number of variables have been associated via correlation analysis with the incidence of oligo/amenorrhea in athletic women. Some have reported that menstrual irregularity is more commonly seen in younger than more mature athletes (Baker, Mathur, Kirk, & Williamson, 1981; Lutter & Cushman, 1982; Speroff & Redwine, 1980). Some report a high relationship between low body weight or a low percentage of body fat and exercise related oligo/amenorrhea (Baker et al., 1981; Dale, Gerlach, & Wilhite, 1979; Lutter & Cushman, 1982; Schwartz, Cumming, Riordan, Selye, Yen, & Rebar, 1981), whereas others report that only weight loss is an important factor (Dale, Gerlach, Martin, & Alexander, 1979; Speroff & Redwine, 1980). Many report that training intensity (mileage) is highly related to oligo/amenorrhea (Dale, Gerlach, Martin, & Alexander, 1979; Dale, Gerlach, & Wilhite, 1979; Feicht, Johnson, Martin, Sparkes, & Wagner, 1978; Feicht, Martin, & Wagner, 1980; Lutter & Cushman, 1982; Speroff & Redwine, 1980). But there is disagreement. Several studies have failed to find a relationship between weight or body composition and amenorrhea in athletes (Baker et al.; Feicht et al., 1978; Wakat, Sweeney, & Rogol, 1982). In amenorrheic ballerinas, menstrual function has been reported to return during vacations and periods of enforced rest without a gain in body weight or fat (Abraham, Beaumont, Fraser, & Llewelyn-Jones, 1982; Warren, 1980). Older age at menarche has been reported to be related to exercise amenorrhea in several studies (Baker et al., 1981; Lutter & Cushman, 1982) but not all (Dale, Gerlach, & Wilhite, 1979; Gray & Dale, 1983).

Another approach to the study of training-related amenorrhea has been to study the direct effects of exercise on the hormonal cycles responsible for the menstrual cycle. Although it is important to have an understanding of the variables associated with exercise-related amenorrhea, hormonal studies have offered a more direct attempt to determine *causal* factors. These studies have been reviewed extensively elsewhere (Wells, 1985, 1986), so results will be only briefly summarized here. The main points of interest are as follows:

- Androgenic hormones (in both men and women) have been found to increase significantly following strenuous exercise.
- Ovarian hormones (estrogen and progesterone) increase in response

to exercise in untrained but not trained women. These changes appear to be more extreme during the luteal phase of the menstrual cycle (when both E and P levels are elevated) than during other phases of the cycle.
- Prolactin levels have been shown to be markedly elevated following exercise that jars the breast (not swimming).
- It is not known whether these changes are due to increased ovarian function, increased adrenal function, or to decreased hepatic clearance.
- Although some studies have reported acute increases in the gonado-tropic hormones (FSH and LH) with exercise, others have not.
- *Chronically* lower androgenic, gonadotropic, and ovarian hormones are found in women distance runners and in teenaged athletes with short-ened luteal phases.

Several hypotheses have been proposed to explain exercise oligo/amenorrhea. The most prominent (once again) is Frisch's critical body weight-body fat hypothesis. According to this theory, a woman must maintain a relative body fat level of 22% to retain menstrual function. If sufficient fat loss occurs due to training (or other reasons), amenor-rhea will result. In order to regain menstruation, sufficient fat will have to be reacquired. Although body fat levels have turned up as an asso-ciated variable time and again, there is really no direct evidence that loss of body fat is the *cause* of exercise-related amenorrhea. The major objec-tions to the theory were discussed above. In our opinion, the critical fat theory has not stood the test of time and criticism. Although it remains the prevailing concept in the popular literature, it is no longer supported in the scientific literature. One reason that low body fat, or loss of body fat, may be so closely associated with amenorrhea is that body fat levels and menstrual function are primarily controlled by the same areas of the brain—the hypothalamus and pituitary. Consequently, one should ex-pect these variables to be highly associated with one another. This does not imply, however, that a causal relationship exists.

Another theory, not well developed in terms of exercise-related amenor-rhea at this time, is the *energy drain theory*. This is sometimes confused with the critical fat theory, but it is not the same thing. Very simply, the energy drain theory states that during times of severe stress—such as in times of famine or other emergency—reproductive function will be tem-porarily lost, to be regained when there is no danger to the prospective mother. The theory does not require a loss of body weight or fat (although that often occurs); it simply implies that the body has sufficient energy to function at a maximal level but *not* to reproduce. Consequently, there is little need for menstrual function during that period of time. The theory has been used extensively by biologists and anthropologists to explain fluctuation in population levels of wild animals and primitive tribes.

Hormonal theories of exercise-related amenorrhea have not been tested experimentally. One concept suggests that elevated ovarian hormone levels following exercise act to inhibit follicular development by activat-ing the negative feedback mechanism between the ovary and the hypothalamic-pituitary axis resulting in inhibition of the gonadotropic hormones. If exercise affects this mechanism, the timing of the LH surge required for ovulation would probably be disrupted. Because many athletes train intensely for 3 to 5 hours per day, often in more than one daily session, it is conceivable that these hormones remain elevated for a sufficient period of time to exert such an inhibitory effect.

The fact that adipose tissue can aromatize androgens to estrogens (Longcope, Pratt, Schneider, & Fineberg, 1978; Nimrod & Ryan, 1975) is often cited in an attempt to integrate some of the concepts presented above with the low body fat levels so often seen in well-trained premenarcheal girls and athletic women. Because well-trained athletes have lower amounts of body fat than nontrained girls and women, possibly less testosterone is being converted to estrogen. This could account for the lower levels of estrogen commonly seen in distance runners, ballerinas, and other athletes with menstrual disorders. Possibly this is a key factor in both the later menarcheal age of athletic girls and exercise-related amenorrhea of the more mature athletic women, but the concept has not yet been experimentally tested.

It should be clear by now that the relationship between training, menarche, and amenorrhea has not yet been satisfactorily described. However, there are several possible ways to pull this information together into an integrated theory. For example, perhaps training overstresses the adrenal glands preventing the release of DHEA, or perhaps training prevents a change in the sensitivity of the hypothalamus to estrogen levels and the resulting stimulation of the gonadotropic hormones. The young, active girl would then experience a retardation in pubertal development as suggested by Figure 8. At a later age, the high levels of energy production that must be maintained for long periods of time throughout an athletic career may lead to low relative body fat levels, and consequently, little aromatization of adrenal androgen to estrogen. Perhaps the hypothalamus adjusts to this by increasing its sensitivity to estrogen. In this way, the mature athletic woman with low chronic estrogen levels might be shifted back to the premenarcheal state of the young girl.

References

Abraham, S.F., Beaumont, P.J.V., Fraser, I.S., & Llewellyn-Jones, D. (1982). Body weight, exercise, and menstrual status among ballet dancers in training. *British Journal of Obstetrics and Gynecology*, **89**, 507-510.

Åstrand, P.-O., Engstrom, I., Eriksson, B.O., Karlberg, P., Nylander, I., Saltin, B., & Thoren, C. (1963). Girl swimmers, with special reference to respiratory and circulatory adaptation and gynaecological and psychiatric aspects. *Acta Paediatrica Scandinavica* (Suppl. 147), 1-75.

Baker, E.B., Mathur, R.S., Kirk, R.F., & Williamson, H.O. (1981). Female runners and secondary amenorrhea: Correlation with age, parity, mileage and plasma hormonal and sex hormone binding globulin concentration. *Fertility and Sterility, 36*, 183-187.

Billewicz, W.Z., Fellowes, H.M., & Hytten, C.A. (1976). Comments on the critical metabolic mass and the age of menarche. *Annals of Human Biology, 3*, 51-59.

Boileau, R.A., Lohman, T.G., Slaughter, M.H., Ball, T.E., Going, S.B., & Hendrix, M.K. (1984). Hydration of the fat-free body in children during maturation. *Human Biology, 56*, 651-666.

Boyer, R.M. (1978). Control of the onset of puberty. *Annual Review of Medicine, 90*, 509-520.

Brisson, G.R., Peronnet, F., Ledoux, M., & Dulac, S. (1982). The onset of menarche: A late event in pubertal progression to be affected by physical training. *Canadian Journal of Applied Sport Sciences, 7*, 60-103.

Cameron, N. (1976). Weight and skinfold variation at menarche and the critical body weight hypothesis. *Annals of Human Biology, 3*, 279-282.

Crawford, J.D., & Osler, D.C. (1975). Body composition at menarche: The Frisch-Revelle hypothesis revisited. *Pediatrics, 56*, 449-458.

Dale, E., Gerlach, D.H., Martin, D.E., & Alexander, D.R. (1979). Physical fitness profiles and reproductive physiology of the female distance runner. *The Physician and Sportsmedicine, 7*(1), 83-95.

Dale, E., Gerlach, D.H., & Wilhite, A.L. (1979). Menstrual dysfunction in distance runners. *Obstetrics and Gynecology, 54*, 47-53.

Drinkwater, B.L. (1984). Athletic amenorrhea: A review. *American Academy of Physical Education Papers, Exercise and Health, 17*, 120-131.

Ellison, P.T. (1981a). Physical growth and reproductive maturity in humans (Abstract). *American Journal of Physical Anthropology, 54*, 216.

Ellison, P.T. (1981b). Threshold hypotheses, developmental age, and menstrual function. *American Journal of Physical Anthropology, 54*, 337-340.

Erdelyi, G.J. (1962). Gynecological survey of female athletes. *Journal of Sports Medicine and Physical Fitness, 2*, 174-179.

Feicht, C.B., Johnson, T.S., Martin, B.J., Sparkes, K.E., & Wagner, W.W., Jr. (1978). Secondary amenorrhea in athletes (letter). *Lancet, 2*(8100), 1145-1146.

Feicht, C.B., Martin, B.J., & Wagner, W.W., Jr. (1980). Is athletic amenorrhea specific to runners? *Federation Proceedings, 39*(3), Part 1, 371. (Abstract 536)

Frisch, R.E., Gotz-Welbergen, A.V., McArthur, J.W., Albright, T., Witschi, J., Bullen, B., Birnholz, J., Reed, R.B., & Hermann, H. (1981). Delayed menarche and amenorrhea of college athletes in relation to age of onset of training. *Journal of the American Medical Association, 246*, 1559-1563.

Frisch, R.E., & McArthur, J.W. (1974). Menstrual cycles: Fatness as a determinant of minimum weight for height necessary for their maintenance or onset. *Science*, **185**, 949-951.

Frisch, R.E., & Revelle, R. (1971a). Height and weight at menarche and a hypothesis of critical body weights and adolescent events. *Science*, **169**, 397-399.

Frisch, R.E., & Revelle, R. (1971b). Height and weight at menarche and a hypothesis of menarche. *Archives of Disease in Childhood*, **46**, 695-701.

Frisch, R.E., & Revelle, R. (1971c). The height and weight of girls and boys at the time of initiation of the adolescent growth spurt in height and weight and the relationship to menarche. *Human Biology*, **43**, 140-159.

Frisch, R.E., Revelle, R., & Cook, S. (1973). Components of weight at menarche and the initiation of the adolescent growth spurt in girls: Estimated total water, lean body weight, and fat. *Human Biology*, **45**, 469-483.

Gray, D.P., & Dale, E. (1983). Variables associated with secondary amenorrhea in women runners. *Journal of Sports Sciences*, **1**, 55-67.

Johnston, F.E. (1982). Relationships between body composition and anthropometry. *Human Biology*, **54**, 221-245.

Johnston, F.E., Malina, R.M., & Galbraith, M.A. (1971). Height, weight and age at menarche and the "critical weight" hypothesis. *Science*, **174**, 1148-1149.

Johnston, F.E., Roche, A.F., Schell, L.M., & Wettenhall, H.N.B. (1975). Critical weight at menarche: Critique of a hypothesis. *American Journal of Disease in Childhood*, **129**, 19-23.

Katch, F.I., & Katch, V.L. (1980). Measurement and prediction errors in body composition assessment and the search for the perfect prediction equation. *Research Quarterly for Exercise and Sport*, **51**, 249-260.

Longcope, C., Pratt, J.H., Schneider, S.H., & Fineberg, S.E. (1978). Aromatization of androgens by muscle and adipose tissue *in vivo*. *Journal of Clinical Endocrinology and Metabolism*, **46**, 146-152.

Loucks, A. (1981, May). *Factors affecting ovulation: Implications for the female athlete*. Unpublished paper presented at The American College of Sports Medicine, Miami Beach, FL.

Loucks, A.B., Horvath, S.M., & Freedson, P.S. (1984). Menstrual status and validation of body fat prediction in athletes. *Human Biology*, **56**, 383-392.

Lutter, J.M., & Cushman, S. (1982). Menstrual patterns in female runners. *The Physician and Sportsmedicine*, **10**(9), 60-72.

Malina, R.M. (1983). Menarche in athletes: A synthesis and hypothesis. *Annals of Human Biology*, **10**, 1-24.

Malina, R.M., Spirduso, W.W., Tate, C., & Baylor, A.M. (1978). Age at menarche and selected menstrual characteristics in athletes at different competitive levels and in different sports. *Medicine and Science in Sports*, **10**, 218-222.

Marker, K. (1981). Influence of athletic training on the maturity process of girls. *Medicine and Sport*, **15**, 117-126.

Mellits, E.D., & Cheek, D.B. (1970). The assessment of body water and fatness from infancy to adulthood. *Monogram of Social Research in Child Development*, **35**, 12-26.

Nimrod, A., & Ryan, K.J. (1975). Aromatization of androgens by human abdominal and breast fat tissue. *Journal of Clinical Endocrinology and Metabolism*, **40**, 367-375.

Root, A.W. (1973). Endocrinology of puberty. *The Journal of Pediatrics*, **83**, 1-19.

Schwartz, B., Cumming, D., Riordan, E., Selye, M., Yen, S., & Rebar, R. (1981). Exercise-associated amenorrhea: A distinct entity? *American Journal of Obstetrics and Gynecology*, **141**, 662-670.

Scott, E.C. (1984). Estimation of total water and fatness from weight and height: Inaccurate for lean women. *American Journal of Physical Anthropology*, **64**, 83-87.

Scott, E.C., & Johnston, F.E. (1982). Critical fat, menarche, and the maintenance of menstrual cycles: A critical review. *Journal of Adolescent Health Care*, **2**, 249-260.

Speroff, L., & Redwine, D.B. (1980). Exercise and menstrual function. *The Physician and Sportsmedicine*, **8**(5), 42-52.

Stager, J.M., Robertshaw, D., & Miescher, E. (1984). Delayed menarche in swimmers in relation to age at onset of training and athletic performance. *Medicine and Science in Sports and Exercise*, **16**, 550-555.

Tanner, J.M. (1962). *Growth at adolescence*. Oxford: Blackwell Scientific Publications.

Tepperman, J. (1980). *Metabolic and endocrine physiology* (4th ed.). Chicago: Year Book Medical Publishers.

Trussell, J. (1978). Menarche and fatness: Reexamination of the critical body composition hypothesis. *Science*, **200**, 1506-1509.

Trussell, J. (1980). Statistical flaws in evidence for the Frisch Hypothesis that fatness triggers menarche. *Human Biology*, **52**, 711-720.

Van't Hof, M., & Roede, H.J. (1977). A Monte Carlo test of weight as a critical factor in menarche, compared with bone age and measures of height, width, and sexual development. *Annals of Human Biology*, **4**, 581-585.

Wakat, D.K., Sweeney, K.A., & Rogol, A.D. (1982). Reproductive system function in women cross-country runners. *Medicine and Science in Sports and Exercise*, **14**, 263-269.

Warren, M.P. (1980). The effects of exercise on pubertal progression and reproductive function in girls. *Journal of Clinical Endocrinology and Metabolism, 51,* 1150-1157.

Wells, C.L. (1985). *Women, sport and performance: A physiological perspective.* Champaign, IL: Human Kinetics.

Wells, C.L. (1986). Menstruation, pregnancy, and menopause. In V. Seefeldt (Ed.), *Physical activity and well-being* (pp. 211-234). American Alliance for Health, Physical Education, Recreation, and Dance.

Osteoporosis Prevention Begins in Childhood

Anne B. Loucks

Most people are aware of the term *osteoporosis*. They may not be aware, however, that osteoporosis is the 12th leading cause of death in the United States, and that this year American women will suffer 700,000 needless fractures due to osteoporosis at a financial cost of $2 billion. Many people think that the prevention of osteoporosis begins at menopause. Osteoporosis, however, is a *pediatric* disease, and the prevention of osteoporosis, like the condition itself, begins in childhood.

The causal chain of events in osteoporosis is shown in Figure 1. There are two sets of factors in this chain of events: involuntary (genetic) and voluntary (life-style). Involuntary factors will not be dealt with in this chapter. However, it should be noted that light-framed Caucasian and Oriental women are genetically most susceptible to osteoporosis.

The focus of this paper is on the voluntary life-style factors. These are factors that can be personally controlled and are of two types: deficiencies that have direct effect on bone density and excesses that influence bone density indirectly by creating or exaggerating these deficiencies. The purpose of this chapter is to explain the role of health educators, physicians, and coaches associated with competitive girls' sports in the effort to reform women's life-styles so that low levels of physical activity and low levels of calcium and reproductive steroids in the blood no longer lead directly to low bone density and to osteoporotic fractures in later life.

Bone as a Dynamic Tissue

Many people mistakenly think of the skeleton as an inert structure. Bone, however, is a dynamic living tissue that is continually being remodeled. The cellular portion of bone provides a matrix for the continual deposition and resorption of large quantities of calcium, phosphate, and carbonate that provide not only structural support but also metabolic reserves of essential minerals.

Figure 2 shows the pattern of bone mineral density as a function of age in men and women and the life-style variables that are associated with this pattern. From childhood to adulthood, bone is deposited faster than it is broken down, and bones become larger and more dense. Bone density increases and peaks at approximately 35 years for both groups. Note

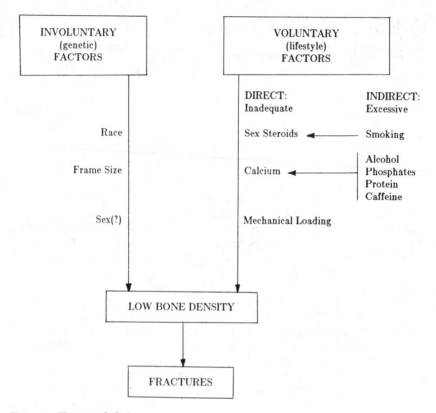

Figure 1 The causal chain.

that bone density increases more slowly in women than in men during adolescence so that the peak at age 35 is lower in women than in men. As a result of reducing habitual activity levels, however, the effect of the remodeling process begins to reverse direction at about age 35. Bone mineral is resorbed and excreted faster than it is deposited, and the same remodeling process decreases bone density. This continues into old age. Note also that the decline with age in women becomes more rapid at the time of menopause if women are not put on sex steroid therapy.

Osteoporosis is usually defined as a quantitative deficiency of bone mineral sufficient to render a bone abnormally susceptible to fracture. Bone density 2 standard deviations below the mean for young adults is regarded as the fracture threshold. There is no evidence of any qualitative difference in osteoporotic bone. This profile, then, points out three goals of a comprehensive osteoporosis prevention program: (a) to prevent the rapid rate of bone loss that occurs in women when sex steroids are inadequate; (b) to prevent the slow rate of bone loss that occurs in older adults as they become less active; and (c) to increase the rate of bone deposition in girls during adolescence.

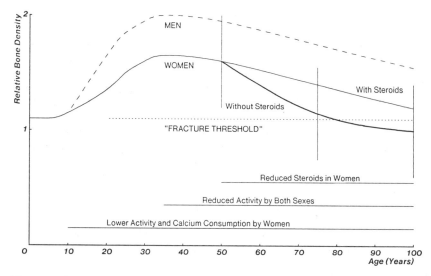

Figure 2 The pattern of bone mineral density as a function of age in men and women.

Direct Influences on Bone Density

Now consider the research related to the factors that have a direct effect on bone density.

Sex Steroids

The rapid loss of bone mineral shown in women at age 50 has been attributed to the decrease in estrogen levels at the time of menopause. The same rapid rate of loss of bone mineral also occurs in premenopausal women whose estrogen levels fall. Lindsay et al. (1976) performed a prospective double-blind study to determine the effect of a synthetic estrogen, mestranol, on bone density in 114 women who underwent premenopausal oophorectomy. Bone density was estimated by annual single photon absorptiometry and analyzed by computing the change in metacarpal mineral density from year to year. Significantly greater metacarpal mineral density was measured in estrogen-treated women than in untreated women after the 1st year. The differences continued to increase throughout the 5-year study. Lindsay et al. (1978) then studied 14 women who began mestranol therapy within 3 years of oophorectomy but who discontinued the estrogen after 4 years of use. Bone mineral content was maintained only as long as the women adhered to the mestranol regimen. Four years after discontinuing the agent, bone mineral content had fallen by 10%.

The same decline in bone density is observed in young women with lactotrophic tumors whose intact reproductive system is suppressed by excessive prolactin concentrations in the blood. In the last 3 years, this same demineralization has been observed and confirmed in an unexpected group: amenorrheic long-distance runners. Four studies have shown decreased bone mineral content in the vertebrae of amenorrheic runners compared to age-matched controls (Cann, Martin, Genant, & Jaffe, 1984; Drinkwater et al., 1984; Lindberg et al., 1984; Marcus et al., 1985). In one cross-sectional study, Drinkwater et al. found amenorrheic runners to have 14% less vertebral mineral than a matched group of regularly menstruating runners. Plotted on a regression line of bone mineral density and age, the bone mineral density of the amenorrheic group, who were in their mid-20s, corresponded to that of 50-year-old women. Cann, Martin, and Jaffe (1985) have also reported the first longitudinal data on the vertebral bone density of such athletes. Just as in other groups of hypo-estrogenic women, amenorrheic runners are losing bone over time, rapidly in the first few years after estrogen depletion (approximately 8% per year) and more slowly in later years. These results have raised grave concern among investigators, physicians, coaches, and athletes alike. They contradict the possibility that the differences observed in cross-sectional studies may have been due to differences in bone density existing before any of the women became athletes, and they contradict the expectation that exercise effectively counteracts the effect of hypoestrogenism on bone density in athletic amenorrhea. They also emphasize the importance of early treatment of amenorrheic athletes to prevent bone loss because mineral losses appear to be irreversible in postmenopausal women after the early rapid phase.

Calcium

The ability to provide mechanical strength and structural properties to bones and teeth is only one important physiological function of calcium. Calcium is also essential for the function of nerves, muscle, and other tissues, and whenever the amount of calcium in the bloodstream falls below a certain level, calcium is removed from the skeleton to satisfy these other needs.

It is important to recognize that calcium is a threshold nutrient (Heaney, 1985). That is, when calcium intake is above a certain level, in the sufficiency range, there is no relationship between calcium intake and bone density. Above the threshold, there is no evidence that larger intakes of calcium will increase bone density. When calcium intake is below this threshold, however, bone density is proportional to calcium consumption.

Retrospective and prospective studies have been done to determine the relationship between calcium intake and bone density. A large number of published reports suggest that patients with clinical osteoporosis consume less calcium than controls. The studies differ widely in quality, method, and rigor but not in their conclusions (Heaney et al., 1982). One study (Matkovic et al., 1979), for example, associated low calcium intakes with distinctly increased prevalences of hip fractures. In this study, bone status and fracture rates were assessed in two Yugoslavian communities distinguished only by their calcium intake. The communities were matched for ethnic origin, physical activity, and living conditions. One community consumed a low-calcium diet (350 to 500 mg/day), whereas the calcium intake for the other community was about twice this amount (800 to 1,100 mg/day). By age 35, greater bone density was indicated in both men and women consuming the high-calcium diet. Both communities lost bone mineral with age, but the community that started with more ended with more. There was a lower incidence of hip fractures among men in the high-calcium district, and women in the high-calcium district had a lower hip fracture rate after age 59. These data suggest that the higher incidence of hip fractures and the lower index of peak bone density of the community consuming the low-calcium diet were related to their reduced calcium consumption.

Now consider calcium intake in the United States. The Health and Nutrition Examination Surveys (HANES I and HANES II) conducted by the U.S. Public Health Service from 1971 to 1974 and from 1976 to 1980 obtained calcium intake values by 24-hr dietary recall administered by trained dieticians to a representative probability sample of over 28,000 persons from the U.S. population (Abraham, Carroll, Dresser, & Johnson, 1977; Carroll, Abraham, & Dresser, 1983). Figure 3 shows the HANES II median and mean intakes plotted against the U.S. Recommended Dietary Allowance (RDA). Note that the RDA is elevated during adolescence when growth rates are rapid. Note also that the average levels for males are a close match to the RDA until old age. The data for females, however, are very different. By age 10 average calcium intake has fallen substantially below RDA. This deficiency continues during the critical period when the bulk of calcium is being deposited in bone and throughout later life.

Figure 4, which compares the calcium consumption of female adolescents as reported in the HANES I and HANES II studies, suggests that women's dietary habits are getting worse instead of better. In the same age group, calcium consumption declines 10% over 5 years. Heaney (1985) attributes this decline to the introduction of low calorie soft drinks. A further 20% difference in calcium consumption between early and late adolescence was evident in both studies. This is a traditional socialization effect. Overall, the girls who were 10 to 14 years of age during HANES I reduced their calcium consumption 30% by the time of HANES II! Because this is the age when dietary habits are formed, these modern "Tab girls" face a gloomy prognosis for skeletal integrity.

Exercise

Bone responds to weight bearing and muscle contraction by increasing its mass and modifying its internal structure. Bone strength depends on both mass and this internal geometric structure. Each bone requires a certain amount and duration of force before it will hypertrophy. The skele-

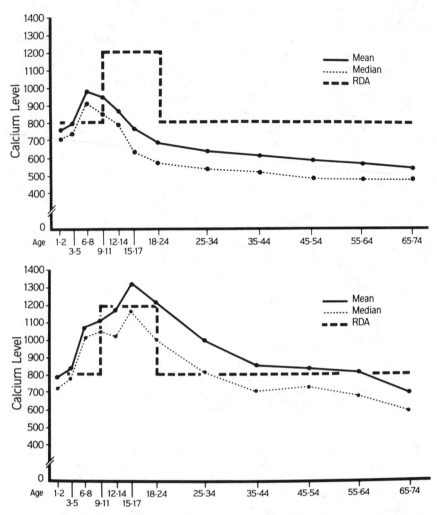

Figure 3 Daily calcium intake (mg) for U.S. females (above) and U.S. males (below) derived from HANES II data 1976 to 1980 (Carroll et al., 1983). (Courtesy of *Calcium: A Summary of Current Research for the Health Professional*, National Dairy Council, 1984.)

tal system, like the muscular system, needs the stimulus of mechanical loading for maintenance of size and strength and for hypertrophy. In fact, the single most important factor in age-related bone loss, after the adult peak at age 35, is decreased activity, which decreases the load on the skeleton. Body composition studies show that while women lose 30% of total body calcium from the age of 50 to 80, they also lose 30% of total body potassium. Potassium serves as an indicator of lean body mass; thus there is an association between loss of bone mass and muscle mass (Heaney, 1985).

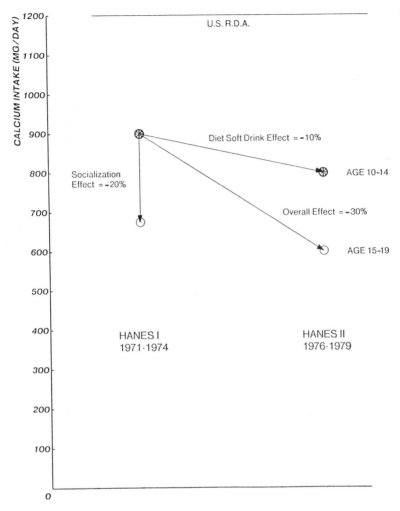

Figure 4 Daily calcium intake for U.S. female adolescents derived from HANES I 1971 to 1974 (Abraham et al., 1977) and HANES II 1976 to 1980 (Carroll et al., 1983) data.

Inactivity has been shown to result in large losses of bone mineral in weight-bearing bones. Rambaut, Dietlein, Vogel, and Smith (1972) found a 25% loss of bone mass in the calcaneus in eight young men after 24 weeks of bed rest. Donaldson et al. (1970) reported a 39% loss in the calcaneus after 36 weeks of bed rest in two young men. These losses following inactivity amount to approximately 1% per week.

The large loss of bone mineral in inactive young men contrasts sharply with the much smaller increases in bone mineral claimed by studies of the effect of exercise on postmenopausal women. Investigators observed increases of 3.5%, 2.29%, and 0% after 32 weeks (Krølner, Toft, Nielsen,

& Tøndevold, 1983), 144 weeks (Smith, Reddan, & Smith, 1981), and 52 weeks (Aloia, Cohn , Ostuni, Cane, & Ellis, 1978) of exercise training in postmenopausal women, respectively. These so-called increases correspond to changes of 0 to 0.1% per week. In fact, none of the increases may be real because they were smaller than the errors in the measurement techniques. Yet, these studies have been widely cited as evidence that exercise increases bone mineral content in postmenopausal women.

Lifelong physical activity, however, has been shown conclusively to increase bone mineral content. The bone mineral content of the tibia and fibula of male and female professional ballet dancers has been found to be 23 to 28% greater than in matched controls (Nilsson, Andersson, Havdrup, & Westlin, 1978). More dramatically, the bone mineral content of male weight lifters is 28 to 38% greater than that of men who do not lift weights (Nilsson et al.). The bone-strengthening effect of exercise, however, is local to the body part under load. For example, Dalén and Olsson (1974) found 21% more bone mineral content in the calcaneus of cross-country runners than in that of a control group, whereas Aloia et al. (1978) found no significant effect of marathon running on the bone mineral content of the radius. Similarly, in tennis players, the bone mineral content of the radius and humerus has ranged from 8 to 13% higher in the dominant arm than in the nondominant arm (Huddleston, Rockwell, Kulund, & Harrison, 1980; Montoye, Smith, Fardon, & Howley, 1980).

Because high levels of physical activity result in high levels of bone mass, the lower activity level of women compared to men plays a major role in predisposing women to osteoporosis. Women acquire their low activity habit amazingly early. Gilliam, Freedson, Geenen, and Shahraray (1981) found that as early as age 6 the heart rate of girls exceeded 160 beats per minute for only half as long per day as did that of boys.

Recommendations

The incidence of osteoporosis in American society can be reduced by avoiding the deficiencies that directly degrade bone density. The efforts of health educators, physicians, and coaches will all be required, however, because the prevention of osteoporosis is a lifelong project that begins by establishing healthful attitudes and habits in childhood.

First, all of these groups must regard it as their professional responsibility to know the reproductive status of the adolescent girls in their care because some unknown factor in the current methods for improving athletic performance also disrupts the reproductive system of a large proportion of the participating girls and women. The delay of menarche beyond age 16 or the cessation of menstruation must not be permitted to result in the undermineralization or demineralization of bone. Hormonal replacement therapy is as essential for young amenorrheic athletes as for postmenopausal women.

Second, the calcium consumption of adolescent girls must be dramatically increased. Milk consumption and dietary calcium supplementation should be actively promoted. Girls should be trained to count milligrams of calcium as rigorously as they count calories. The self-destructive substitution of high phosphate soft drinks for milk should be vigorously discouraged. Legislation for the calcium supplementation of other beverages should be passed.

Without adequate estrogen and calcium, a woman cannot even begin to prevent osteoporosis. With adequate estrogen and calcium, her success in preventing osteoporosis will depend on her habitual level of physical activity. Therefore, a third recommendation is to increase the physical activity of girls and women in order to increase their peak adult bone mass. Efforts after menopause are too little and too late. Women cannot pursue an ideal of delicate passivity while avoiding osteoporosis. Dense bones are the product of a large strong muscle mass.

Competitive girls' sports can play a major role in the effort to improve women's skeletal integrity. The goal should be to promote lifelong enthusiasm for physical activity in girls that matches that of boys. In particular, because mechanical loading is local in its effect upon the skeleton, complex activities that load the entire body should be promoted. Activities such as running and cycling, which load only certain body parts, are not sufficient to protect the entire skeleton. Because a properly designed weight training program is an effective means for total body loading, this author recommends that weight training be incorporated into girls' compulsory physical education classes.

Osteoporosis begins as a pediatric disease and is a cultural affliction. Prevention of it will require a cultural change in ideals and behavior. The traditional ideals and habits of most women are self-destructive in this respect, and reducing the incidence of osteoporosis in America will require the concerted effort of educators, physicians, and coaches, as well as parents.

References

Abraham, S., Carroll, M.D., Dresser, C.M., & Johnson, C.L. (1977). *Dietary intake findings, United States 1971-1974*. Hyattsville, MD: National Center for Health Statistics.

Aloia, J.F., Cohn, S.H., Babu, T., Abesamis, C., Kalici, N., & Ellis, K. (1978). Skeletal mass and body composition in marathon runners. *Metabolism, 27*, 1793-1796.

Aloia, J.F., Cohn, S.H., Ostuni, J.A., Cane, R., & Ellis, K. (1978). Prevention of involutional bone loss by exercise. *Annals of Internal Medicine, 89*, 356-358.

Cann, C.E., Martin, M.C., Genant, H.K., & Jaffe, R.B. (1984). Decreased spinal mineral content in amenorrheic women. *Journal of the American Medical Association, 251*, 626-629.

Cann, C.E., Martin, M.C., & Jaffe, R.B. (1985). Duration of amenorrhea affects rate of bone loss in women runners: Implications for therapy. *Medicine and Science in Sports and Exercise, 17*, 214.

Carroll, M.D., Abraham, S., & Dresser, M. (1983). *Dietary intake source data: United States 1976-1980.* Hyattsville, MD: U.S. Department of Health and Human Services, Public Health Service, National Center for Health Statistics.

Dalén, N., & Olsson, K.E. (1974). Bone mineral content and physical activity. *Acta Orthopaedica Scandinavica, 45,* 170-174.

Donaldson, C.L., Hulley, S.B., Vogel, J.M., Hattner, R.S., Bayers, J.H., & McMillan, D.E. (1970). Effect of prolonged bed rest on bone mineral. *Metabolism, 12,* 1071-1084.

Drinkwater, B.L., Nilson, K., Chestnut, C.H. III, Bremner, W.J., Shainholtz, S., & Southworth, M.B. (1984). Bone mineral content of amenorrheic and eumenorrheic athletes. *The New England Journal of Medicine, 311,* 277-281.

Gilliam, T.B., Freedson, P.S., Geenen, D.L., & Shahraray, B. (1981). Physical activity patterns determined by heart rate monitoring in 6- to 7-year-old children. *Medicine and Science in Sports and Exercise, 13,* 65-67.

Heaney, R. (1985, May). *Dietary and pharmacological maintenance of skeletal integrity.* Paper presented at "Skeletal integrity: Exercise and amenorrhea," a symposium conducted at the meeting of the American College of Sports Medicine, Nashville, TN.

Heaney, R.P., Gallagher, J.C., Johnston, C.C., Neer, R., Parfitt, A.M., Chir, B., & Whedan, G.D. (1982). Calcium nutrition and bone health in the elderly. *The American Journal of Clinical Nutrition, 36,* 986-1013.

Huddleston, A.L., Rockwell, D., Kulund, D.N., & Harrison, B. (1980). Bone mass in lifetime tennis athletes. *Journal of American Medical Association, 244,* 1107-1109.

Krølner, B., Toft, B., Nielsen, S.P., & Tøndevold, E. (1983). Physical exercise as prophylaxis against involutional vertebral bone loss: A controlled trial. *Clinical Science, 64,* 541-546.

Lindberg, J.S., Fears, W.B., Hunt, M.M., Powell, M.R., Boll, D., & Wade, C.E. (1984). Exercise-induced amenorrhea and bone density. *Annals of Internal Medicine, 101,* 647-649.

Lindsay, R., Hart, D.M., Aitken, J.M., MacDonald, E.B., Anderson, J.B., & Clarke, A.C. (1976). Long-term prevention of postmenopausal osteoporosis by oestrogen. *Lancet, i,* 1038-1040.

Lindsay, R., Hart, D.M., MacLean, A., Clark, A.C., Kraszewski, A., & Garwood, J. (1978). Bone response to termination of oestrogen treatment. *Lancet, i,* 1325-1327.

Marcus, R., Cann, C., Madvig, P., Minkoff, J., Goddard, M., Bayer, M., Martin, M., Gaudiani, L., Haskell, W., & Genant, H. (1985). Menstrual function and bone mass in elite women distance runners. *Annals of Internal Medicine, 102,* 158-163.

Matkovíc, V., Kostial, K., Simonovíç, I., Buzina, R., Brodarec, A., & Nordin, B.E.C. (1979). Bone status and fracture rates in two regions of Yugoslavia. *The American Journal of Clinical Nutrition, 32*, 540-549.

Montoye, H.J., Smith, E.L., Fardon, D.F., & Howley, E.T. (1980). Bone mineral in senior tennis players. *Scandinavian Journal of Sport Science, 2*, 26-32.

National Dairy Council. (1984). *Calcium: A summary of current research for the health professional*. Rosemont, IL: Author.

Nilsson, B.E., Andersson, S.M., Havdrup, T., & Westlin, N.E. (1978). Ballet dancing and weight-lifting—Effects on BMC. *American Journal of Roentgenology, 131*, 541-542.

Rambaut, P.C., Dietlein, L.F., Vogel, J.M., & Smith, M. (1972). Comparative study of two direct methods of bone mineral measurement. *Aerospace Medicine, 43*, 646-650.

Smith, E.L., Jr., Reddan, W., & Smith, P.E. (1981). Physical activity and calcium modalities for bone mineral increase in aged women. *Medicine and Science in Sports and Exercise, 13*, 60-64.

PART VI

Physical Characteristics of the Young Athlete

Competitive Youth Sports and Biological Maturation

Robert M. Malina

The growth and maturation of the organism depend on the integration of many factors. Among these factors, regular physical activity such as that involved in training for sport is believed by many to have favorable influences on the organism during growth and maturation and into adulthood. Physical activity, for example, is a significant factor in the regulation of body weight and composition and in the growth and integrity of skeletal and muscular tissues. On the other hand, regular activity has no apparent effect on stature, skeletal proportions and physique, or biological maturation as commonly assessed in growth studies (Malina, 1980, 1983a).

Comparisons of young athletes of local, national, and international caliber with reference data for the general population of children and youth generally indicate that young athletes, on the average, grow and mature in a similar manner as nonathletes; that is, the experience of athletic training and the stress of competition do not advance or delay the growth and maturation of the physically active youngster. There is, however, variation in size, physique and body composition, and in maturity status associated with specific sports (see Malina, 1982, in press; Malina, Meleski, & Shoup, 1982; Malina et al., 1984). Part of the variation in size, physique, and body composition is due to variation in maturity status. This variation may be more significant at certain ages and in specific sports (e.g., the size advantage of the early maturing boy and girl in fifth and sixth grade football and volleyball, respectively). Conversely, the size disadvantage of the late maturing youngster may be a factor directing him or her to other sports such as track or gymnastics.

The preceding relates to selection, which is a significant contributory factor when considering the growth and maturity of young athletes. Successful young athletes are a highly selected group, primarily on the basis of skill but sometimes on the basis of size and physique in some sports or positions within a sport. Selection may be by the child, parents, coaches, or a combination of the three. Self-selection is a critical factor because it can influence the youngster's motivation to train and be receptive to coaching. Selection also occurs to some extent by default; that is, there are dropouts who choose not to participate for reasons unrelated to sport even though they may have the skill to be successful. And as competition becomes more rigorous, selection is probably a more important factor.

Delayed Menarche in Athletes

Given the reasonable body of literature on the growth and maturity characteristics of young athletes, concern is, nevertheless, often expressed about the effects of prolonged intensive training and the stress of competition on the growth and maturation of youngsters who specialize in sport at an early age. The concern is most often focused on delayed menarche, which is common in elite athletes. Because athletes who began training before menarche tend to have later ages at menarche than those who began training after menarche, training is implicated as the causative factor (see Malina, 1983b).

The data dealing with the inferred relationship between training and delayed menarche, however, are associational, are generally based on small samples of postmenarcheal athletes (an exception is the report of Stager, Robertshaw, & Miescher, 1984), do not specify training load, and do not consider other factors that are known to influence menarche. As an example, the influence of family size (i.e., number of children in the family) on the age at menarche in nonathletes and athletes is shown in Table 1. Although the estimated effects vary, the influence of family size on the age at menarche of athletes is well within the range of that for samples of nonathletes. There is, however, variation in family size among athletes in different sports (Malina, 1983b).

Correlation between years of training before menarche and age at menarche obviously does not imply a cause-effect sequence; rather, the association is likely an artifact. The older a girl is at menarche, the more likely she would have begun her training prior to menarche, and conversely, the younger a girl is at menarche, the more likely she would have begun training after menarche or would have had a shorter period of training prior to menarche (Stager et al., 1984). It may also be that delayed maturation is a contributing factor in the young girl's decision to take up sport rather than the training causing the lateness (Malina, 1983b).

In contrast to delayed menarche commonly observed in athletes and the inferred relationship with training, training as a factor influencing the maturation of males is not ordinarily considered an important issue. It is somewhat puzzling why one would expect training to delay the maturation of girls and not boys, even though the processes underlying maturation are quite similar in both sexes. Further, there is a reasonable body of literature that suggests that the growth and maturation of males are more susceptible to environmental alteration whereas that of females is better buffered against environmental stress (Bielicki & Charzewski, 1977; Stinson, 1985).

Maturity Indications

Thus, issues related to biological maturation and the effects of training for sport and perhaps the stress of competition on maturation merit more detailed consideration. It is first necessary to distinguish maturation from

Table 1 Estimated Effects of Family Size on the Age at Menarche in Samples of Nonathletes and Athletes

Sample	Reference	Years per additional sibling
Belgian	Wellens (1984)	0.11
English	Roberts et al. (1971)	0.18
Rumanian	Štukovsky et al. (1967)	0.17
Welsh	Roberts & Dann (1967)	0.15
High school athletes, U.S.	Davidson (1981)	0.12
Olympic athletes	Malina (1983b)	0.22

growth because the two concepts are fundamentally different. Maturity implies progress toward the mature state, which varies with the biological system considered. Skeletal maturity, for example, is a fully ossified skeleton; sexual maturity is reproductive capability; somatic maturity is often defined as adult stature. Growth, on the other hand, refers to changes in the size of the organism or of its parts. All individuals attain adult stature, skeletal maturity, and sexual maturity. However, the age of attaining each is variable. Thus, progress toward maturity implies time or variation in rate, whereas growth is size oriented. This is the fundamental distinction between the two terms, which are often used synonymously in developmental studies. Both processes are probably under separate genetic regulation, yet they are related. For example, children advanced in biological maturity status are closer to adult size at all ages compared to children who are delayed, so that at any given age during childhood the former are, on the average, taller and heavier than the latter. Youngsters advanced in maturity also differ in physique, body composition, and physical performance compared to those delayed in maturity (Malina, 1984). The differences between contrasting maturity groups are especially pronounced during early and middle adolescence, the ages during which youth sports are most popular.

It should be emphasized that growth and maturation are processes, and only the outcomes of these processes are measured and observed. Thus, it is difficult to make direct statements on the effects of training on the cellular processes that underlie the events that are measurable and observable. Further, a variety of factors other than training are capable of influencing these processes.

The most commonly used indicators of maturity are skeletal maturation, the development of secondary sex characteristics, including the age at menarche, and the timing of maximum growth in height or peak height velocity. The hand-wrist complex is the most commonly used area of the skeleton for maturity assessments, but methods of evaluating maturity vary. One can inquire, of course, as to how representative of the skeleton are the hand and wrist. For example, there may be discrepancies of

1 or more years between skeletal ages of the knee and of the hand and wrist in individual children (Roche, Wainer, & Thissen, 1975).

Sexual maturation is monitored primarily via the development of secondary sex characteristics: pubic hair development in both sexes, breast development in girls, and genital development in boys. The development of each of these characteristics is rated on the basis of five-stage scales, with the criteria of Tanner (1962, 1969) for these scales the most widely used. Stage 1 indicates the preadolescent state of development (i.e., absence of pubic hair, breast, or genital development). Stage 2 indicates the initial development or appearance of each particular characteristic. Stages 3 and 4 indicate continued development of each and may be difficult to assess, especially for pubic hair. Stage 5 indicates the adult state. Ratings of stages of sexual development are generally made from standardized photographs or by visual inspection on clinical examination. Such ratings obviously have limitations because the method requires invasion of individual privacy, which is a matter of much concern to adolescents. It should be emphasized that the development of these characteristics is a continuous process upon which discontinuities or stages are imposed.

The initial appearance of breast and genital development is the first overt sign of impending sexual maturation in girls and boys, respectively. Mean and/or median ages for initial development of the breast in American and European girls vary between 10.6 and 11.4 years, whereas corresponding ages for initial genital development in boys vary between 11.0 and 12.2 years (Malina, 1978).

The age at menarche is perhaps the most commonly reported developmental milestone of female adolescence. However, most studies of athletes use the retrospective method, which has the limitation of error in recall. Menarche is a rather late maturational event. It occurs after peak height velocity and while most girls are in Stage 4 of breast and pubic hair development (Marshall, 1978). The average difference between age at menarche and age at peak height velocity is about 1.2 to 1.3 years (Tanner & Davies, 1985).

Somatic maturity is most often viewed in terms of the timing of maximum growth during the adolescent growth spurt, that is, age at peak height velocity. This requires longitudinal data, and methods of estimating peak height velocity vary, for example, single, double, and triple logistic models, the spline technique, graphical estimates, polynomials, and so on. Estimated ages at peak height velocity vary with the method used, for example, double logistic estimates are consistently lower than the others, but the ages are, on the average, reasonably similar in American and European samples, respectively (Table 2).

Interrelationships Among Maturity Indicators

There is variation in the development of secondary sex characteristics, skeletal maturity, and peak height velocity within each sex during adolescence. Nevertheless, these maturity indicators are related. Several ex-

Table 2 Estimated Ages (Mean ± Standard Deviation) at Peak Height Velocity in North American and European Youth

Sample	Reference	Method	Males			Females		
			n	M	SD	n	M	SD
North American:								
Berkeley, CA	Bock & Thissen (1980)	Triple logistic	66	13.7	1.1	70	11.6	0.9
Berkeley, CA	Thissen et al. (1976)	Double logistic	65	13.1	1.1	64	11.0	0.8
Boston, MA	Thissen et al. (1976)	Double logistic	54	12.9	0.9	54	11.1	0.9
Denver, CO	Thissen et al. (1976)	Double logistic	54	13.3	0.9	49	11.0	0.9
Yellow Springs, OH	Thissen et al. (1976)	Double logistic	83	13.0	0.9	74	11.0	0.8
Newton, MA	Zacharias & Rand (1983)	Preece-Baines I				332	11.6	1.2
Saskatchewan, SK	Mirwald et al. (1981)	Preece-Baines I	14	14.2	1.2[a]			
		Preece-Baines I	11	14.1	0.7			
European:								
UK, Harpenden	Tanner et al. (1966)	Graphical	49	14.1	0.9	41	12.1	0.9
UK, Harpenden	Tanner et al. (1976)	Single logistic	55	13.9	0.8	35	11.9	0.9
UK, Harpenden	Preece & Baines (1978)	Preece-Baines I	35	14.2	0.9	23	11.9	0.7
		Preece-Baines IV	35	13.6	0.8	22	11.4	0.9
Belgium, National	Beunen et al. (in press)	Nonsmooth Polynomials	432	14.2	1.0			
Belgium, Brussels	Hauspie et al. (1980)	Preece-Baines I				35	11.6	1.0
		Double logistic				34	10.9	1.0
		Single logistic				35	11.4	1.0
		Graphical				35	11.7	1.0
Netherlands, Leiden	Wafelbakker (1970)	Graphical (?)	81	14.4				
Sweden, Stockholm	Taranger et al. (1976)	Moving increments	122	14.1		90	11.9	
Sweden, Urban	Lindgren (1978)	Midyear velocity	373	14.1	1.1	357	11.9	0.9
Switzerland, Zurich	Largo et al. (1978)	Splines	112	13.9	0.8	110	12.2	1.0
Poland, Wrocław	Bielicki (1975)	Graphical				234	11.7	0.9
Poland, Wrocław	Bielicki et al. (1984)	Graphical	177	14.0	1.2			

Note. [a]The boys were classified as physically active (n = 14) and inactive (n = 11).

Table 3   Correlations Between Ages at Reaching Certain Maturity Indicators During Adolescence

Source	Girls						Boys	
	PHV			B2		PH2	PHV	
	B2	PH2	M	PH2	M	M	G2	PH2
Reynolds & Wines (1948)	.80		.71	.66	.86	.70		
Nicolson & Hanley (1953)	.78	.75		.75	.74	.74	.67	
Deming (1957)	.82		.93					.56
Marshall & Tanner (1969)			.91		.64			
Bielicki (1975)	.76	.77	.76	.77	.72	.73		
Taranger et al. (1976)	.80	.73	.84	.70	.74	.58	.78	.49
Tanner et al. (1976)	.78	.77	.84				.47	.84
Bielicki et al. (1984)							.87	.84

amples are shown in Table 3. The correlations are generally moderate to high, and the correlations for boys tend to be somewhat lower than those for girls. Skeletal maturity is also related to the development of secondary sex characteristics. This is clearly evident in the reduced variation in skeletal age at menarche. In an early study, for example, Simmons (1944) noted that 80% of the Brush Foundation sample of girls had skeletal ages within 6 months of the mean skeletal age at menarche. More recently, Marshall (1974) reported mean chronological and skeletal ages at menarche of 13.2 and 13.3 years, respectively, in the Harpenden Study, but the standard deviation for skeletal age was less than one half (0.39 year) of that for chronological age (0.84 year).

The interrelatedness among maturity indicators and their independence are reasonably well illustrated in results of principal component analyses of sexual, skeletal, and somatic indicators of maturity in boys and girls followed longitudinally. Sex-specific analyses of ages at attaining a variety of maturity indicators in males and females of the Wroclaw Growth Study (Bielicki, 1975; Bielicki, Koniarek, & Malina, 1984) resulted in two principal components. The first, which accounted for 77% and 68% of the total sample variance in boys and girls, respectively, had high loadings on almost all indices. It appears to be a general maturity factor that discriminates among individuals who are early, average, or late maturing. The second principal component accounted for 12% and 7.5% of the total sample variance in boys and girls, respectively. Among boys, this component, which had high positive loadings on skeletal maturity at 11 and 12 years of age and lower loadings at 13, 14, and 15 years of age, appears to be a rather specific factor for the rate of skeletal maturation during preadolescence. The second principal component in girls was somewhat similar in that it had moderate loadings for skeletal maturity scores that systematically decreased from 10 through 14 years of age. But this component also differed between the sexes, particularly in the magnitude and sign of loadings for indices of linear growth and secondary sex characteristic development.

Although there are some differences in the two separate analyses, the results suggest that the indices of sexual, skeletal, and somatic maturation are sufficiently interrelated to indicate a general maturity factor during adolescence. The evidence also suggests variation among the indicators. Thus, although there is a general maturity factor underlying the tempo of maturation and growth during adolescence in both sexes, there is sufficient variation so that no single system (i.e., sexual, skeletal, or somatic maturation) provides a complete description of the tempo of maturation of an individual boy or girl during adolescence. These results are consistent with the earlier observations of Nicolson and Hanley (1953) on California adolescents, although the analytic methods differed.

The apparent "disharmony" among the indicators probably reflects real biological variation and perhaps methodological concerns. The five-stage scale for rating secondary sex characteristics is somewhat arbitrary. An individual in the early phase of Stage 3 of breast development, for example, is rated the same as an individual in the late phase of this stage. The variation also relates to individual variability in the timing and duration of events used to document the adolescent spurt. The 3rd percentile for the total duration of genital development from Stages 2 through 5 in British boys is 1.9 years, whereas the 97th percentile is 4.7 years. Thus, some boys may pass from genital Stages 2 through 5 in about 2 years, whereas others may take about 5 years (Marshall, 1978). Further, there is no consistent relationship between the age at which secondary sex character development begins and the rate of progress through the stages.

The variation may also reflect differences in the nature of hormonal control in prepubertal and pubertal phases of development. This is suggested in the correlations between the timing of the beginning or takeoff of the adolescent height spurt and skeletal maturity at successive ages (Table 4). The correlations become systematically greater with increasing levels of skeletal maturity so that the age at takeoff of the height spurt (mean ages: 9.7 years in girls and 11.8 years in boys) is more closely correlated with the age at reaching the skeletal maturity for 14 and 15 years of age in girls and boys, respectively, than it is with the age at reaching the skeletal maturity score for 10 and 12 years, respectively (Bielicki, 1975; Bielicki et al., 1984). In other words, the age at takeoff of the adolescent height spurt is more closely related to an event that occurs, on the average, more than 3 or 4 years later than it is with an event that occurs, on the average, at the same time. The earlier phases of skeletal maturation are principally dependent on the stimulation of growth hormone, whereas the later stages, which include epiphyseal capping and fusion, are chiefly under the influence of steroid hormones (Tanner, Whitehouse, Marshall, Healy, & Goldstein, 1975). Thus, the later phases of skeletal maturation are under the control of the same hormones that underlie the adolescent growth spurt and sexual maturation.

Genetic and Endocrine Regulation

Although the twin model has limitations (see Bouchard & Malina, 1983), the evidence indicates generally high heritabilities for indicators of sexual, skeletal, and somatic maturity (Fischbein, 1977a, 1977b; Kimura, 1981, 1983; Skład, 1973, 1977). This would suggest that under adequate environmental conditions, the adolescent growth spurt and sexual maturation are genetically determined. Although the evidence is less extensive, plasma hormonal levels of luteinizing hormone (LH), follicle-stimulating hormone (FSH), and testosterone also show a significant genotypic contribution in male monozygotic pubescent twins (Parker, Judd, Rossman, & Yen, 1975).

The preceding discussion of interrelationships among maturity indicators must be considered within the context of the neuroendocrine hypothesis for the regulation of sexual maturation and the adolescent growth spurt. Gonadotropin-releasing hormone (GnRH) is secreted by the hypothalamus and stimulates the secretion of gonadotropins by the anterior pituitary. The latter in turn initiates the maturation of the gonads and the process of sexual maturation. The process is gradual and probably begins in the late prepubertal period, long before any overt signs of

Table 4 Correlations Between Skeletal Maturity at Successive Ages and the Age at Takeoff of the Height Spurt in Wrocław Boys and Girls[a]

Boys skeletal maturity[b]	Age at takeoff	Girls skeletal maturity[b]	Age at takeoff
11	.19	10	.46
12	.33	11	.55
13	.57	12	.58
14	.71	13	.62
15	.78	14	.68

[a]Adapted from Bielicki (1975) and Bielicki et al. (1984). [b]For boys, skeletal maturity is the age at which the median skeletal maturity score for each chronological age was reached; for girls, it is the skeletal maturity score attained at each chronological age. Hence, for girls the signs of the correlations were reversed.

sexual maturation are evident. Further, the initiation of the changes in the hypothalamic-pituitary-gonadal axis resides in the central nervous system (Wierman & Crowley, 1986).

The gonadal steroids that underlie sexual maturation also influence the adolescent growth spurt and skeletal maturation. Adrenal sex steroids provide additional hormonal regulation. Hence, there is considerable potential for variation among indicators of sexual, skeletal, and somatic maturity. Target organ responsiveness to the hormonal changes and hormone receptor concentration are perhaps other sources of variation among maturity indicators.

Environmental Influences

The timing of sexual maturation and the adolescent growth spurt can also be influenced by environmental factors. The delaying effects of chronic undernutrition are well documented. Stressful life events are also significant. They are especially evident in the growth and maturation of youngsters experiencing disturbed home environments (Patton, 1962) and in the "unusually 'fractured' curves of growth and pubertal development in girls translated to unfamiliar boarding schools at various times in puberty" (Tanner, 1978, p. 102). Studies of secular change in the age at menarche (Ellison, 1981; Liestøl, 1982) suggest that environmental effects on menarche may be programmed by conditions early in life and not necessarily by those conditions that may be operating circumpuberally. Liestøl (1982) suggests the following:

During the period around or after birth, the processes leading to menarche are sensitive to a set of environmental stimuli. After this period, the reproductive system becomes clearly less susceptible. During adolescence, the maturation process may be influenced somewhat, but probably not to any great extent as long as conditions are not adverse. If the situation becomes adverse, menarche may be delayed considerably and postmenarcheal women will be at risk of becoming amenorrhoeic. (p. 535)

A question of concern, therefore, is whether intensive training for sport and the stress of competition during sexual maturation and the adolescent growth spurt produce conditions that are sufficiently "adverse" to influence the progress and thus the timing of these maturational events. A related question is whether regular, intensive prepubertal training for sport and regular competition is sufficiently stressful to prolong the prepubertal state and in turn delay sexual maturation and the adolescent growth spurt.

The data available to adequately answer these questions are not extensive. As noted earlier, most concern is for delayed menarche commonly observed in athletes, with little attention to other maturity indicators and virtually no concern for possible effects of intensive training on the maturation of boys. Some consider the questions moot, for example:

There is controversy in the literature whether heavy training resulting in a lean physique is related to delayed maturation, or if the qualities of smallness and leanness are selective factors in certain sports.
    The question appears moot since experimental data are generally not available. (Ross & Marfell-Jones, 1982, p. 99)

The questions, however, are not moot because biological maturation does not occur in a social vacuum. Individual variation in biological maturation and associated changes in size, physique, and body composition, as well as associated changes in behavior are the backdrop against which youth ultimately evaluate and interpret their own growth, maturation, and self-concept. However, the psychological importance of menarche has no counterpart in the maturation process of boys. Menarche has important cultural values associated with its attainment.

Further, the conclusion offered by Frisch et al. (1981) that "intense physical activity (before menarche) does in fact delay menarche" has been widely disseminated in the popular press, even though the data are limited and the authors made the error of drawing a cause-effect relationship from a correlation that was at best moderate (i.e., $n = 18$ and $r = +.53$ between age at menarche and years of training before menarche) (p. 1562). Nevertheless, this view has persisted even though the available data are only associational and are not based on developing girls. Bullen et al. (1985), for example, recently opened a report with the following statement: "High-intensity athletic performance has become an accepted addition to the defined *causes* [italics added] of . . . delayed menarche" (p. 1349). As mentioned earlier, correlation or association does not imply a cause-effect sequence of events.

Given parental concern for the well-being of their children, one can only wonder if some parents may withdraw their daughters from sport or may experience undue anxiety because of such a questionable conclusion! Moreover, there are thousands of premenarcheal girls involved in sports training, and this questionable conclusion may, perhaps, have a negative impact at a time when young girls are increasingly encouraged to be physically active in sports. Hence, the questions are not moot; rather, they merit serious consideration.

Training and Delayed Menarche

The suggested mechanism for the association between training and delayed menarche is hormonal, that is, intensive training influences circulating levels of gonadotrophic and ovarian hormones and, in turn, menarche. A role for "energy drain" has also been suggested.

However, hormonal data for prepubertal or pubertal athletes are limited. Premenarcheal ballet dancers show extremely low gonadotropin secretion in association with only "mild" growth stunting (Warren, 1980). Prepubertal 11-year-old gymnasts have lower plasma levels of estrone, testosterone, and androstenedione than prepubertal swimmers of the same age, but the two groups of young athletes do not differ in gonadotropin levels. Among those gymnasts and swimmers in the initial stage of puberty (i.e., Stage 2 of breast development), none of the plasma hormone levels differ. It is of interest that the prepubertal gymnasts and swimmers have similar levels of dehydroepiandrosterone-sulphate, which suggests that both groups are in a similar stage of adrenarche, although the gymnasts have been training longer than the swimmers (Peltenburg et al., 1984). This observation does not support the suggestion that training delays adrenarche and prolongs the prepubertal state (Brisson, Dulac, Peronnet, & Ledoux, 1982). Further, recent evidence does not support the view that secretion of adrenal androgens triggers sexual maturation (Wierman & Crowley, 1986).

The preceding provides descriptive profiles of several hormones in young female athletes. Data are necessary, however, on the acute hormonal responses to exercise and on changes, if any, in basal levels of hormones associated with training in young athletes. In small samples of pre- and postmenarcheal competitive swimmers 13 to 18 years of age (Carli et al., 1983a), changes in adrenocorticotrophic hormone (ACTH), cortisol, prolactin, and testosterone occur in response to training, but the patterns of response are generally similar in the pre- and postmenarcheal girls. Basal estradiol levels, as expected, differ between the maturity groups, but both groups experience a decrease in basal levels during the first 12 weeks of training and an increase after 24 weeks. Basal levels of estradiol at the beginning and end of the training program do not differ in the premenarcheal swimmers but are lower in the postmenarcheal swimmers at the end of the 24-week training program (Carli et al., 1983a).

Results of these studies of young female athletes are variable and not conclusive. They are based on plasma hormonal levels. The simple presence of a hormone, however, does not necessarily imply that it is physiologically active. There is variation in tissue responsiveness, and the tissue probably must be sufficiently mature in order to respond in developing youngsters.

Data on the hormonal profiles of young male athletes are not extensive. Changes in plasma levels of ACTH and testosterone over two competitive seasons are evident in competitive male swimmers 12 to 16 years of age (presumably pubertal) but not in plasma levels of growth hormone and gonadotrophic hormones (Carli et al., 1983b). Results are variable, however, from one season to the next, and the hormonal changes are variable and generally within the physiological range. In a sample of nonathletes, no differences are apparent in postmaximal exercise concentrations of serum testosterone and growth hormone among boys grouped by stage of pubertal development (Fahey, Valle-Zuris, Oehlsen, Trieb, & Seymour, 1979). This observation would suggest that a critical pubertal state with enhanced hormonal responsiveness to exercise does not exist.

Clearly, data on hormonal profiles of young athletes and hormonal responses of young athletes to regular training are not extensive. Hence, it is difficult to draw conclusions about the effects of intensive training for sport at young ages on the underlying neuroendocrine changes that trigger sexual maturation and the adolescent growth spurt.

The general interrelatedness of indices of sexual, skeletal, and somatic maturation was indicated earlier. Hence, it is somewhat surprising that the effects of training for sport on other maturity indicators are not ordinarily considered. If the hormonal responses to regular training are considered important as modifiers of sexual maturation, one might expect them to influence skeletal maturation as well. Evidence from two studies of young athletes in Czechoslovakia, however, indicates no effects of training for sport and sports competition on skeletal maturity of the hand and wrist (Kotulán, Reznickova, & Placheta, 1980; Novotny, 1981). Thus, the process of skeletal maturation in the hand and wrist is not seemingly affected by regular training for sport in adolescent boys and girls.

Maturation of Active Youngsters

Longitudinal data are obviously required to examine the effects of training for sport and sports competition on the maturation of young athletes. Given the logistical difficulties of conducting longitudinal studies, it might be worthwhile to more closely examine available longitudinal data. In other words, are there young athletes in the available longitudinal series? To this end, the longitudinal data from the Wroclaw Growth Study (Poland) were examined (Malina & Bielicki, unpublished data). The subjects were followed from 8 through 18 years of age and subsequently interviewed at 24 (females) and 27 (males) years of age. The interview included questions on present physical activity habits in addition to sport activities in elementary and secondary school. The records indicated 16 males

Table 5   Standard Scores ($M \pm SE$) for Ages at Attaining Certain Pubertal Events in 13 Active Boys[a]

Pubertal event	M	SE
Peak height velocity	+0.36	.25
Peak weight velocity	+0.37	.26
Skeletal maturity, 11 years	+0.05	.28
Skeletal maturity, 15 years	+0.23	.33
80% adult height	-0.10	.32
90% adult height	+0.25	.25
Genital II	+0.25	.20
Genital IV	+0.29	.22
Pubic hair II	+0.50	.22
Pubic hair IV	+0.59	.23

[a]Malina & Bielicki (unpublished data).

who were active in sports (usually at the club level) during the elementary and high school years, and who were active in sport at the time of the interview. Thus, it is assumed that the individuals had trained for and competed in sport during their immediate prepubertal and pubertal years. As a group the subjects participated primarily in team sports, and one played for the national basketball team in international competition. Complete records, which included secondary sex characteristic development, skeletal maturity, and somatic indicators, were available for 13 of the 16 individuals. The data were converted to z scores using the means and standard deviations for the larger series (Bielicki et al., 1984). Mean standard scores and standard errors for ages at attaining certain pubertal events in this sample of 13 active males are shown in Table 5. With the exception of the age at attaining the median skeletal maturity score for 11 years and the age at attaining 80% of adult height (both of which are prepubertal events and probably under different hormonal control; see above discussion of the principal components analyses), all average standard scores are advanced relative to the population means by about one fourth of a standard deviation or more. This would suggest that as a group, this sample of males who were active in sport during childhood and adolescence were generally advanced in sexual, skeletal, and somatic maturity relative to the longitudinal series as a whole.

In contrast to the data for males, only five females who indicated physical education as a favorite subject in elementary and high school and who were active in club sports as young adults could be identified. Ages at attaining certain developmental landmarks were converted to z scores using the means and standard deviations for the longitudinal series (Bielicki, 1975). Means and standard errors are shown in Table 6. Note the generally large standard errors, which indicate considerable variation in this small sample. Nevertheless, these active females tend to be, on

Table 6 Standard Scores ($M \pm SE$) for Ages at Attaining Certain Pubertal Events in 5 Active Girls[a]

Pubertal event	M	SE
Peak height velocity	−0.25	.26
Skeletal maturity, 12 years	−0.32	.49
Skeletal maturity, 14 years	−0.22	.61
Breast II	−0.24	.45
Breast V	−0.65	.49
Pubic hair II	−0.44	.49
Pubic hair V	−0.56	.36
Menarche	−0.32	.37

[a]Malina & Bielicki (unpublished data).

the average, delayed in the ages at attaining selected indices of sexual, skeletal, and somatic maturation.

Although the preceding data are limited, they are generally consistent with information on the maturity characteristics of young athletes (Malina, 1982, 1988). The results would seem to emphasize constitutional factors in successful sports participation at young ages. Constitutional factors imply variation in size, physique, body composition, maturity, and performance among individuals, all of which have a significant genotypic component under adequate environmental conditions. Training is a significant factor influencing body composition and performance but not size (stature), physique, and biological maturation. Thus, given the available data, it is difficult to implicate intensive training for sport and the stress of sports competition as critical influences on the biological maturation of children and youth.

References

Beunen, G., Malina, R.M., Van't Hof, M.A., Simons, J., Ostyn, M., Renson, R., & Van Gerven, D. (in press). *Physical growth and motor performance of Belgian boys followed longitudinally between 12 and 19 years of age*. Champaign, IL: Human Kinetics.

Bielicki, T. (1975). Interrelationships between various measures of maturation rate in girls during adolescence. *Studies in Physical Anthropology*, 1, 51-64.

Bielicki, T., & Charzewski, J. (1977). Sex differences in the magnitude of statural gains of offspring over parents. *Human Biology*, 49, 265-277.

Bielicki, T., Koniarek, J., & Malina, R.M. (1984). Interrelationships among certain measures of growth and maturation rate in boys during adolescence. *Annals of Human Biology*, 11, 201-210.

Bock, R.D., & Thissen, D. (1980). Statistical problems of fitting individual growth curves. In F.E. Johnston, A.F. Roche, & C. Susanne (Eds.), *Human physical growth and maturation* (pp. 265-290). New York: Plenum.

Bouchard, C., & Malina, R.M. (1983). Genetics for the sport scientist: Selected methodological considerations. *Exercise and Sport Sciences Reviews*, **11**, 275-305.

Brisson, G.R., Dulac, S., Peronnet, F., & Ledoux, M. (1982). The onset of menarche: A late event in pubertal progression to be affected by physical training. *Canadian Journal of Applied Sport Sciences*, **7**, 61-67.

Bullen, B.A., Skrinar, G.S., Beitins, I.Z., Mering, G. von, Turnbull, B.A., & McArthur, J.W. (1985). Induction of menstrual disorders by strenuous exercise in untrained women. *New England Journal of Medicine*, **312**, 1349-1353.

Carli, G., Martelli, G., Viti, A., Baldi, L., Bonifazi, M., & Lupo di Prisco, C. (1983a). The effect of swimming training on hormone levels in girls. *Journal of Sports Medicine and Physical Fitness*, **23**, 45-51.

Carli, G., Martelli, G., Viti, A., Baldi, L., Bonifazi, M., & Lupo di Prisco, C. (1983b). Modulation of hormone levels in male swimmers during training. In A.P. Hollander, P.A. Huijing, & G. de Groot (Eds.), *Biomechanics and medicine in swimming* (pp. 33-40). Champaign, IL: Human Kinetics.

Davidson, A.E. (1981). *The age at menarche and selected familial and menstrual characteristics of high school varsity athletes.* Unpublished master's thesis, The University of Texas at Austin.

Deming, J. (1957). Application of the Gompertz curve to the observed pattern of growth in length of 48 individual boys and girls during the adolescent cycle of growth. *Human Biology*, **29**, 83-122.

Ellison, P.T. (1981). Morbidity, mortality, and menarche. *Human Biology*, **53**, 635-643.

Fahey, T.D., Valle-Zuris, A. del, Oehlsen, G., Trieb, M., & Seymour, J. (1979). Pubertal stage differences in hormonal and hematological responses to maximal exercise in males. *Journal of Applied Physiology*, **46**, 823-827.

Fischbein, S. (1977a). Onset of puberty in MZ and DZ twins. *Acta Geneticae, Medicae et Gemellologiae*, **26**, 151-157.

Fischbein, S. (1977b). Intra-pair similarity in physical growth of monozygotic and dizygotic twins during puberty. *Annals of Human Biology*, **4**, 417-430.

Frisch, R.E., Gotz-Welbergen, A.V., McArthur, J.W., Albright, T., Witschi, J., Bullen, B., Birnholz, J., Reed, R.B., & Hermann, H. (1981). Delayed menarche and amenorrhea of college athletes in relation to age of onset of training. *Journal of the American Medical Association*, **246**, 1559-1563.

Hauspie, R.C., Wachholder, A., Baron, G., Cantraine, F., Susanne, C., & Graffar, M. (1980). A comparative study of the fit of four different functions to longitudinal data of growth in height of Belgian girls. *Annals of Human Biology*, **7**, 347-358.

Kimura, K. (1981). Skeletal maturity in twins. *Journal of the Anthropological Society of Nippon*, **89**, 457-477.

Kimura, K. (1983). Skeletal maturity and bone growth in twins. *American Journal of Physical Anthropology*, **60**, 491-497.

Kotulán, J., Řezničková, M., & Placheta, Z. (1980). Exercise and growth. In Z. Placheta (Ed.), *Youth and physical activity* (pp. 61-117). Brno: J.E. Purkyne University Medical Faculty.

Largo, R.H., Gasser, T., Prader, A., Stuetzle, W., & Huber, P.J. (1978). Analysis of the adolescent growth spurt using smoothing spline functions. *Annals of Human Biology*, **5**, 421-434.

Liestøl, K. (1982). Social conditions and menarcheal age: The importance of early years of life. *Annals of Human Biology*, **9**, 521-537.

Lindgren, G. (1978). Growth of schoolchildren with early, average and late ages of peak height velocity. *Annals of Human Biology*, **5**, 253-267.

Malina, R.M. (1978). Adolescent growth and maturation: Selected aspects of current research. *Yearbook of Physical Anthropology*, **21**, 63-94.

Malina, R.M. (1980). Physical activity, growth, and functional capacity. In F.E. Johnston, A.F. Roche, & C. Susanne (Eds.), *Human physical growth and maturation* (pp. 303-327). New York: Plenum.

Malina, R.M. (1982). Physical growth and maturity characteristics of young athletes. In R.A. Magill, M.J. Ash, & F.L. Smoll (Eds.), *Children and sport* (pp. 73-96). Champaign, IL: Human Kinetics.

Malina, R.M. (1983a). Human growth, maturation, and regular physical activity. *Acta Medica Auxologica*, **15**, 5-23.

Malina, R.M. (1983b). Menarche in athletes: A synthesis and hypothesis. *Annals of Human Biology*, **10**, 1-24.

Malina, R.M. (1984). Physical growth and maturation. In J.R. Thomas (Ed.), *Motor development during childhood and adolescence* (pp. 2-26). Minneapolis: Burgess.

Malina, R.M. (1988). Biological maturity status of young athletes. *Proceedings of the Conference on Child and Sport*. Urbino, Italy, 1984. Champaign, IL: Human Kinetics.

Malina, R.M., & Bielicki, T. Sexual, skeletal and somatic maturation of active boys and girls. Unpublished manuscript.

Malina, R.M., Little, B.B., Bouchard, C., Carter, J.E.L., Hughes, P.C.R., Kunze, D., & Ahmed, L. (1984). Growth status of Olympic athletes less than 18 years of age: Young athletes at the Mexico City, Munich, and Montreal Olympic Games. In J.E.L. Carter (Ed.), *Physical structure of Olympic athletes. Part II. Kinanthropometry of Olympic athletes* (pp. 183-201). Basel: S. Karger.

Malina, R.M., Meleski, B.W., & Shoup, R.F. (1982). Anthropometric, body composition, and maturity characteristics of selected school-age athletes. *Pediatric Clinics of North America*, **29**, 1305-1323.

Marshall, W.A. (1974). Interrelationships of skeletal maturation, sexual development and somatic growth in man. *Annals of Human Biology*, **1**, 29-40.

Marshall, W.A. (1978). Puberty. In F. Falkner & J.M. Tanner (Eds.), *Human growth. Volume 2. Postnatal growth* (pp. 141-181). New York: Plenum.

Marshall, W.A., & Tanner, J.M. (1969). Variations in pattern of pubertal changes in girls. *Archives of Disease in Childhood*, **44**, 291-303.

Mirwald, R.L., Bailey, D.A., Cameron, N., & Rasmussen, R.L. (1981). Longitudinal comparison of aerobic power in active and inactive boys aged 7.0 to 17.0 years. *Annals of Human Biology*, **8**, 405-414.

Nicolson, A.B., & Hanley, C. (1953). Indices of physiological maturity: Derivation and interrelationships. *Child Development*, **24**, 3-38.

Novotny, V. (1981). Changes in skeletal age with sport training over several years. *Medizin und Sport*, **21**, 44-47.

Parker, D.C., Judd, H.L., Rossman, L.G., & Yen, S.S.C. (1975). Pubertal sleep-wake patterns of episodic LH, FSH and testosterone release in twin boys. *Journal of Clinical Endocrinology and Metabolism*, **40**, 1099-1109.

Patton, R.G. (1962). Growth and psychological factors. In *Mechanisms of Regulation of Growth*, Report of the Fortieth Ross Conference on Pediatric Research (pp. 58-61). Columbus, OH: Ross Laboratories.

Peltenburg, A.L., Erich, W.B.M., Thijssen, J.J.H., Veeman, W., Jansen, M., Bernink, M.J.E., Zonderland, M.L., Brande, J.L. van den, & Huisveld, I.A. (1984). Sex hormone profiles of premenarcheal athletes. *European Journal of Applied Physiology*, **52**, 385-392.

Preece, M.A., & Baines, M.J. (1978). A new family of mathematical models describing the human growth curve. *Annals of Human Biology*, **5**, 1-24.

Reynolds, E.L., & Wines, J.V. (1948). Individual differences in physical changes associated with adolescence in girls. *American Journal of Diseases of Children*, **75**, 329-350.

Roberts, D.F., & Dann, T.C. (1967). Influences on menarcheal age in girls in a Welsh college. *British Journal of Preventive and Social Medicine*, **21**, 170-176.

Roberts, D.F., Rozner, L.M., & Swan, A.V. (1971). Age at menarche, physique and environment in industrial North East England. *Acta Paediatrica Scandinavica*, **60**, 158-164.

Roche, A.F., Wainer, H., & Thissen, D. (1975). *Skeletal maturity: The knee as a biological indicator*. New York: Plenum.

Ross, W.D., & Marfell-Jones, M.J. (1982). Kinanthropometry. In J.D. MacDougall, H.A. Wenger, & H.J. Green (Eds.), *Physiological testing of the elite athlete* (pp. 75-115). Ottawa: Canadian Association of Sport Sciences.

Simmons, K. (1944). The Brush Foundation study of child growth and development. II. Physical growth and development. *Monographs of the Society for Research in Child Development*, **9**, no. 1.

Sklad, M. (1973). Genetic foundation of certain manifestations of puberty (based on twin studies). *Zeitschrift für Morphologie und Anthropologie*, **65**, 192-211.

Sklad, M. (1977). The rate of growth and maturing of twins. *Acta Geneticae, Medicae et Gemellologiae*, **26**, 221-237.

Stager, J.M., Robertshaw, D., & Miescher, E. (1984). Delayed menarche in swimmers in relation to age at onset of training and athletic performance. *Medicine and Science in Sports and Exercise*, **16**, 550-555.

Stinson, S. (1985). Sex differences in environmental sensitivity during growth and development. *Yearbook of Physical Anthropology*, **28**, 123-147.

Štukovsky, R., Valsik, J.A., & Bulai-Stirbu, M. (1967). Family size and menarcheal age in Constanza, Roumania. *Human Biology*, **39**, 277-283.

Tanner, J.M. (1962). *Growth at adolescence* (2nd ed.). Oxford: Blackwell Scientific.

Tanner, J.M. (1969). Growth and endocrinology of the adolescent. In L.I. Gardner (Ed.), *Endocrine and genetic diseases of childhood* (pp. 19-60). Philadelphia: Saunders.

Tanner, J.M. (1978). *Fetus into man*. Cambridge: Harvard University Press.

Tanner, J.M., & Davies, P.S.W. (1985). Clinical longitudinal standards for height and height velocity for North American children. *Journal of Pediatrics*, **107**, 317-329.

Tanner, J.M., Whitehouse, R.H., Marshall, W.A., Healy, M.J.R., & Goldstein, H. (1975). *Assessment of skeletal maturity and prediction of adult height*. New York: Academic Press.

Tanner, J.M., Whitehouse, R.H., Marubini, E., & Resele, L.F. (1976). The adolescent growth spurt of boys and girls of the Harpenden Growth Study. *Annals of Human Biology*, **3**, 109-126.

Tanner, J.M., Whitehouse, R.H., & Takaishi, M. (1966). Standards from birth to maturity for height, weight, height velocity, and weight velocity: British children, 1965. I and II. *Archives of Disease in Childhood*, **41**, 454-471, 613-635.

Taranger, J., Engström, I., Lichtenstein, H., & Svennberg-Redegren, I. (1976). Somatic pubertal development. *Acta Paediatrica Scandinavica* (Suppl. 258), 121-135.

Thissen, D., Bock, R.D., Wainer, H., & Roche, A.F. (1976). Individual growth in stature: A comparison of four growth studies in the U.S.A. *Annals of Human Biology, 3*, 529-542.

Wafelbakker, F. (1970). Adolescent growth spurt in relation to age and maturation. In J. Kral & V. Novotny (Eds.), *Physical fitness and its laboratory assessment* (pp. 49-52). Prague: Charles University.

Warren, M.P. (1980). The effects of exercise on pubertal progression and reproductive function in girls. *Journal of Clinical Endocrinology and Metabolism, 51*, 1150-1157.

Wellens, R.E. (1984). *The influence of sociocultural variables and sports participation on the age at menarche of Flemish girls (the Leuven Growth Study of Flemish girls)*. Unpublished master's thesis, The University of Texas at Austin.

Wierman, M.E., & Crowley, W.F., Jr. (1986). Neuroendocrine control of the onset of puberty. In F. Falkner & J.M. Tanner (Eds.), *Human growth. Volume 2. Postnatal growth* (rev. ed.). (pp. 225-241). New York: Plenum.

Zacharias, L., & Rand, W.M. (1983). Adolescent growth in height and its relation to menarche in contemporary American girls. *Annals of Human Biology, 10*, 209-222.

Physical Characteristics of Elite Young Distance Runners

Vern Seefeldt
John Haubenstricker
Crystal F. Branta
Sharon Evans

The potential detrimental effects of distance running on children have recently been called to the attention of parents, coaches, and race directors. The medical committee of the International Athletics Association Federation (IAAF), as reported in "Not Kids Stuff" in the *Sportsmedicine Bulletin* (1983), and the American Academy of Pediatrics (1982) have issued statements regarding the potential for injury to children who run long distances. Of primary concern to these medical groups is the possibility of microtrauma to the epiphyses of the long bones, the inability of children to adequately dissipate heat in warm temperatures, and the potential for psychological damage when parents compel children to train and compete beyond the children's natural interests. Recommendations from the IAAF (1983) contained the following quote:

> It is the opinion of the committee that training and competition for long-distance track and road running events should not be encouraged. Up to the age of 12, it is suggested that not more than 800 meters should be run in competition. An increase in this distance should be introduced gradually with, for example, a maximum of 3000 meters in competition for 14-year-olds. (p. 11)

The IAAF recommendations seem unusually restrictive, especially when the *Health Related Physical Fitness Test Manual* (1980), which describes tests that are administered in many of our public schools, contains standards on the mile run for children as young as 5 years of age. The statement by the American Academy of Pediatrics (1982) lists the potential dangers of distance running, but it does not recommend specific age-distance relationships.

A review of the scientific literature provides little evidence that long-distance running is detrimental to children's growth (Caine & Lindner, 1984; Lopez & Pruett, 1982; Mayers & Gutin, 1979). Conversely, neither does it give any reassurance that these intensive training regimens are harmless (Paty & Swafford, 1984; Rowland & Walsh, 1985). The vulnerability of the epiphyseal cartilage during adolescence has been documented (Larson, 1973; Schwab, 1977), but whether there is a direct relationship between injuries of this type and growth impairment is unknown. Investigators have also been unable to define the level or intensity of training in children at which the beneficial effects cease and injuries, which are our first indications of potential growth impairment, begin to accumulate.

Reports of running injuries in children generally deal with acute problems, without the associated long-term follow-up of their influence on growth. On the other hand, it is possible that growth retardation due to strenuous training in children is not manifested by injuries. If growth retardation or impairment is associated with strenuous training, perhaps the consequences are so subtle and latent that their effects cannot be detected by methods other than longitudinal growth records. If the long-term record of growth is to be a useful comparison for running-related effects, it must begin before the child becomes involved in running.

Availability of longitudinal growth records, per se, during the course of training does not permit us to assume cause and effect relationships. As Malina (1986) has indicated in his recent chapter pertaining to this problem, there are many environmental variables that may influence growth. Of primary concern are the timing and velocity of the adolescent growth spurt. These genetically controlled phenomena are also influenced by strenuous physical activity. The potential confounding effects of these environmental variables make attributions of increases or decreases in growth rates a questionable practice. A more defensible procedure, in view of the difficulties associated with attributing growth to specific causes, is to accurately describe the growth rates of children who train and compete as long-distance runners and then compare their growth to that of other children who do not practice or participate in long-distance running but who live in a similar geographic area. Such a comparison permits us to examine absolute and relative growth and to speculate about marked differences if they occur.

Purpose

This study posed the question, Is the training and competition of long-distance running by children sufficiently stimulating or stressful to influence their physical growth rates? The focus was on rates of growth in selected parameters. The evidence consisted of pure longitudinal data on runners and two control groups. A previous paper examined the initial differences between the runners, who are also the subjects of this report, and a control group to which the runners had been matched on a subject-by-subject basis by chronological age and standing height (Seefeldt, Haubenstricker, Branta, & McKeag, 1986). The previous report indicated that, although the runners were slightly shorter in stature, they had absolutely and relatively longer legs than the control groups. They also had less body fat, as determined by 10 skinfolds, and had smaller circumferences as reflected in 15 body and segmental girths. The accumulation of growth over a 1-year period of time in this subsequent report provides the opportunity to test for differences in rates of growth.

Method

Subjects involved 32 runners (18 males and 14 females) between the ages of 9 and 15 years, drawn from a pool of 45 runners in the study. A criterion for inclusion involved the availability of complete data from two annual measurements. Control subjects included a group of 9 males and 8 females who were matched, in the initial year, to runners by height and age. In addition, standards for comparison were computed from the pure longitudinal data of 75 males and 65 females who participated in a local program designed to study the interrelationship of physical growth and motor performance. The children in the latter group were measured twice yearly over a period of years encompassed by the age range of the runners.

Runners and their controls were measured annually in the Center for the Study of Human Performance, Michigan State University. During the annual evaluation, they also completed a battery of tests that assessed their psychological, biomechanical, motoric, and physiological characteristics. Due to differences in the time interval between measurement dates for some of the subjects, all data were plotted on growth charts and interpolated to annual increments by manually fitting the plots to the trajectories of growth.

Limitations of space precluded a comparison of the runners and their control group on each of the 50 anthropometric variables assessed. Therefore, five measures—standing height, sitting height, biacromial diameter, biiliac diameter, and the sum of subscapular, triceps, and abdominal skinfolds—were selected as representative of stature, shape, and body fat, respectively.

Results

Statistical comparisons were made by group and gender in the following categories: all runners versus all controls, male runners versus male controls, female runners versus female controls, male runners versus female runners, and male controls versus female controls. Because the question focused on rates of growth during the annual interval, it was essential to determine if initial differences existed between the runners and controls on each of the five variables. Separate one-way analysis of variance (ANOVA) indicated that the groups differed significantly ($p < .05$) on each variable except standing height and biiliac diameter (see Table 1), thereby necessitating a follow-up statistical procedure involving analysis of covariance (ANCOVA) to adjust for the initial differences between the groups.

Table 1   Differences Between Runners and Control Subjects on Selected Physical Growth Variables as Determined by One-Way ANOVA Procedures

Variable	F	Significance of F
Standing height	3.59	$p > .064$
Sitting height	7.68	$p < .008$
Biacromial diameter	8.80	$p < .005$
Biiliac diameter	3.26	$p > .078$
Sum of skinfolds	25.22	$p < .000$

Table 2   Differences Between Runners and Control Subjects in Rate of Growth on Selected Physical Characteristics as Determined by ANCOVA Procedures

Variable/effect	F	Significance of F
Standing height		
Group	0.55	$p > .46$
Gender	2.42	$p > .13$
Group by gender	1.41	$p > .24$
Sitting height		
Group	3.34	$p > .07$
Gender	0.003	$p > .95$
Group by gender	0.20	$p > .66$
Biacromial diameter		
Group	0.64	$p > .43$
Gender	0.72	$p > .40$
Group by gender	0.64	$p > .43$
Biiliac diameter		
Group	0.63	$p > .43$
Gender	0.05	$p > .83$
Group by gender	0.18	$p > .67$
Sum of skinfolds		
Group	0.09	$p > .76$
Gender	5.39	$p < .02$
Group by gender	1.63	$p > .21$

Results of the ANCOVA indicated that there were no group by gender interactions when the growth rates of the runners were compared with those of the controls on any of the variables (see Table 2). There also were no significant group differences in any of the five variables, but there was a significant gender difference in the sum of skinfolds, with controls having significantly larger skinfolds.

Table 3 Group Differences in Rates of Growth on Selected Physical Characteristics Using ANCOVA Procedures

Groups	Standing height		Sitting height		Biacromial diameter		Biiliac diameter		Sum of skinfolds	
	F	Significance	F	Significance	F	Significance	F	Significance	F	Significance
Male runners vs. male controls	0.0006	$p > .98$	3.76	$p > .06$	0.68	$p > .42$	0.35	$p > .56$	0.05	$p > .82$
Female runners vs. female controls	1.21	$p > .28$	0.77	$p > .39$	0.04	$p > .85$	0.06	$p > .81$	0.49	$p > .49$
Male runners vs. female runners	0.41	$p > .53$	0.003	$p > .96$	0.25	$p > .62$	0.03	$p > .87$	0.89	$p > .35$
Male controls vs. female controls	4.19	$p > .06$	0.17	$p > .69$	0.68	$p > .42$	0.15	$p > .71$	3.17	$p > .10$

None of the other comparisons by group (male runners vs. male controls, female runners vs. female controls, male runners vs. female runners, and male controls vs. female controls) revealed any significant differences in rates of growth on any variable (see Table 3). Therefore, the only distinction between the runner and control groups in rates of growth was that the control subjects gained more body fat, as measured by skinfolds, during the year than the runners. Two other comparisons are worthy of note: Differences in sitting height between male runners and male controls approached significance, with a p of .06, and the standing height for male and female control subjects also had a p value of .06, with the greater gains evident in the male subjects.

Discussion

Illustrations (see Figures 1 to 8) confirm the results of the statistical analyses; there were no marked differences in the growth rates of runners and controls, and neither group differed markedly from the larger longitudinal sample from whose data the standards were computed. However, some information that is masked by the method of analysis is worthy of comment:

- On the illustrations for absolute standing height for males (see Figure 1), note that the tallest individuals were control subjects and the shortest were runners. However, in terms of relative gains (see Figure 2), the greatest gains appeared to be made by the runners. These greater gains reflect their later maturation. The controls most likely had already experienced their growth acceleration in these variables.
- The illustration for standing height of females (see Figure 3) indicates that the tallest and shortest individuals were runners, whereas all of the controls were within ±1 standard deviation of the mean. The figure for annual gains (see Figure 4) shows that the control females had smaller growth increments, probably due to their earlier maturation. This suggests that the height spurt of the control females had occurred by approximately 12 years of age.
- In absolute sitting height for males (see Figure 5), the controls had the tallest subjects, whereas all of the cases below −1 standard deviation of the mean were runners. However, the incremental growth plots (see Figure 6) show that the runners had equally large increments and appeared to be extending these large increments beyond the time when the controls were growing rapidly. This also suggests that the runners were later maturing individuals. The later maturation of the runners had been confirmed by hand-wrist X rays, although that portion of the study will not be reported here.
- Absolute measures of sitting height for females (see Figure 7) indicated that the runners were still growing, as is evident by the upward slant of their curves, whereas the incremental gains for the controls beyond 12 years of age had a flatter trajectory. Substantial incremental gains (see Figure 8) of the female runners also appeared to be present at a time when many of the control subjects had completed their growth.

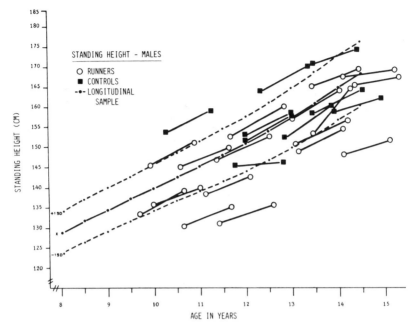

Figure 1 One-year increments of standing height for male runners and control subjects compared to the mean, ±1 standard deviation, for a longitudinal sample of boys.

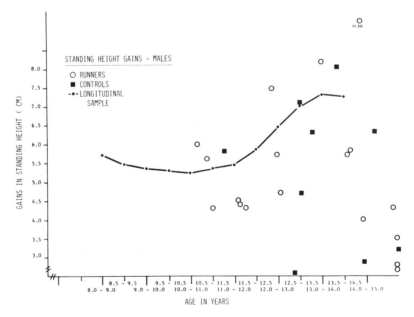

Figure 2 Annual gains in standing height for male runners and control subjects compared to the average gains of a longitudinal sample of boys.

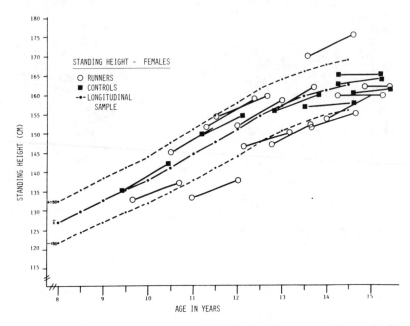

Figure 3   One-year increments of standing height for female runners and control subjects compared to the mean, ±1 standard deviation, for a longitudinal sample of girls.

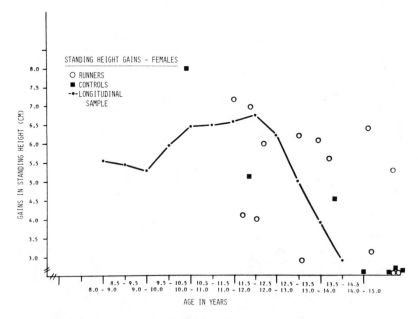

Figure 4   Annual gains in standing height for female runners and control subjects compared to the average gains of a longitudinal sample of girls.

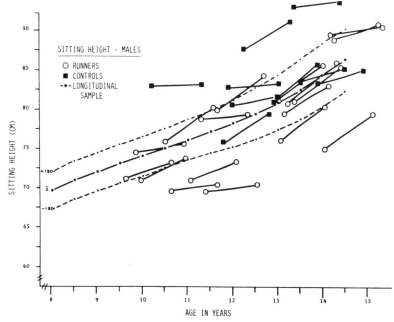

Figure 5 One-year increments of sitting height for male runners and control subjects compared to the mean, ±1 standard deviation, for a longitudinal sample of boys.

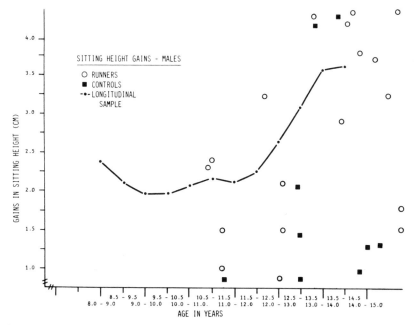

Figure 6 Annual gains in sitting height for male runners and control subjects compared to the average gains of a longitudinal sample of boys.

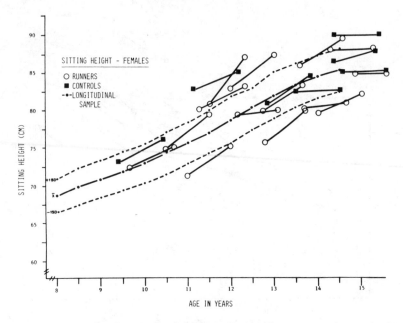

Figure 7   One-year increments of sitting height for female runners and control subjects compared to the mean, ±1 standard deviation, for a longitudinal sample of girls.

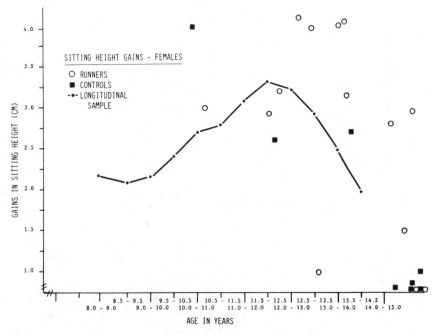

Figure 8   Annual gains in sitting height for female runners and control subjects compared to the average gains of a longitudinal sample of girls.

Summary

Two-year data on rates of growth for five selected variables (standing height, sitting height, biacromial diameter, biiliac diameter, and the sum of three skinfolds) indicated that young runners were not significantly different in their growth rates than children from similar geographical areas who engaged in regular physical activity but who were not involved in distance running. On the basis of these data, there was no apparent detrimental effect of training or competitive running, as represented in the life-styles of this group of young runners, on their rates of physical growth as indicated in the five measures.

Initial differences between the runners and controls in the five variables were adjusted by ANCOVA. When equated for initial differences, there were no group by gender interactions nor were there any group differences, except for a gender difference in skinfolds, favoring the control groups of males and females.

Although the statistical analyses did not detect any significant differences in rates of skeletal growth, individual plots of these incremental data suggested that the runners were still growing rapidly during the time when many of the control subjects were experiencing smaller increments of growth. The suggestion that the runners achieved skeletal maturation at later ages than the control subjects had been confirmed by hand-wrist X rays. Control subjects had significantly greater gains in total skinfold than their runner counterparts of the same gender.

References

American Academy of Pediatrics. (1982). Risks in long-distance running for children. *The Physician and Sportsmedicine, 10,* 82-86.

Caine, D., & Lindner, K. (1984). Growth plate injury: A threat to young distance runners? *The Physician and Sportsmedicine, 12,* 118-124.

Health Related Physical Fitness Test Manual. (1980). Reston, VA: The American Alliance for Health, Physical Education, Recreation and Dance.

Larson, R. (1973). Epiphyseal injuries in the adolescent athlete. *Orthopedic Clinics of North America, 4,* 839-851.

Lopez, R., & Pruett, D. (1982). The child runner. *Journal of Physical Education, Recreation and Dance, 53,* 78-81.

Malina, R. (1986). Physical growth and maturation. In V. Seefeldt (Ed.), *Physical activity and well being* (pp. 4-38). Reston, VA: American Alliance for Health, Physical Education, Recreation and Dance.

Mayers, N., & Gutin, B. (1979). Physiological characteristics of elite prepubertal cross-country runners. *Medicine and Science in Sports, 11,* 172-176.

Not kids stuff. (1983, January). *Sportsmedicine Bulletin,* p. 11.

Paty, J., & Swafford, D. (1984). Adolescent running injuries. *Journal of Adolescent Health Care*, **5**, 310-313.

Rowland, T., & Walsh, C. (1985). Characteristics of child distance runners. *The Physician and Sportsmedicine*, **137**, 45-53.

Schwab, S. (1977). Epiphyseal injuries in the growing athlete. *Canadian Medical Association Journal*, **117**, 626-629.

Seefeldt, V., Haubenstricker, J., Branta, C., & McKeag, D. (1986). Anthropometric assessment of body size and shape of young runners and control subjects. In M. Weiss & D. Gould (Eds.), *Sport for children and youths* (pp. 247-254). Champaign, IL: Human Kinetics.

Longitudinal Cardiorespiratory Performance Testing in Young Swimmers

Douglas B. McKeag

The subject of endurance training and the subsequent aerobic response in children and adolescents continues to remain a controversial subject in the scientific literature of exercise medicine. It is known through recent research that children and adolescents possess higher weight-related maximal oxygen consumption ($\dot{V}O_2$max) levels than older individuals (Rowland, 1985). The capacity of children, whether prepubescent or pubescent, to improve aerobic fitness with endurance training remains unclear with conflicting evidence on both sides of the issue. Numerous authors have studied this question with variable results. Hamilton and Andrew (1976) reported no difference in levels of aerobic fitness between prepubescent hockey players and inactive children. These authors concluded that the lack of a training effect in the hockey players was more due to the high innate levels of activity in the control children. Bar-Or (1983) emphasized that aerobic trainability prior to puberty was less than expected. Kaboyishi et al. (1978) noted a definite increase in $\dot{V}O_2$ response to training at the time of the adolescent growth spurt. However, Weber, Kardodihardja, and Klissouris (1976) failed to demonstrate such a phenomenon.

On the other side of the issue, Shephard (1982) reported typical adult-like improvement in aerobic fitness in the prepubescent and pubescent age group. Pate and Blair (1978) suggest that conflicting data regarding training ability of children might be attributed to differences in exercise intensity and duration of training programs. They concluded that improvements in aerobic power were possible in pubescent children, but only after prolonged and vigorous regimens. Rowland (1985) summarized the results of 14 reports focused on the aerobic responses of prepubescent children to physical training. Of major concern to this author was the fact that a number of these studies did not involve training regimens that satisfied current guidelines for eliciting an adult training effect. In addition, the ones that did conform to adult criteria involved small numbers of children (the longest study involved 16 children). Another major drawback of these studies was the lack of any longitudinality in research design with the majority of research completed after only a 12- to 16-week period. The longest cited study was that of Daniels and Oldridge (1971) lasting 88 weeks. There indeed appear to be few longitudinal studies

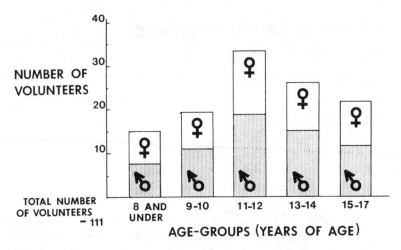

Figure 1   Age and sex distribution of project.

involving cardiorespiratory endurance and its correlation to supervised exercise programs.

This study was attempted for the purpose of investigating the effects of measured exercise (competitive swimming) on the cardiorespiratory performance of adolescents and preadolescents. It represents the longest, largest study on a formal training program known.

Method

Ninety male and female competitive or beginning competitive swimmers and 21 control volunteers were tested over the 2 years from 1974 to 1976. Age group and sex distribution of the project are shown in Figure 1. Age range was from 5 to 18 years of age. Each subject was asked to obtain both parental and medical permission prior to undergoing the series of graded exercise tests. Each volunteer was screened with a health questionnaire that included pertinent physical statistics, past medical history, a cardiorespiratory review of systems, and previous swimming experience. Then a screening physical exam emphasizing the cardiorespiratory and musculoskeletal systems was done on each project participant. Each subject was also subjectively rated by his or her swimming coach based on each volunteer's swimming ability compared to others in his or her age group. Finally, the purpose and procedure of this study were explained to each volunteer and interested parents.

Repeat multistage treadmill testing using the modified Bruce (1974) protocol before, during, and following each swim season furnished the necessary data used in this analysis. A total of seven separate treadmills were done, the first four surrounding the 1975 swimming season and the last three, the 1976 season. Figure 2 illustrates where each treadmill fell on

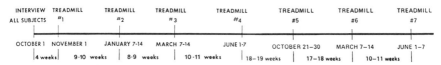

Figure 2 Timeline of study.

Table 1 Total Tests Done

$$
\left.
\begin{array}{l}
T_1 - 111 \\
T_2 - 85 \\
T_3 - 109 \\
T_4 - 77 \\
T_5 - 104 \\
T_6 - 95 \\
T_7 - 88
\end{array}
\right\} \quad \text{Total} - 669
$$

the project timeline. A total of 669 treadmills were done (see Table 1). Controls were not tested for Tests 2 and 4. Height, weight, and recent medical history including medication intake were recorded each time. Baseline electrocardiograms were obtained prior to the start of each treadmill test. Each youth was reminded of the test protocol prior to the start of testing itself. In addition, prior to the start of the first treadmill, each participant was given the opportunity to participate in a "dry run" for the purpose of acclimatization.

Blood pressure, heart rate, and electrocardiogram lead V5 were monitored continuously throughout the test and during recovery. An arbitrary maximum heart rate of 200 beats/min was designated the automatic stopping point for all participants. However, the subject could stop the test himself at any time. Duration on the treadmill and length of time for recovery to pretest blood pressure and pulse levels were measured. Lead V5 was investigated primarily for any arrhythmia, conduction, or repolarization abnormalities. Duration of exercise ranged from 4 to 24 min, recovery time from 1 to 15 min.

Results

Results represent statistical analyses (Student's t test) done on the data from this project. Treadmill duration and recovery for swimmers versus controls over all seven treadmills is summarized in Tables 2 and 3, respectively.

There was no significant difference in swimmers or controls between the 2 years tested. No total difference was noted between the groups in duration of testing or recovery time. Longitudinally taking each tread-

Table 2   Treadmill Recovery Means

Treadmill	Date	Mean recovery (min) Swimmers	Controls
T_1	10/74—start season	5.4	5.2
T_2	1/75	5.2	—
T_3	3/75—end season (peak)	3.9	4.3
T_4	6/75	3.4	—
T_5	10/75—start season	5.2	4.9
T_6	3/76—end season (peak)	3.6	4.4
T_7	6/76	4.2	4.8

Table 3   Treadmill Duration Means

Treadmill	Date	Mean duration (min) Swimmers	Controls
T_1	10/74—start season	12.9	12.7
T_2	1/75	14.7	—
T_3	3/75—end season (peak)	14.9	14.6
T_4	6/75	14.6	—
T_5	10/75—start season	13.2	13.3
T_6	3/76—end season (peak)	14.9	14.5
T_7	6/76	14.0	14.2

mill into account, there are significant differences and an indication of a trend correlating performance with degree of swimming activity. These differences are most striking in the 9 to 10, 11 to 12, and 13 to 14 age groups (Table 4). All age groups showed a decrease in recovery time at peak season. A small difference was noted in duration, with swimmers lasting slightly longer on the treadmill and requiring slightly less time than controls. These differences increase slightly when data secondary to lack of motivation or poor subject performance are eliminated from the results. This was accomplished by culling out all data from volunteers who did not attain a level of 90% maximum arbitrary heart rate prior to stopping the treadmill. Swimmers who achieved heart rates of 180 beats/min or greater lasted longer and recovered sooner than controls achieving the same submaximal target heart rate (see Table 5). The trend mentioned earlier seems to show the best treadmill performance at times when better swimming performance and a greater amount of exercise (swimming) were present. Also, the phenomenon of decondition-

Table 4 Treadmill Duration (TD) and Recovery Time (RT) by Age Groups (in Minutes)

Group	TD_1	RT_1	TD_2	RT_2	TD_3	RT_3	TD_4	RT_4
8 and under	10.1	4.2	12.9	4.1	13.5	2.8	11.7	2.0
9-10	13.3	4.7	15.5	4.9	15.6	3.1	15.5	3.3
11-12	12.9	5.9	14.5	4.4	15.1	4.3	15.0	3.8
13-14	13.7	5.4	15.6	6.6	15.6	4.2	15.5	3.6
15-18	13.7	6.0	15.1	6.2	14.6	4.9	14.5	4.6

Table 5 Mean Duration and Recovery Considering 90% Maximum Heart Rate

	Mean duration (min)		Mean recovery (min)	
	Swimmers	Control	Swimmers	Control
Total	14.3	13.8	4.4	4.8
> 180-HR max	14.9	14.6	5.0	5.3
< 180-HR max	11.1	13.3	2.4	2.3

ing seems to be present with a mild decrease in performance coinciding with the absence of structured exercise.

Slopes of heart rate, diastolic blood pressure, and systolic blood pressure rise and fall during the testing procedure were considered (Figure 3). Although again it was evident that the acceleration heart rate rise of the swimmers and nonswimmers decreased with each succeeding treadmill, no statistical difference was noted between the two groups. The negative slopes resulting from heart rate decrease during recovery did indicate that swimmers recover faster than the control group. No significant difference was noted in either systolic or diastolic blood pressure rise or fall between the two groups. The phenomena of conditioning and deconditioning seem to be illustrated by the examination of pulse pressure differences of swimmers during the first season treadmill tests (see Figure 4). T_1, done prior to the swimming season, had a similar slope but greater initial readings than subsequent treadmills. Conversely, T_3, done at the end of the season (peak conditioning time), shows better performance than any other tests. T_4 results (done 3 to 4 months after the season) may actually indicate degradation of fitness has begun.

Further analysis was conducted using various physiological parameters as subgroups and comparing the performance of swimmers and controls:

1. **Chronologic age.** Analysis here was incomplete and unsatisfactory secondary to the small cell size of most groups. Where significant

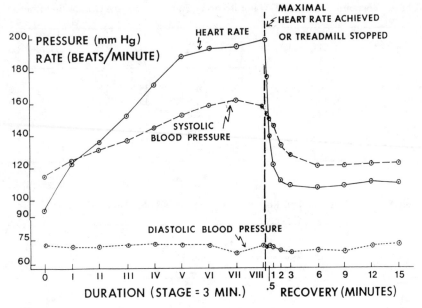

Figure 3 Mean heart rate and blood pressure values.

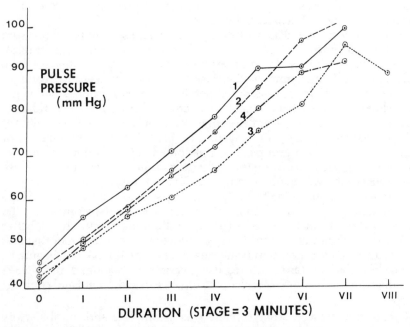

Figure 4 Mean pulse pressure means by stage for 4 first-year tests.

Table 6   Treadmill Analysis by Age Groups

Group	Mean duration (min)		Mean recovery (min)	
	Swimmers	Control	Swimmers	Control
8 and under	12.0	12.3	3.4	2.5
9-10	15.0	10.5	4.0	5.0
11-12	14.3	13.9	4.8	3.5
13-14	15.2	14.0	5.1	4.3
15 and over	14.4	14.4	5.2	7.2

Table 7   Total Age-Group Results

Group	Total number of treadmills	Mean duration (min)	Mean recovery (min)
8 and under	111	12.2	3.8
9-10	117	14.4	4.3
11-12	118	14.4	4.9
13-14	144	14.7	5.3
15-18	119	14.9	5.6

differences were able to be analyzed, they again reflected the same trend as previously stated; that is, swimmers lasted longer and took less time recovering than controls.

2. **Age group** (arbitrarily determined on the basis of current United States competitive swimming age group standards).

- First analyzing the swimmers versus controls for all treadmills by each age group, we discovered significant differences in all age groups except the 8 and under (Table 6). In the older age groups, differences in duration or recovery followed the same trend as earlier stated; that is, swimmers last longer and recover more quickly (or both) than the control group.
- When all subjects were considered together and analyzed by age group, the results once again proved interesting (Table 7). There was a gradual, but significant, almost step-wise increase in both duration and recovery time as one progresses from younger to older age groups. The fact that slope analysis of heart rate and systolic blood pressure increased during the treadmill test as well as decreased during recovery also reinforces the above statement. Please note, however, the "failure" of the 8 and under age group to achieve a similar duration on the treadmill in comparison with other

Table 8 Treadmill Duration and Recovery by Sex

Sex	Mean duration (min)		Mean recovery (min)	
	Swimmers	Control	Swimmers	Control
Male	13.6	11.9	4.9	5.3
Female	14.8	15.1	4.2	4.4

age groups. Consequently, the recovery time for this age group is less than other age groups.

3. **Sex.** Forty-five percent of the project volunteers were male, 55% female. Consistently, females outperformed males in each year of the study and in the total overall study (Table 8). There was no significant difference in performance between female swimmers and controls. Male swimmers, however, did last significantly longer and recover more quickly than their control groups. Additionally, heart rate and systolic blood pressure were slower to increase during testing and quicker to recover for these same male swimmers.

4. **Height and weight.** Significant trends were seen in both parameters. Generally the greater the height or weight, the longer the duration or recovery.

5. **Electrocardiographic findings.** On a basis of findings of the baseline electrocardiograms, two groups were artificially formulated—those with normal EKGs and those with abnormal asymptomatic findings. No symptomatic patients were accepted for this study. No significance between the two groups was found although diastolic blood pressure and heart rate fall during recovery were significantly accentuated in the abnormal group.

6. **Resting cardiac rhythm.** Initial rhythm at the beginning of each testing period was used as criteria to separate project volunteers. Sixty-three percent of the subjects started their treadmill test in normal sinus rhythm, whereas 37% began theirs in sinus tachycardia. For the purposes of this study sinus tachycardia was defined as any resting heart rate greater than 95 beats per minute. Those volunteers in sinus rhythm at the start of the test lasted longer and recovered quicker than those who began in sinus tachycardia. Swimmers with sinus tachycardia had longer durations than controls.

7. **Reasons for stopping the test.** Approximately 46% of the subjects stopped their respective tests after requesting to do so. The remaining achieved the arbitrary maximal heart rate of 200 beats per minute. Those attaining maximum heart rate response, as expected, lasted significantly longer on the treadmills and also took longer to recover. The percentage of self-imposed cessation of testing versus achievement of maximum heart rate remains constant for each of the seven treadmills.

Table 9 Treadmill Duration and Recovery Considering Competitive Swimming Experience

	Mean duration (min)		Mean recovery (min)	
	Swimmers	Control	Swimmers	Control
≤ 3	13.2		4.2	
> 3	14.8		4.8	

Table 10 Analysis of Duration and Recovery Time by Athlete Rating

	Mean duration (min)		Mean recovery (min)	
	Swimmers	Control	Swimmers	Control
0	—	13.7		4.9
1	12.7		4.7	
2	14.9		5.2	
3	14.5		3.9	
4	13.8		4.5	
5	15.6		4.6	

Analysis of testing was also accomplished on the basis of nonphysiologic groupings of volunteers determined solely on the basis of past medical history and other parameters. The results indicate the following:

1. **Significant medical history.** Thirty-three percent of the subjects had positive past or present medical histories. Chronic illness, medications, and past injuries were all considered potentially significant and affected the results of graded exercise testing. Although there was no performance difference between children without positive histories, swimmers with a positive history did not perform as well, and controls with a positive history had significantly poorer performance on a treadmill.
2. **Competitive swimming experience.** The average number of years' experience in competitive swimming for the swimmer in this project was 3.4 years with males averaging 3.9 and females 2.8 years. Beginning swimmers without any previous experience were included, but controls were not. Swimmers with greater than 3 years of experience had longer durations but also longer recovery times than the control groups (Table 9).
3. **Rating.** As mentioned earlier, each project volunteer was subjectively rated prior to the swimming season and initiation of the project. This rating was based on past performance, overall ability, and how this

ability compared to other competitive swimmers of the same age for the state of Michigan. From analysis of duration and recovery time, the control group had the lowest performance of any group (Table 10). As expected, beginning swimmers were next, with groups graded 2 to 5 closely bunched together. Swimmers rated 5 obviously showed the best performance and below-average swimmers the worst performance of these four rated groups. Overall, however, treadmill performance did not closely reflect the preseason ability ratings.

4. **Activity.** When the level of sports activity was analyzed, there appeared to be a correlation between treadmill performance and greater activity levels. Subjects engaging in swimming and other activities ranked highest, followed by those children engaged in swimming as the only sport, followed by those controls engaged in other activities only, followed finally by a group of inactive children.

Discussion

This study provides information concerning the aerobic response to endurance training for prepubescent and pubescent children. Although the controversy surrounding this study area will continue, this project did allow a look at a large group of children (N = 111) over a long period of time (2 years). It was also able to look at various biological and epidemiological parameters and their relationship to exercise. Because of the size of this project as well as the physical and equipment limitations, the actual measurement of respiratory performance (V_E and $\dot{V}O_2$) was sacrificed. Although this represents a major methodologic flaw of this study, a significant data set was obtained. Additionally, a point might be made for the adjustment of swimmers having to be tested while running. Once again, in the interest of the project size, time, and money constraints, no other choices seemed feasible.

This study did show that competitive swimmers generally lasted longer on the treadmill and took less time recovering to a pretest cardiac level than controls. However, these differences were not significant, and mean values for both the experimental and control groups were surprisingly close together. Each group improved treadmill performance as a result of two major factors: (a) acclimation to the treadmill testing procedure and (b) improved physical endurance secondary to physical activities and age. A critical look at the control group reveals perhaps a third reason for this group's surprisingly high performance level. Almost all of these individuals were the nonswimming siblings or friends of project swimmers, and most were just as athletically inclined in their own respective sport as their swimming siblings were in their sports.

The major interpretations of results from this study include the following points:

• Treadmill testing can be successfully done on preadolescents and adolescents.

- Continued strenuous exercise in a structured exercise program does show improved performance of those taking part.
- Correlations of treadmill endurance and recovery with amount of exercise by means of longitudinal serial testing have been shown. Both conditioning and deconditioning are evident.
- The above may not be true for younger participants (the 8 and under age group). Could they already be at peak efficiency as several studies suggest (American Academy of Pediatrics, 1976; Hamilton & Andrew, 1976)? If this is true, no amount of exercise would affect their performance.
- Females outperformed males.
- As growth and development progressed, treadmill duration increased. So did the recovery phase. If optimal performance on graded exercise testing is to be measured by the longest duration followed by the shortest recovery, then the author would suggest that growth and development lends itself to only one half of the performance combination, namely increase in duration. Training and the aerobic response to endurance are necessary to achieve the other half of the combination (shortened recovery time).
- An increase in initial heart rate generally indicated a decreased treadmill duration.
- Significant medical history did adversely affect the treadmill performance of some nonswimming volunteers.
- The "better" rated swimmers performed better, as did the more experienced.
- The level of sports activity of the youngster was a factor in the treadmill performance.

Summary

The subject of whether or not pubescent and prepubescent children can improve aerobic fitness with endurance training, that is, achieve a training effect, remains controversial. Review of the literature on this subject reveals a number of studies indicating no difference between controls and exercising children. Other studies reportedly do show the typical adult improvements in fitness. This study has taken a thorough look at 111 prepubescent and pubescent children over a 2-year period of time involving 669 treadmill tests. The results would indicate that a training and detraining effect can be achieved in most children corresponding to a particular formal training program, in this case competitive swimming. The exception for this study appeared to be the younger volunteers (specifically, those 8 years old and younger) who may have already been at peak efficiency because of their age, activity, and maturity. They showed neither conditioning nor deconditioning in response to chronic aerobic exercise.

References

American Academy of Pediatrics. (1976). Fitness in the preschool child. *Pediatrics, 58,* 88-89.

Bar-Or, O. (1983). *Pediatric sports medicine for the practitioner* (p. 30). New York: Springer-Verlag.

Bruce, R.A. (1974). Methods of exercise testing. *American Journal of Cardiology, 33,* 715-720.

Daniels, J., & Oldridge, N. (1971). Changes in oxygen consumption of young boys during growth and running training. *Medicine and Science in Sports and Exercise, 3,* 161-165.

Hamilton, P., & Andrew, G.M. (1976). Influence of growth and athletic training on heart and lung functions. *European Journal of Applied Physiology, 36,* 27-38.

Kaboyishi, K., Kitamura, K., Miuri, M., Sodeyama, H., Murase, Y., Miyashita, M., & Matsui, H. (1978). Aerobic power as related to body growth and training in Japanese boys: A longitudinal study. *Journal of Applied Physiology, 44,* 666-672.

Pate, R.R., & Blair, S.N. (1978). Exercise and the prevention of otherosclerosis: Pediatric implications. In W.B. Strong (Ed.), *Atherosclerosis: Its pediatric aspect.* New York: Grune and Stratton.

Rowland, T.W. (1985). Aerobic response to endurance training in prepubescent children: A critical analysis. *Medicine and Science in Sports and Exercise, 17*(5), 493-497.

Shephard, R.J. (1982). *Physical activity and growth* (Chap. 10). Chicago: Yearbook Medical Publishers.

Weber, G., Kardodihardja, W., & Klissouris, V. (1976). Growth and physical training with reference to heredity. *Journal of Applied Physiology, 40,* 211-215.

PART VII

Social and Medical Issues in Youth Sports

Some Ethical Issues for the Physician in Youth Sports

Paul G. Dyment

This chapter will discuss several ethical issues as perceived by the author, who is a pediatrician, a high school hockey team physician, and a specialist in adolescent medicine, and who has a particular interest in the factors influencing character development during adolescence. Character, in this context, encompasses such traditional virtues as responsibility, honesty, loyalty, compassion, courage, and initiative. Several recent ethical questions faced by this particular team physician will be discussed as examples of the ubiquity of moral issues faced by physicians active in youth sport. Also to be addressed will be the questions of whether sports are truly character-building experiences, and whether the level of violence in certain sports should make a physician hesitate before extolling the virtues of all sport in instilling character into youth.

Cheating Issues

Youth who concede during their sports preparticipation physical examinations that they are taking steroids for muscle size and strength can raise ethical issues for the physician. What should a physician do after finishing a discussion of the dangers of this practice? Give a brief sermon that you believe this is a form of cheating? Urge the athletes to keep returning regularly if the steroid is going to be continued so that their liver function can be monitored through blood tests? In this latter case the word may spread throughout the local weight-lifting community that there is a physician who will monitor the ill effects of steroids, making it safer to take them, and then others might begin to take them knowing they could receive similar ongoing care.

Recently, while performing a high school sports preparticipation examination in August, a colleague of mine wondered why a physical examination for basketball was being done so early in the season. The youth was tactfully asked about what the team was doing. The boy conceded that the team was practicing with the coach, months before the "legal time" when they could begin to have organized practices. What is the role of the physician when faced with evidence of cheating? Discuss the moral implications with the athlete? "Blow the whistle" anonymously by reporting the offending school to the state association? Say nothing?

A recent example of my being faced with privileged knowledge of cheating was when one of my high school hockey players "went down" in a pileup after a vigorous check into the boards. It was at a time when the team was shorthanded because of a penalty, and the other team was "on a roll" and about to score. The player's apparent injury caused the whistle to be blown. When I hurried over to the boy who was still stretched out on the ice, he whispered, "I'm OK doc, I just had to stop the play." Does the confidentiality of the doctor-patient relationship (whether actually stated or just implied because of your status as a physician and the player's status as a patient) preclude the reporting of these rule violations?

Since Hippocratic days, the answer to the above dilemmas has been simple and the same for all: The sanctity of the doctor-patient relationship takes precedence over the physician's duties as a good citizen in fighting corruption and immorality. Physicians should not be the watchdogs of athletes' morals, at least in the individual situation. So I believe the physician in the above instances has an obligation to stay quiet and forego even the modest pleasure of a facial expression of moral disapprobation. To do otherwise could lead to the player-patient's reluctance to discuss anything of a personal nature with this or any other physician on later occasions. Physicians should no more express moral disapproval regarding these practices than they should if the youth confessed to sexual activity or drug abuse. In the case of steroid use, the physician should continue to care for the athlete and to monitor possible side effects. Physicians should be sympathetic, not moralistic.

Tolerating cheating in the form of the use of ergogenic aids like androgenic steroids and amphetamines must be vigorously opposed in general by physicians, both because they can produce toxic side effects and because taking them may give that competitor an unfair advantage. Physicians should also speak out against such recent innovations as blood doping and "soda loading." Cheating is cheating; it occurs whenever a competitor obtains an unfair advantage over an opponent, whether or not it is in technical violation of the current rules. The American competitors at the Los Angeles Olympics in 1985 who received transfusions of their own cryopreserved blood just prior to competing apparently did not think it was wrong because an autotransfusion was not then specifically listed as a banned ergogenic drug! Coaches should talk to their players early in each athletic season and express their personal commitment against, and intolerance of, all forms of cheating. This should include proscribed preseason practices. We should cooperate with, and even initiate if it is our responsibility, drug-screening programs of athletes, at least at the college level. However, I do have grave reservations about programs that include testing for so-called recreational drugs such as cocaine, marijuana, and alcohol, in addition to ergogenic aids. It does not seem fair to single out athletes for evidence of their being drug abusers and not test the nonathletes on the same campus. As a profession, we need to insure that state licensing boards are effectively removing from practice incompetent and unethical physicians who are the source of many illicit ergogenic drugs.

Violence Issues

One important ethical issue involves the role that violence in sports may play in the development of character in youth. If sports are accompanied by a degree of violence (which I'll define as the deliberate production of physical or mental damage) that would be a negative character-building experience, then all of us who are active in youth sport share a degree of responsibility.

Although it is part of received wisdom that we are living today in one of the most violent periods in history, only a nodding acquaintance with world history would seem to disprove this perception. Although it is regrettably true that this century has brought genocide as an art form to an all-time high, and war-related losses of life have been catastrophic (20 million during World War II alone), everyday violence in the streets is probably occurring less now than during most of the preceding centuries. There is a perception that on-the-field violence on the part of athletes is increasing; but is this really true? Perhaps what is actually happening involves the magnification effect of television. When a well-known college football coach punched a member of the opposing team a few years ago, the incident was recorded by a television camera and replayed again and again over the next few days around the world during the evening news. It has been estimated that over 100 million people watched him throw that punch. We must remember that it was only one punch viewed through a million TV screens and in newspaper pictures, not a million punches (Yeager, 1979).

The early history of aggressive sports has been recently recorded by Yeager (1979) and Atyeo (1979). Historically, we tend to view early Greek and Roman athletics as relatively nonviolent with clean-limbed youth exercising at school. But the early Romans introduced leaded and spiked gloves into boxing, and they also invented gladiatorial contests with death being the fate of the loser. The direct heirs of the gladiators during the Middle Ages were the knightly jousts. In 1249, 60 knights lost their lives in a single tournament near Cologne. Mob-ball, the ruleless forerunner of football in which half the town tried to move a ball through the other half, was accompanied by so many deaths and injuries that Edward II of England outlawed it in 1314. And it remained proscribed during the next 500 years in England, although it was played often enough and with so many injuries that it was necessary to keep the law on the books.

In 1883, Harvard, claiming that football had become ''brutal, demoralizing to teams of spectators, and extremely dangerous,'' pulled out of the league (Atyeo, 1979, p. 205). At the first Rose Bowl in 1901, Stanford was forced to request an early end to the match as it had run out of able-bodied players. By 1905 college games were still quite brutal. For example, a flying wedge of players could run in front of the ballcarrier, knocking opponents down en masse. That year 18 college and high school students lost their lives, and in 1909 33 players were killed. The worst toll was in 1931 when 40 players were lost. Because of the many rule changes and the use of safer equipment such as scientifically designed helmets, deaths on the field are extremely rare occurrences today. However, a tragic number of catastrophic neck injuries were occurring in high school and college football in this country prior to 1976 when new rules prohibiting spearing (using the head as a battering ram while blocking or tackling) were introduced. The number of quadriplegias dropped dramatically from 34 in 1976 to only 5 in 1984. But injuries are not necessarily directly related to the level of violence or aggressiveness. Certain sports such as mountain climbing are associated with high risks, but they are not considered to be violent.

But if American football is less violent than it used to be, an arguable thesis at least, professional hockey is another story. Excessive violence still remains a serious problem in this sport. This was graphically shown during the 1979 All-Star Game between the Soviet Union and our National Hockey League team, in which the Soviets won with a game emphasizing skill, whereas the North Americans' game was characterized by overly aggressive play. It seems that most professional hockey games today are interrupted by several fist fights. If these fights are not actually tolerated by fans, officials, judges, and players, then the penalties are so minor that youth watching the games on television certainly receive the message that aggressive playing is part of the game. This behavior has now regrettably permeated amateur and youth hockey, and in Canada this has resulted in at least two government commissions looking into the problem.

But in the last 5 years I have only seen a single high school hockey game marred by a fight. These youthful players watch National Hockey League games on television, and they see plenty of fists thrown. But they know that in our state players are ejected from high school games as soon as the first punch is thrown, and there is an automatic suspension for the next game as well. This has been an extremely effective way of preventing fighting. We must therefore insure that there are immediate and appropriate penalties for violent behavior in youth sport, and professional hockey leagues should do likewise. At the end of our high school games all of the players shake hands with each other. Although I am not sure this heals many personal feuds, at least it introduces a thin layer of civilization into this potentially violent sport and emphasizes to the boys that the match was just a game.

Professional boxing is also a problem. It is the only sport in which injuring the opponent is one of the goals, and we would all be well to have this country rid of this latter-day gladiatorial contest. As a character-building instrument, there is nothing to be said for it. It has led countless inner-city youth to toss away their chances of an education as they enter this sport in the vain hope that it will carry them to big earnings and be an escape from their impoverished life. Medically, the overwhelming concern is the chronic brain damage so often seen in long-time fighters. All physicians have an ethical imperative to discourage youth from taking part in professional boxing at least, in which the evidence for chronic brain damage is fairly conclusive. The American Medical Association, the American Academy of Pediatrics, and the British Medical Association have all recently called for its abolishment. However, boys have probably been fighting with each other for as long as there have been boys, and they will probably continue to do so until there is another major evolutionary advance for Homo sapiens. If they must fight, we should encourage them to take part in either wrestling or one of the martial-art forms of fighting, such as judo or karate. The injuries in these sports are such things as strained muscles and broken ribs and collar bones, all of which heal; the brain does not. In our medical practices we should discourage youth from boxing, and our professional organizations should continue to speak out against professional boxing at least.

Character Formation

How did team sports get their reputation as developers of character? We need to look back to Thomas Arnold, the great British headmaster of Rugby School in the early 1800s. He revolutionized education by regarding it the duty of a school to instill into its pupils (i.e., upper-class boys) lofty intangibles such as character, morality, and manliness, rather than just teach them the ancient languages and simple arithmetic that had comprised the educational curriculum of the preceding centuries. He believed that these virtues could be taught by the lessons learned on the playing field; the rougher the game, the more enduring and worthwhile the lesson. A boy's life in his school was graphically described in Thomas Hughes' novel, *Tom Brown's School Days*, written during the Victorian era. Tom Brown, the new boy at Rugby School, was told, "it's no joke playing-up in a match, I can tell, Why there's been two collarbones broken this half, and a dozen fellows lamed" (Hughes, 1984, p. 95). The games were furious battles, pitting perhaps 60 boys of one house against the rest of the school. Thomas Arnold began to develop the rules that changed mobball into rugby football (named after his school), and he truly believed that it was a force that could help shape a boy's character.

Do sports really do much to develop character, as Thomas Arnold had expounded? I believe they do but concede they are no more likely to do so than other activities allowing young people experiences in competition, socialization, cooperation, winning, and losing. Physicians should, therefore, not shrink from taking part in youth sport, as these experiences can be very valuable to youth. But physicians should also be prepared to face a variety of ethical dilemmas, some of which I have just discussed.

References

Atyeo, D. (1979). *Blood and guts: Violence in sports*. New York: Paddington Press.

Hughes, T. (1984 reprint). *Tom Brown's schooldays*. London: Penguin.

Yeager, R.C. (1979). *Seasons of shame. The new violence in sports*. New York: McGraw Hill.

The Incidence of Injuries in Children's Sports: A Medical Perspective

Lyle J. Micheli

There is general agreement on the part of coaches, parents, and physicians that we are seeing more injuries in young athletes. Opinions differ, however, as to why this is and, perhaps more importantly, what can be done to prevent this (Micheli, 1984).

There appear to be a number of different factors responsible for this increased number of injured young athletes. Certainly, many more children are participating in organized sports, so it would appear reasonable that more injuries are occurring. What is more critical and much more difficult to determine, however, is if the rate of injury in organized children's sports is increasing. In addition, are we encountering new types of injuries in organized sports, not seen in the free play situation, as a result of sports training itself (Micheli, 1983)?

The prime feature of the organized sport situation is the use of systematic repetitive training to improve fitness or sport skills. It is in the training of young athletes, in particular, and not in the actual playing situation that new patterns of sport injuries may be occurring. These questions can only be answered by the application of proper epidemiological techniques to children's sports and sport injuries.

Epidemiology is the science concerned with the distribution and determinants of illness, injury, and death in population groups. It evolved from the study of communicable infectious diseases in population groups. The application of classical epidemiological techniques to traumatic injury was pioneered by Haddon (1966).

An essential technique of epidemiology is the determination of not only the population injured or affected by the disease process but also the accurate determination of the population at risk in order to determine the rate or incidence of injury. As will be seen, most studies of children's sport injuries have recorded episodes of injury occurrence. Some have subclassified injuries into different levels of severity, but few have accurately determined the population at risk. Despite this, much can be learned from presently available studies.

Another important epidemiologic technique is factoring—determining the host and environmental factors contributing to the occurrence of illness or injury. Once again, studies of youth sport injuries have often done little more than record the occurrence of injury, giving little attention to risk factoring. An exception to this are the pioneering studies of Mueller and Blythe (1981) done on football injuries among adolescents in North Carolina. As an example, they determined that the football helmet was the most prevalent risk factor in the occurrence of injury.

An additional problem in factoring injuries in sports is the mixing of macrotrauma and repetitive microtrauma, or overuse, injuries. These two very different classes of injury often have quite different host and environmental factors contributing to their occurrence (Micheli, 1983).

Host factors in youth sport injury include the size, body proportions, anatomic alignment, body composition, level of maturation, fitness level, and sex. Environmental factors include the rules and techniques of the games played, the quality and content of coaching and officiating, the quality of playing surface and equipment, and protective equipment used by the player in a given sport.

In organized sports, as in free play, acute injuries (the result of a single impact macrotrauma) occur. These include sprained ankles, twisted knees, fractured wrists, or a whole variety of similar types of injury. Whether there is a greater or lesser chance of this occurring in the sport situation as opposed to the free play situation is very difficult to compare because a common population at risk is rarely definable (Jackson, Jarrett, Bailey, Kausek, Swanson, & Powell, 1978). The National Electronic Injury Survey System, which compares compiled data of injuries to children admitted to emergency rooms, is really only recording the occurrence of injury or the relative occurrence of injury between various activities including organized sports and free play (U.S. Consumer Product Safety Commission, 1975). The assumption is made that the populations at risk are similar, but this is totally unfounded because the number of children in a given community participating in free play as opposed to organized sport activities may vary dramatically. At present, there is no evidence that the risk of acute traumatic injuries is greater in organized sports than it is in free play activities (Zaricznyi, Shattuck, Mast, Robertson, & D'Elia, 1980).

In addition, the potential for these acute accidental injuries may vary dramatically between different sports and different free play situations. Fortunately, these comparisons can be made much more easily because the population at risk for a given sport activity can often be determined, particularly in the school setting. Garrick and Requa (1978) compared the rates of injuries in high school sports in a group of Seattle schools. Although the absolute rate of injury in a number of these sports has been criticized as being artificially high because of the minimal definition of injury, the comparison of true rate of injury between different sports is most probably valid. Their studies demonstrated a relatively high risk of injury in sports such as gymnastics and basketball, and showed that although football is high in risk, it was rivaled by a number of other supposedly "safe sports."

The second type of injury now occurring in children participating in organized sports appears specific to the organized sport situation. These so-called overuse injuries are the result of repetitive training and, in the case of the injured child, the repetitive microtrauma to tissues of the upper or lower extremity overstressed by this training (Micheli, 1983). These injuries do not occur in the free play situation. However, they appear to occur with particular frequency in sports with a repetitive pattern to their training or participation. Thus, ironically and in contrast to the macrotrauma situation, swimming training may have a greater chance of overuse injury than soccer training and rowing a greater incidence of this type of injury than football.

Children can sustain many of the same injuries as adult athletes, including fractures, dislocations, and musculotendinous injuries, as well as similar types of overuse injuries. In addition, however, they appear to have a special risk of both macrotrauma and microtrauma injury because they are growing. Growth appears to increase the chance of injury in two ways: first, because of the presence of the growth cartilage, which is more susceptible to injury as a tissue, and second, because of the presence of the growth process itself.

Growth occurs in the long bones and vertebral end plates of the spine. Soft tissues and muscle tendon units spanning these bones lengthen secondarily in response to the stretching forces applied as bony growth takes place, so soft tissue-lengthening lags behind skeletal growth. This process can result in a dramatic loss of flexibility in the rapidly growing child. In the presence of tight muscles and tendons, the apophysis, which is the site of insertion of tendon into bone in the child, may become inflamed, or a frank avulsion fracture at the apophyseal site can occur as a result of a single superimposed stretch or contraction (Ogden & Southwick, 1976). Growth cartilage is located at three sites in the child: at the apophysis, as noted, and also at the growth plate at the ends of the long bones and on the joint surface itself. The articular surface is also growing in the child and is also more susceptible to stress and, in particular, shear stress, than the articular cartilage of the adult (Bright, Burstein, & Elmore, 1974).

One of the traditional concerns regarding the participation of immature athletes in sports has been the fact that the child does indeed have growth cartilage and is susceptible to growth cartilage injury. This concern has been particularly evident in the debate over whether growing children should safely participate in contact or collision sports such as gridiron football.

Because of this concern for growth plate fractures in contact sports, in 1956 the Committee on School Health of the American Academy of Pediatrics recommended that body contact sports be "avoided" by children. Despite this recommendation, the growth of youth football and Pop Warner football has continued in this country. Other organized sports have followed suit. Fortunately, studies done to review the incidence of serious growth plate injuries in sports have been reassuring. In 1966, Larson and McMahon reviewed the growth plate fractures presented to their group's private practice and sports medicine clinic. They found that only 6% of sport-related injuries in children under the age of 14 involved the growth plate. Once again, these types of data are not true epidemiologic data but are "pooled data." This is a selected injury group at a single treatment center in which the population at risk is not known. Despite this, these observations are reassuring to those concerned about the high potential for growth plate injury in sports. We reviewed all serious growth plate injuries treated in our own clinic between 1964 and 1974. Of the 153 cases reviewed, only one third were due to participation in organized sports (McManama & Micheli, 1977). Of these, approximately half of the sport-related injuries at the knee were due to cross-body blocking in football, and just under one half of those occurring at the ankle were due to sliding in baseball. Once again, although this represents pooled data and not a true incidence of injury, we might reasonably conclude from these data that the maneuvers of cross-body blocking in gridiron football and sliding in baseball are best avoided by growing athletes.

In addition, three studies done specifically on youth football have shown a very low rate of injury. Roser and Clauson (1970), Godshall (1975), and Goldberg, Rosenthal, and Nicholas (1984) found the rate of injury in junior football was less than 5%, and most of these were of low severity. These studies have confirmed the impressions of many people involved in children's sports, including youth football, that the lower rate of acute injury may be due to the smaller size of the children and the lower kinetic energy of impact.

Of additional reassurance are several studies that compare the injury rates in organized children's sports with those of unorganized or recess-type activities. Zaricznyi et al. (1980) showed that nonorganized sports and physical education classes produced nearly twice as many injuries as organized sports. Other studies by Collins (1967) in Texas and Garrick and Requa (1978) in Seattle support this.

These findings on the risk of serious acute injury from contact sports in children are certainly reassuring. However, the long-term effects of those acute injuries that do occur, as well as the overuse injuries occurring in some children participating in such sports, are not yet known (Micheli, 1983).

An additional area of debate in children's sports concerns the relative safety of contact versus noncontact sports. As noted, the impact or collision sports may not be nearly as dangerous as suspected in this age group. Ironically, some of the noncontact sports that emphasize repetitive training, such as gymnastics or even swimming, may now have higher rates of injury than contact sports because of increasing numbers of overuse injuries. In such high skill sports, in particular, the quality of the adult supervision and training appears to be a critical determinant of the risk of injury. Thus, a swimming program in one community may be relatively safe with a low rate of injury, whereas that in another community may be relatively dangerous with a high rate of shoulder and knee problems occurring from the training regimen.

Similarly, comparisons of injury rates for soccer and gridiron football are also surprising in this age group. Sullivan, Gross, Grana, and Garcia-Moral (1980) found a 2.6% incidence of acute injury in youth soccer in Oklahoma, comparable to injury rates in youth football. In addition, clinical observation would suggest that the rate of overuse injuries is higher in soccer than in many other children's field sports.

When the technique of factoring is applied to the youth sport situation, a number of very interesting observations can be made. This appears to be particularly true when the level of maturation is factored out. It has been well demonstrated that both boys and girls grow at different rates of speed and mature at different times. Thus, competition based on relative maturity level might prove to be safer and more fair. Hafner (1975) found that when athletes are matched by size and skill level, injury rates in a variety of sports are actually decreased.

An additional constitutional factor that has gained much attention has been that of the relative increased risk of injury associated with ligamentous laxity. Nicholas (1970) first drew attention to this risk factor when he observed that studies of professional football players suggested that players with lax ligamentous structures have an increased risk of serious knee injuries, whereas those with tight muscle-tendon units have an increased risk of muscle-tendon strains and sprains, particularly in the hamstrings. However, when similar studies were done on groups of young athletes, no association was found between relative flexibility and the potential for joint injury (Jackson et al., 1978).

A final area of controversy related to risk factors and potential for injury is that of gender of the participants. Clinical observations have suggested that, at the prepubescent level, the relative risk of injury is similar in boys and girls. However, Sullivan et al. (1980) found a greater rate of injury in girls participating in soccer than in boys. The rate of injury was similar in the adolescent age groups. Similarly, Garrick and Requa (1978) compared the injury rate of females competing against females in noncontact sports and compared them with male events. They found a similar rate of injury, suggesting that females were not at a greater risk of injury from noncontact sports than males when competing against members of their own gender.

We are not aware of studies done comparing the rate of injuries in contact sports between young male and female athletes. A study of the rate of injuries about the head, neck, and shoulder in women versus men in rugby football found a similar rate of injury in these groups (Havkins, 1986). Recent clinical observations of girls and boys engaged in similar intensive athletic training programs suggest that, with proper preparation, girls have no greater risk of injury than boys in competitive athletics (Micheli, 1983).

References

Bright, R.W., Burstein, A.H., & Elmore, S.M. (1974). Epiphyseal plate cartilage—A biomechanical and histological analysis of failure modes. *Journal of Bone and Joint Surgery*, **56A**, 668-703.

Collins, H.R. (1967). Contact sports in junior high school. *Texas Medical*, **63**, 67-69.

Committee on School Health. (1956). Competitive athletics. *Pediatrics*, **18**, 672-675.

Garrick, J.G., & Requa, R.H. (1978). Injuries in high school sports. *Pediatrics*, **61**, 465-469.

Godshall, R.W. (1975). Junior league football: Risks vs. benefits. *Journal of Sports Medicine*, **3**(4), 139.

Goldberg, B., Rosenthal, P.P., & Nicholas, J.A. (1984). Injuries in youth football. *Physician and Sports Medicine*, **12**, 122-132.

Haddon, W., Jr. (1966). Principles in research on the effects of sports on health. *Journal of American Medical Association*, **197**, 885-888.

Hafner, J. (1975). Problems in matching young athletes: Body fat, peach fuzz, muscle, and moustache. *Sports Medicine*, **3**, 96-98.

Havkins, S.B. (1986). Head, neck, face, and shoulder injuries in female and male rugby players. *The Physician and Sports Medicine*, **14**(7), 111-118.

Jackson, D.W., Jarrett, H., Bailey, D., et al. (1978). Injury prediction in the young athlete: A preliminary report. *American Journal of Sports Medicine*, **6**, 6-16.

Larson, R.L., & McMahon, R.O. (1966). The epiphysis and the child athlete. *Journal of American Medical Association*, **196**, 607-612.

McManama, G.B., & Micheli, L.J. (1977). The incidence of sport related epiphyseal injuries in adolescents. *Medicine and Science in Sports and Exercise*, **9**(1), 57.

Micheli, L.J. (1983). Overuse injuries in children's sports: The growth factor. *Orthopedics Clinics of North America*, **14**, No. 2.

Micheli, L.J. (Ed.). (1984). *Pediatric and adolescent sports medicine*. Boston: Little, Brown.

Mueller, F., & Blythe, C. (1981). Epidemiology of sports injuries in children. *Clinics in Sports Medicine*, **15**, 229-233.

Nicholas, J.A. (1970). Injuries to the knee ligaments: Relationships to looseness and tightness in football players. *Journal of American Medical Association*, **212**, 2236-2239.

Ogden, J.A., & Southwick, W.D. (1976). Osgood Schlatter's Disease and tibial tubercle development. *Clinical Orthopaedics*, **116**, 180-189.

Roser, L.A., & Clauson, D.K. (1970). Football injuries in the very young athlete. *Clinical Orthopaedics*, **69**, 212.

Sullivan, J.A., et al. (1980). Evaluation of injuries in youth soccer. *American Journal of Sports Medicine*, **8**, 325.

U.S. Consumer Product Safety Commission. (1975). NEISS: An overview. *NEISS News*, **3**, 1-8.

Zaricznyi, B., et al. (1980). Sports-related injuries in school-aged children. *American Journal of Sports Medicine*, **8**, 318.

The Moral of the Youth Sport Story

Brenda Jo Bredemeier

If we are to examine the effects of competitive sport experience on the moral development of young participants, we must first determine what morality means.

There are essentially two different ways scientists approach the question of morality and moral growth. The first approach takes society as the reference point for what is moral. Morality is viewed as whatever is valued by a given culture. Moral development, according to this approach, involves teaching the young to value what society values. Thus, we can refer to this approach as the internalization approach. Within the internalization viewpoint, there are two basic theoretical paradigms.

The first of these paradigms is *psychoanalytic theory*. The critical event in moral development according to Freud is the child's resolution of the Oedipal complex: First the child is attracted to the opposite sex parent, then the child experiences guilt brought on by the real or imagined reprimands by the same sex parent, and finally, the child identifies with the same sex parent and internalizes the values of that person. Such is the origin of the superego, which functions to control primitive and hedonistic impulses.

The second of the internalization paradigms is *social learning theory*. Modeling and reinforcement are emphasized in this approach. A social learning theorist might offer the following scenario to illustrate the process of a young sport participant's moral growth: A girl watching a tennis match observes the players as they exhibit prosocial behavior by shaking hands with each other; after the girl's own game, she exhibits the same behavior she had earlier seen modeled; finally, she is rewarded by the coach for her prosocial behavior.

Thus, although both psychoanalytic theorists and social learning theorists view morality as the internalization of social norms and values, they diverge in their explanation of how that internalization takes place. Psychoanalytic theory emphasizes psychodynamic processes tied to the id, ego, and superego. Social learning theory, on the other hand, points to the role of socializing agents who model and reinforce appropriate behavior.

There has not been an abundance of theoretically grounded research on the topic of moral development among sport participants, and until recently, internalization studies predominated. I would like to take this opportunity to focus on an alternate approach, one that has served as a framework for our moral development research program.

Internalization approaches to morality emphasize the learning of existing social norms. A second major approach to moral development is that of the *constructivists*. These theorists hypothesize that individuals do not internalize the viewpoint of society; rather, people construct their own moral understandings, which become—through developmental periods—increasingly sophisticated and adequate.

The constructivist view is held by structural/developmental theorists who might illustrate moral growth by offering this example: A young girl playing alone with a basketball is asked by a boy if she will share the ball and play with him. At first our young female athlete hogs the ball, but then she reconsiders. Something is going on inside her head. She is reorganizing her understanding of what is appropriate behavior. This reorganization of thought may be stimulated by noticing that the boy is upset, or maybe it came about as a result of previous discussions about sharing. Whatever the source, she is experiencing some confusion, and subtle changes are occurring in the way she understands appropriate moral action. Finally, she decides to share the ball. This is not so much because she has learned that society does not approve of young girls who do not share athletic equipment with young boys; rather, her own ability to recognize and integrate her moral rights and responsibilities with those of another has changed.

Structural/developmental theory is based on a theoretical distinction between the *content* of thought and the underlying *structure* that gives coherence and order to that content. For example, the girl's belief that she should share the ball was an item of moral content. That belief, however, came from an organized pattern of thought, or moral understanding, that led her to interpret the moral rights and duties of self and others in a particular way. The underlying pattern is referred to as structure.

According to structural/developmental theorists, qualitative changes in the underlying structure, in the pattern of organized meanings, are what constitutes moral growth. This may be contrasted with the internalization theorist's emphasis on the quantitative addition of more and more bits of moral information (e.g., more frequent modeling and reinforcement of prosocial behaviors like sharing or shaking hands).

The view that experience in competitive games and sports will enhance the moral growth of young participants has been supported by a diverse group of theorists, including Dewey (1962), Erickson (1965), Mead (1934), Piaget (1932), and Sutton-Smith (1965). Conversely, the little empirical research that has been conducted suggests that these activities, in certain circumstances, may be associated with undesirable moral development.

Moral development has been assessed both in terms of moral thought and moral behavior. Structural/developmentalists have offered limited evidence that youth sport participation may be negatively related to mature moral reasoning. Romance (1984) found a low negative correlation between length of youth sport participation and fifth-grade children's moral reasoning maturity about hypothetical sport dilemmas. This finding is consistent with the results of studies with high school and college students in which basketball players were found to reason at a significantly lower moral level than nonathletes (Bredemeier & Shields, 1984,

1986; Hall, 1981). Horrocks (1979), on the other hand, in a study of fifth- and sixth-grade children, found a positive correlation between sport involvement and reasoning about one hypothetical sport dilemma.

The relationship between sport involvement and various dimensions of moral behavior has occasionally been investigated. Athletic aggression has been the focus of several of these studies. Nelson, Gelfand, and Hartmann (1969) conducted a laboratory experiment with 5- and 6-year-old children who either observed an aggressive or a nonaggressive model and then participated in a competitive game with experimentally controlled outcomes. It was found that competition increased aggression even above levels expected from modeling alone. In a second experiment, Christy, Gelfand, and Hartman (1971) found that competition increased aggression only for those children who also observed an aggressive model. These laboratory findings are consistent with several field studies in which aggression was observed to increase as a result of participation in competitive games or sports (Rausch, 1965; Rausch, Dittman, & Taylor, 1959; Sherif, Harvey, White, Hood, & Sherif, 1961; Sherif & Sherif, 1953).

In addition to direct participation in sport, observation of sports may be related to children's aggression tendencies. In a study of 604 young male ice hockey competitors, Smith (1978) found that over one third of the respondents had learned and used illegal hits by watching professional hockey. Similarly, Mugno and Feltz (1984) found that youth league and high school male football players learned aggressive sport acts by observing college and professional football. Those young athletes who described themselves as having observed a greater number of aggressive acts also exhibited more aggression in their own play.

Special interest in particular athletes also may be related to the aggression tendencies of young sport participants. Smith's (1974) interviews with 83 Toronto male high school ice hockey players revealed that those who perceived their favorite NHL performer as "rough and tough" exhibited higher levels of athletic aggression than players whose favorite performers were perceived as less aggressive. In contrast, Russell (1979) found that, among 205 male amateur ice hockey competitors in the 1975 Canadian Winter Games, those displaying higher levels of physical and/or nonphysical aggression were no more likely to select as heroes NHL individuals and teams having high penalty totals than less aggressive Games competitors.

Several limitations are characteristic of this literature on the moral aspects of youth sport involvement. Investigators often have confined their analyses to a single sport or have indiscriminately lumped all sports together into a single index of sport participation. Because each sport is characterized by a particular complex of relationships and roles that may have differing impact on the participants, it is unsound to generalize from one type of sport experience to another. Thus, for example, a noncontact sport like swimming may have substantially different implications for moral growth or tendencies to aggress than a high-contact sport like football.

Another limitation, characteristic of studies on aggression, is that sport and daily life contexts have not been studied in conjunction with one another. Thus, it is difficult to determine whether children who are aggressive in sport will be correspondingly high in their daily life aggression tendencies and vice versa. Similarly, if a factor is reported to be associated with increased aggressiveness in sport, we do not know whether it also will be associated with greater aggressiveness in everyday life.

Youth Sport Involvement and Moral Development

I would like to discuss results of a research project designed to investigate the relationship of children's participation and interest in low-, medium-, and high-contact sports with their moral reasoning maturity, self-described tendencies to aggress, and legitimacy judgments about the injurious sport acts of others. The setting for this study was a summer sport camp sponsored by the University of Oregon, Eugene.

Assessment of Sport Involvement and Morality Variables

Participants in this study included 106 camp participants in Grades 4 through 7. The girls and boys responded to a sport involvement questionnaire, participated in a moral interview, described their tendencies to aggress in sport and daily life contexts, and recorded judgments about the legitimacy of injurious sport acts.

Sport development. Their sport involvement was assessed through the administration of the Sport Involvement Questionnaire (SIQ), which provided information regarding sport participation and interest. In the first section of the SIQ, children were asked to list each of the organized sport teams on which they had participated and to indicate the number of seasons that they had participated in each sport. In the second section, children were asked to name their favorite athlete and what sport they most enjoyed watching.

Each sport listed by SIQ respondents was coded as being included in one of three categories, depending upon the relative frequency and intensity of physical contact associated with it. Low-contact sports included baseball/softball, gymnastics, swimming, tennis, track; medium-contact sports included basketball and soccer; high-contact sports included football, judo, and wrestling. For the first section of questionnaire responses, the number of seasons that children participated in each category of sport was recorded. If a child listed one season of swimming, three seasons of basketball, and two seasons of football, for example, that child would receive scores of 1, 3, and 2 for low-, medium-, and high-contact sports, respectively.

Responses to the second section of the SIQ were simply assigned to one of the three sport categories and given a score of 1, 2, or 3 corresponding to low, medium, and high contact. For example, a child who identified Martina Navratilova as his favorite athlete received a 1 on that item because Martina Navratilova participates in the low-contact sport of ten-

Table 1 Levels of Interactional Morality

Assimilation Phase

Level 1: Power Balancing. The person is unable to sustain a view of others' interests apart from self-interest and vacillates between compliance with others when forced and thwarting others when able to do so. Balances reflect self-interest except for situations where the self is indifferent or forced to compromise.

Level 2: Egocentric Balancing. The person is able to differentiate others' interests from self-interest but does not understand that both may coincide in a mutual interest. People are viewed as essentially self-interested and out for their own good. To get what the self wants, trade-offs or compromises are made.

Accommodation Phase

Level 3: Harmony Balancing. The person differentiates others' interests from self-interest but assumes that a harmony of these interests can be found because most people are believed to possess essentially altruistic motives. Balances are sought that rest on the good faith of all. People of bad faith are considered odd and dismissed from moral consideration.

Level 4: Common Interest Balancing. The person differentiates all parties' self-interests from the common interests of the group. Balances of compromise are sought that conform to the system-maintenance requirements of the group. Because the moral culpability of all is recognized, externally regulated patterns of exchange are sought that benefit all while limiting personal vulnerability.

Equilibration Phase

Level 5: Mutual Interest Balancing. The person coordinates all parties' self-interests and the common interest of the group in a search for a situationally specific moral balance that will optimize everyone's interests. In such a search, the person recognizes the need to consider the specific values and desires, strengths, and vulnerabilities of the parties involved. Solutions may achieve harmony of interests or may represent compromises of interests, whatever the particularities of the situation and participants allow.

---

nis. Similarly, if a child said she most enjoyed watching the game of football, a score of 3 was assigned to that response.

Moral reasoning. The children's moral reasoning was assessed by means of 45-min individual interviews in which four hypothetical moral dilemmas were presented. Children's reasoning about the dilemmas was evaluated in light of Haan's (1977, 1978) interactional model of moral development. Her interactional model (see Table 1) consists of a five-level characterization of an individual's ability to engage in differentiated dialogical processes to achieve intersubjective "moral balances" concerning respective rights and obligations. Development moves from an assimilative orientation (Levels 1 and 2) in which moral balances are egocentrically constructed, through an accommodative orientation (Levels 3 and 4), where self-interest is subordinated to others' interest, until equilibration is reached at Level 5.

Aggression tendencies. Deluty's (1979) Children's Action Tendency Scale (CATS) was administered to assess children's self-reported aggression tendencies in daily life conflict situations. This instrument presents 10 situations involving provocation, frustration, loss, or conflict in the home or at school. Each situation is followed by three response alternatives—one aggressive, one assertive, and one submissive—that are offered in a paired-comparisons format, thereby yielding three pairs of choices for each situation. The following is an example of one CATS item:

> You're standing in line for a drink of water. A kid your age and size walks over and just shoves you out of line.
>
> What would you do?
>
> A. Push the kid back out of line.
> *Circle A or B*   or
> B. Tell the kid, "You've no right to do that."
>
> A. I'd go to the end of the line.
> *Circle A or B*   or
> B. Push the kid back out of line.
>
> A. Tell the kid, "You've no right to do that."
> *Circle A or B*   or
> B. I'd go to the end of the line.

The aggression responses can be subdivided into physical and nonphysical aggression.

Bredemeier's (1985a) Scale of Children's Action Tendencies (SCATS) was administered to assess children's self-reported aggression tendencies in sport-specific contexts. The SCATS format is identical to that of the CATS, but SCATS stories are set in game or sport contexts. As with the CATS, the aggression scores can be divided into physical and nonphysical aggression subscales.

Legitimacy judgments. To assess children's judgments regarding the legitimacy of potentially injurious sport acts, a series of nine slides, the Injurious Sport ACT Slide Series (ISASS), was presented in conjunction with a questionnaire. The slides, which depicted male athletes participating in medium- or high-contact sports at the collegiate or professional level, had been judged by a panel of experts to present acts with high potential for injury. Children were asked to record on their questionnaires, among other things, (a) the sport being played, (b) whether the action depicted was against the rules, (c) whether someone was likely to get hurt as a result of the act, and (d) whether the act was OK. Scoring of the ISASS consisted of simply adding the number of times a child indicated approval of an act perceived as likely to cause injury.

Associations Between Sport Involvement and Morality Variables

The major issue investigated in the present study pertained to the

Table 2 Associations Between Participation and Interest in Low-, Medium-, and High-Contact Sports With Moral Reasoning, With Aggression Tendencies in Sport (SCATS) and Daily Life (CATS), and With Legitimacy Judgments

| | Participation[a] | | | | | | Interest[b] | | | |
| | Low | | Medium | | High | | Fav. spectate | | Fav. athlete | |
	Female	Male	Female	Male	Female	Male	Female	Male	Female	Male
Moral reasoning	−.20	−.18	−.30***	−.08	—	−.28***	−.11	−.26	−.10	−.34**
Physical aggression										
CATS	.18	.22	.36***	.02	—	.39*	.23***	.47*	.27	.37**
SCATS	.03	.20	.37**	−.05	—	.39*	.09	.37*	.20	.30***
Nonphysical aggression										
CATS	.33***	.20	.36***	−.11	—	.32**	.21	.34**	.25	.07
SCATS	.00	.16	.36***	.01	—	.24***	.01	.35**	.01	.17
Legitimacy judgments	.10	.10	.03	.09	—	.27***	.21	.39**	.21	.39**

* = $p < .001$; ** = $p < .01$; *** = $p < .05$.

[a]Female $N = 42$, male $N = 64$. Analyzed with partial r, controlling for school level. [b]For Favorite Sport to Watch: Female $N = 42$, male $N = 64$. For Favorite Athlete: Female $n = 18$, male $n = 37$. Analyzed with tau-c.

relationship between sport involvement, on the one hand, and moral reasoning and aggression tendencies, on the other. Correlation analyses revealed that sport participation and sport interest were related to moral reasoning to self-described aggression tendencies in both sport and daily life contexts and to judgments regarding the legitimacy of injurious sport acts. (See Table 2 for a presentation of these results.) After discussing associations with sport participation, I will briefly highlight relations with sport interest.

Sport participation.   Girls did not report any high-contact sport experience; as a group, boys described themselves as having participated in low-, medium-, and high-contact sports. Boys' participation in high-contact sports and girls' participation in medium-contact sports were related to less mature moral reasoning and greater tendencies to aggress both physically and nonphysically in sport and daily life contexts. High-contact sport participation by boys was also positively associated with the number of injurious sport acts they perceived as legitimate.

A structural/developmental interpretation of these clearly patterned relationships incorporates the interaction between the environment of contact sports and the meaning-construction of sport participants. Sport structures that allow higher levels of contact encourage rough physical play that can be perceived at times as aggressive. Participants learn that they must physically dominate opponents, who are often objectified as mere obstacles in the quest for victory, if they are not to be dominated themselves. Not surprisingly, participation in these sports was associated with increased aggressiveness in sport. The fact that participation in higher contact sports was also related to tendencies to aggress in everyday life suggests that these sport experiences may be related to behavioral tendencies that extend beyond the bounds of the playing field. Future studies will be needed to investigate the patterns of causality among these variables.

If the sport structure itself were the only significant factor, we would have expected girls' and boys' participation in medium-contact sports to be similarly related to the moral variables. However, medium-contact sport participation was significantly related to the moral reasoning and aggression tendencies of girls but not of boys, leading us to posit that the boys and girls attached different meanings to actions within similar sport structures. Perhaps medium-contact sport behaviors were not interpreted by boys as particularly aggressive in light of the spectrum of contact sport actions with which boys are often involved. Because medium-contact sports were the "roughest" girls had experienced, girls may have been more inclined than boys to interpret acts within these sports as aggressive, especially in light of females' tendencies to express and accept less aggression (Hyde, 1984). Thus, it may not be the amount of physical contact encouraged by a particular sport structure that directly relates to moral reasoning and aggression tendencies but rather an interaction between actual physical contact and the meaning participants attach to that contact based on their experience with and valuing of aggression. A second explanation of the weak findings for girls may be that the girls were less able to identify with the male athletes presented in the ISASS slides than were the boys.

The inverse relationship between relatively high-contact sport participation and moral reasoning also emphasizes the need for an interactional interpretation of the present findings. The moral reasoning of most study participants ranged between the second and third developmental levels. Movement to Level 3 moral reasoning is facilitated by the development of concern for other people, a view of others as basically good moral beings, and an acceptance of responsibility for one's own moral integrity, defined in terms of altruistic giving to others. Participation in relatively high-contact youth sports may impede the transformation to Level 3 moral reasoning in a variety of ways. High-contact sports raise the moral issue of others' welfare in a salient manner, yet the highly regulated and controlled structure often encourages the projection of personal responsibility onto coaches and officials. Also, dialogue among competitors is minimized, facilitating a depersonalization of opponents. Finally, the informal "combat mentality" that often accompanies high-contact sports encourages a negative view of others and discourages altruistic interaction. It is not surprising that participation in high-contact youth sports was more closely associated with assimilative than accommodative moral reasoning, the former also being linked with greater acceptance of aggression (Bredemeier, 1985b; Bredemeier & Shields, 1984).

The significant correlations of legitimacy judgments with boys' participation in high-contact sports, but not other sports, suggests that the normative structure of sport plays a key role in legitimating aggressive game tactics and/or encouraging the involvement of boys who believe athletic aggression is appropriate. For boys participating in sports where more forceful body contact is normative, a greater acceptance of potentially injurious acts is likely.

The general lack of significant legitimacy judgment relations with girls' sport participation may reflect the less significant role that sport plays in female socialization. Relegated to a peripheral role, sport experience may not be as integrated with the general psychosocial development of girls as with boys.

Sport interest. Boys' interest in higher-contact sports was related to less mature moral reasoning, to greater tendencies to aggress both physically and nonphysically in sport and daily life contexts, and to more acceptance of injurious sport acts. We do not know why a particular athlete or sport was appealing to study participants. The general pattern for boys, which closely parallels associations with their sport participation, may indicate that boys' sport interests were motivated by a desire to learn game skills and/or by an appreciation of aggression itself. It also may be that the correlations between sport interests and moral variables reflect the influence of significant others, such as parents or peers, who place a premium on certain types of physical expression for boys. High-contact sport and its elite participants may be elements used in the socialization of boys into men. Thus, boys' interests in high-contact sport may be reflective of their perceptions of what is valued for them by others.

Girls' sport interests were not related to the morality variables, with the exception of physical aggressiveness in daily life settings. These non-significant relationships may indicate that girls' sport interests were not well established or that the girls were less influenced than the boys by factors such as the learning of contact sport skills, an appreciation of aggression, or the influence of strong socializing agents. Because high-contact sport experience often is not available for girls, a correlation between sport interest and morality variables is less likely.

The one notable correlation for girls' sport interest and physical aggression in daily life may reflect a pattern of deviance. It is probably less socially approved for girls to identify higher-contact sport athletes as favorites or to enjoy watching higher-contact sports; similarly, physical aggression is less stereotypically feminine than nonphysical aggression, and aggression in everyday life is less accepted than aggression in sport. For a few girls, these deviations seemed to form a coherent pattern.

Implications and Conclusions

The present study suggests that sport involvement may have important implications for the development of children's morality. Although the possible interactive effect of participating in more than one form of sport was not controlled in this study, the results appear to have a clear pattern. In particular, participation in relatively high-contact sports was associated with less mature moral reasoning, greater tendencies to aggress physically and nonphysically in both sport and daily life, and boys' judgments about the legitimacy of injurious sport acts. The relationship between boys' interest in high-contact sports and their moral reasoning, aggression tendencies, and legitimacy judgments generally fit this pattern also. Although cause-effect relationships between sport involvement and morality variables cannot be illuminated in the present study, potential implications need to be carefully examined.

Based on the structural/developmental interpretation of our findings, we suggest that involvement in sports characterized by a relatively high degree of physical contact may be developmentally counterproductive for children beginning to construct accommodative reasoning patterns. Because development is derived from an interaction between the active structuring processes of the mind and environmental experiences that push against the boundaries of current cognitive structures, it is important to reflect on the significance of sport involvement in light of its meaning for individuals at various levels of development. The types of social interactions fostered by relatively high-contact sports in typical settings may provide little stimulus for—or even impede—moral growth. Future research is necessary to determine whether or in what ways high-contact sport involvement can be beneficial and/or detrimental to the moral growth of participants and spectators reasoning predominantly at the assimilative phase.

Sport involvement does not necessarily impede participants' moral development. In fact, in a previous field experiment we were able to facilitate children's moral reasoning during an 8-week summer camp program by training teachers/coaches to employ theoretically grounded instructional strategies designed to promote moral growth (Bredemeier, Weiss, Shields, & Shewchuk, 1986). I believe that experience in competitive youth sport can enhance the children's development, but the ball is in the court of adults—researchers, coaches and teachers, parents—who must do their part to create a sport structure conducive to moral growth.

Acknowledgments

I would like to acknowledge the important contributions of Dr. Maureen Weiss, director of the University of Oregon summer sport camp, as well as those of David Shields and Bruce Cooper, both of the University of California, Berkeley.

References

Bredemeier, B.J. (1985a). *Children's moral reasoning and action tendencies in daily life and sport-specific contexts.* Manuscript submitted for publication.

Bredemeier, B.J. (1985b). Moral reasoning and the perceived legitimacy of intentionally injurious sport acts. *Journal of Sport Psychology, 7,* 110-124.

Bredemeier, B., & Shields, D. (1984). The utility of moral stage analysis in the understanding of athletic aggression. *Sociology of Sport Journal,* **1,** 138-149.

Bredemeier, B., & Shields, D. (1986). Moral growth among athletes and nonathletes: A comparative analysis of females and males. *Journal of Genetic Psychology,* **147,** 7-18.

Bredemeier, B., Weiss, M., Shields, D., & Shewchuk, R. (1986). Promoting moral growth in a summer sport camp: The implementation of theoretically grounded instructional strategies. *Journal of Moral Education,* **15,** 212-220.

Christy, P.R., Gelfand, D.M., & Hartman, D.P. (1971). Effects of competition-induced frustration on two classes of modeled behavior. *Developmental Psychology,* **5,** 104-111.

Deluty, R.H. (1979). Children's action tendency scale: A self-report measure of aggressiveness, assertiveness, and submissiveness in children. *Journal of Consulting and Clinical Psychology,* **47,** 1061-1071.

Dewey, J. (1962). Theory of valuation. In H.W. Burns (Ed.), *Philosophy of education.* New York: The Ronald Press.

Erickson, E. (1965). *Childhood and society.* New York: W.W. Norton Co.

Haan, N. (1977). *A manual for interactional morality.* Unpublished manuscript, Institute of Human Development, Berkeley.

Haan, N. (1978). Two moralities in action contexts: Relationship to thought, ego regulation, and development. *Journal of Personality and Social Psychology*, **36**, 286-305.

Hall, E. (1981). *Moral development levels of athletes in sport specific and general social situations*. Unpublished doctoral dissertation, Texas Woman's University, Denton.

Horrocks, R.N. (1979). *The relationship of selected prosocial play behaviors in children to moral reasoning, youth sports participation, and perception of sportsmanship*. Unpublished doctoral dissertation, University of North Carolina, Greensboro.

Hyde, J.S. (1984). How large are gender differences in aggression? A developmental meta-analysis. *Developmental Psychology*, **20**(4), 722-736.

Mead, G.H. (1934). *Mind, self, and society*. Chicago: University of Chicago Press.

Mugno, D., & Feltz, D. (1984, July). *The social learning of aggression in youth football*. Paper presented at the 1984 International Olympic Scientific Congress, University of Oregon, Eugene.

Nelson, J., Gelfand, D., & Hartmann, D. (1969). Children's aggression following competition and exposure to an aggression model. *Child Development*, **40**, 1085-1097.

Piaget, J. (1932). *The moral judgment of the child*. New York: Harcourt.

Rausch, H. (1965). Interaction sequences. *Journal of Personality and Social Psychology*, **2**, 487-499.

Rausch, H., Dittman, A., & Taylor, T. (1959). Person, setting, and change in social interaction. *Human Relations*, **12**, 361-379.

Romance, T. (1984). *A program to promote moral development through elementary school physical education*. Unpublished doctoral dissertation, University of Oregon, Eugene.

Russell, G.W. (1979). Hero selection by Canadian ice hockey players: Skill or aggression? *Canadian Journal of Applied Sport Science*, **4**, 309-313.

Sherif, M., Harvey, O., White, B., Hood, W., & Sherif, D. (1961). *Intergroup conflict and cooperation: The robbers' cave experiment*. Norman: University of Oklahoma Press.

Sherif, M., & Sherif, C. (1953). *Groups in harmony and tension*. New York: Harper & Row.

Smith, M.D. (1974). Significant others' influence on the assaultive behavior of young hockey players. *International Review of Sport Sociology*, **3**, 45-56.

Smith, M.D. (1978). Social learning of violence in minor hockey. In F.L. Smoll & R.E. Smith (Eds.), *Psychological perspectives in youth sports*. Washington: Hemisphere.

Sutton-Smith, B. (1965). Play preference and play behavior: A validity study. *Psychological Reports*, **16**, 65-66.

Helping Children Become Independent, Responsible Adults Through Sports

Rainer Martens

Why do adult-organized children's sport programs exist? What are our society's objectives for these programs? Are the answers obvious, even though they are seldom discussed? When adult-organized children's sport programs first emerged in this country, we spoke of their value in developing strong men so our nation would be better prepared in the event of war. This may have been a useful purpose in the past, but today few accept preparation for war as an objective of children's sport programs.

Is the purpose of children's sport programs to provide a feeder system for higher levels of sport that entertain our society? Is the purpose of children's sports, as some have charged, to give adult coaches an opportunity to relive their youth vicariously, or to give parents an opportunity to compare their combined genetic endowments with those of other parents through their offspring? These may be purposes, but I doubt they are primary objectives.

What do YMCAs hope to accomplish by offering sport programs to 2 million children? What does USA Wrestling seek from its kids' wrestling program in which 500,000 children participate? Why does the Champaign, IL, Park District spend close to $85,000 to offer sport opportunities to the youth of the community? What do parents hope will be accomplished by sending their sons and daughters to America's playing fields and gymnasia? What do concerned professionals consider to be the objectives of children's sport programs? All these questions lead to one compelling query: What effects do we want well-designed children's sport programs to have on the young people who participate?

The presentations at this conference have focused extensively on research related to children's sports, and research is sorely needed. But scholars who are concerned about improving children's sports and about seeing the research implemented into practice should also be concerned about the objectives our society holds for children's sports. The preceding questions are value questions that give the research direction and meaning. A scientist does not study the etiology of sport injuries for the sheer sake of it. He or she hopes that in some way the results will lead to an improvement in children's sports. And so it should be.

I believe that existing sport science and medicine research is underutilized because our society is unclear about the objectives children's sport

297

programs should have in our society. Not only will our society's objectives for children's sports influence what research will be utilized and how, they will also influence the type of research conducted by guiding the questions asked. If the objective is primarily to win by demonstrating excellence, then the research that addresses performance enhancement will be used. If the objective is to help young people to develop physically, psychologically, and socially, then the research that addresses human development will receive greater emphasis.

My purposes in this paper are as follows:

- To emphasize the importance of defining clearly our society's objectives for children's sport programs
- To state my opinion abut what these objectives should be
- To offer some examples of how coaches fail to achieve these objectives
- To suggest how they may be achieved

Why Objectives Are Important

When I first began developing the American Coaching Effectiveness Program (ACEP), I placed total emphasis on teaching coaches the basics of sport medicine and science and the techniques specific to their sport. But the information did not fit together well; it lacked perspective. What was missing, I discovered, was that ACEP did not espouse a philosophy. Although coaches need the technical facts that come from science, much of what coaches deal with concerns making judgments, often value judgments. After hundreds of coaching seminars, I finally realized with what coaches were struggling. They were requesting assistance in formulating a philosophy of coaching. Not only is our society vague about the objectives sought from children's sports, but coaches are equally unclear. Left without direction, coaches tend to adopt the most prevalent philosophy or objective, which, of course, is the professional or elite sport model that emphasizes winning. If society is indecisive, if as professionals dedicated to children's sports we are ambiguous or nondirective, then we cannot expect coaches of children's sports to have objectives contrary to the objectives in the most visible sport programs—professional sports, including the high school and college feeder systems. We all know what the prevailing objective is in professional sports.

I shall attempt to make the case that the most important task to be accomplished by professionals involved in children's sports is to influence society to adopt more appropriate objectives than those embraced in professional sports. Not all the answers to the problems in children's sports rest in science. I deeply respect science for what it can contribute to our understanding, but I also appreciate what science cannot do. Polanyi (1958) wrote in *Personal Knowledge*:

> In the days when an idea could be silenced by showing that it was contrary to religion, theology was the greatest single source of fallacies. Today, when any human thought can be discredited

by branding it as unscientific, the power previously exercised by theology has passed over to science; hence science has become in its turn the greatest single source of error. (p. 24)

What brought coherence, then, to the hundreds of bits of information contained in ACEP, was its philosophy: "Athletes first, winning second." It became the cornerstone of the program. What I mean by these four words is simply this: Every decision a coach makes should be made first in the best interest of the athlete and then in the pursuit of victory. This philosophy is carefully explained in program materials and through exercises that give coaches an opportunity to try out this perspective. Many coaches and sport administrators have told me that this philosophy, more than the technical information, leads them to change the way they coach.

Objectives to Which Children's Sports Programs Should Aspire

It is risky to state, "These are my objectives for children's sports." Who am I to declare what they should be? I am no more qualified to do so than anyone else, but I am no less qualified either. My opinions are not dictums; you can take them or leave them. My purpose is to stimulate thought about these objectives in order first to urge some consensus for certain objectives, and second to emphasize the need to help coaches, parents, and society as a whole formulate a philosophy that enhances these objectives. With this in mind, I share my objectives.

The immediate short-term objective is to win. Striving to win within the rules of the game should be the objective of every athlete and coach. But striving to win the game is an objective of the *contest*, not an objective of *participation* in children's sport programs. Keeping these two types of objectives distinct is not always easy. Sometimes they complement each other (e.g., when winning helps develop confidence), and sometimes they conflict (e.g., when further injury is risked by playing injured athletes in the belief that their talents may enhance the team's chance to win).

Winning the contest, the league, or a tournament, I believe, must always be seen as secondary in importance to the objectives of the program, and those objectives should include the following:

- To help young people become physically skillful and gain an appreciation for these abilities
- To develop an active life-style and a lifelong commitment to such a life-style
- To play for sheer fun, to enjoy themselves
- To come to know themselves and to like what they come to know
- To develop interpersonal skills
- To enhance their self-worth by developing a positive self-concept and self-confidence
- To become a responsible, autonomous contributor to society

In this chapter I would like to emphasize the latter objective, which to me incorporates all the other objectives. I would like to see every child experience sport so that it moves him or her a little closer to being a responsible, autonomous person. Borrowing from Carl Rogers (1983), I would like to see our children become fully functioning persons who are open to their experiences, meaning they are not defensive.

I hope that children emerge from sport being less dependent on others, having learned how to make it on their own in the world. This is not to imply that the youngster is uncooperative. Becoming an autonomous person means knowing when to work with others and knowing how to help oneself.

I hope athletes emerge from sport perceiving that they are responsible for themselves and responsible to society. The sport experience should help athletes perceive that they are in control of their fate, that they are the cause of their behavior. De Charms (1976) would say that children should see themselves as the *origin* of their behavior, not as *pawns* who are used by others. When children feel they are in control of their fate, they feel free to pursue their goals.

Werner Erhard captured the significance of becoming responsible when he wrote, "When you accept that you are responsible for your life, you find out you just didn't happen to be lying there on the tracks when the train passed through. You are the [person] who put yourself there."

The development of responsibility goes hand in hand with becoming competent. I believe humankind possesses an innate disposition to be competent. From birth, the infant begins the ongoing process of striving to develop the requisite skills of our society. As the child becomes more competent, more responsibilities are given. The more responsibilities children are given, the more competent they are likely to become. And the cycle continues. The more competent individuals become, the more autonomous they become. The more autonomous individuals are, the more freedom they have to pursue their goals.

Freedom is an important concept related to responsibility and autonomy. Some argue that humans are never free. B.F. Skinner contends that we are a product of our environment, and this environment is a fully determined, cause-and-effect environment. I would agree that all of us are constrained by our environment, but the freedom I am talking about is the freedom espoused by Carl Rogers. It is, as he says, "essentially an inner thing, something that exists in the living person quite aside from any of the outward choices of alternatives that we so often think of constituting freedom. It is the realization that I can live myself, here and now, by my own choice" (Rogers, 1983, p. 39).

Becoming responsible, then, means that the child must give up the notion of complete freedom to do anything, regardless of the consequences to others. The youngster must learn to take responsibility for his or her actions. The difficult lesson of responsibility is learning to seek self-determined goals while at the same time promoting the goal seeking of others. Thus, the responsible person learns he or she is not free to do anything he or she wants but is free to make choices within the constraints of the environment.

Responsible, autonomous persons view the world as one where they determine their goals and constantly strive to influence the external forces to enhance the probability of attaining them. "Unresponsible" (not irresponsible) people, the pawns of society, have neither clear goals nor a concept of personal striving. Instead they focus on the constraints inherent in their environment.

Becoming a responsible, autonomous person is an idealistic goal, seldom to be fully achieved. Yet it is a goal that all adults who make children's sports possible should strive to achieve. It is a goal not only to be pursued through sport but also through other institutions of society whose purpose it is to help young people become successful adults. The sport experience must be judged a failure unless at least some progress is made in achieving autonomy.

Why Children's Sports Programs Seldom Reach This Goal

The problem resides, as I have suggested, with society being vague about its objectives for children's sport programs and thus with many coaches adopting the objective that prevails in professional sports, namely winning. If the alternative objective advocated in this chapter is to be implemented on a large scale, children's sport scholars and administrators need to support it. But most of all, coaches need to embrace it into their coaching philosophy.

What is coaching in the minds of most who practice this profession? It is not primarily concerned with helping athletes become responsible, autonomous individuals. For too many coaches, coaching is Xs and Os. It is teaching skills, running drills, conditioning athletes, and disciplining those who do not follow the rules. Coaching is organizing details and motivating children to pursue victory, in some cases at the expense of those children's physical and psychological development.

This view of coaching is badly in need of change. The most difficult aspect of coaching is this: Coaches must learn to let athletes learn. Sport skills should be taught so they have meaning to the child, not just meaning to the coach. Coaches must learn to involve the athletes more in what they are learning—both the motor and cognitive aspects. Athletes need to be given the opportunity to initiate learning, to make mistakes, and to learn from them. True coaching has no room for the authoritarian dictator nor the person who is on an ego trip. The true coach serves as a guide and a partner in the competitive sport experience. Through the courageous act of sharing decision making, coaches can nurture the development of responsible, autonomous members of society.

Now I would like to describe a few ways in which coaches deny athletes the opportunity to develop autonomy by denying them the opportunity to exercise responsibility by making their own decisions.

Responsibility Through Winning

Most coaches would subscribe to the objective that athletes should become more responsible for themselves, yet they apparently do not understand what is involved in helping young people learn self-responsibility. Some coaches seem to put all their stock in winning. They believe that if athletes learn to win and to put in the hard work to win, then they will accrue all types of wonderful physical and psychological benefits. That simply is not the case, and countless numbers of winning athletes are witness to this absurdity. The outcome of winning does not develop the psychological qualities we consider here; the *process* used in pursuing winning does. But in the minds of some coaches, the end is more important than the means.

Responsibility Through Decision Making

Responsibility begins by giving the athletes the opportunity to make some of their own decisions, and the degree to which they are given the right to make their own decisions depends on how well they use this right. Too many coaches never permit athletes to have the opportunity to exercise this right because they fear it risks winning. Coaches are probably correct in this assumption, at least initially.

Young athletes will not exercise the newly granted right of making decisions for themselves perfectly the first time it is given to them. Errors are likely, and they can have serious consequences for the outcome of a game. Coaches who feel the pressure to win from society, or who simply coach for their own ego enhancement, will be quick to withdraw such decision-making responsibilities from their athletes.

When Greg Johnson was fired as head wrestling coach at the University of Illinois, he was quoted as saying, "With the guys who really wanted to wrestle for Illinois, I was effective. But the guys who weren't willing to put in the effort I had a hard time motivating. I probably should have been stricter. In the end it sold me down the drain."

Is being stricter or more authoritarian a better way to build motivation? From what sport psychologists have learned, it is not. Motivation is developed by building positive feelings within the athletes throughout the sport experience. When athletes feel more worthy as individuals, they have the self-confidence to risk all out effort in sport. This inner self-worth is the source of intrinsic motivation—the type of motivation that refuels itself because it is built on personal pride. A coach becoming stricter or more domineering may serve as a source of extrinsic motivation, but such motivation is transient and fickle.

Consider some other ways coaches deny athletes the right to make decisions and therefore deny them the opportunity to develop responsibility. I know coaches in many sports who make all the decisions for their athletes with regard to the training program. The schedule of miles to run, laps to swim, kilometers to ski are fixed, now often by computer. The athletes have no input into the training regimen; they simply follow it. This seems ludicrous, especially when an athlete is in high school or college. By then athletes should have a reasonably good understanding of the elements to consider in a training program if coaches through the years have explained why the training program contains what it contains. The athlete knows his or her body better than anyone. Given that he or she has been taught how, it makes sense that the athlete is the best person to develop and to implement the training program in consultation with the coach. Sometimes I wonder if coaches purposely choose not to teach their athletes the ingredients of a training program, perhaps unconsciously fearing they will no longer be needed. Could it be that some coaches like having athletes dependent on them?

Responsibility Through Communication

Responsibility cannot be developed in young athletes unless coaches communicate with them and, in particular, listen to them. Athletes learn responsibility by having input into the program and seeing the consequences of their input. Athletes learn responsibility by sharing their ideas, by probing for information through countless questions. Unfortunately, too many coaches are great talkers and poor listeners.

Of course, coaches need not be good listeners if they never consider what athletes say anyway. If they listen to an athlete suggesting how practice could be made more effective to meet the athletes' needs, then this would be sharing some of the decision making. From some coaches' perspective this again threatens their power; it diminishes their authority. Some coaches have come to think of themselves as the experts, the keepers of order, the evaluators, the rule makers, as all-knowing.

Actually, many coaches who assume such roles know they do not know it all; they have good or bad days like all of us. These coaches, however, believe that if they let their mask slip or show themselves as they are, then there would be questions by the athletes to which they would have to answer "I don't know." This would show the coach to be a real person, but our society expects coaches to be infallible, and some coaches begin to believe this expectation is true.

Coaches who are concerned with helping athletes learn to become responsible for themselves will facilitate this process by listening to their athletes, by admitting to errors, and by being a real adult without a mask.

Responsibility Through Learning Skills

Opportunities to learn responsibility are denied athletes by some coaches, even in the learning of skills. When coaches teach skills, they sometimes become impatient, unable to leave the athlete alone, unable to let the athlete learn the skill at his or her own pace. I have seen coaches who overinstruct and are constantly yelling instructions. Every trial of a skill is followed with a list of things done incorrectly. Rather than being helpful, these comments are distractions that will never permit athletes to experience flow. The athlete never has the opportunity to discover the skill for him- or herself. The athlete is deprived of making another important decision: how to make adjustments to perform in a desired way.

If coaches embrace the objective of helping athletes to become more responsible, they should view their role as being available to the athlete when needed, assisting when the athlete recognizes the need for assistance, and minimizing the athlete's dependency on the coach. Such an approach places emphasis on athletes becoming responsible for the learning of skills rather than on coaches being responsible for teaching skills.

Responsibility Through Decisions About Strategy

Part of the joy of sport is learning to make decisions about strategy. Planning strategy is also an excellent way to learn responsibility for one's own decisions and to learn to exercise good judgment. But coaches too often keep this joyful part of the game for themselves. Wherever possible, coaches will make the decisions about strategy, especially in sports like football and basketball. (Could we not make a rule that made it illegal for coaches to call the plays in football? It is unlikely because the coaches make the rules and would never give up this enjoyable part of the game.)

A fair question to ask again, though, is, How are athletes to learn to make important decisions if they are never given the opportunity? Don Meredith, former quarterback for the Dallas Cowboys, says that the Dallas Cowboy system "doesn't encourage the individuality of a player; it's more of a conforming thing." Perhaps this is the way it must be in professional sports. But must it be this way in children's sports?

Coaches at every level defend the making of strategy decisions by claiming it increases their chances of winning. They probably are right, at least in children's sports. But here is an example where the short-term objective of winning supercedes and therefore obstructs the ultimate objective: to provide athletes with the opportunity to develop decision-making skills and thus responsibility.

Responsibility in Life

Young athletes who show promise of becoming stars are given considerable assistance in developing their physical talent, but at the same time they are often so sheltered that their psychological and social development is hindered. Coaches are sometimes guilty of taking control over an athlete's total life, telling him or her what courses to study, when and where to study, whom he or she can see socially, and so forth. Athletes who endure such coddling often have exceptional difficulty reentering society when their playing days are over. Coaches are guilty in these cases of using these athletes to win at the expense of helping these athletes develop decision-making skills so they can become responsible, autonomous individuals.

Coaching to Enhance Responsibility Development

What are the qualities of coaches that are likely to result in children becoming responsible, autonomous human beings? The most important quality is believing deeply that the athlete is more important than winning. Facilitating the development of an athlete into an autonomous human being is very much a long-term objective. Such development is achieved by countless little events that cumulatively permit the child to experience life and to grow from these experiences. It requires the coach to communicate that he or she cares for the athlete as a human being, accepting and trusting the person.

To be able to help youngsters to become responsible, coaches must drop the role of coach that is now so prevalent in America. They must become real or genuine people. They must be able to enter into a relationship without a front, a facade, a mask.

Coaches must also have empathy—the ability to understand the emotions and attitudes of the athletes, to see the world as they see it. Empathy creates the trust between coach and athlete that is essential for both to have if decision making is going to be shared.

Coaches need to coach less and to focus more on facilitating children's development. Coaches need to ask themselves not how they can facilitate winning, but how they can create a psychological environment in which children will feel free to be curious, to make mistakes, and to learn from the surroundings, fellow players, and the coach.

Athletes coached by adults who create this nurturing environment will learn that:

- they are valued persons,
- they can risk error in order to learn,
- their curiosity is welcomed and prized,
- the coach is friendly and caring,
- they can learn at their own pace,
- they can contribute to the goals of the team, and
- sport is fun.

Athletes who emerge from this type of sport environment will likely be:

- more motivated,
- more skilled,
- more responsible, and
- more autonomous.

Importance of Coaching

You may conclude from my comments that I am anti-children's sports. This would be an erroneous conclusion. I am highly supportive of children's sports, but I recognize some of the problems and want to work toward some solutions.

You may conclude from these comments that I am opposed to coaching. I am not opposed to good coaching: I am opposed to coaching that is based on a "win first, athletes second" philosophy. I believe coaching is extremely important; it is why I have expended much effort to prepare coaches for the challenging task of leading our youth.

Not long ago I received a copy of a letter written by a young man studying to be a coach. The letter was passed on to me by Jim Elwanger, the ACEP state director in Iowa. I cannot begin to communicate the significance of coaching as well as this coach-to-be has.

My philosophy of coaching has taken an about face, much like my life. For the past 5 years I've been dead against competition of any kind, I didn't like what it did for me, or the coaches I had. So the chip on the shoulder was heavy and I carried it. I wasn't ever first in the lineup, although I felt that's where I was supposed to be because of my size.

After failing, and disappointing myself and others I turned to drugs. It was something I could do, feel good (except for the days after), and be high. I didn't have to worry about being #1 because when I was high I was #1.

This term at college has changed my life; I'm no longer playing with drugs because someone very special to me has coached me, not at basketball, but in gaining control of my life again, instead of drugs. A coach is someone that tells you you're important, and needed. He knows when you need to be yelled at, for sloughing off, exactly what I've been doing for years. He instills confidence in you when you feel totally worthless. A coach has the right things to say, is a counselor, a buddy, a pal, and someone that you feel will never let you down.

He's emotionally stable when everytings [sic] seems to be going hog wild. He's a setter of limits to make athletes feel comfortable in knowing what is expected from them and what they should expect from themselves. He gets angry, only when he has a right to, because he's been let down, by me. He's a friend that listens to our problems, joys, and shares a shoulder to cry on and a good hearty laugh to relieve the everyday pressures. He's someone who compliments you when you deserve it, and let's you know the potential that you have, not far fetched, but realistic. He lets you know that you can be anything (all that you can be— without the Army). He's a teacher that experiences new things with you, at a level that you can comprehend.

I love my coach, and pray that any athlete that I should ever have on my team, can love me the same.

This paper is the hardest paper I've ever written, because it's me. Sometimes we don't like to look at our past, but that is something that has to be looked at, thought about, and learned from. Now comes my part of teaching others to learn from my mistakes and be the best that they can be. (Author unknown)

Closing Comment

The most significant problems in children's sports are not in reducing injuries, in discovering ways to teach skills better, in finding better training methods, or in employing innovative motivational techniques. The most significant task is changing the values society has imposed upon the coaches of America. If we want to improve children's sports, we must first change the philosophy of coaches to athletes first, winning second. Only when coaches adopt this perspective can we hope to see young people emerge from the sport experience who are responsible, autonomous human beings.

Acknowledgment

I would like to thank Linda Bump for her critique of the manuscript and for presenting the paper on my behalf.

References

de Charms, R. (1976). *Enhancing motivation*. New York: Irvington Publishers.

Polanyi, M. (1958). *Personal knowledge*. Chicago: University of Chicago Press.

Rogers, C.R. (1983). *Freedom to learn for the 80's*. Columbus, OH: Charles E. Merrill.

Perspective on Children's Sports With Suggestions for Future Directions

Allan J. Ryan

The extreme positions in the ongoing discussions regarding children's participation in sports might be defined as forbidding sports completely and allowing unrestricted participation of children of all ages at any level possible for them. It would probably be difficult to find anyone who would take either position. Among all those assuming positions somewhere between, most would come down closer to one side than the other. Failure to reach a realistic and satisfactory compromise between these divergent opinions appears to be based on differing ideas as to (a) the age at which an individual can be considered a child, (b) how sport is defined, (c) what differences exist in the experiences of children participating in sports from those who do not, (d) whether the balance between favorable and unfavorable effects produced in children by sports participation is unequal, and (e) if unfavorable effects do occur, whether the results are temporary or long-lasting physical, emotional, or mental instability.

Participation of young persons in high-level sport competition is hardly new; it extends back to the time of the ancient Greek festivals and games. Although this generally accepted concept during those times classified a young male as a child until he reached his 12th birthday and as a boy until he reached his 18th birthday, the upper limit was based more on the fact that he could then be trained for military service than any medical or pedagogical consideration. The term *ephebos* was applied only to sons of the patrician class who were subject to formal education, which included academic studies; training in speaking, practical sciences, and the arts; as well as what is now called physical education. There was some vaguely defined distinction between boy and youth, and for purposes of some sport participation there were as many as five different age groups. In Asia Minor boys were allowed to enter men's events if they felt qualified. A principal reason for the involvement of boys in high-level sport competition was that there was no opportunity for sports as a leisure activity as exists today. The exercises in the gymnasium were not sports. Although they could be competitive, the ephebos could compete only in their own gymnasiums. Aristotle favored physical education for the young but decried early specialization. He pointed out that most of those who won the boys' events in the games did not go on to win the men's events later. Milo of Croton was an exception.

In the Olympic Games they adhered to the classification of boys between the ages of 12 and 18, even though the decisions had to be made chiefly by the eyes of the judges in the absence of written records in most instances. The afternoon of the third day in the early years of the Olympic Games was devoted to three boys' events: wrestling, boxing, and a 200-m race. Milo won the boys' wrestling in 540 B.C. and subsequently the men's wrestling three times. A 12-year-old boy won the sprint in 368 B.C. A pentathlon for boys was held only in 628 B.C. and it is not known why it was never held again. In 200 B.C. a pankration, a combination of wrestling and boxing for boys, was instituted and continued.

Relatively little is known about sports for girls and young women in ancient Greece because the Greek men, with the exception of the Spartans, did not feel that they were important. Women were never allowed as competitors in the Olympic Games except as owners of racing chariots. The principal festival involving sports for women was the Games of Hera, established by Hippodamia. Sixteen unmarried girls and women of unspecified ages were recruited to maintain the veil of Hera's temple. At these Games the 16 females were divided into three groups for a race of 160 m. Races for women were established at three other sacred festivals (Isthmia, Nemea, and Pythia), but it is not known who was involved. Wrestling was an activity for girls and women only in Sparta.

Over the centuries different patterns of youth involvement in sport have appeared and disappeared based on social conditions and the development of sports as competitive, recreational, and professional activity. Children have continued to invent and play games, some of which have become established sports. Physical education has also passed through a great variety of forms, ranging from calisthenics to competitive sports and including such specialized activities as movement education, rhythmic gymnastics, and water exercise. Competitive sports in modern times developed principally along two lines: (a) adolescent and young adult sports allied primarily with educational institutions and (b) adult sports, both amateur and professional. Recreational sports run generally across age boundaries.

In recent times there has been a remarkable growth in the numbers of very young athletes in highly organized and competitive sports throughout the world. This has caused physicians, educators, and parents to wonder whether these children are too young to be involved in such activities, and if so, why they are too young. Do modern-day professionals have any better ideas than the Greeks did about how the terms boy, youth, girl, adolescent, and young adult are properly defined, and do such definitions tell us anything about what they can or should do? On the one hand, some young people are involved in school and community sport programs within their home environments, and on the other hand, some leave their homes to be enrolled and maintained full time in special sport schools or in the homes of professional sport coaches in places far distant from their homes and families.

Dr. Ommo Grupe (1988) of the University of Tübingen put the controversy on youth involvement in sport into an appropriate perspective in his presentation, "Top-Level Sports for Children From an Educational

Viewpoint,'' at the 1984 conference on children and sport in Urbino, Italy. He said that the chief purpose for children's participation in top-level sports is to retain the top-level sport system and to better athletic performances continuously for reasons that are indigenous to the system as well as for political, ideological, and commercial reasons rather than to contribute to the education and development of children. The number and intensity of training sessions involved in many sports on a year-round schedule—particularly in gymnastics, swimming, ice skating, and tennis—together with the competitions requiring extended absences from school and home for travel create problems for the education and development of the child. Those who are highly intelligent and strongly motivated may be able to overcome these problems, but others lose out in their education and development, even if they are temporarily successful in a sport.

Advocates of early extensive and intensive training of children contend, Grupe says, that with proper supervision, failures do not have to occur and that what can be accomplished during a phase that is favorable to learning sports skills cannot be made up entirely at an older age, even with more intensive training. They say that the whole development of the child is not affected by the temporal, physical, and emotional demands of sport at the top level, but he says they omit saying that these demands do not stimulate this development and perhaps misdirect or retard it.

In many cases it means loss of contact with their age peer group and learning to associate with an older age group from whom they may derive and adopt ideas and practices that are less appropriate to them. Education, he says, cannot orientate itself to what physical proficiency can be attained with a child but rather what is important for the child's development and general education.

Although a number of studies have reported the functional performance improvements made in child athletes subjected to specific training procedures compared to nonsport age-group controls, there is little specific information about how the two groups compare emotionally and intellectually. Richard Weinberg (1985), codirector of the University of Minnesota's Center for Early Education Development, told the second National Behavioral Pediatrics Conference that a study of school-age children showed that sport participation ranked very low on a long list of activities that they found stressful. This runs contrary to the popular impression that competitive sports are stressful for children. Children will find ways to compete with each other even if no sports are available. If cooperation rather than competition is emphasized, they will compete at cooperation. Joan Duda (1985) of Purdue University said recently that children can enjoy sport participation and competition when they feel that (a) they have the ability to meet physical requirements of the sport situation, (b) they can meet their personal goals and successfully demonstrate competence, and (c) they are in effective control in the sport context.

Are children more susceptible to injury in sports than adolescents or adults? A belief that they might be has concerned physicians, especially pediatricians, for many years and has led to statements from the American Academy of Pediatrics (''Competitive athletics,'' 1968) recommending major restrictions on sports participation for children. Physicians have modified their position now to the point where recommendations instead concern how sports can be made more safe for children. A major source of fear was that injuries to the growth centers (epiphyses) of long bones could result in permanent joint deformities or retardation of normal growth. The study reported by Larson and McMahon (1966) of over 1,000 consecutive childhood injuries showed that the risk to the epiphyseal area was low in children (1.2% overall) and high only in adolescents over the age of 15. Overuse injuries in baseball and swimming are reasonably common in children, but most can be treated successfully, and few result in permanent disability. The occurrence and seriousness of overuse injuries in adults seem to be greater because children are more inclined to stop when something begins to hurt, whereas highly motivated adults will continue. Whether or not the occurrence of arthritis is greater among adults who had been very active in sports as children when compared to adults who were not very active is unknown. Most traumatic arthritis in adults appears to be the result of injuries sustained in late adolescence.

Some recent developments indicate concern about the direction in which youth sport competition has been going. Several countries are currently reevaluating whether or not they should send teams of competitors to world junior tournaments in soccer and ice hockey. The International Tennis Federation recently accepted a special commission report (Schonborn, 1985) recommending restrictions on youths under 16 years old competing on the world circuit, a ban on professional play by youths under 14, and abolition of international tournaments for youths under 12. These measures will have to be enacted by the men's and women's professional councils to become effective. West Germany and Sweden have already withdrawn from tournaments for youths under 12 years old. This was based on a study by Richard Schonborn, the German federation head coach, who found that of 203 top West German players aged 11 to 16, 66 had evidence of spinal damage and less than 27% had escaped foot troubles. He concluded that many young players had inadequately developed musculature, leading to premature damage to the spine, hips, knees, and ankles. The German federation is now requiring that under-12 tennis players must participate in other sports, and tennis will account for only 40% of the rating of their progress.

If we were still in an era of largely amateur sport competition, the problems of the child and youth in top level sports might not be so difficult to handle. When thousands of dollars in prizes and endorsements can be obtained by a person who is not yet of voting age or old enough for military service, and not even of an age to be legally married in some states, the pressures to obtain these financial rewards from the parents who have made substantial investments in these youngsters and from the athletes themselves are enormous. They may overcome all other considerations.

The issue of whether the parents are exploiting the children for their own satisfaction as well as for personal gain is one that has been largely manufactured by the press. A few blatant abuses have been recognized and stopped. There may have been more that have not been obvious and have escaped attention. By and large the intelligent parent who sees potential talent for sports in a child would feel neglectful if he or she did not make a serious attempt to help the child realize it. It would be difficult to find an athlete who has attained some degree of success in sports and who was given an early start by his or her parents who has not publicly announced gratitude. For everyone who had not been successful and might be inclined to blame the parent for pushing them into an activity they did not want, you would probably find as many to say that the parent had not done enough to help and push them. Jim Easton, who has been a principal factor in developing the Junior Olympic Archery Program for youths from 8 to 18 years of age by providing free instruction and equipment to more than 7,000 youngsters between 1981 and 1984, has said, "The key to the program's success lay in parent involvement." Isn't that true for any youth sport program? This author has seen much more disagreement between parents in these programs than between parent and child.

For the future I do not see any decrease in the involvement of children and youth of all ages in sport at all levels of competition. The National Children and Youth Fitness Study released in October 1984 (Ryan, 1985) showed in a statistically designed random study of 10,275 students from 140 schools in 19 states that among 8,800 boys and girls in Grades 5 through 12 who were given a questionnaire and five fitness tests, the average student gets more than 80% of his or her physical activity outside the school education program, and an estimated 58.9% participate in appropriate physical activity year-round. About 46.9% engaged in one or more lifetime sports or exercise activities. Although on the average their scores in the fitness tests fell below some expectations, they felt fit enough to play sports, and they were doing it. To me this was an encouraging report. In international sports competition our U.S. athletes stack up well against those from any other country in the world, and they will continue to do so.

References

Competitive athletics for children of elementary age. (1968, October). *Pediatrics*, p. 4.

Duda, J.L. (1985). Consider the children—Meeting participants' goals in youth sport. *Journal of Physical Education, Recreation, and Dance, 56*(6), 55-56.

Grupe, O. (1988). Top-level sports for children from an educational viewpoint. In R. Malina (Ed.), *Child and sport*. Champaign, IL: Human Kinetics.

Larson, R.L., & McMahon, R.O. (1966). The epiphyses and the childhood athlete. *Journal of the American Medical Association, 196*, 607-612.

Ryan, A.J. (1985). America's youth not in bad shape. *The Physician and Sportsmedicine, 13*(1), 41.

Schonborn, R. (1985, July 29). Tennis anyone? *Sports Illustrated*, **63**(5), 11.

Weinberg, R. (1985, June 30). Stress not a big factor in children's sports. Quoted by Gordon Slovut in *Minneapolis Star and Tribune*, p. 14C.